DATE DUE

Melville's Later Novels

Melville's Later Novels

William B. Dillingham

THE UNIVERSITY OF GEORGIA PRESS
ATHENS AND LONDON

This publication has been supported by the
National Endowment for the Humanities,
a federal agency which supports the study of such fields
as history, philosophy, literature, and languages.

Set in 11 on 12 Linotron 202 Garamond with Weiss Display

The paper in this book meets the guidelines for
permanence and durability of the Committee on
Production Guidelines for Book Longevity of the
Council on Library Resources.

Printed in the United States of America

90 89 88 87 86   5 4 3 2 1

Library of Congress Cataloging in Publication Data

Dillingham, William B.
Melville's later novels.

Includes index.
1. Melville, Herman, 1819–1891—Criticism and
interpretation. I. Title.
PS2387.D525 1986   813'.3   85-1192
ISBN 0-8203-0799-8

For

| Rebecca Lynn | Judith Ann | Paul Christopher |
| Warren | Briggs | Dillingham |

in quō probitas naturalis est

The spirit of man is the candle of the Lord,
searching all the inward parts of the belly.
—Proverbs 20:27

Contents

Contents

Preface

This book argues that the central subject of Melville's later novels is survival through self-knowledge. My hope is to show something of the depth and richness of Melville's art and thinking by suggesting the varied and sophisticated ways he explores this subject in *Moby-Dick, Pierre, Israel Potter, The Confidence-Man,* and *Billy Budd, Sailor.* Surprisingly, in the many years of prolific scholarly activity since 1960, when Merlin Bowen's *The Long Encounter* was published, little has appeared that directly supports and extends Bowen's claim for the centrality in Melville of "the problem of self-discovery, self-realization." My book does so, but I concentrate on the later novels only. Though Bowen and I seem to be starting on the same journey and though I agree with him on what it is that we are seeking, our methods of exploration are greatly different, and the way that we interpret the terrain makes it a matter to marvel at that we could have started with the same destination in mind. Nevertheless, his work remains one of the most provocative books on Melville.

This volume completes a trilogy of books on Melville's fiction begun over fifteen years ago, a project that has fascinated me with its elusiveness and—on occasion—threatened to do me in with its leviathanic proportions. However, Herman Melville yields so much of the rich oil of truth that a hunt for him, even a prolonged one that has little of the lee shore and much of the howling infinite, is worth to the pursuer the risk of being stove.

During the long course of publication of these three volumes, the University of Georgia Press has exercised consistently good judgment in advice, a spirit of cooperation in accepting my suggestions about nearly every aspect of production, and a benevolent patience in dealing with a prodigal son. To all of those excellent people at that excellent press, I am grateful. I wish to express my thanks as well to the John Simon Guggenheim Memorial Foundation and to the National Endowment for the Humanities for the fellowships that enabled me to bring this volume to its conclusion. I am much indebted to my friends and colleagues at Emory University for their encouragement and support—to Floyd C. Watkins for his reading of the entire manuscript, to Frank Manley for his unrelenting faith in me and in the project, to Trudy Kretchman and her staff, who spent long hours on the manuscript, and to others too numerous to list by name.

Melville's Later Novels

Chapter 1

Ishmael's is a highly complicated mind—not because it was Melville's deliberate artistic scheme to make him that way but because the author poured so much of his own complexity into the fictional character.[1] Ishmael is not only one of the characters

1. The issue of point of view in *Moby-Dick* is a long-standing and complex one in Melville criticism. Early readers tended to ignore Ishmael in favor of Ahab and to think of Melville as the narrator. Later the question of inconsistency in point of view was much debated. In recent years many critics have pushed Melville out of the novel in favor of Ishmael. Three quotations will serve to illustrate this trend. Alfred Kazin writes that "Ishmael is not only a character in the book; he is also the single voice, or rather the single mind, from whose endlessly turning spool of thought the whole story is unwound." Introduction to *Moby-Dick* (Boston: Houghton Mifflin, 1950). According to Paul Brodtkorb, Jr., Ishmael is not only "the vessel that contains the book," but "in a major sense he *is* the book." Consequently, there is "no necessity to blame Melville for the book's inconsistencies" since they belong to Ishmael. *Ishmael's White World: A Phenomenological Reading of Moby-Dick* (New Haven: Yale University Press, 1965), pp. 4, 5. The "root assumption" of Robert Zoellner's book on *Moby-Dick* is that "every word" of the novel "including even the footnotes, comes from Ishmael rather than Melville." *The Salt-Sea Mastodon: A Reading of Moby-Dick*

in *Moby-Dick*; he is also a type. There are several Ishmaels in Melville's works. This one, however, is the master portrait and at the same time largely a portrait of the master, his creator. Melville calls a later Ishmael-like figure in one of his short works a "seedsman," literally because the man's occupation is selling seeds, but figuratively and more importantly because something within him compels him to look beyond the surface for the seed, that is, for his own essence.[2] This is a strong tendency in the

---

(Berkeley and Los Angeles: University of California Press, 1973), p. xi. While such a view holds obvious advantages in analyzing the book, it also seems to me a somewhat artificial distinction because Ishmael and Melville are so much alike that one fades into the other. As Charles Feidelson, Jr., puts it, behind Ishmael "always present as a kind of Doppelgänger, stands Herman Melville," and Ishmael "is often indistinguishable from the mind of the author himself." *Symbolism and American Literature* (Chicago: University of Chicago Press, 1953), p. 31. James Guetti concludes his perceptive chapter on *Moby-Dick* as follows: "Ishmael's gods are Melville's gods. The ineffable of Ishmael is the ineffable of *Moby-Dick*, and the difference between author and narrator—as a reader has perhaps suspected all along—is only nominal." *The Limits of Metaphor: A Study of Melville, Conrad, and Faulkner* (Ithaca: Cornell University Press, 1967), p. 45. That it is possible to think of Ishmael as the narrator and to analyze him as a character but at the same time to recognize that he is essentially Melville is illustrated by Harrison Hayford's incisive analysis of the first chapter of *Moby-Dick*. After discussing Ishmael's imagery and patterns of thought, Hayford concludes: "I suppose readers have been at least as uneasily aware all along as I have of the limitations of some of my strategical assumptions, and especially do I sense the artificiality of my main working assumption that everything in the book is coming to us from its narrator Ishmael. When one should ascribe such elements as imagery, syntax, rhetoric, and their implications for thought and character in *Moby-Dick* to the fictional narrator Ishmael and when to his creator Melville is, I suspect, perhaps more of a matter of critical strategy and relevance than of inherent propriety." Much in *Moby-Dick* often ascribed specifically to Ishmael occurs also in Melville's other works "from *Typee* to *Billy Budd,* where of course he is not. The total imaginative coherence of these works must have as its ground the mind of Melville, as author of them all." " 'Loomings': Yarns and Figures in the Fabric," in *Artful Thunder: Versions of the Romantic Tradition in American Literature,* ed. Robert J. DeMott and Sanford E. Marovitz (Kent: Kent State University Press, 1975), pp. 136, 137. My own method of dealing with Ishmael is closer to that of Feidelson, Guetti, and Hayford than that of others who tend either to ignore Ishmael or to make him the sole consciousness behind *Moby-Dick,* as if Melville did not exist.

2. "The Paradise of Bachelors and the Tartarus of Maids," in *The Complete Stories of Herman Melville,* ed. Jay Leyda (New York: Random House, 1949), pp. 185–211.

Ishmael of *Moby-Dick* (as it was in Melville himself). He is fascinated with things hidden from the eye, with what may be below, with an invisible world, and this characteristic manifests itself in the very imagery with which he expresses himself. To understand this side of Ishmael—and Melville—it is therefore necessary first to isolate and study some of these patterns of internality in the novel before approaching the larger question of cause.

Ishmael speaks frequently of things that are hidden. Captain Ahab hides below deck for the early part of the voyage. We know he is aboard, but he does not show himself. Fedallah and his tiger-yellow crewmen remain clandestinely in the hold until the first whale of the voyage is sighted. Father Mapple's sermon is pervaded with suggestions of hiding. He depicts Jonah as a man in hiding. The best are hidden and sometimes the worst, the "choice hidden handful of the Divine Inert" (p. 129) and the "Most dreaded creatures" that "glide under water, unapparent for the most part, and treacherously hidden beneath the loveliest tints of azure" (p. 235).[3] The list of such references is long because hiding projects an aspect of Ishmael's way of perceiving: wherever he looks, he has a strong desire to know what may or may not exist within or below what he actually sees.

This is why he seems so inordinately fond of secrets. His very first words create the aura of secrecy that hangs over the whole story—never mind what his real name may be, he says in the beginning; just call him Ishmael, and never mind how long it has been since the events about to be narrated; just say some years ago. There appears no good reason why Ishmael should be secretive about these details, but he, like the mind that conceived him, is plainly given to this way of dealing with reality. In fact, there are so many secrets in *Moby-Dick* that it is a tribute to Melville's genius that the book is not melodramatic to the point of absurdity. Ahab's background, though hinted at, is largely secret. Elijah, who accosts Ishmael and Queequeg in chapter 19, seems to hold some great secret about Ahab which he will not reveal. References to riddles, mazes, and labyrinths abound in the novel. The "secret part of the tragedy," involving Macy, the mate

---

3. All references to *Moby-Dick* are to the Norton Critical Edition, ed. Harrison Hayford and Hershel Parker (New York: Norton, 1967).

of the *Town-Ho,* never reaches "the ears of Captain Ahab and his mates" (p. 208). Ahab's "unabated rage" is called a "mad secret" (p. 162), and the wound to his groin is a secret "unwittingly . . . divulged" (p. 386). Through the albatross Ishmael imagines that he "peeped to secrets which took hold of God" (p. 165). *Secret* is one of Ishmael's favorite words; on one page alone he uses it three times (p. 406).

Very much a part of this same tendency in Ishmael to think and talk in terms of the hidden and the secret is his predilection toward mystery, the mystical, and the magical.[4] He finds "magic" in the appeal water has for human beings, a "mystical vibration" (p. 13). Therein is the "ungraspable phantom of life" (p. 14). To him the whale is a "mysterious monster" (p. 16). He tells of the strange experience he had as a youth when he felt a supernatural hand placed in his, and he claims that he lost himself in "confounding attempts to explain the mystery" (p. 33). He finds himself "mysteriously drawn" to Queequeg (p. 53). He indicates that he believes in ghosts as do other and "far deeper men than Doctor Johnson" (p. 262). He refers to the youth who insisted on trying to see what mystery was beneath the "dread goddess's veil at Sais" (p. 286). Fedallah, he says, "remained a muffled mystery to the last" (p. 199). The source of the "spirit-spout" in chapter 51 is unsolved to the end. Throughout his narrative, Ishmael creates mysteries (such as Queequeg as he marvels at the large number of pages in a book or Ahab as he puzzles over the riddle of Saint Elmo's fire) and speaks of familiar sights (such as the sea) in terms of deep mystery.

Ishmael's concern with the hidden is also evidenced in his projection of inner states through character doubles. In several ways Queequeg is a manifestation of tendencies hidden within Ishmael; he is as much a doppelgänger as he is a separate and distinct character.[5] As Ishmael puts it: "Queequeg was my own insepara-

---

4. As Walter E. Bezanson puts it: "His rich imagination is stirred by all that is secret, mysterious, and undecipherable in the great riddles of mankind." "*Moby-Dick*: Work of Art," in *Moby-Dick: Centennial Essays,* ed. Tyrus Hillway and Luther S. Mansfield (Dallas: Southern Methodist University Press, 1953), p. 39.

5. See, for example, John Halverson, "The Shadow in *Moby-Dick,*" *American*

ble twin brother" (p. 271). An even more obvious example of a double is Fedallah, who projects the dark and terrible monomania of Ahab. He is Ahab's shadow.[6] Melville's interest in the recesses of the mind (*his* mind, to be more accurate) was real and profound, as Henry A. Murray recognized as far back as 1929. In a review, Murray objected to Lewis Mumford's biography of Melville because it was "not mysterious or ambiguous" and thus did not truly reflect Melville's commitment to the hidden world of the irrational mind.[7] The creation of double figures and other indications that Melville is exploring what Murray called "the world of the mind" are but aspects of his wider puzzling over *all* that is hidden away.

One principal image that reflects this interest is that of concentric circles. The whirlpool in which Ishmael is caught in the epilogue is a good example. The outside rings move him rapidly and against his will, but the inner circles are calmer. Movement slows and the hidden center is tranquil. The center of a vortex, like the eye of a hurricane, is calm, but from that motionless point outward reverberate the ever-widening circles of destruction. In chapter 87, "The Grand Armada," Ishmael recounts another experience involving the image of a calm center. In the vicinity of Sumatra and Java the *Pequod* encounters a great herd of sperm whales that form themselves into concentric circles. Queequeg's harpoon strikes a whale that heads "straight for the heart of the herd" (p. 323). The outside rings are marked by a flourish of activity, but as Ishmael and his companions move inward toward the hidden center, they get "further and further from the circumference of commotion" (p. 324). Finally they glide "into

---

Quarterly 15 (1963): 440; Daniel G. Hoffman, *Form and Fable in American Fiction* (New York: Oxford University Press, 1961), p. 264; James Kirsch, "The Engima of *Moby-Dick*," *Journal of Analytical Psychology* 3 (1958): 135; and Martin Leonard Pops, *The Melville Archetype* (Kent: Kent State University Press, 1970), p. 82.

6. "And Ahab chanced so to stand, that the Parsee occupied his shadow; while, if the Parsee's shadow was there at all it seemed only to blend with, and lengthen Ahab's" (p. 278).

7. Henry A. Murray, book review, *New England Quarterly* 2 (1929): 526.

the innermost heart of the shoal" (p. 324). From there they faintly perceive in the "distracted distance" the "tumults of the outer concentric circles" where frantic whales go "round and round, like multiplied spans of horses in a ring" (p. 324). In this center position, they observe the playful infant whales with their mothers and "young Leviathan amours in the deep" (p. 326). It is a place of joy and tranquility amid outer rings of panic and destruction: "And thus, though surrounded by circle upon circle of consternations and affrights, did these inscrutable creatures at the centre freely and fearlessly indulge in all peaceful concernments" (p. 326). The image is similar in a passage where Ishmael describes the eyes of ill Queequeg, who has wasted away and is almost at the point of death. His eyes "seemed rounding and rounding, like rings of Eternity." They are "like circles on the water" (p. 395). But looking into the center of them, Ishmael sees there not disease and destruction but an "immortal health in him which could not die or be weakened" (p. 395).

In moments like these, Ishmael is truly a seedsman; he senses that there is a core of his existence where may be found a peace that passes understanding, a center of calm amid all the meaningless uproar of the outside. Repeatedly he comes back to this center, referring to it in different ways but always speaking of it as an unchanging essence. In one place it is "that immaculate manliness we feel within ourselves, so far within us, that it remains intact though all the outer character seem gone" (p. 104). In another passage it is an "ever vernal endless . . . [landscape] in the soul; in ye,—though long parched by the dead drought of the earthly life,—in ye, men yet may roll, like young horses in new morning clover; and for some few fleeting moments, feel the cool dew of the life immortal on them. Would to God these blessed calms would last" (p. 406). In "The Grand Armada," he compares the tranquil center of the circles of whales with a center deep within himself: "Amid the tornadoed Atlantic of my being, do I myself still for ever centrally disport in mute calm; and while ponderous planets of unwaning woe resolve round me, deep down and deep inland there I still bathe me in eternal mildness of joy" (p. 326).

6

Ishmael is not always confident, however, of reaching the hidden center: "For as this appalling ocean surrounds the verdant land," he writes, "so in the soul of man there lies one insular Tahiti, full of peace and joy, but encompassed by all the horrors of the half known life. God keep thee! Push not off from that isle, thou canst never return!" (p. 236). When Ishmael makes this statement, he is overwhelmed by "the universal cannibalism of the sea; all whose creatures prey upon each other, carrying on eternal war since the world began" (pp. 235–36). He is speaking of the cannibalism that he has observed in the ocean, of what that represents figuratively in terms of mankind's aggressive relationship with its own kind, and finally of what that in turn suggests about his personal internal turmoil—the warring within. In the "one insular Tahiti" passage, he may be saying, uncharacteristically, that one is better off not to "dive," not to set out into the dangerous sea of self but to remain on the calm and protected land, an idea in direct contradiction to his theme in chapter 23, "The Lee Shore."[8] However, he is, as Melville was himself, a man of moods, and in such a moment of depression as he is experiencing he is as capable of advising against intellectual and spiritual deep-diving, noble though it be, as the steely Ahab is of shedding a tear in a rare moment of human warmth.[9] He may not be referring to internal journeys at all, however, but to the fruitless and frustrating metaphysical treks into external reality where nothing is knowable for sure and where confusion causes the probing mariner to lose his way so that return to one's own understanding of self becomes impossible.

But this passage has another dimension that relates it more directly to the group of references in the novel to calm centers amid circumferences of turmoil. When Ishmael says "in the soul of man there lies one insular Tahiti," he seems to mean not that

8. It would simplify matters if we could say about this passage, as one critic does, "Ishmael is of course being facetious in that advice," but the tone of genuineness argues strongly against such a view. Richard Finholdt, *American Visionary Fiction* (Port Washington, N.Y.: Kennikat Press, 1978), p. 69.

9. For a discussion of moods in Ishmael's way of perceiving, see Brodtkorb, pp. 12–18.

there is a Tahiti within the soul but that the soul itself is a kind of Tahiti hidden among the stormy aspects of our being. [10] The soul is that calm center he refers to in other places by other names. And when he says "God keep thee! Push not off from that isle, thou canst never return!" he is actually saying that it is better never to be born. [11] At birth the soul is with God, and would that it would stay there, he indicates in good Platonic fashion, for birth is the beginning of a journey, a pushing off "from that isle," the soul. The personal center, or soul, he suggests, becomes covered over with stifling layers of time, materialism, and deadening experience. There is also a kind of collective soul of mankind, of which the fundamental and primitive creative impulses are a part, and this soul, too, has been covered over through the passing of ages—the center, the essence, of both the individual and the race is hidden almost beyond detection.

Ishmael's references to calm centers, therefore, are often linked with ancient periods, as if to seek the essence is to return in time. Whenever he mentions the distant past, there is an excellent chance that he is again yearning for that "eternal mildness of joy," that "mute calm," which centrally exists "amid the tornadoed Atlantic" of his being. He is speaking of himself as much as Ahab when he describes the "deeper part," the "very heart," in terms of a captive king, buried beneath the ages:

> This is much; yet Ahab's larger, darker, deeper part remains un- hinted. But vain to popularize profundities, and all truth is pro- found. Winding far down from within the very heart of this spiked Hotel de Cluny where we here stand—however grand and wonderful, now quit it;—and take your way, ye nobler, sadder souls, to those vast Roman halls of Thermes; where far beneath the fantastic towers of man's upper earth, his root of grandeur, his

10. "*In* the soul" is used here as one might say, for example, "*In* him you have the perfect friend."

11. Melville made the same point in "Bartleby," where the scrivener regresses to a state resembling infancy and then dies in a fetal position. When the grub man asks if Bartleby is asleep, the narrator replies "with kings and counsellors," a quotation from Job, who laments that he was born and wishes he were still in the state of pre-birth.

whole awful essence sits in bearded state; an antique buried beneath antiquities, and throned on torsoes! So with a broken
throne, the great gods mock that captive king; so like a Caryatid,
he patient sits, upholding on his frozen brow the piled en-
tablatures of ages. Wind ye down there, ye prouder, sadder souls!
question that proud, sad king! A family likeness! aye, he did beget
ye, ye young exiled royalties; and from your grim sire only will the
old State-secret come. (p. 161)

Melville had visited the Hotel de Cluny in Paris in 1849 and was
struck not only with the medieval building itself, but also with
what was under it. He "descended," he recorded in his journal,
"into the vaults of the old Roman palace of Thermes," over which
the museum then stood.[12] There was some evidence that the Roman palace itself had been constructed over the ruins of still earlier buildings.[13] By going below, therefore, he also felt himself
going back in time, back toward something more fundamental
both in the race of man and in himself toward a center. This
passage in *Moby-Dick* that resulted from Melville's visit to the
Hotel de Cluny is both a metaphorical map pointing the way
toward essence and an admonition to "wind ye down there" to
those proud enough and gifted enough to make the journey
within self.

So strong is this idea in Ishmael that he expresses it or hints at
it frequently through a myriad of references to inward or down-
ward movements. To read *Moby-Dick* is to feel oneself constantly
being taken inward to some enclosed space—through two sets of
doors into a Negro church, into the snug small room and the big
bed of Peter Coffin, under the bed with Queequeg while he puts
on his boots, into the Whaleman's Chapel with its pulpit "a self-

12. *Journal of a Visit to London and the Continent by Herman Melville, 1849–
1850,* ed. Eleanor Melville Metcalf (Cambridge: Harvard University Press,
1948), p. 58.

13. "It was the contention of the private owner before this became public
property in 1843 that just as the Hotel de Cluny had been built c. 1490 upon
the ruins of an old Roman palace as the level of Paris had been raised, so the
palace itself had been built on top of yet earlier ruins." Luther S. Mansfield and
Howard P. Vincent, eds., *Moby-Dick* (New York: Hendricks House, 1952), p.
698.

containing stronghold," into the bowels of the ship on which Jonah sailed, into the whale that swallowed Jonah, into the cave of Elephanta, into a whale's skeleton that is in turn within a green grove, into Ahab's cabin, and so on almost endlessly. Even the mass of information about the whale's anatomy has a general pattern to it, a movement inward. [14]

Ishmael is particularly fascinated with two activities that suggest inward movement—diving and digging. Melville's fondness for the metaphor of deep diving is obvious to anyone familiar with his works and letters. His comment to Evert Duyckinck that he loved "all men who *dive*" is typical, and whaling is in part a representation of that activity of the mind in *Moby-Dick*. [15] The water-gazers that Ishmael speaks of in the first chapter come as close to the water as possible, as if "bound for a dive" (p. 13). Though digging is less romantic perhaps than deep diving, Ishmael uses it as a metaphor with almost equal fervor. He describes an impulse that sways man against his will as "the subterranean miner that works in us all," and he asks, "how can one tell

14. Early in the novel (chapter 32, "Cetology"), Ishmael classifies whales according to their outer aspects. He discusses how their appearance has been represented in written documents and in pictures in chapters 55 and 56. In chapter 57 he speaks of reproductions of whales "in paint; in teeth; in wood; in sheet-iron; in stone; in mountains; in stars" (p. 231). Their quality as food is partly the subject of chapters 64 and 65. In chapter 68, the whale's blanket of blubber is described. From there Ishmael moves on to the whale's head in chapters 70, 74, and 75, to the brow or battering ram in chapter 76, and to the cask, or inside of the head, in chapter 77. Then he returns briefly to the brow in chapter 79 to comment on its interest phrenologically and on its mystery. He then moves further inward from the cask to the brain in chapter 80. Though not steady and unswerving, the movement in these several chapters is principally from the outside to the inside, from the sizes and shapes of whales to the size and shape of the whale's brain. Ishmael appears to return to the outer aspects of the whale as he discusses the spout in chapter 85 and the tail in 86, but even here he is still within, for respiration is the subject of the one chapter and the whale's sense of touch largely the subject of the other.

15. Melville's full comment was as follows: "I love all men who *dive*. Any fish can swim near the surface, but it takes a great whale to go down stairs five miles or more; & if he dont attain the bottom, why, all the lead in Galena can't fashion the plumet that will." He adds that he is speaking of "the whole corps of thought-divers, that have been diving & coming up again with bloodshot eyes since the world began." *The Letters of Herman Melville*, ed. Merrell R. Davis and William H. Gilman (New Haven: Yale University Press, 1960), p. 79.

whither leads his shaft by the ever shifting, muffled sound of his pick?" (pp. 162–63). Stubb's discovery of valuable, sweet-smelling ambergris in a diseased whale is described in terms of an excavation: "Seizing his sharp boat-spade, he commenced an excavation in the body. . . . You would almost have thought he was digging a cellar" (p. 341). The ambergris is still another representation of the seed, the sweet, calm center, the essence, arrived at this time by digging through the stench of animal rottenness: "Now that the incorruption of this most fragrant ambergris should be found in the heart of such decay; is this nothing? Bethink thee of that saying of St. Paul in Corinthians, about corruption and incorruption; how that we are sown in dishonor, but raised in glory" (p. 343). The seedsman Ishmael is ever on the alert for ways to project his vision. He can scarcely describe even such a mundane activity as going within the hold in search of leaky casks without suggestions of excavating the distant past and thus moving toward a center of truth: "They broke out deeper and deeper, disturbing the slumbers of the huge ground-tier butts; and from black midnight sending those gigantic moles into the daylight above. So deep did they go; and so ancient, and corroded, and weedy the aspect of the lowermost puncheons, that you almost looked next for some mouldy cornerstone cask containing coins of Captain Noah" (pp. 394–95). In a mood of displeasure with both the visible world and with the mass of human beings that can never see beyond it, Ishmael contrasts the ship's carpenter, a shallow and simple man, with those who dig beyond the visible to that hidden within: "For nothing was this man more remarkable, than for a certain impersonal stolidity as it were; impersonal, I say; for it so shaded off into the surrounding infinite of things, that it seemed one with the general stolidity discernible in the whole visible world; which while pauselessly active in uncounted modes, still eternally holds its peace, and ignores you, though you dig foundations for cathedrals" (p. 388). [16]

Melville may not have been fully aware of just how much these

16. That Ishmael (and Melville) is referring to himself as the digger here is clear when we remember that he earlier compared his creation of a "cetological System" to the great unfinished Cathedral of Cologne (pp. 127–28).

various aspects of imagery that Ishmael creates have in common. The recurrent pattern of internality and encapsulation that I have traced may not reflect so much conscious artistry as Melville's compulsion to manifest even in minor details his perceptional proclivities. Jung paid *Moby-Dick* the compliment of calling it "the greatest American novel," and he included it in that category of art that reveals the depths of authors' minds without the writers deliberately doing so.[17] *Moby-Dick* reveals, among other things, Melville's compulsion to travel beyond the world of rational and sensuous experience. When Ishmael says that he is "tormented with an everlasting itch for things remote" (p. 16), he is echoing Melville's own desire to explore within himself some deep realm, entirely different from the ordinary world. "I love to sail forbidden seas and land on barbarous coasts. Not ignoring what is good, I am quick to perceive a horror, and could still be social with it—would they let me—since it is but well to be on friendly terms with all the inmates of the place one lodges in" (p. 16). It is the "wonder-world" he speaks of here, and by the act of writing *Moby-Dick,* he enters it—or, rather, it enters him: "the great flood-gates of the wonder-world swung open, and in the wild conceits that swayed me to my purpose, two and two there floated into my inmost soul, endless processions of the whale . . ." (p. 16).

To a very great degree, Ishmael's numerous references to hiding, secrets, and mystery, his creation of double or shadow figures, his imagery involving concentric circles with a calm center, diving and digging all derive from his tendency toward what William Johnston calls "vertical thinking," a "process in which the mind goes silently down *into its own center,* revealing cavernous depths ordinarily latent and untouched by the flow of images and concepts that pass across the surface of the mind" (italics mine). In such an experience, one goes down to the "still point" or "the ground of the soul, thus finding a type of knowledge that is supra conceptual and therefore ineffable, a species of superthinking."[18]

17. C. G. Jung, "Psychology and Literature," in *The Spirit in Man, Art, and Literature,* trans. R. F. C. Hull (New York: Pantheon Books, 1966), pp. 88–89.

18. William Johnston, *The Still Point* (New York: Fordham University Press, 1970), pp. 124–25.

Melville's brand of "superthinking," however, is not to be confused with transcendental moments so prized by romantic visionaries and mystics in which one's individual identity is lost and where a sense of well-being usually is pervasive. The difference is fundamental: Melville's deep diving is into *self* with the goal of discovering at the center a hidden but powerful and sublime identity; transcendental or mystical experience takes one without and merges individual identity with the whole. Melville clearly expresses his opinion of visionaries in a letter to Hawthorne where he speaks of Goethe's advice to *"Live in the all."* Goethe was unquestionably a great genius, Melville readily confesses, but he adds, "there is an immense deal of flummery" in him. Goethe's notion was to let go of "your separate identity," to "get out of yourself, spread and expand yourself, and bring to yourself the tinglings of life that are felt in the flowers and the woods, that are felt in the planets Saturn and Venus, and the Fixed Stars." To this Melville replies, "What nonsense!" He does not, however, deny the reality of the experience: "This 'all' feeling, though, there is some truth in. You must often have felt it, lying on the grass on a warm summer's day. Your legs seem to send out shoots into the earth. Your hair feels like leaves upon your head. This is the *all* feeling."[19] What Melville objects to most strongly with respect to the *all* feeling is that it seduces one into a loss of consciousness whereas what he seeks most intensely is a heightened consciousness. It takes away that which he so highly prizes—individual identity. It also has a hangover effect and causes a separation from the real world: "But what plays the mischief with the truth is that men will insist upon the universal application of a temporary feeling or opinion."[20] To extend the sense of well-being that characterizes a mystical experience into a euphoric optimism and then apply it to all of existence is to wear permanently rose-colored glasses.

Whereas Melville represents metaphorically the journey within self as consciously diving or willfully plunging, he describes transcendental moments in terms of falling and associates them with

19. *Letters*, pp. 130–31.
20. *Letters*, p. 131.

sleeping. The seedsman impulse leads to discovery, to an awakening, to superthinking; transcendental experience is a falling asleep to the self as imagined merger with the "all" takes place. The one is a finding; the other is a losing. There is an extrarational and deeply emotional aspect of deep diving, but it is knowingly undertaken whereas the other kind of experience seems almost opium-induced and is described as an enchantment. Ishmael recounts in detail the steps that lead to the "all feeling" in chapter 35 ("The Mast Head) and leaves no doubts about his distrust of it. "To a dreamy meditative man," he says, standing the masthead is "delightful" (p. 136). The "tranced ship indolently rolls; the drowsy trade winds blow; everything resolves you into languor" (p. 137). The words are calculatingly selected to convey the sense of a lotus-caused irresponsibility. The outside world fades; there are no "domestic afflictions" to shatter the peace and utter security of such moments on "these seductive seas" of the southern fishery (p. 139).[21] In this passage, and elsewhere, discovering the whale and knowing the "all feeling" are presented as mutually exclusive experiences because the former act metaphorically stands for the discovery of one's own center of power and sublimity whereas the latter experience of merging with nature negates individual identity. Though the whale of self may be within reach, the "sunken-eyed young Platonist" will not discover it. In the following lines Melville is actually pointing to the difference between those who alertly journey after the whale—the hidden self—and those who desire to lose personal identity and indulge in the artificial experience of transcendence. "Very often do the captains of such ships take those absent-minded young philosophers to task, upbraiding them with not feeling sufficient 'interest' in the voyage; half-hinting that they . . . in

21. Luther S. Mansfield and Howard P. Vincent point out that Melville probably based this passage on one in J. Ross Browne's *Etchings of a Whaling Cruise* (1846). It is clear, however, that Browne does not distrust his masthead revery but romanticizes it. It was disconcerting, Browne writes, "to be suddenly startled from a delicious revery, abounding in those ethereal and refined fancies which Rousseau has so beautifully described as part of the inspiration derived from an elevated atmosphere." *Moby-Dick* (New York: Hendricks House, 1952), p. 682.

their secret souls would rather not see whales than otherwise. But all in vain; those young Platonists have a notion that their vision is imperfect; they are short-sighted; what use, then, to strain the visual nerve? They have left their opera-glasses at home" (p. 139).

What happens to such a person is that he is "lulled into such an opium-like listlessness of vacant, unconscious reverie" that "at last he loses his identity." Then he "takes the mystic ocean at his feet for the visible image of that deep, blue, bottomless soul, pervading mankind and nature; and every strange, half-seen, gliding beautiful thing that eludes him; every dimly-discovered, uprising, fin of some undiscernible form, seems to him the embodiment of those elusive thoughts that only people the soul by continually flitting through it." While in "this enchanted mood," one's consciousness seems to become "diffused through time and space, like Wickliff's sprinkled Pantheistic ashes, forming at last a part of every shore the round globe over" (p. 140). Melville's account of such a transcendent moment is different from those given by well-known mystics because he insists upon the deceptiveness and perniciousness of the experience. He calls it a "trance" or an "enchantment" and always stresses its flimsiness: "But while this sleep, this dream is on ye, move your foot or hand an inch; slip your hold at all; and your identity comes back in horror." It thus takes only the slightest interruption to bring you back to earth from this glorious but artificial trance; then you are worse off than ever because consciousness is not nearly so pleasant. But an even more horrible prospect to Ishmael is that of not coming back at all, of somehow falling into this state permanently and therefore losing his personal individual identity: "And perhaps, at mid-day, in the fairest weather, with one half-throttled shriek you drop through that transparent air into the summer sea, no more to rise for ever. Heed it well, ye Pantheists!" (p. 140). To the seedsman, this other kind of extrarational experience is always tempting, false as it may be. Even Ishmael nearly falls in chapter 61 ("Stubb Kills a Whale"), when he is standing watch at the masthead: "I idly swayed in what seemed an enchanted air. . . . In that dreamy mood losing all consciousness, at last my soul went out of my body. . . . Suddenly bubbles seemed bursting beneath my closed eyes; like vices my hands grasped the shrouds; some invisible, gracious agency preserved me; with a shock I came back to life" (pp. 241–42).

The state Ishmael finds himself in is thus a kind of death-in-life, pleasant though it may be; and to "fall" because of it is to be lulled into forgetting that glimpses of divine reality and eternal truth come only from deep within the self. What characterizes the fall into delusive self-forgetfulness is effortlessness. It takes no thinking, no pain; it is a falling asleep that is at the same time an ostensible psychological fusing with nature which smothers individual identity. Ishmael's most poignant description of it is his account of "the delicious death of an Ohio honey-hunter, who seeking honey in the crotch of a hollow tree, found such exceeding store of it, that leaning too far over, it sucked him in, so that he died embalmed. How many, think ye, have likewise fallen into Plato's honey head, and sweetly perished there?" (p. 290).

If transcendental moments of the type Ishmael describes in his masthead experiences have to be distinguished from deep diving, so does another kind of visionary state that is much more unpleasant than the "all feeling" but just as artificial and delusive. Ishmael describes two such instances, both associated with sleep. He remembers having to spend a day in his bed when he was a child. "Half steeped in dreams," he says, "I felt a shock running through all my frame. . . . A supernatural hand seemed placed in mine. My arm hung over the counterpane, and the nameless, unimaginable, silent form or phantom, to which the hand belonged, seemed closely seated by my bed-side. For what seemed ages piled on ages, I lay there, frozen with the most awful fears, not daring to drag away my hand" (p. 33). He "shudderingly" remembers this terrifying delusion after he awakes the next morning and cannot dismiss the thought of the "horrid spell" for months afterward. His other "unnatural hallucination of the night" (the "all feeling" seems to come at midday) occurs one evening while he is at the helm of the *Pequod*. As he watches the activity around the tryworks, the "fiend shapes before me, capering half in smoke and half in fire," they "at last begat kindred visions in my soul, so soon as I began to yield to that unaccountable drowsiness which ever would come over me at a midnight helm." But this particular night he had a horrible experience. "Uppermost was the impression, that whatever swift, rushing thing I stood on was not so much bound to any haven ahead as rushing from all havens astern. A stark, bewildered feeling, as of death, came over me" (p. 354). He finds that he has turned himself around and is facing the stern of the ship, which is about to founder. He wakes and grasps the tiller just in time to save himself and the ship. "Believe not," he warns, " the artificial fire, when its redness makes all things look ghastly" (p. 354).

Ishmael's two fearful visionary experiences represent a threat equal to that of the transcendental states but opposite in nature. Whereas the "all feeling" is seductive and sugared and would destroy the individual self by engulfment, the other experience in its unspeakable horror would destroy by paralysis. Both states are well known to students of mysticism. Emanuel Swedenborg referred to the nightmarish vision as a "vastation" (but he felt that it served a positive function). Henry James, Senior, recounts an experience in his own life that is close to Ishmael's:

> One day . . . I remained sitting at the table after the family had dispersed, idly gazing at the embers in the grate, thinking of nothing, and feeling only the exhilaration incident to a good digestion, when suddenly—in a lightning-flash as it were—"fear came upon me, and trembling, which made all my bones to shake." To all appearance it was a perfectly insane and abject terror . . . and only to be accounted for, to my perplexed imagination, by some damned shape squatting invisible to me within the precincts of the room, and raying out from his fetid personality influences fatal to life. The thing had not lasted ten seconds before I felt myself a wreck, that is, reduced from a state of firm, vigorous, joyful manhood to one of almost helpless infancy. The only self-control I was capable of exerting was to keep my seat.[22]

So affected was James by this experience that he suffered severe mental anguish for two years afterward.

When Ishmael speaks of diving, then, he is not referring to a pursuit of the "all feeling" or of "unnatural hallucinations of the night," which are both false and misleading. "Falling overboard,"

---

22. *Henry James, Senior: A Selection of His Writings*, ed. Giles Gunn (Chicago: American Library Association, 1974), pp. 55–56.

he says in chapter 68 ("The Blanket"), one becomes only "as a fly . . . glued in amber" (p. 261). Nobility and sublimity are within, not without. Thus "we see the rare virtue of a strong individual vitality, and the rare virtue of thick walls, and the rare virtue of interior spaciousness. Oh, man! admire and model thyself after the whale! Do thou, too, remain warm among ice. Do thou, too, live in this world without being of it. Be cool at the equator; keep thy blood fluid at the Pole. Like the great dome of St. Peter's, and like the great whale, retain, O man! in all seasons a temperature of thine own" (p. 261). Finding that inner spaciousness, power, self-confidence, and divine stability is the goal of the seedsman, but he realizes that few have these qualities within: "Of erections, how few are domed like St. Peter's! Of creatures, how few vast as the whale!" (p. 261).

To say that Melville distrusted these two forms of visionary experience as being destructively misleading is not to say that he found no dangers in the act of deep diving. The seedsman is nobler and certainly less deluded than persons who succumb to temporary transcendental or hallucinary states, but he must be perceptive enough and strong enough both to understand and control the forces he encounters within the wonder-world of self. Otherwise, he may simply unleash usurping powers and fall prey to their rage for control. Narcissus, in Melville's use of the myth, did not fall but "plunged" with anticipation into the water where he had glimpsed the image of his deepest self.[23] He was not in a trance like the "young Platonist" who, lulled by nature into an enchantment, loses his identity and falls into the "all." On the contrary, his is a conscious act, and he is diving after his identity, not giving it up. Melville's treatment of the story of Narcissus illustrates both the magnetic appeal of the sublime central self once it has been glimpsed and the fate of one who cannot handle what he discovers within.

Even with its dangers, however, self-probing is clearly for Melville the only viable method of arriving at what truth may be available to mortal man. As constantly curious as he is about the

---

23. Melville departs significantly from the Greek myth, in which Narcissus simply pines away and dies after he sees his reflection in the water.

nature of external reality, the universe around us, he ultimately suspects either that it cannot be fathomed or that there is nothing there to be fathomed. In another letter to Hawthorne, he wrote: "We incline to think that the Problem of the Universe is like the Freemason's mighty secrets, so terrible to all children. It turns out, at last, to consist in a triangle, a mallet, and an apron,— nothing more!"[24] And this is really what chapter 42 ("The Whiteness of the Whale") is about. Nowhere else in *Moby-Dick* does Ishmael manifest so urgently his desire to remain reasonable though confronted with blankness. Like many other chapters in *Moby-Dick,* this one is confessional in nature and written perhaps for the therapeutic purpose not only of expressing what most disturbs but also of convincing himself that his is a universal experience. The most notable thing about this chapter is the subjectivity of its argument. It is deep and compelling, brilliant in its use of allusions and associations, fascinating in its myriad suggestiveness, virtuoso in style, but altogether the outcry of a troubled mind expressing a highly personal vision, not human common denominators. It is permeated with rationalizations.

Ishmael begins by saying that he will try to indicate what the white whale "at times" meant to him, that is, not always but in times of meditation on whiteness. He is not concerned here with the things about Moby Dick that ordinarily create alarm but only its color, which is to Ishmael the cause of "vague, nameless horror" (p. 163). What Ishmael experiences when he contemplates whiteness is "well nigh ineffable," but his purpose is to come as close as he can to explaining it.[25] In one long sentence where example is piled upon example, he points out that white represents beauty, royalty, gladness, nobility, innocence, the benignity of age, honor, justice, and divinity—"whatever is sweet, and honorable, and sublime" (p. 164). But he ends this sentence of some forty-four lines with another expression of the horror whiteness evokes at times. Then he proceeds to discuss mostly the negative aspects of whiteness, in actuality putting off the naming

24. *Letters,* p. 125.

25. Walter E. Bezanson comments that "The narrator's whole effort to communicate the timeless, spaceless concept of 'The Whiteness of the Whale' is an act of dream analysis" (p. 48).

of what that horror is. He claims that in destructive things, such as the bear and shark, whiteness heightens the terror we feel. In mysterious things, like the albatross and White Steed of the Prairies, whiteness heightens the sense of the supernatural. In ugly things whiteness heightens the maliciousness. In superstitious things, it heightens the superstition. Halfway through the chapter, Ishmael then summarizes his argument so far: in one mood he sees white as the symbol of whatever is "grand or gracious"; in another mood, whiteness "calls up a peculiar apparition" (p. 166).

The summary is misleading, however. He seems to imply in it that his "horror" of whiteness results from the fact that this grand and gracious hue symbolizes also whatever is ignoble and evil. Yet his presentation so far has suggested that this is not the source of his horror. To be sure, in one mood he does see white as representative of goodness, and in another, he does associate it with "human malice" and ugliness. But he is clearly speaking of something other than evil or the combination of good and evil when he describes "a peculiar apparition," "an elusive something" that appalls. Just what this is he is not yet prepared to say.

The second half of the chapter continues to raise the question of what it is in whiteness that so disturbs, but he continues to delay the real answer. He says that the mere mention of the word *white* is enough to depress or frighten. It calls up things that are woeful and oppressive. Although people might not admit it, it is the whiteness that disturbs them most in a view of milky water, frosty mountains, or snow-covered prairies. Like a buffalo robe shaken behind a colt, the word *white* calls up in Ishmael "the knowledge of the demonism in the world" (p. 169). But then he insists that the problem has not been solved; he admits that he still has not really answered the question he began with. It is not the fact that white symbolizes goodness that bothers him or that white symbolizes demonism. It is not even the fact that white can symbolize both things. "Not yet have we solved the incantation of this whiteness," he says in the penultimate paragraph. Therefore, it appalls for a reason not yet given. In the last paragraph he finally directs himself to this reason: white is the concrete of all colors and also the absence of color, which is to say, it represents the spectrum (good and evil) and *denies that the spectrum is there.* Under the variety and color of the visible universe lies blankness, and the "vague nameless horror" he experiences is not the fear of evil but the dread of that insanity which results from the contemplation of blankness.[26]

"The Whiteness of the Whale" chapter thus expresses what sometimes bothers Ishmael—his concern over "the woe that is insanity"—and depicts him in the process of dealing in one way with the problem. Throughout, he tries very hard to expunge the specter that haunts him, the "peculiar apparition," by universalizing his disturbance. If he can express and explain away this "panic to the soul" that he experiences, he can perhaps alleviate it. He is so persuasive that his departure from normalcy escapes a great many readers who do not stop to question his assertions. His tactic is to *assume,* that is, to make agreement with his premises a foregone conclusion, and then to raise the question of why all of humanity feels this way. In reality his own view is aberrant, not representative. For example, he questions what it is in the albino man that "so peculiarly repels and often shocks the eye," what it is that "makes him more strangely hideous than the ugliest abortion" (p. 166). His answer is whiteness, and it is a perfectly logical conclusion *if* one accepts Ishmael's premise that an albino is more horrible in appearance than any twisted, humped, scarred, or otherwise malformed member of the human race that can be imagined. The possibilities are so great for human ugliness that Ishmael surely exaggerates the horror that most people feel when observing an albino. *He* feels it, however, and he would like to believe that he is normal in doing so, but in fact he is not.[27] He seldom admits that he is speaking just for himself but rather pretends to be describing the "common, hereditary experience of all mankind" (p. 166). Consequently, he frequently utilizes the

26. William Ellery Sedgwick came close to recognizing this truth when he commented that Ishmael's horror of whiteness is "the soul's fear of itself." *Herman Melville: The Tragedy of Mind* (Cambridge: Harvard University Press, 1944), p. 122.

27. Paul Brodtkorb, Jr., observes that Ishmael "has overwhelmed us with examples, some of them so farfetched they clearly reflect the ponderings of a man trying to think the unthinkable by surrounding it" (p. 118).

first-person plural pronoun: "Can *we* thus hope to light upon some chance clue to conduct *us* to the hidden cause *we* seek?" (p. 167, italics mine).

He leaves no openings for disagreement about whiteness. "No man can deny," he positively asserts, that it "calls up a peculiar apparition." And he assumes that there will be no disagreement: "But though without dissent this point be fixed, how is mortal man to account for it?" (p. 166). Passages like these reveal a mind confronted with a strong suspicion of madness trying to rationalize and to fit what it secretly suspects may be lunacy into the pattern of normal response. "To analyze it," he says, meaning his reaction to whiteness and therefore his concern over insanity, "would seem impossible" (p. 166). So he talks himself and others into believing that what he feels, all sensitive human beings feel.

In doing so, he utilizes the ancient and proven device of snob appeal. One must be "subtle" and "imaginative" in "a matter like this," he claims, and without these qualities one cannot hope to grasp what he is saying and accept it. Thus he has indirectly charged those who might not follow him "into these halls" with lacking adequate mental powers to do so, and he is indirectly congratulating and flattering those who do go along by bestowing upon them the qualities of subtlety and imagination. If that is not enough, he uses still another device to win acceptance of his argument. The feeling he is about to describe, he claims, has probably "been shared by most men," but it was subconscious, and they therefore cannot now recall it. It is an argument impossible to refute because anyone can assert, without fear of being disproved, that anyone else feels anything *subconsciously.*

In the last half of the chapter, Ishmael makes a number of statements about whiteness that reveal his own peculiar state of mind. He suggests that to a person of "untutored ideality" even the mention of the word *Whitsuntide* calls up "dreary, speechless processions of slow-pacing pilgrims" (p. 167). All one has to do is say *White Friar* or *White Nun* to any "unread, unsophisticated Protestant," and he will immediately see in his imagination a frightening "eyeless statue." Through a kind of word association game, Ishmael tells what feelings the word *white* evokes *in him* but he professes again to be speaking for all mankind. *White Mountains* produces ghostly responses whereas *Blue Ridge* does not. *White Sea* brings on "spectralness," though *Yellow Sea* pleasantly "lulls us." Other examples follow to show over and over again the subjectivity of Ishmael's views. All this is true, he suggests, *if* you are imaginative enough to grasp it; all this is true, though it is so deep that you may not consciously realize it. That mind in which whiteness does not produce "terror" is an "unimaginative mind," and with this bit of name-calling Ishmael claims that sailors will not admit that when they see milky water below their ship they are not as much frightened by the prospect of striking hidden rocks as by "that hideous whiteness" (p. 168). His reasoning is thin, but his language and his tactics compelling. He wants to believe himself and to be believed. He even jokes toward the end of the chapter about being unbalanced in order to appear perfectly normal: "But thou sayest . . . thou surrenderest to a hypo, Ishmael" (pp. 168–69). In this moment he indeed has, but by admitting to it only jokingly, he hopes to dismiss the charge.

One of the great dramas of *Moby-Dick*, as great as the overt one of a tenacious and revenge-ridden whaling captain chasing the whale that dismembered him, is the hidden drama of a genius struggling hard to avoid drowning—and succeeding in the end, though just barely. "The Whiteness of the Whale" is an expression of Ishmael's most desperate moment in *Moby-Dick* and probably Melville's in the writing of it, for it reveals just where probings into the nature of universal truth, explorations not into self but into *external* reality, can lead. Nowhere else does his speculation about all truth external to the self bring on a sensation of such profound disturbance, and nowhere else is the struggle so great to stay afloat, to avoid the drowning of "the infinite of his soul," as Ishmael describes Pip's departure into madness. This is not the only time, however, that Ishmael is aware of the same basic danger; elsewhere he tries to handle the problem much in the same way.

If Melville feels alternately that answers to the riddle of the universe are unobtainable and that there really are no answers because nothingness underlies mere appearances, and if he realizes with a shiver where persistent attempts to solve the problems lead, he also is aware that uninterrupted probings into the one place where truth is available—the inner world of self—are also dangerous. He knows that unalleviated self-concern separates from the ordinary world and that that prolonged separation brings on personal destruction. Thus he suggests that one must be both a pale usher and a sub-sub-librarian.

The words *etymology* and *extract,* which serve as titles to the introductory sections of *Moby-Dick,* have in common the idea of essence; the former is the analysis of the elements of words and the latter is an essential constituent or concentration. Melville used the terms not only as the titles of those sections where he shows the derivation of the word *whale* and where he quotes some eighty passages from various writings having to do with whales and whaling but also as the headings for his brief descriptions of the pale usher and the sub-sub-librarian, which in the first American edition are on separate pages from the actual etymology and extracts.[28] He entitled his comment on the pale usher "Etymology" because therein he reveals an essential part, an element, and it is within himself. Similarly, his passage on the sub-sub-librarian is entitled "Extracts" because it contains an essence, again another aspect of his being. What he does in these much neglected introductory sections, then, is highly significant. With a deceptively condescending tone, he actually lays himself bare; both the sub-sub-librarian and the pale usher are within him.

The sub-sub-librarian of the "Extracts" section personifies the seedsman in Melville.[29] He goes beneath. He is a "burrower." What he says one must not always take literally: "You must not, in every case at least, take the higgledy-piggledy whale statements, however authentic, in these extracts, for veritable gospel

---

28. In the Norton Critical Edition of *Moby-Dick,* the editors placed the description of the usher on the same page as the words for *whale* in several languages, and similarly they did not devote a separate page to the comments about the librarian.

29. Edgar A. Dryden takes a different view of the sub-sub-librarian, considering him not a reflection of Ishmael but a contrast to him. See *Melville's Thematics of Form: The Great Art of Telling the Truth* (Baltimore: Johns Hopkins University Press, 1968), p. 84.

cetology. Far from it." A seedsman is concerned with a "glancing bird's eye view" and with what has been "fancied." The rest of the commentary on the sub-sub-librarian is especially revealing, for it depicts him as not really of this world and as never truly appreciated by ordinary people. Though he is superficially facetious, Melville is describing something within himself and making one of his most sympathetic statements about other seedsmen: "Give it up, Sub-Subs! For by how much the more pains ye take to please the world, by so much the more shall ye for ever go thankless! Would that I could clear out Hampton Court and the Tuileries for ye!" (p. 2).

The Sub-Sub, however, is always in danger of burrowing too long without returning to the surface. The usher within him must prevent this. Melville had been an "usher," a teacher, in his younger days, but he is describing an aspect of himself in a more fundamental way in the "Etymology" section: "The pale Usher— threadbare in coat, heart, body, and brain; I see him now. He was ever dusting his old lexicons and grammars, with a queer handkerchief, mockingly embellished with all the gay flags of all the known nations of the world. He loved to dust his old grammars; it somehow mildly reminded him of his mortality" (p. 1). Unlike the sub-sub-librarian, the pale usher deals in facts, in definitions and rules that are readily before him in his lexicons and grammars. He is not a burrower but a duster, lightly sweeping over life. In contrast to the sub-sub-librarian, the pale usher is of the world and reminds himself of his linkage with it constantly. His handkerchief is a symbol of that connection, and his dealing in measurable truth assures him that he is a mortal, an ordinary human being. He values this feeling that he is not against the world but part of it. Though both represent essences, tendencies in Melville himself, the two are diametrical opposites.[30]

30. In his letter of early June 1851 to Hawthorne, Melville revealed an important truth about himself as a writer. "The calm, the coolness, the silent grass-growing mood in which a man *ought* always to compose,—that, I fear, can seldom be mine. Dollars damn me; and the malicious Devil is forever grinning in upon me, holding the door ajar" (*Letters,* p. 128). Melville seems to mean that he was frustrated because he needed money and therefore had to write what would please the public. And that is the way biographers and critics have gener-

The pale usher is present, as is the sub-sub-librarian, in a hundred different ways in *Moby-Dick,* pouring forth data, even boring us at times with his storehouse of information, reminding himself and others that he is no introspective hermit but much a citizen of the world, a wise, mature, and sensible fellow, a down-to-earth mortal. He is a wit, a humorist, a humanitarian, an objective observer. The usher is not the real Ishmael, however, any more than is the librarian. They are both parts of Ishmael's overall personality, and one is just about as dangerous to his mental balance as the other. When the usher becomes too dominant, Ishmael experiences an enervation of body, mind, and spirit, a great depression. As *Moby-Dick* opens, Ishmael has become tired of letting the usher in him have his way. Consequently, his motivation for going to sea is to "see the watery part of the world," to allow himself now those diving experiences which ultimately become perilous but which also vitalize when life close to the ordinary world has become oppressive.[31] His description of himself after

---

ally read this remark. But the word *dollars* represents far more than money in what he says. He is "damned" because he cannot write the book he wants to write, and what is damning him is not just a desire for money but his desire to remain mentally stable. Otherwise he could leave the dull, materialistic, ordinary world—symbolized by dollars in his letter—and dive into the wonderworld.

31. Numerous critics have viewed Ishmael as undergoing some basic and permanent change in the course of the novel. Merlin Bowen, for example, says that "we must distinguish . . . between the experiencing actor and the more sophisticated narrator, between Ishmael-then and Ishmael-now." Ishmael-then, according to Bowen, was a "splenetic fellow, rather 'grim about the mouth,'" whereas Ishmael-now represents a "transformation" and is a mature and mellowed man who has moved from "resentment to acceptance." *The Long Encounter: Self and Experience in the Writings of Herman Melville* (Chicago: University of Chicago Press, 1960), pp. 240–41, 248. Howard Vincent feels that Ishmael undergoes "a symbolic resurrection" after he learns to accept things as they are. *The Trying-Out of Moby-Dick* (Boston: Houghton Mifflin, 1949), p. 203. This is a view largely shared by M. O. Percival in *A Reading of Moby-Dick* (Chicago: University of Chicago Press, 1950) and by John Seelye, *Melville: The Ironic Diagram* (Evanston: Northwestern University Press, 1970), p. 8. And Robert Zoellner speaks of Ishmael's redemption, gained through "a revolution in perception" (p. 164). Carl F. Strauch suggests that Ishmael undergoes change by curing "his suicidal neurosis." "Ishmael: Time and Personality in *Moby-Dick,*"

having been dominated by the pale usher for a while is remarkably effective for projecting his sense of being "threadbare" in heart, body, and brain. He needs to regulate his "circulation." He is "growing grim about the mouth." It is "a damp, drizzly November" for him. He feels he has nothing to live for. This depression is the result of following too long and too obediently the way of the world. That Melville knew this state of mind intimately is evidenced by the fact that he describes it in such similar terms in other places as well as in *Moby-Dick*. Various narrators in his work suffer the same malaise, and they follow the same course as Ishmael into the wonder-world. Like Ishmael, the narrator of "Cock-A-Doodle-Doo!" is "full of hypos," enervated, in need of divorcing himself from the affairs of the world. His highly subjective description of the surrounding countryside with its "damp, disagreeable air," its "oozy sod," and "humped hills" reveals a man almost smothered by his mortality.[32] Pale usher thus yields to sub-sub-librarian, and the narrator enters the wonder-world through the agency of a crowing cock. A similar situation develops in "The Piazza," where the narrator has grown so tired of his dull life that he becomes physically ill. His weariness is extreme, and his attitude pessimistic. He describes it as "ingrate peevishness." He, too, goes in search of the inner world,

---

Studies in the Novel, 1 (1969): 468–83. John Halverson represents the view of many critics when he writes: "Moving within himself closer to the human collectivity, he changes radically from the man who feels the urge to go about 'methodically knocking people's hats off' to the celebrant of brotherly love who squeezes his neighbors' hands along with the spermaceti" (p. 440). Martin Leonard Pops agrees that Ishmael changes, but he sees it as not toward greater maturity: "Ishmael not only does not grow older (i.e. overripe with fulfillment) as the quest continues but . . . he grows younger and younger" (p. 87). In contrast to these critics, Harrison Hayford writes that Ishmael "did not change and has not changed, from then to now, in his essential nature. Ishmael is forever Ishmael" (" 'Loomings,' " p. 121). If his "essential nature" is understood to embody conflicting forces and a manifest struggle, then I find Hayford's position much closer to my own than that of other critics who argue that a drastic and permanent change takes place in Ishmael (and often as a corollary that he alone is saved because of this transformation).

32. "Cock-A-Doodle-Doo!, or, the Crowing of the Noble Cock Beneventano," in *Complete Stories*, p. 119.

which he thinks of as "fairyland," represented by a "spot of radiance" that he discerns from afar, "dazzling like a deep-sea dolphin,"[33] In each instance, however, the journey into self, uplifting as it is for a while, proves to be as perilous as a life lived too long without access to the wonder-world. The question posed in many of Melville's works is whether it is nobler to perish in one place rather than in the other, for both the lee shore and its opposite, the howling infinite, are destructive. For Melville, however, and actually for Ishmael in the novel, survival—sanity with dignity—is ultimately the goal, not naked heroism, and that aim can be achieved only by keeping both tendencies alive within, by preventing either from destroying or permanently dominating the other as each would like to do.

Moby-Dick mirrors this struggle in a number of obvious ways: the factual part of the whaling material alongside passages of metaphysical speculation, straight narrative with Elizabethan theatrics, dirty jokes with cosmic jokes, prose with poetry, and so forth. Its most persistent manifestation, however, is also one of the most neglected aspects of the book: the strange combination of pervasive implausibility on the one hand and on the other hand Ishmael's frequent insistence upon its being believed. He is like another kind of Hawthorne who is writing a "romance" but insisting all the time that it be accepted as a "novel." Nothing in *Moby-Dick* produces a more profound sense of puzzlement than these conflicting forces. It is one thing to write a symbolic novel; it is something else to write a symbolic novel and claim repeatedly that it is pure realism, and that is what Melville has done. The brief epilogue is a good example. In it Ishmael tells how he survived the destruction of the *Pequod*. He explains that he was previously tossed from his boat and therefore was far enough away when the ship sank to avoid the resultant suction. He did get caught in the vortex, but it was already subsiding, and when he reached the center, he found Queequeg's unused airtight coffin to float on. This short chapter is essentially an explanation that Ishmael seems to feel he owes his readers, an accounting in sensible

---

33. "The Piazza," in *Complete Stories,* p. 444.

terms of how it happened that he and only he survived.[34] Yet that sensible explanation is undercut, for Ishmael cannot resist the temptation to add an unrealistic detail. Though the waters were filled with sharks, they did not harm him. They "glided by as if with padlocks on their mouths" (p. 470). Ishmael thus clears up a puzzle only to create a new one. This pattern occurs in many places throughout the book. Ishmael's writing is marked by recurrent desires both to explain himself and to foist off on the reader many farfetched details.

Modern readers, aware as they usually are of the immense reputation of *Moby-Dick* as one of the greatest novels of all time and conditioned to read symbolic literature in an entirely different manner from realistic writings, appear largely to miss a truth that certain early reviewers were struck with, namely that despite documented instances of whales sinking ships in the nineteenth century,[35] *Moby-Dick* is incredible. The reviewer for the London *Morning Post* commented on the "improbable character of the incidents," and added that "there are occasions when the reader is disposed to believe that the whole book is one vast practical joke." Nevertheless, he confessed that the novel is so compelling that "we bolt down all events, however unlikely . . . as an ostrich of potent digestion gobbles down bullets and gun-flints." Even so, "there are many things in this work which appear to us extravagant and unlikely." Ahab "devotes his life to the vindictive purpose of hunting the identical fish that mutilated him through all the waters of the globe. . . . It seems as though the man who would undertake such a pursuit would be engaged in a search about as hopeful as that of the Brahmin in the Eastern tale, whose wife sent him all over the world on a fool's errand to look for the

34. Furthermore, without the epilogue, as some reviewers noted when the British edition appeared without it, there would be no one left to tell the story, and that would strain the novel's credibility.

35. See Howard P. Vincent, *Trying-Out*, pp. 163–77. Added to the accounts Vincent cites should be the one-hundred-page narrative of Thomas Nickerson, a survivor of the *Essex* tragedy, whose work was not discovered until the spring of 1981.

fifth volume of the Hindoo Scriptures, there never having been but four."[36]

His point is well taken. The search for the white whale and the success in finding that one particular whale must have appeared utterly fantastic to actual whalemen of the time. And although whaling ships were noted for the unusual mixtures of nationalities among their crew members, Ahab's crew is strictly mythical. Queequeg, Daggoo, and Tashtego present incredible extremes in themselves, but Fedallah could be nothing but an inhabitant of Melville's wonder-world. That this unbelievable creature could be secreted aboard a relatively small whaling ship with his tiger-yellow cohorts without anyone knowing it, all of them fed and cared for, and then brought out suddenly upon the first lowering for whales—all this is of the hidden inner world, not the actual. A reviewer in 1851 was struck with another fact that little bothers modern readers, but one that leads to a legitimate question nevertheless regarding the novel's believability: "From the Captain to the Cabin-boy, not a soul amongst them talks pure seaman's lingo."[37] One need look only at the speech of the crew members in chapter 39 ("First Night-Watch") or that of Pip throughout to understand the reviewer's objection. No less a writer than Joseph Conrad was repelled by *Moby-Dick* because of what he considered its lack of authenticity. *Moby-Dick* was to Conrad what Cooper's *The Deerslayer* was to Mark Twain. When he was asked to write a preface for a new edition of the book to be published by the Oxford University Press, Conrad refused and replied that there was "not a single sincere line in the 3 vols of it."[38] What he meant by a lack of sincerity is clear from a later comment to Jacob Epstein, who was sculpturing a bust of him. According to Epstein, "We talked of books, and I mentioned Melville's *Moby-Dick*, expecting him to be interested. Conrad

36. London *Morning Post,* November 14, 1851. Reprinted in *Moby-Dick as Doubloon,* ed. Hershel Parker and Harrison Hayford (New York: Norton, 1970), pp. 28–31.

37. New York *Albion,* November 22, 1851. Reprinted in *Doubloon,* pp. 42–47.

38. Letter from Conrad to Humphrey Milford, January 15, 1907, in Frank Macshane, "Conrad on Melville," *American Literature* 29 (1957–58): 463–64.

burst into a furious denunciation of it. 'He knows nothing of the sea. It's fantastic, ridiculous,' he said."[39]

Measured even by a loose standard of plausibility, the book is still in many places "fantastic," as Conrad put it.[40] Incident after incident is questionable once this kind of examination has been initiated—Queequeg's rescue of Tashtego in the whale's head, the explanation Ishmael gives for the stone lance found in a captured whale, his eating of the "plum pudding," Tashtego's actions with the flag at the end, the sharks having padlocked jaws in the epilogue, and so on. The point here, however, is not that Melville has violated the laws of realism and that consequently the book has been weakened. Conrad and others notwithstanding, the depth and richness of *Moby-Dick* stand despite a certain lack of verisimilitude. It is obvious that Melville derives his power from sources other than those of the realist, and it may be beside the point to hold him to that which is readily believable on the literal level. But it is important to recognize that *Moby-Dick* is indeed a farfetched book *because Ishmael claims with such fervor that it is not.*

The strongest and most consistent emotion that Ishmael displays in *Moby-Dick* is a desire to be believed. Indeed, this is his primary motivation in telling the story. He must express himself, but he must do it in such a way that others will understand and accept whether he is being reasonable and literal or not.[41] One of his most telling remarks occurs in the "The Whiteness of the Whale": "But how can I hope to explain myself here; and yet, in some dim, random way, *explain myself I must else all these chapters might be naught*" (p. 163, italics mine). This same hunger is pres-

---

39. Jacob Epstein, *Let There Be Sculpture* (New York: Putnam's, 1940), p. 66.

40. Richard Chase, who discusses ways in which *Moby-Dick* is related to the tall tale of the American frontier and to the hoax, writes: "*Moby-Dick,* it does the book no disservice to admit it, is a literary-scientific extravaganza with very clear affinities to Barnum's showmanship. The fact that the tale winds up in anything but a hoax does not invalidate the relationship. Indeed, that is Melville's point: it looks like a hoax, but woe to him who allows himself the comfortable belief that it *is* a hoax." *Herman Melville: A Critical Study* (New York: Macmillan, 1949), p. 77.

41. It is this serious, sincere, and urgent need to be believed by others which Ishmael often displays that makes his characterization different from that of a host of famous truth-stretchers in literature, such as Lemuel Gulliver.

ent in many places in the book, especially when Ishmael is preparing for the fatal meeting between Ahab and Moby-Dick. In fact, he is given to taking solemn oaths on his veracity. When he discovers that his listeners question whether his account of Moby Dick, Steelkilt, and Radney is "really true," he sends out for a priest and Bible, places his hand upon the Holy Book, and swears: "So help me heaven, and on my honor, the story I have told ye, gentlemen, is in substance and its great items, true" (p. 224). This somewhat extreme action is meant to convince not only his audience at the Golden Inn in Lima but also the readers of *Moby-Dick*.[42]

He provides another oath in chapter 45, this time the legal equivalent of the oral statement he made before a priest with his hand on the Bible in "The *Town-Ho*'s Story." He entitles the chapter "The Affidavit," which, of course, is in law a written statement, its truth sworn to before some authorized official. His purpose is to substantiate his contention in the previous chapter ("The Chart") that one certain whale could indeed be sought out and encountered in the vast oceans. As he often does in his attempts to convince, he plays upon the reader's ignorance of whaling: "Now, to any one not fully acquainted with the ways of the leviathans, it might seem an absurdly hopeless task thus to seek out one solitary creature in the unhooped oceans of this planet" (p. 171). Since his credibility rests so heavily upon proving that Ahab's actual finding of Moby Dick with such dispatch once he reaches the line is not farfetched, he offers his affidavit "in order to be adequately understood, and moreover to take away any incredulity . . . as to the natural verity of the main points of this affair" (p. 175). Seldom has there appeared a character in fiction so thoroughly obsessed with being believed. As he presents instances in this chapter where whalemen have met a particular whale more than once, where certain whales have had names and were sometimes avoided and sometimes specifically sought out,

42. Heinz Kosok makes the convincing observation that Melville is dramatizing in Ishmael's audience at the Golden Inn what he anticipated would be the general reaction of incredulity among the readers of *Moby-Dick*. "Ishmael's Audience in 'The *Town Ho*'s Story,'" *Notes and Queries*, n.s., 14 (1967): 54–56.

he displays nothing less than a compulsion to establish "in all respects the reasonableness of the whole story of the White Whale" (p. 177). Otherwise, he says, those "ignorant" of the wonders of the sea "might scout at Moby Dick as a monstrous fable, or still worse and more detestable, a hideous and intolerable allegory" (p. 177). This is no fable or allegory, he protests with excessive heat, for "the most marvellous event in this book [is] corroborated by plain facts of the present day" (p. 181). Whales did indeed sink a few ships, as the story of the *Essex* and others make clear, and there apparently were fierce whales that sailors named, like Mocha Dick, Timor Tom, and New Zealand Jack; but all this is nothing compared to the feats of Moby Dick, which make for as incredible a tale as was ever told of whales, Ishmael's fervid desire to be believed notwithstanding.[43]

No matter how fantastic he becomes, Ishmael says in a later chapter, you *must* accept his word as truth: "So that when I shall hereafter detail to you . . . this expansive monster . . . I trust you will have renounced all ignorant incredulity, and be ready to abide by this; that though the Sperm Whale stove a passage through the Isthmus of Darien, and mixed the Atlantic with the Pacific, you would not elevate one hair of your eye-brow" (p. 285). Whenever Ishmael suspects his readers will elevate an eyebrow, he pauses to offer assurance that he is not being either facetious or unreasonable. For example, when darkness overtakes the *Pequod* while it is chasing Moby Dick, Ahab is still able to follow the whale through the night. At this point Ishmael stops to make sure he has not lost his credibility: "Here be it said, that this pertinacious pursuit of one particular whale, continued through day into night, and through night into day is a thing by no means unprecedented in the South sea fishery" (p. 453). The

43. A comment by Morton L. Ross suggests another way in which Ishmael manifests this yearning to be credible. In the "Cetology" chapter, Ishmael makes "the reader believe both that all available information has been here assembled for him and that the definitive limits of such information have been brought into view. Melville promotes this belief by frequent reminders of the scope of Ishmael's labors, such reminders credibly supported by the sheer wealth of data, but also slyly raising the bounds of such data by exaggerating the effort to reach them." "*Moby-Dick* as an Education," *Studies in the Novel* 6 (1974): 63.

question of whether Ishmael is actually being realistic is less significant than the obvious manifestation of his intense wish that his readers think he is. He displays this yearning also in matters that do not involve the search for the white whale. For example, after narrating Queequeg's miraculous rescue of Tashtego, who had fallen into the head of a decapitated whale and was sinking into the sea within it, he admits that "this queer adventure of the Gay-Header's will be sure to seem incredible to some landsmen" (p. 290), and so it does appear. Ishmael argues that it is not at all unbelievable, but he addresses himself not to the most farfetched aspect of the affair—Queequeg's superhuman feat—but to the secondary questions of why the head should sink rather than float and why it should sink slowly. He has given the illusion of proof to a tall tale that he most urgently wants everyone to believe is true.[44]

Ishmael's compulsion to be believed derives from two principal causes. The first is an aesthetic theory he develops during the course of the novel. He suggests that, ironically, the closer a work of art follows actual life, the more deeply symbolic it is. Since life is complex and inexplicable, so is that art most like life. Nothing could thus be more ineffably complicated than a simple fact. This view lies behind chapter 56 ("Of the Less Erroneous Pictures of Whales, and the True Pictures of Whaling Scenes"). Ishmael's interest in the more accurate representations of whaling life grows out of his conviction that, as he expresses it in a later chapter, "in this world it is not so easy to settle these plain things. I have ever found your plain things the knottiest of all" (p. 312). Melville came back to this idea repeatedly in his works. In Pierre, for example, he wrote: "This world we live in is brimmed with wonders, and I and all mankind, beneath our garbs of common-placeness, conceal enigmas that the stars themselves, and perhaps the highest seraphim can not resolve."[45] Ishmael sums up this posi-

44. As far back as his first novel, Melville evinced the same conflict seen in Ishmael, a desire to be completely sane and communicative—to be believed— and a yearning to involve himself totally in otherworldly experience. Typee is far from a literal account of Melville's experiences, though he went to great lengths to try to prove that it was.

45. Pierre, ed. Harrison Hayford, Hershel Parker, and G. Thomas Tanselle

tion when he says, "All truth is profound" (p. 161). Consequently, he respects authentic, lifelike art though his own frequently moves with force in the opposite direction.

His second and more important reason for desiring to be totally credible is more emotional and psychological than it is aesthetic or philosophical. The pervasive implausibility in *Moby-Dick* derives chiefly from the seedsman's aspect of Ishmael's personality, a factor in his makeup that sometimes deeply troubles him, sometimes makes him defiantly proud. If Ishmael can make himself believed, however, then he will feel that he has not cut off communication with the workaday world. He recognizes also that as long as others believe him, he will be considered reasonable; if his credibility disappears, his mental stability will come into question. He is aware that he must not sever communication with those who dwell on the ordinary plane of existence (no matter how superior he may feel to them) and that his remaining too long in the wonder-world will result in this isolation. The sub-sub-librarian in him repeatedly creates much in his narrative that is implausible; he then has to combat this tendency and try to make all appear rationally acceptable. Ishmael must convince others and himself that he is still afloat, a survivor in his perilous subjective world. If we dismiss the implausibility of *Moby-Dick* as unimportant since Melville was a symbolist rather than a realist, or if we accept without serious questioning Ishmael's frequent insistence that all he says is actually plausible, then what is going on within Ishmael—the dramatic interaction between pale usher and sub-sub-librarian—is obscured and the book is deprived of one of its richest and most fascinating dimensions.

(Evanston and Chicago: Northwestern University Press and the Newberry Library, 1971), p. 139.

The High and Mighty
Business of Whaling

Chapter 2

W hen Melville completed *Moby-Dick,* he wrote Hawthorne: "I have written a wicked book, and feel spotless as a lamb."[1] Critics have debated for years what exactly he meant, but one thing seems obvious: although he was not entirely pleased with *Moby-Dick,* writing it had a therapeutic effect on him, at least for a short time.[2] That was probably because he chose a subject that offered him a needed opportunity to give vent to his diving urges while retaining to some extent his grounding in the ordinary world. He discovered a subject that he could write about from both perspectives. It may have been "wicked" of him to use his art so personally and, in a way, so selfishly, but he did it, and he did not feel guilty about it. Both Melville's compulsion to dive and his desire to keep his connection with the real, workaday

1. *The Letters of Herman Melville,* ed. Merrell R. Davis and William H. Gilman (New Haven: Yale University Press, 1960), p. 142.

2. Though he rationalized that "grand erections" were never completed in a single age, it nevertheless seemed to bother him that *Moby-Dick* was unpolished if not, indeed, unfinished. In it he wrote: "This whole book is but a draught— nay, but the draught of a draught. Oh, Time, Strength, Cash, and Patience!"

world are manifested in his treatment of the whaling material of *Moby-Dick,* which is the subject of this chapter.

Through much of the novel, Ishmael offers praise of the whaling industry in America and expresses his personal indebtedness to it. "As for me," he says, "if, by any possibility, there be any as yet undiscovered prime thing in me; if I shall ever deserve any real repute in that small but high hushed world which I might not be unreasonably ambitious of: if hereafter I shall do anything that, upon the whole, a man might rather have done than to have left undone; if, at my death, my executors, or more properly my creditors, find any precious MSS. in my desk, then here I prospectively ascribe all the honor and the glory to whaling; for a whaleship was my Yale College and my Harvard" (p. 101).[3] Crucial to an understanding of whaling in *Moby-Dick* is an awareness that in such a statement as the above, Melville is addressing himself more to metaphoric than to literal whaling. While seeming to laud those who pursue actual whales, he often is extolling the nobility of deep diving in an intellectual and spiritual sense.

Chapter 24, "The Advocate," and chapter 82, "The Honor and Glory of Whaling," illustrate this form of double-dealing especially well. Both purport to sing the praises of the whaling industry, but Ishmael's language has a quality of double entendre about it. While defending literal whalemen—and seeming more flippant than sincere—he is making an indirect but heartfelt and impressive case for his own fraternal order of deep divers. If "The Advocate" is read (as critics usually read it) as an attempt to ennoble ordinary whalemen,[4] it is illogical and unconvincing. Ishmael says that the whaling industry should be honored because there is "something puissant" in it. On the level of common sense, this is weak because that which is big and powerful is not necessarily noble and attractive. But it is a highly appropriate remark to make about figurative whaling. As Ishmael tries to praise the influence of literal whalemen on civilization, he fails to be con-

---

3. All references to *Moby-Dick* are to the Norton Critical Edition, ed. Harrison Hayford and Hershel Parker (New York: Norton, 1967).

4. See, however, Joseph Flibbert, *Melville and the Art of Burlesque* (Amsterdam: Rodopi, 1974), pp. 97–98. Flibbert is one of a very few critics who comment on the illogicality and mock heroic tone of "The Advocate" chapter.

vincing because his examples raise serious questions. What if whaling ships did bring the white man's way to primitive parts, as Ishmael asserts, and what if they did carry the first missionaries to South Sea islands? We know from reading *Typee* and *Omoo* that these are not necessarily the beginnings of enlightenment. On the other hand, his argument does seem convincing when we recognize that he is speaking of the other kind of whaleman: "For in their succorless empty-handedness, they, in the heathenish sharked waters, and by the beaches of unrecorded, javelin islands, battled with virgin wonders and terrors that Cook with all his marines and muskets would not willingly have dared" (p. 100).

Toward the end of the chapter, Ishmael lists several objections commonly raised against real whalemen, and he responds to each charge. His answers, if taken literally, are tricky, humorous, or even irrelevant. For example, he says that it is not true that the whale has no famous "chronicler," but the names he comes up with seem farfetched examples—Job, Alfred the Great, and Edmund Burke. They are not facetious or absurd choices, however, if we understand Ishmael actually to be referring to metaphoric whaling. In response to the charge that whalemen have "no good blood in their veins," Ishmael genuinely defends his own kind: "They have something better than royal blood" (p. 101). Then he moves on to the issue of respectability. The first comment is a deeply felt generalization that whalemen—divers—are "imperial." The example that follows is that "by old English statutory law," the king gets the tail and the queen the head of all whales taken on the beaches. This curious fact does not prove anything at all in regard to the respectability of real whaling, but to say that the whale is "a royal fish" is suggestive and meaningful in a metaphoric sense, for Ishmael believes he has some royal essence. To defend whaling against the charge that it has no dignity, Ishmael states that there is a constellation named Cetus, which has little to do with real whalemen but much to do with those who voyage into the wonder-world (the dignity of whom "the very heavens attest"), his deeper and truer subject of this chapter. Ishmael thus stands up for two kinds of whale hunters in "The Advocate," but it is only his impassioned sympathy for the deep divers of the world that rings true. His defense of the other kind comes across as halfhearted or facetious.

As Melville confessed to Hawthorne, there is, indeed, something "wicked" about *Moby-Dick,* a sort of duplicity. When he composed "The Honor and Glory of Whaling," he wanted to brag, to place himself high above the members of the commonality—not among them—in the company of heroes and demigods. When this feeling came over him, he told himself that he was actually part of the Godhead, which had been broken up into a few choice pieces (at one time he believed Hawthorne was another piece). His attitude during these periods was little short of theomania.[5] In periods of melancholy and at times when he felt unaccepted and generally isolated, he cultivated this mood of spiritual arrogance to lift himself as well as to defy almost spitefully the cloddish world around him. "The Honor and Glory of Whaling" reflects this mood. It is a sneaky performance because Melville is boasting of his own genius while seemingly raising the American whaling industry to mythic and heroic levels.

If read as praise for actual whaling, the tone of the chapter can only be called mock heroic, and the evidence given for the nobility of whaling ridiculous. Perseus was the first whaleman, the father of the industry. St. George fought a whale that had crawled up on the land. Since both Hercules, "that antique Crockett and Kit Carson," and Jonah were swallowed by whales, that makes them "of our clan." And so on.[6] The entire chapter appears to be a hoax. Yet it is not: the whalemen that Ishmael is referring to are those few like himself. He is praising himself, not the whaling industry, when he says: "The more I dive into this matter of

5. This feeling is reflected sometimes in his marginalia. For example, in his copy of the New Testament, the following lines appear in his handwriting: "In Life he appears as a true Philosopher—as a wise man in the highest sense. He stands *firm to his point;* he *goes on his way inflexibly;* and while he exalts the lower to himself, while he makes the ignorant, the poor, the sick, partakers of his wisdom, and his riches, of his strength, he, on the other hand, in no wise conceals his divine origin; and he dares; he dares to equal himself with God; nay, to declare that he himself is God."

6. After quoting passages from this chapter in *Moby-Dick,* Robert Zoellner makes the following point: "It is distressing to discover that this arrant Ishmaelian nonsense has been used as the foundation for readings of *Moby-Dick* almost certainly at odds with what Melville actually intended." *The Salt-Sea Mastodon: A Reading of Moby-Dick* (Berkeley and Los Angeles: University of California Press, 1973), p. 176.

whaling, and push my researches up to the very spring-head of it, so much the more am I impressed with its great honorableness and antiquity; and especially when I find so many great demigods and heroes, prophets of all sorts, who one way or other have shed distinction upon it, I am transported with the reflection that I myself belong, though but subordinately, to so emblazoned a fraternity" (p. 304).[7] He was not accepted at that time as America's great genius of literature—far from it. He should have been, and he knew it, but he could at least comfort himself by placing his name among the great. Flighty as it seems, "The Honor and Glory of Whaling" is an act of defiant self-justification. It might be farcical to include Perseus, St. George, Hercules, Jonah, and Vishnoo as members of the same profession that includes as well Stubb, Flask, Gabriel, the crew of the *Bachelor,* and a host of others, but Melville was dead serious in believing that these heroes and demigods were brothers with himself in a far more exalted fraternity, not the fishery but "high" whaling.

This is not to say that Melville did not like some features of the American whaling industry. He respected the courage and uncomplaining toughness of its sturdy sailors, and he was impressed with its importance to America's economic well-being. He had himself been a whaleman and therefore felt somewhat defensive about the much maligned profession. But coeval with these attitudes, he held other, and perhaps deeper, opposing feelings. A clue to these may be his review (*Literary World,* March 6, 1847) of J. Ross Browne's book about whale hunting, *Etchings of a Whaling Cruise.* He liked Browne's book because it contains "unvarnished facts" and "presents a faithful picture of the life led by the twenty thousand" American whalemen.[8] So much romantic nonsense had been written about the sea, he says, that this book brings refreshing reality. The truth that it offers, however, does not do much to further the reputation of whalemen. The captain of the whaling

7. Edgar A. Dryden notices that Ishmael is speaking of being more than an ordinary whaleman in this chapter, but he takes Ishmael's other meaning to be that he is a writer of books. *Melville's Thematics of Form: The Great Art of Telling the Truth* (Baltimore: Johns Hopkins University Press, 1968), pp. 92–93.

8. *Herman Melville: Representative Selections,* ed. Willard Thorp (New York: American Book Co., 1938), p. 320.

ship is a monster and the crew an ignorant and beastly bunch who are "incessantly quarrelling and fighting."[9] Melville seemed delighted that Browne's book pointed up the difference between the image of whaling that the industry wanted and the "sort of vocation whaling in truth is."[10] The public relations men of whaling would have us believe, Melville writes in the review, that a whaleship "is the home of the unfortunate—the asylum of the oppressed."[11] Browne, in fact, was himself "duped" (Melville's word) by this falsehood when he was talked into joining the crew of a whaling ship.

Melville's comments on the American whaling industry in his review of Browne's book do not sound like those of a spokesman for whaling. He "shudders" to think of what awaits young men who are deceived into believing there is wealth, excitement, dignity, and nobility awaiting them in the fishery. He sneers with delight that after Browne's exposé, the shipping agents of the whaling companies will have to find some new tricks to entice unsuspecting and "unsophisticated striplings" into joining the crew of a whaling ship.[12] Since aside from *Moby-Dick* Melville

---

9. Ibid., p. 324.

10. Ibid., p. 326.

11. Ibid., p. 323.

12. Ibid., p. 322. Though Melville looked back with a degree of pride at having been a sailor himself, he did not enjoy his days at sea as much as is commonly believed, and he had no illusions about the kinds of men who spent their lives before the mast. The narrator of *Typee* describes the crew of his ship as "a parcel of dastardly and mean-spirited wretches, divided among themselves, and only united in enduring without resistance the unmitigated tyranny of the captain" (Northwestern-Newberry ed., p. 21). In *Redburn* the narrator is no kinder in his general view of sailors: "Consider, that, with the majority of them, the very fact of their being sailors, argues a certain recklessness and sensualism of character, ignorance, and depravity" (Northwestern-Newberry ed., p. 138). During his seagoing period, Melville no sooner got aboard a ship than he was dying to get off. After a brief but unpleasant voyage as a merchant seaman, he signed on as a whaler, only to abandon his ship at Nukuhiva in the South Seas. He left the Marquesas Islands aboard another whaling ship on which he found conditions so deplorable that he joined in a bloodless mutiny. For that he was arrested and jailed on the island of Tahiti, but confinement was so loose he was able to escape. He enlisted in the American navy for a miserable voyage on the frigate *United States*, which brought him back to America. He became more

wrote so little about whaling, this review offers a valuable insight into some of his negative feelings about the industry.

There persists, however, the widespread conviction that Melville unequivocally loved and respected the whaling profession and that *Moby-Dick* is an epic glorifying the ordinary whale hunter. Newton Arvin, for example, senses a "loving manner in which Melville lingers over his imagery of lances, harpoons, and cutting-spades, of whaleboats, whale-lines, and blubber-hooks." He says that all this "recalls again the epic minstrel."[13] Richard Chase takes *Moby-Dick* to be "intransigently a story of the whaling industry; a hymn to the technical skill of the heroes and the marvelous perfection of their machine."[14] The novel, Lewis Mumford believes, "recorded the last heroic days of whaling,"[15] and William Ellery Sedgwick perceives "patriotism" in the book, "the happier because it is identified not with a warlike navy but the great American whale fishery, which exemplified American daring and democratic independence."[16] Robert Zoellner has rightly questioned the validity of this view,[17] but the notion that *Moby-Dick* is an epic of the common American whaleman remains, as H. Bruce Franklin's comment on the book indicates: "It is a celebration of the transcendent dignity and nobility, in fact, divinity, of the most oppressed members of the proletariat."[18]

Melville gives ample support for such views if one takes him

---

appalled with each experience aboard ship; consequently, when he arrived home, he vowed never again to go down to the sea in ships (except as a passenger).

13. Newton Arvin, *Herman Melville* (New York: Sloane, 1950), p. 159.

14. Richard Chase, *Herman Melville: A Critical Study* (New York: Macmillan, 1949), p. 101.

15. Lewis Mumford, *Herman Melville* (New York: Harcourt, Brace, 1929), p. 184.

16. William Ellery Sedgwick, *Herman Melville: The Tragedy of Mind* (Cambridge: Harvard University Press, 1944), p. 89. A more recent critic continues the same line of argument that Melville "elevates whaling to heroic proportions," that Melville insists that "there is the greatest dignity in whaling." Ray B. Browne, *Melville's Drive to Humanism* (Lafayette: Purdue University Studies, 1971), p. 57.

17. Zoellner, pp. 166–90.

18. H. Bruce Franklin, *The Victim as Criminal and Artist: Literature from the American Prison* (New York: Oxford University Press, 1978), p. 45.

strictly at his word. If one can read, say, "The Advocate" chapter or "The Honor and Glory of Whaling" as serious and sincere praise of the whaling industry, then Melville certainly is, as many believe, the champion of the common whaleman. But he was a much more complicated man than that position allows for. *Moby-Dick* is really about two kinds of whaling, material and non-material. When Melville is speaking of the latter, whether glorifying it or warning against it, his voice has the unmistakable ring of passion, awe, inspiration, and depth. When he is describing the former, his tone ranges all the way from the objective and down-to-earth to the mock heroic. He felt ambivalently about actual whaling—both favoring it and disapproving of it. He goes on an energizing but dangerous metaphoric voyage, the object of which is to locate and experience the whale. Literally whalemen pursue the whale not to experience it but to kill it for petty material gain. Consequently, Melville could like some of the things about the whaling industry, but inevitably it had to come into conflict in his mind with metaphoric whaling, and that clash produced the strong note of insincerity in much of his praise of actual whaling.

Furthermore, Melville had such a profound reverence for the sanctity of life and such a sensitivity to the similarities between whales and human beings that his descriptions of whales often reveal a sympathy for them that appears incongruous with a role he may have wanted to play (but could not): a staunch supporter of the whaling industry. To be sure, he does have Ishmael sometimes treat whales merely as objects to be hunted, sliced up, and boiled down. He can be very coldhearted. For example, Ishmael describes in one place how the "precious parts" of a nursing whale are cut and how the milk pours forth mixed with blood. Then, without the slightest apparent sympathy, he comments on the whale's milk as food. It is sweet and "might do well with strawberries" (p. 326).[19] He is similarly detached from any emotional

19. Darrell E. Griffiths comments on "Ishmael's lack of compassion" in this passage. See "Circles and Orphans," *Books at Brown*, 24 (1971): 71. In their edition of *Moby-Dick* (New York: Hendricks House, 1952), Luther S. Mansfield and Howard P. Vincent point out that Melville derived his statement on the

considerations when he describes the use of a device in whaling called the "drugg": "It is chiefly among gallied whales that this drugg is used. For then, more whales are close around you than you can possibly chase at one time. But sperm whales are not every day encountered; while you may, then, you must kill all you can. And if you cannot kill them all at once, you must wing them, so that they can be afterwards killed at your leisure" (pp. 323–24). Spoken like a true whaleman—sensible, practical, efficient in getting the bloody job done, experienced in his worldly trade. There are other passages like these in *Moby-Dick* where we hear Ishmael speaking merely as whale killer.

But at other times Ishmael makes whales seem more like human beings than brute beasts and consequently the killing of them more like murder than a heroic profession.[20] He says that whales have "profound" heads like those of Plato or Dante and other men who think "deep thoughts" (p. 313). The cows and calves among whales are "the women and children" (p. 324). As if speaking of human youngsters, he says that small whales are "young, unsophisticated, and every way innocent and inexperienced" (p. 325). It might not be unusual to describe an animal as "young," but calling it "unsophisticated" or "inexperienced" links it with humanity. In the same chapter, "The Grand Armada," Ishmael draws the whale even more into the human circle by comparing cubs with infants:

> But far beneath this wondrous world upon the surface, another and still stranger world met our eyes as we gazed over the side. For, suspended in those watery vaults, floated the forms of the

richness of whales' milk from passages in Thomas Beale, *The Natural History of the Sperm Whale* (1839), and William Scoresby, Jr., *An Account of the Arctic Regions, with a History and Description of the Northern Whale-Fishery* (1820). As another possible source, one that Melville may have read earlier than the above, Kendra H. Gaines offers a passage that paraphrases such sources as Beale and Scoresby in *The Penny Cyclopaedia* (1843). See "A Consideration of an Additional Source for Melville's *Moby-Dick*," *Melville Society Extracts*, no. 29 (1977): 6–12. The comment, however, that "it might do well with strawberries" is apparently Melville's own.

20. The details of my argument that follows about Melville's treatment of whales sometimes parallel those of Robert Zoellner in *The Salt-Sea Mastodon*, but we reach different conclusions.

nursing mothers of the whales, and those that by their enormous girth seemed shortly to become mothers. The lake, as I have hinted, was to a considerable depth exceedingly transparent; and as human infants while suckling will calmly and fixedly gaze away from the breast, as if leading two different lives at the time; and while yet drawing mortal nourishment, be still spiritually feasting upon some unearthly reminiscence;—even so did the young of these whales seem looking up towards us, but not at us, as if we were but a bit of Gulf-weed in their new-born sight. . . . One of these little infants . . . seemed hardly a day old. . . . He was a little frisky; though as yet his body seemed scarce yet recovered from that irksome position it had so lately occupied in the mater- nal reticule; where, tail to head, and all ready for the final spring, the unborn whale lies bent like a Tartar's bow. The delicate side- fins, and the palms of his flukes, still freshly retained the plaited crumpled appearance of a baby's ears newly arrived from foreign parts. (p. 325)

These are not merely creatures to be disposed of unfeelingly for profit. An aura of mystery surrounds them. "Some of the subtlest secrets of the seas," writes Ishmael, "seemed divulged to us in this enchanted pond" (p. 326). He is referring to "young Levia- than amours in the deep." Melville points out in a footnote— without specifically stating the comparison—that whales copu- late, gestate, and give birth in a manner almost identical to that of human beings: "The sperm whale, as with all other species of the Leviathan, but unlike most other fish, breeds indifferently at all seasons; after a gestation which may probably be set down at nine months, producing but one at a time; though in some few known instances giving birth to an Esau and Jacob:—a con- tingency provided for in suckling by two teats" (p. 326).

In other places, Ishmael describes whales in a way that resem- bles the technique used in a series of once popular paintings, each one of a poker game in progress. Many of the recognizable types of humanity are there—the scared bettor, the sharper, the bluffer, and so forth. The participants in the game, however, are not people but dogs.[21] Generations of amused viewers have studied

21. These are popular paintings of dogs by Cassius Marsellus Collidge (1844–1934). In the late nineteenth and early twentieth centuries, they were to

these pictures with a double sensation: love of dogs and mild disgust with fellow humans. The dogs in the paintings are more than dogs because they are often decked out in human clothes and are involved in a human situation (one that satirizes humanity at the same time that it humanizes the animals). Melville uses the same technique in *Moby-Dick*. He has fun at the expense of whales just as the painter did with dogs. He dresses them up exaggeratedly in human costumes; he forces them into human situations; he types them in human terms. Consequently, he causes them to look ridiculous. The net result, however, is that they are brought into the human circle by this verbal costuming of them in comic human terms.

The most extended treatment of whales in this manner is chapter 88 ("Schools and Schoolmasters"), which describes certain domestic habits of whales, especially in groups. "In cavalier attendance upon the school of females, you invariably see a male in full grown magnitude, but not old; who, upon any alarm, evinces his gallantry by falling in the rear and covering the flight of his ladies" (p. 328). With whimsical delight, Ishmael continues his account, using nouns and adjectives more appropriate for a sultan and his wives than for whales: "In truth, this gentleman is a luxurious Ottoman, swimming about over the water world, surroundingly accompanied by all the solaces and endearments of the harem. . . . It is very curious to watch this harem and its lord in their indolent ramblings. . . . My lord whale keeps a wary eye on his interesting family." Ishmael next describes the intrusion of an outsider into the whale pod: "Should any unwarrantably pert young Leviathan coming that way, presume to draw confidentially close to one of the ladies, with what prodigious fury the Bashaw assails him, and chases him away! High times, indeed, if unprincipled young rakes like him are to be permitted to invade the sanctity of domestic bliss; though do what the Bashaw will, he cannot keep the most notorious Lothario out of his bed" (p. 329). The incongruities Ishmael evokes by calling whales "Lothario," "Bashaw," or "Solomon" and his description of their

---

be found in great numbers in such places as barber shops, small stores, and bars, many of them reproduced on calendars and posters.

domestic bliss in terms of a pasha's harem all work—somewhat ironically—to create sympathy for them through condescending anthropomorphizing.

Because of his sympathy for these humanlike sea forms, Ishmael occasionally comes close to an outright condemnation of whaling when he depicts vividly the suffering of wounded whales. In chapter 81 ("The Pequod Meets the Virgin"), Ishmael describes the wounding and killing of a "huge, humped old bull" whale with an "unnatural stump" for his "starboard fin." Although Ishmael treats this infirmity and others of the old whale with some levity, he becomes serious when he speaks of the whale's desperate and futile attempt to escape: "It was a terrific, most pitiable, and maddening sight. The whale was now going head out, and sending his spout before him in a continual tormented jet; while his one poor fin beat his side in an agony of fright. Now to this hand, now to that, he yawed in his faltering flight, and still at every billow that he broke, he spasmodically sank in the sea, or sideways rolled towards the sky his one beating fin" (p. 298). The pity is intensified by his realization that the creature in all his panic cannot cry out: "He had no voice, save that choking respiration through his spiracle, and this made the sight of him unspeakably pitiable" (p. 298). It is not sporting or humane to hunt an aged and mutilated creature. This one is also blind: "From the points which the whale's eyes had once occupied, now protruded blind bulbs, horribly pitiable to see" (p. 301). But whalemen are not sportsmen, and pity for whales is to them a foreign emotion. Ishmael recognizes these facts in one of his rare direct statements against the cruelty of whaling: "But pity there was none. For all his old age, and his one arm, and his blind eyes, he must die the death and be murdered" (p. 301). In *Moby-Dick* Melville certainly was not composing the great American epic of the whaling industry. What he did write turned out to be largely an attack on civilization with its blatant hypocrisy and high folly. Whales had to be "murdered," he writes, in order to light the churches that "preach unconditional inoffensiveness by all to all" (p. 301).

If the killing of whales is "murder," three acts that whalemen perform on the bodies of whales are described in terms that suggest desecration: tearing out the tongue, severing and mutilating the penis, and eating whale flesh. Ishmael treats these events lightly on the surface, but the total effect is serious. Whalemen come off looking not only barbarous but cruelly profane as well. One of the main reasons for this is that Ishmael describes all three actions in contexts of holiness and reverence, making the acts seem blasphemous. The whale's tongue is violently ripped from a mouth that Ishmael pictures as a great church (The Grote Kerk in Haarlem). He uses clerical terms when he describes the use made of the whale's penis. And he shows Stubb in the act of eating whale meat while giving Fleece orders about how to preach a sermon to sharks, a sermon that blasphemes against the principles of Christianity. Chapters 95 and 64 ("The Cassock" and "Stubb's Supper") in particular reveal an Ishmael who is ostensibly joking and having a good time but cringing somewhere deep within himself at the spectacles of violated sanctity.

"The Cassock" chapter has been snickered over a good deal, but it has not received the primacy it deserves in analyses of *Moby-Dick*.[22] Many readers regard it as a dirty joke. Others take Melville's intent more seriously but still read the tone as a "locker-room leer."[23] Melville's treatment of his subject is frequently described as "Rabelaisian."[24] One critic says that the chapter is outrageously humorous, that it possesses an "ingeniously comic effect."[25] What humor there is does not come from a locker room,

22. D. H. Lawrence, however, was greatly impressed with this chapter. It is, he wrote, "surely the oldest piece of phallicism in all the world's literature." *Studies in Classic American Literature* (New York: Thomas Seltzer, 1923), p. 231. "Some day," writes Howard P. Vincent, "a critic will properly explain the full significance of this chapter, perhaps the most amazing in an amazing book." *The Trying-Out of Moby-Dick* (Boston: Houghton Mifflin, 1949), p. 328.

23. Paul Brodtkorb, Jr., *Ishmael's White World: A Phenomenological Reading of Moby Dick* (New Haven: Yale University Press, 1965), p. 155n. Generally, however, Brodtkorb's comments on this chapter are—as is his entire book—provocative.

24. See, for example, Brodtkorb, p. 154n, and Vincent, *Trying-Out*, p. 328.

25. Mario L. D'Avanzo, "'The Cassock' and Carlyle's 'Church-Clothes,'" *ESQ* 50 (1968): 76. John Stark, "'The Cassock' Chapter in *Moby-Dick* and the Theme of Literary Creativity," *Studies in American Fiction* 1 (1973): 105–11, refers to "The Cassock" as "a sly, amusing chapter" but discovers much meaning

nor is it truly comic. It is sardonic black humor, an indirect but devastating charge against civilization for its treatment of whales. The *cassock* is Ishmael's name for the skin cut from the penis of a whale and dried out. It is then worn by a crewman called a mincer, who slices whale blubber into small pieces in preparation for the trying-out process. This unusual garment apparently shields out the oil he is exposed to and also protects him from the black smoke of the tryworks. Insofar as scholars have been able to determine, Melville did not derive information about the *cassock* from his usual sources; it came either from his own experience aboard whale ships or from his imagination.[26]

The effect of "The Cassock" is not amusement but shock. It is bizarre, grotesque, even macabre. If it is not widely considered as such, it is probably because of two major reasons. The first is that many readers never realize what the "strange, enigmatical object" is that Ishmael is describing.[27] It is never called a whale's penis. The second is that among those sophisticated readers who know that Ishmael is describing a whale phallus, the reputation of the chapter as an irreverently bold and naughty joke dilutes what should be the full impact. After all, how can any of it be taken seriously when Ishmael creates, as numerous critics have pointed out, such a mischievous pun as "archbishoprick," his label for the mincer who wears the "cassock" (a garment worn by the clergy), and who cuts "Bible leaves," as the slices of whale blubber are called? The word *archbishoprick* has probably been the most important single influence in the reading of this chapter as mainly a phallic joke.[28]

---

in it nevertheless. It is about, he says, "the growth of the artist." Leslie Fiedler finds "something a little childish" about it. *Love and Death in the American Novel* (New York: Criterion Books, 1960), p. 533.

26. "None of Melville's fish documents was particularly helpful to Melville in 'the Cassock.'" Mansfield and Vincent, p. 797. "The whaling sources," comments Vincent in *Trying-Out*, "give no indication, physiological or otherwise, of the facts of Melville's chapter" (p. 328).

27. Vincent comments that "ninety percent of Melville's readers miss entirely the meaning of 'The Cassock'" (*Trying-Out*, p. 328).

28. Yet the word may not be so obviously a phallic pun as it seems. The spelling "archbishoprick" was still perfectly legitimate in Melville's day, if

Melville probably did intend a pun, but the most important term, weighted heavily with baggage of meaning beyond that of "archbishoprick," is the word *mincer*. Ishmael centers his attention on this word, which he uses several times in the chapter. The word strongly appealed to him. How appropriate, he seems to be saying, that this man into whose desecrating hands the "grandissimus" is placed should be known among whalemen as the "mincer"! Ishmael profits by the multiple and suggestive meanings of the word. A mincer is one who "diminishes or disparages" (OED), which is what the mincer is doing to the whale. Melville may have also been familiar with the use of *mince,* then popular as a slang term in medicine for the dissecting of a human body (OED). To underscore further this suggestion of an autopsy— albeit an atrocious one—he refers to the penis as "a dead comrade" carried off the field of battle. It is not afforded any last rites with dignity, however, for in a shocking and perverse "post-mortemizing" process, as Ishmael calls it, this comrade is subjected to the most debasing mutilation imaginable. The mincer is the high priest, the pope, of whale killers who emasculate and mutilate for the sake of a materialistic religion of utilitarianism. [29]

Ishmael deals with the third act of desecration, the eating of the whale, in chapter 64 ("Stubb's Supper") and in chapter 65 ("The Whale as a Dish"). Again, he makes it sound as if the dead whale were not once just an animal but a fellow human being. He says that Stubb is eating a "corpse." [30] In the chapter that follows,

---

somewhat outdated. The *Oxford English Dictionary* gives several examples of the spelling "bishoprick," and *Murray's Grammar,* a contemporary text Melville knew, lists the -*rick* ending as indicating "dominion, jurisdiction, or condition: as, 'Bailewick, bishiprick. . . .'" See Donald Drury, "Melville, Pip, and *Murray's Grammar," Melville Society Extracts,* no. 31 (1977): 9.

29. Melville's feeling that whale mutilation was a reflection of mankind's insensitivity appears eminently justified by a news story in the Atlanta *Journal,* January 18, 1978: "Sightseers ripped away patches of flesh from a beached [at Juno Beach, Florida] 50-foot sperm whale, children scrambled over its tail and teen-agers tried to pull out its teeth before marine officers chased them away. . . . By [the time] they finished, the whale looked like a bloody rock. . . . No one was arrested."

30. Stubb's cannibalism is also suggested by his comment in chapter 81 concerning Captain Derick De Deer of the ship *Virgin:* "I'd like to eat that villanous Yarman" (p. 297).

Ishmael finds it abhorrent "that a man should eat a newly murdered thing of the sea, and eat it too by its own light" (p. 255).
Stubb is not to be singled out, however, as a special ogre; he is
representative of the dead level of the mass: "Go to the meat-
market of a Saturday night and see the crowds of live bipeds
staring up at the long rows of dead quadrupeds. Does not that
sight take a tooth out of the cannibal's jaw? Cannibals? who is not
a cannibal?" (p. 255).

Here Ishmael is speaking of a cannibal in a literal sense of one
who actually feeds on his own kind. But he establishes a clear
difference between cannibals like the natives of Typee who eat
other human beings and those more "civilized" cannibals who in
his view are actually doing pretty much the same thing but who
hypocritically refuse to recognize it. In a direct attack on civilization, Ishmael caustically remarks: "I tell you . . . it will be more
tolerable for that provident Fejee, I say, in the day of judgment,
than for thee, civilized and enlightened gourmand, who nailest
geese to the ground and feastest on their bloated livers in thy
'paté-de-foie-gras'" (pp. 255–56). This is not to say that Ishmael
approves of the cannibalism of the Fejees any more than Christ
approved of the atrocities of Sodom and Gomorrha when he made
a strikingly similar statement about those in a "city" who refuse
to accept the Word of God, a passage on which Ishmael's words
are obviously based: "Verily I say unto you, It shall be more tolerable for Sodom and Gomorrha in the day of judgment, than for
that city" (Mark 6:11). Ishmael, too, is speaking out against
those who do not see, those who are smug in their disgusting
hypocrisy. Some of them will criticize Stubb for eating "the whale
by its own light" and thus "adding insult to injury," but they
themselves carve the flesh of animal with a knife the handle of
which is made from that animal's bone. They eat a goose and pick
their teeth with a goosefeather, and the "Secretary of the Society
for the Suppression of Cruelty to Ganders" writes his circulars
with a gander quill.

Ishmael considers Stubb cannibalistic in eating the whale steak
not only because whales are so much like human beings but also
because they simply are fellow living creatures. With the ardor of
an evangelistic vegetarian, he denounces the eating of all flesh. In
words that imply a terrible act of violation, that of robbing a

grave, he describes how in order to obtain the brains of small sperm whales for eating, "the *casket* of the skull is *broken into with an axe,* and the two plump, whitish lobes" taken out (p. 255, italics mine). He then broadens his attack by linking whalemen who relish whale brains with people on land who feast on calves' brains: cannibals all! He further suggests that it "requires uncommon discrimination" to tell the calves' heads from their own, "and that is the reason why a young buck with an intelligent looking calf's head before him, is somehow one of the saddest sights you can see" (p. 255). Though supposedly civilized, they are no more so than the animals they are eating. Melville's word to describe the young eater of the calf's head—*buck*—is well chosen. "The head looks a sort of reproachfully at him," Ishmael continues, "with an 'Et tu Brute!' expression" (p. 255). *Brute* suggests the murderous treachery of Brutus, but it has the double meaning of brute—the eater of the head is no less a brute than the creature he is consuming. The sailor eating whales' brains and the landsman eating calves' heads are both in a sense cannibals. Ishmael never says that he is a vegetarian, but he has the sensibilities of one.

How, then, is Ishmael's own admission of cannibalism to be taken? "I myself am a savage," he says, "owning no allegiance but to the King of the Cannibals" (p. 232). Furthermore, he claims to have actually eaten part of a whale himself. After describing "plum-pudding" as "certain fragmentary parts of the whale's flesh, here and there adhering to the blanket of blubber" when it is pulled from the whale's carcass, he says in an oddly facetious way: "I confess, that once I stole behind the foremast to try it. It tasted something as I should conceive a royal cutlet from the thigh of Louis le Gros might have tasted, supposing him to have been killed the first day after the venison season, and that particular venison season contemporary with an unusually fine vintage of the vineyard of Champagne" (p. 349). If Ishmael actually did what he says he did, he is nothing short of a madman, but this passage is neither the literal account of what a crazy man did nor a simple spoof. Here as in several other places, such as the curious passage in the same chapter where he tells of his experience while squeezing sperm, Ishmael has taken leave of actual whales and is speaking of moments in what he calls the wonder-world. Stubb eats the whale literally; Ishmael eats it figuratively.

Though it would be a mistake to make this figurative whale in *Moby-Dick* equivalent to Christ or to God or in any Judeo-Christian sense to give it religious meaning except on the broadest level, Melville is using the same metaphor as that found in the Bible when Christ describes the eating of his flesh: "Verily, verily, I say unto you, Except ye eat the flesh of the Son of man, and drink his blood, ye have no life in you. . . . For my flesh is meat indeed, and my blood is drink indeed. He that eateth my flesh, and drinketh my blood, dwelleth in me, and I in him" (John 6:53, 55–56). Melville had a deep appreciation for Christian symbolism, and he understood its wide implications and vast profundities with rare insight. Consequently, the words, symbols, and parables of the King James Bible find their way often into *Moby-Dick*. Melville profits from their weighty and brilliant suggestiveness, their incomparable richness in collective cultural traditions, and their sometimes strange, if not shocking, associations (as in the case of Christ's cannibalistic metaphor) while turning them to his own specific purposes. Ishmael is not uniting with Christ when he eats the whale, but the metaphor is similar. He is describing a kind of transubstantiation, for he seeks to find his true spiritual identity in that which he "eats," not mere whale flesh but what it represents.

Eating the whale, or squeezing its sperm, is thus for Ishmael a metaphorical way of expressing his attempts to discover it, to taste it, to feel it *within himself.* It is, in other words, a symbolic handling of the act of self-discovery. In this sense whaling is the process by which one embarks upon the adventure of finding out who one is, not only in the personal and individualistic sense but also in terms of one's basic human nature when it can be detached from the effluvium of civilization. This is what Ishmael means when he says that there may yet be some "undiscovered prime thing in me." Whaling takes him to that prime thing, and the result is an experiencing of magnitude, power, and sublimity. The whale represents what is on the inside, great primal strength.

Ishmael spends a good deal of time extolling this pristine and primal inner force and bemoaning its loss in ordinary civilized man. To argue that Melville was attacking civilization in *Moby-Dick,* and more specifically the nature of ordinary man, is to swim against a current of opinion, for many critics see him as a believer in the principles of democracy and thus temperamentally a friend of the masses. In his rare complexity, he was and he was not. He spoke frequently in favor of democracy, but just as often he revealed a deep distrust of the masses and their civilization. Ironically, his lack of respect for the common man sometimes even followed from his belief in democracy. On June 1, 1851, he wrote to Hawthorne: "Let any clergyman try to preach the Truth from its very stronghold, the pulpit, and they would ride him out of his church on his own pulpit bannister. . . . Truth is ridiculous to men." Recognizing that he had spoken out for democracy in the past (notably in *White-Jacket*), he added: "It seems an inconsistency to assert unconditional democracy in all things, and yet confess a dislike to all mankind—in the mass. But not so." Breaking off at this point, he refused to explain further: "But it's an endless sermon,—no more of it."[31] He did not want to preach an endless sermon here on how his dim view of the masses could be reconciled to his assertions of unconditional democracy, but in a sense that was what he was doing at that precise time with the novel he was writing—*Moby-Dick.* In the book he made it clear that all men are not created equal; Ahab certainly towers over his crewmen.[32] Among ordinary men there are some differences, but the distinction between a truly exceptional person, like Ahab, and a member of the masses is much greater than that among individual members of the commonality. "For be a man's intellectual superiority what it will, it can never assume the practical, available supremacy over other men, without the aid of some sort of external arts and entrenchments, always, in themselves, more or less paltry and base. This it is, that for ever keeps God's true princes of the Empire from the world's hustings; and leaves the highest honors that this air can give, to those men who become

31. *Letters,* p. 127.
32. Ahab himself puts it this way to Starbuck: "Ye two are the opposite poles of one thing; Starbuck is Stubb reversed, and Stubb is Starbuck; and ye two are all mankind; and Ahab stands alone among the millions of the peopled earth, nor gods nor men his neighbors!" (p. 452).

famous more through their infinite inferiority to the choice hidden handful of the Divine Inert, than through their undoubted superiority over the dead level of the mass" (p. 129).

Praise of the ordinary and glorification of the principle of democracy are directed not toward men as they actually are in the world but toward some idealized concept of what may lie within them dormant and covered up, some "undiscovered prime thing," the whale. Ishmael recognizes in chapter 26 ("Knights and Squires") that the world contains "knaves, fools, and murderers," that "men may seem detestable as joint stock-companies and nations" and have "mean and meagre faces," but he finds something "noble" and "sparkling" in "man in the ideal." Then it becomes clear that he considers this essence of nobility within idealized man as the same quality which the whale symbolizes throughout the book: "that immaculate manliness . . . within . . . so far within . . . that it remains intact though all the outer character seem gone" (p. 104).

Therefore, when Ishmael breaks forth in effulgent praise for the humble masses in passages defending democracy, he is likely to be using the same tactics as in his glorification of whaling and the whaling industry. If a passage like the following is read literally, it appears ridiculous, but it is not. Ishmael is not really speaking sincerely of the glories of humble and ordinary folk but camouflagedly of himself and those like him who are in search of the whale within:

> If, then, to meanest mariners, and renegades and castaways, I shall hereafter ascribe high qualities, though dark; weave round them tragic graces; if even the most mournful, perchance the most abased, among them all, shall at times lift himself to the exalted mounts; if I shall touch that workman's arm with some ethereal light; if I shall spread a rainbow over his disastrous set of sun; then against all mortal critics bear me out in it, thou just Spirit of Equality, which has spread one royal mantle of humanity over all my kind! Bear me out in it, thou great democratic God! who didst not refuse to the swart convict, Bunyan, the pale, poetic pearl; Thou who didst clothe with doubly hammered leaves of finest gold, the stumped and paupered arm of old Cervantes; Thou who didst pick up Andrew Jackson from the pebbles; who didst hurl

him upon a warhorse; who didst thunder him higher than a
throne! Thou who, in all Thy mighty earthly marchings, ever
cullest Thy selectest champions from the kindly commons; bear
me out in it, O God! (pp. 104–5)[33]

As actual praise for the humble this passage seems insincere
because what Ishmael says that he is going to do for "meanest
mariners, and renegades and castaways" he simply does not do.[34]
He does not make the common sailors of the *Pequod* tragic, ascribe high qualities to them, or show the most abased among
them lifted to exalted heights; quite the contrary.[35] Consequently, this paragraph, like most of the chapter on "The Honor
and Glory of Whaling," seems a hoax of sorts.[36] What Ishmael
does in this passage, however, is to show that even through the
"kingly commons" there runs a shared thread of royal, divine
origin. He finds it startling that men like Bunyan, Cervantes,

33. Critics generally take this invocation quite literally. See, for example,
Leon Howard, "Melville and the American Tragic Hero," in *Four Makers of the
American Mind: Emerson, Thoreau, Whitman, and Melville,* ed. Thomas Edward
Crawley (Durham: Duke University Press, 1976), p. 78. Robert Milder feels
that "Ishmael's appeal to the 'great democratic God' in the first 'Knights and
Squires' [chapter] is a conscious recognition that the 'meanest mariners, and
renegades and castaways' who comprise the *Pequod*'s crew must and indeed *can* be
endowed with the 'high qualities' appropriate to heroic literature." "The Composition of *Moby-Dick:* A Review and a Prospect," *ESQ* 23 (1977): 209. In
Melville's Quarrel with God (Princeton: Princeton University Press, 1952), however, Lawrance Thompson argues that this passage is "caustically sarcastic" in tone
and "heretical and blasphemous" in purpose (p. 175).

34. For a perceptive and sensible treatment of Melville's "democratic" attitudes, see Larry J. Reynolds, "Kings and Commoners in *Moby-Dick,*" *Studies in
the Novel* 12 (1980): 101–13.

35. Melville was to perform a similar deception on his readers three years
later in "The Encantadas," where the narrator expresses his love for common
humanity but in a context that makes the confession seem convictionless. His
exaltation of the spirit of humanity is undercut by his otherwise tragic view of
life and by his depiction of Hunilla's fate.

36. The probable source for Ishmael's Spirit of Equality invocation should in
itself be enough to make one question Melville's sincerity with regard to his
ostensible purpose. Mansfield and Vincent point out that Melville's likely source
was comic—the humorous invocation in Laurence Sterne's *Tristram Shandy,*
book 9, chapter 25.

Jackson (and himself), men of humble origins, could be blessed with the pearl of great price, untarnishable gold, and royal inner thunder. The tragedy is that so few go whaling in this sense to discover it. In writing the novel, Melville was himself engaged in the search to know more of himself and to extol what he found there.

Moby-Dick is a wicked book because in many places it is such an arrogant one, and its wickedness is intensified by the fact that its arrogance is so often clothed in the garments of praise for the humble and ordinary. It is a wicked book because it is frequently deceptive and seductive—it entices its very victims into loving and acclaiming it for what it is not. It is a statement of high treason that sounds like a patriotic pledge. And at the same time, it is the undisputed fictional masterwork of American literature, a glimpse into the workings of a brilliant and rare (if not unique) mind in action.

Internal whaling, however, is not the only form of deep diving represented in the novel. The whale was Melville's most ambitious and most comprehensive symbol, for to him it stands not only for the core of being but also for all that is outside. The whale is totality—all that is inside and all that is external to self. When it is clear that Ishmael is speaking of metaphoric whaling rather than the literal sort, one still must distinguish between statements about inner and outer probing, about the attempt to gain self-knowledge as opposed to knowledge about all matters external to self. Metaphysical whaling, or the search for truth, is courageous and noble, but Melville insists that answers will not be forthcoming, even to the deep and sensitive seeker who refuses to be taken in by dogma and oversimplifications. Such a person would do well to leave off the fast and furious pursuit of answers to all those universal questions that have troubled man since the beginning of the race and to assume, insofar as this particular form of whaling is concerned, the stance Ishmael describes at the end of chapter 85: "Doubts of all things earthly, and intuitions of some things heavenly; this combination makes neither believer nor infidel, but makes a man who regards them both with equal eye" (p. 314).

The two forms of figurative whaling are consequently different, for Melville feels that he might discover through inner voyaging some "prime thing" that might have as yet remained unfound, but metaphysical speculation and deep intellectual probings into the riddles of human existence, the cosmos, and the divinity result in frustration, disillusionment, and sometimes an all-pervasive bitterness. The reason for this is that the whale as it represents all reality external to self simply is unknowable. This theory is the basis for all of those admonitions in *Moby-Dick* that no matter how close you think you are getting to understanding the whale, you are still in the dark. "Dissect him how I may," says Ishmael, "I go but skin deep; I know him not, and never will," for though he may seem to have a face, he does not, or if he does, he will not let it be seen (p. 318). The Egyptian hieroglyphics were finally deciphered, but his great whale of truth will never be: "How may unlettered Ishmael hope to read the awful Chaldee of the Sperm Whale's brow? I but put that brow before you. Read it if you can" (p. 293). Whaling in this sense is finally unproductive and threatening to survival because it ends in a maddening conviction of ambiguity or a blinding preoccupation with nothingness. "For all these reasons," Ishmael concludes, "any way you may look at it, you must needs conclude that the great Leviathan is that one creature in the world which must remain unpainted to the last. True, one portrait may hit the mark much nearer than another, but none can hit it with any very considerable degree of exactness. So there is no earthly way of finding out precisely what the whale really looks like." Of course, you might embark on a whaling voyage into the howling infinite, "but by so doing, you run no small risk of being eternally stove and sunk by him. Wherefore, it seems to me you had best not be too fastidious in your curiosity touching this Leviathan" (p. 228). Later Ishmael suggests that at one time this Leviathan will seem to be related to heaven, but at other moments, it will appear like "Satan thrusting forth his tormented collossal claw from the flame Baltic of Hell." So in contemplating the whale, "it is all in all what mood you are in; if in the Dantean, the devils will occur to you; if in that of Isaiah, the archangels" (p. 317). The mood, what is inside you, and not the objective and unswerving nature of the thing itself dictates how you see this whale, which is so massive, elusive, and unpredictable "that his very panics are more to be dreaded than his most fearless and malicious assaults!" (p. 62). The perilous situation of the seeker who looks outward, away from himself, for truth instead of inward is manifested memorably in a painting that Ishmael describes in chapter 3. Near the entry of the Spouter-Inn hangs "a very large oil-painting so thoroughly be-smoked, and every way defaced, that in the unequal cross-lights by which you viewed it, it was only by diligent study and a series of systematic visits to it, and careful inquiry of the neighbors, that you could any way arrive at an understanding of its purpose. Such unaccountable masses of shades and shadows, that at first you almost thought some ambitious young artist, in the time of the New England hags, had endeavored to delineate chaos bewitched. But by dint of much and earnest contemplation, and oft repeated ponderings, and especially by throwing open the little window towards the back of the entry, you at last came to the conclusion that such an idea, however wild, might not be altogether unwarranted." In the center of this ambiguous scene is a dark mass that is too hazy to be defined: "But what most puzzled and confounded you was a long, limber, portentous, black mass of something hovering in the centre of the picture over three blue, dim, perpendicular lines floating in a nameless yeast. A boggy, soggy, squitchy picture truly, enough to drive a nervous man distracted." Indeed, for this is Melville's representation of universal truth, which attracts and invites interpretation but remains undefined. "You involuntarily took an oath with yourself to find out what that marvellous painting meant. Ever and anon a bright, but, alas, deceptive idea would dart you through.—It's the Black Sea in a midnight gale.—It's the unnatural combat of the four primal elements," and so on. Ishmael never knows for sure what this strange painting is supposed to depict, but as if he is reading an ink-blot, he theorizes that the force or mass at the center is Leviathan about to destroy a vessel that has been seeking it (pp. 20–21). Nowhere in the novel does Ishmael suggest more directly the noble compulsion to try to solve the riddles of the universe, the utter impossibility to do so, and the danger in pursuing them without relief.

Three forms of whaling thus intertwine in *Moby-Dick:* "high" whaling (metaphysical speculation), "mighty" whaling (the pursuit of self-knowledge and rediscovery of the powerful and noble aspects of a largely lost human nature), and the "business" of whaling (the physical pursuit of actual whales). The most widely accepted explanation of how *Moby-Dick* was composed, the "two *Moby-Dicks*" theory, posits that Melville did not have the usable imaginative powers before he discovered Hawthorne and reread Shakespeare (in August of 1850) to create the novel as we know it. Those who espouse the theory believe that Melville wrote first the greater part of a rather simple book, such as "a literal account of the whaling industry," and then added to it a second and more complicated book after his remarkable creative growth.[37] The hypothesis has evolved through the years since Leon Howard first expressed it in 1940 into a sophisticated and tightly argued position. Details have been added and some shifts have taken place, but the basic assumptions remain intact.[38] One of the most

37. Leon Howard, "Melville's Struggle with the Angel," *Modern Language Quarterly* 1 (1940): 195–206. Howard expanded the theory in his *Herman Melville: A Biography* (Berkeley and Los Angeles: University of California Press, 1951). In *Call me Ishmael* (San Francisco: City Lights Books, 1947), Charles Olson boosted the theory by stating bluntly as fact: "*Moby-Dick* was two books written between February, 1850 and August, 1851" (p. 35). The early book, he says, was an "account of the Whale Fishery" (p. 38). In 1949 Howard P. Vincent agreed: "Melville began to write a book which in no way stretched his powers and which by no means met his deepest wish. *Moby-Dick* was first intended to be a whaling story pure and simple." It was begun, he continues, "as a whaling document." *Trying-Out,* pp. 22–23. In "The Two *Moby-Dicks*," *American Literature* 25 (1953–54): 417–48, George R. Stewart first used the term by which the theory has come to be known, and he offered the fullest discussion of the idea up to that time.

38. James Barbour, "The Composition of *Moby-Dick,*" *American Literature* 47 (1975): 343–60, argues for three stages in the writing of the book instead of two: first Melville wrote "a Whaling story," then added in the last four months of 1850 much of the cetology, then in the first seven months of 1851 wrote under the influence of Shakespeare and Hawthorne what early proponents of the theory had called the "second" *Moby-Dick*. In designating which chapters belong in which phase, Barbour disagrees somewhat with Stewart. He disagrees with all previous holders of the theory in saying that Melville did not begin to write the metaphysical *Moby-Dick* until after the first of the year 1851. Apparently convinced by this argument, Leon Howard states that he has "learned better" since his early belief that the "second" *Moby-Dick* was begun in August 1850

important of these is that Melville's descriptions of whales and his treatment of the whaling industry are largely the products of his early intention, of the first and simpler *Moby-Dick*.[39] The difficulty with this premise is that the whaling material is not straightforward and uncomplicated; indeed, it is multilayered and complex.[40] Literal whaling is in itself a complex subject for Melville because his sensitivity and deep compassion, his reverence for life, could not allow him always to write about it with the enthusiasm he may have wanted to convey. This situation may be what he had in mind when well into his writing of *Moby-Dick*, he complained to Hawthorne that "the product" of his artistic endeavors was always "a final hash."[41] He was right, as Hawthorne recognized,[42] but his friend also knew that it was one of

---

and that he now agrees that it was delayed until January 1851. "Melville and the American Tragic Hero," pp. 71–74.

39. Barbour feels that "the material [on whales] and whaling written in the first stage may occur in *Moby-Dick* as late as Chapter 90" (p. 348). Much of the whaling material I have discussed in this chapter, such as that in chapter 88, "Schools and Schoolmasters," was, according to Barbour, part of the "original story." Puzzlingly, he finds chapter 61, "Stubb Kills a Whale," and chapter 66, "The Shark Massacre" (both part of the "first" *Moby-Dick*), "fanciful and often humorous accounts of whaling adventure" (p. 356).

40. The "two *Moby-Dicks*" theory has become widely accepted as fact despite the warning of a few skeptical critics like Jerome M. Loving, "Melville's Pardonable Sin," *New England Quarterly* 47 (1974): 262-78; and Edwin M. Eigner, *The Metaphysical Novel in England and America: Dickens, Bulwer, Melville, and Hawthorne* (Berkeley and Los Angeles: University of California Press, 1978), pp. 25–26. Loving argues that the influences on Melville suggested by the "two *Moby-Dicks*" theory are greatly overplayed and that Melville might well have set out to write an allegory to begin with, not a mere sea narrative. For an excellent history of the theory as it has evolved and a perceptive analysis of its flaws, see Robert Milder's "The Composition of *Moby-Dick*." Milder feels that "one must . . . be skeptical of a theory of composition which regards the cetological chapters as so much novelistic blubber, conceived and written before Melville imagined a tragic *Moby-Dick* and at best tangentially related to Ahab's quest" (p. 207). In looking back upon the several discussions espousing the "two *Moby-Dicks*" theory, he concludes: "The question which concerns us is how far we should be willing to impoverish our reading of *Moby-Dick* to accommodate compositional speculation founded upon insufficient evidence and doubtful methodology" (p. 213).

41. *Letters*, p. 128.

42. Hawthorne had already discovered the source of Melville's anxiety

the richest and most nourishing hashes that he had ever consumed. Melville may not have done quite what he wanted to do, especially with his handling of literal whales and whalemen—in his letter to Hawthorne he also referred to the book as a "botch"—but his conflicts and irresolutions were more artistically procreative than the single-minded and consistent urges of many another writer. Precisely how Melville first conceived his novel, the order in which he wrote its words down, and how he then revised them, these matters and dozens of others involving the evolution of *Moby-Dick* are as much a mystery—and perhaps will always remain so—as the inner workings of the creative imagination itself.

---

through reading *Mardi.* He confided to E. A. Duyckinck that the novel was "so good that one scarcely pardons the writer for not having brooded long over it so as to make it a great deal better." *The American Notebooks,* ed. Randall Stewart (New Haven: Yale University Press, 1932), p. 307. Ironically, Melville's making a "hash" of *Moby-Dick,* his partial failure of expression—at least from his own point of view—resulted perhaps in a more profound book than it might have been otherwise. No one has stated this theory better than James Guetti: "Ishmael's failures, in their suggestiveness and ultimate inconclusiveness, become the evidence for the existence of what is beyond them, something expressed because it is not expressed, which we can only call the ineffable. This communication of the ineffable, however, is not only negative, for—although it depends upon the negation of Ishmael's imaginative efforts—his 'failures' always work in two ways: to give partial form to what is beyond them and to assert that this form itself is artificial. The ineffable thus exists for a reader as a vast potential of significances which are irreducible, provisional, and unrealizable in any defined or final way." *The Limits of Metaphor: A Study of Melville, Conrad, and Faulkner* (Ithaca: Cornell University Press, 1967), p. 29.

Ahab's Phantom Limb

Almost the first detail about Ahab to appear in *Moby-Dick* is that he is one-legged. When Ishmael explains to Captain Peleg that he wants "to see what whaling is," Peleg replies: "Clap eye on Captain Ahab, young man, and thou wilt find that he has only one leg" (p. 69).[1] From that point onward, even before he has a chance to clap eye on Ahab, Ishmael focuses his attention and his imagination often on his captain's one-leggedness. Elijah, the crazy sailor prophet, brings up the subject just after Ishmael has learned of Ahab's misfortune from Peleg. Ishmael claims to know "all about the loss of his leg," but Elijah suggests by his question that he knows little of the deeper implications: *"All about it, eh—sure you do?—all?"* (p. 87). This aspect of his as yet unseen captain begins to loom huge in Ishmael's mind. He departs from Elijah with "all kinds of vague wonderments" as he considers "Captain Ahab; and the leg he had lost" (p. 88).

Ahab hobbles through the novel, maneuvering but poorly with the whalebone leg the ship's carpenter provides for him. He can stand steadily on deck only after he has holes drilled in which to put the tip of his artificial limb. Even then, he has to support

1. All page references to *Moby-Dick* are to the Norton Critical Edition, ed. Harrison Hayford and Hershel Parker (New York: Norton, 1967).

himself constantly. He bumps along the deck so awkwardly and noisily that Stubb complains about being kept awake. He cannot board another ship in the customary way during a gam. He cannot climb the mastheads as others do. He is constantly in danger of falling, and in fact he does fall before the voyage begins, breaking his whalebone leg and injuring himself severely in the groin. He is hampered at every turn. When he returns to his ship from the *Samuel Enderby*, he lands on deck with such force that he again cracks his leg. On the second day after Moby Dick has been spotted, the artificial leg is once again splintered, and again Ahab has to be fitted for another one.

Despite his severe handicap, Ahab continues to act as if he had two good legs. He does go aboard other ships, and he does go to the masthead, though special arrangements have to be made for him. He equips a whaleboat for himself, though the owners of the *Pequod* would certainly have considered it unwise "for any maimed man to enter a whaleboat in the hunt" (p. 197). Ahab is indeed "maimed," but he insists upon behaving as if he were not. One of the most striking evidences of his holding on to the idea that he is a man with both legs is his experiencing sensation in a limb which is no longer there. "When I come to mount this leg thou makest," he says to the carpenter, "I shall nevertheless feel another leg in the same identical place with it; that is, carpenter, my old lost leg; the flesh and blood one, I mean." The carpenter responds: "Yes, I have heard something curious on that score, sir; how that a dismasted man never entirely loses the feeling of his old spar, but it will be still pricking him at times. May I humbly ask if it be really so, sir?" "It is, man," answers Ahab. "Look, put thy live leg here in the place where mine once was; so, now, here is only one distinct leg to the eye, yet two to the soul. Where thou feelest tingling life; there, exactly there, there to a hair, do I" (p. 391).

What Ahab is describing is known as the "phantom limb" sensation, a phenomenon probably first recorded by a French surgeon of the sixteenth century, Ambrose Paré, who amputated the limbs of many soldiers wounded in battle.[2] Studies of the phan-

---

2. Warren Gorman, *Body Image and the Image of the Brain* (St. Louis: Warren H. Green, 1969), pp. 29–30.

tom limb have occupied the attention of modern psychologists who deal with what they term the "body image." Much is still unknown about the phantom limb sensation. For example, amputees unaccountably feel it for different durations. Psychiatrists and psychopathologists generally agree, however, that "the phantom is the result of a psychic striving by the individual to replace a missing part of the body image. . . . *No physical cause* that is regularly reproducible has yet been identified."[3] An amputee who experiences this feeling may be so convinced that the lost limb has been restored that he will act accordingly, as Ahab does. In his book on body image, Seymour Fisher writes: "It is as if the amputated member were still part of the body and a source of sensations. The individual may feel that he can still move it and will unthinkingly undertake sequences of action which assume its reality."[4] This "maladaptation" occurs frequently in persons of strong pride.[5]

These clinical observations about actual amputees shed much light on Melville's reasons for focusing on Ahab's one-leggedness, and once again Melville's remarkable intuitive understanding of the mind is revealed. Psychiatrists know that especially in exceptional persons the loss of a limb represents a violation of the body image which is in turn a severe threat to one's overall self-concept. It often results in a traumatic sense of being changed suddenly into a new and undesirable identity. In the cases of men, the amputation can be accompanied by a feeling of emasculation.[6] That Melville instinctively realized all this is evidenced by his use of amputation—both in literal and figurative senses—in his works. It is one of the principal motifs in *White-Jacket,* where by and large it carries the suggestion of a loss of essence, of manhood. The scene where a robust seaman is deprived of his leg by a withered surgeon, Cadwallader Cuticle, is one of the most horrible spectacles in all of Melville's works. A less bloody form of amputation, beard cutting, is also treated in *White-Jacket.* The

3. Ibid, p. 99, italics mine.

4. Seymour Fisher, *Body Experience in Fantasy and Behavior* (New York: Appleton-Century-Crofts, 1970), p. 59.

5. Lawrence C. Kolb, "Disturbances of the Body-Image," in *American Handbook of Psychiatry,* ed. Silvano Arieti (New York: Basic Books, 1959), 1:764.

6. Ibid.

command of the unmanly captain to cut all beards is considered by the crew members as degrading, and a near-mutiny results. After a long voyage the beards have become a part of their body image.

Not everyone reacts to amputation in the same way as Ahab. The manly young sailor aboard the *Neversink* cannot stand the shock of Cuticle's butchery and he dies. The sailors who object to cutting away their beards finally give in (with one exception) and adjust to their new image. In *Moby-Dick* Captain Boomer of the *Samuel Enderby* has had his arm removed after an encounter with the white whale. Unlike Ahab he retains a sensible and cheerful attitude and prefers thereafter to leave Moby Dick alone. His loss of limb has not left a permanent psychic wound. The blacksmith Perth has lost the "extremities of both feet" (p. 401). His response is the opposite of Captain Boomer's but still unlike Ahab's. He reacts to amputation, which is symbolic of his loss of almost everything he holds dear—his occupation, his wife, his children—with paralyzing grief and bitterness. He ships aboard the *Pequod* a broken man. The two responses to amputation represented by Boomer and Perth, eventual personal adjustment and surrender to a sense of defeat, are those most often encountered in actual amputees. Ahab is different. He reacts to amputation with unsuccorable woe and untamable aggression; and he persists in feeling a leg that is no longer there. To understand why he does so, to probe the separate sources of his woe and aggression, is to go far into the recesses of this great and mysterious character.

Ahab's "close coiled woe" is primarily the result of his loss of balance. His has been a lifelong pursuit of equilibrium. No wonder, then, at the shock he feels from sudden one-leggedness. The idea of imbalance is intolerable to him. His posture, his very way of standing—despite his being crippled—reveals his affinity for balance. Ishmael is "struck with the singular posture he maintained" (p. 110), erect and balanced, the whale bone leg in an auger hole, an arm holding a shroud, his head steady and fixed on the horizon. In crucial scenes, he strikes such postures of balance, difficult though they be for him. When he defies the corposants, he stands with a mainmast link in his left hand, with his foot upon Fedallah, and with his right arm upward, covering all the bases, as it were. His lowest moments in the novel are those in which he loses his balance. Physical clumsiness is unspeakably disgusting to him, and his own loss of body control produces his severest mental depression. Thus when before the *Pequod* sets sail, he falls and injures himself, his physical pain is less than his mental anguish. He hides himself away, and for this interval seeks "speechless refuge . . . among the marble senate of the dead" (p. 386). On the third day of the chase after Moby Dick, he is spilled into the sea. When he is picked up, he lay "all crushed in the bottom of Stubb's boat like one trodden under foot of herds of elephants. Far inland nameless wails came from him, as desolate sounds from out ravines" (pp. 450–51).

Ahab shows his rage for balance in numerous other ways. After a sperm whale is killed and the head hoisted up on one side, he has a right whale killed so that its head can be placed on the other side bringing the *Pequod* back on an even keel. He believes that a balance exists between externality and internality, between nature and mind. "Not the smallest atom stirs or lives in matter," he says, "but has its cunning duplicate in mind" (p. 264). References to balancing books and accounting occur in his speech. He refers to fate as "the accountants" (p. 143). He is impatient, however, with a lower, petty form of bookkeeping, of profit and loss on a literal and materialistic level: "Cursed be that mortal inter-debtedness which will not do away with ledgers. I would be free as air; and I'm down in the whole world's books. I am so rich, I could have given bid for bid with the wealthiest Praetorian at the auction of the Roman empire (which was the world's), and yet I owe for the flesh in the tongue I brag with" (p. 392). His rage for true balance and his impatience with the world's ledgers are what the narrator of Melville's short story "I and My Chimney" refers to as a love of the "higher mathematics" and a contempt for lower arithmetic that leads not to ultimate understanding but to a shallow knowledge of the commonplace world.

The phantom limb that Ahab feels is an indication of great emotional upheaval. He persists in sensing that his old leg is still there because, as psychiatrists would point out, he so desperately *wants* it to be there; its loss has thrown him completely off balance, forcing on him a new body image he cannot accept. And since the body image is so totally a part of the way one views all of reality, his physical imbalance projects frustrating mental and spiritual imbalance against which he is struggling with all his strength.

His desire to hunt down and kill the white whale is a part of this tormented struggle to find balance. His lust for vengeance is related to his profound affinity for justice, and for him justice is synonymous with balance. As Georgio Del Vecchio puts it: "The very nature of justice . . . [is] essentially a virtue of balance and equilibrium."[7] If one motto could sum up Ahab's deepest convictions and emotional proclivities, it would be "fair play." In all things, however, he makes a distinction between "higher" and "lower" forms. Since he is "gifted with the higher perception," he says, he lacks the lower (the "low, enjoying power"). He believes in a higher democracy and thinks of himself—as Starbuck points out—as being on equal terms with the gods, but he has no patience with lower democracy in which most men are created equal (and inferior). He believes in pursuing the higher mathematics, and in breaking the quadrant he feels that he is doing just that, for to him that instrument symbolizes a mechanical and petty arithmetic. So, too, he embraces the concept of a higher fair play while rejecting the lower. In his mind, belief in the higher justice frees him from trivial restrictions and the world's fear-ridden admonitions. When Starbuck accuses him of blasphemy, he answers: "Talk not to me of blasphemy, man; I'd strike the sun if it insulted me. For could the sun do that, then could I do the other; since there is ever a sort of fair play herein, jealousy presiding over all creations" (p. 144). If he were in a fight with the sun, he would refuse to take an unfair advantage or to have any special assistance. When lightning threatens the *Pequod* and Starbuck commands the protective rods be dropped into the water, Ahab—faithful to his own concept of justice—countermands him: "Let's have fair play here, though we be the weaker side. Yet, I'll contribute to raise rods on the Himmalehs and Andes, that all the world may be secured; but out on privileges! Let them be, sir" (p. 415).

7. Georgio Del Vecchio, *Justice: An Historical and Philosophical Essay,* ed. A. H. Campbell (Edinburgh: Edinburgh University Press, 1952), p. 6.

This distinction between higher and lower fair play is important in Melville's treatment of the Golden Rule in *Moby-Dick*. Though the Golden Rule is generally considered the highest standard of justice in civilization, Melville satirizes its users in one episode and then depicts Ahab in the act of openly breaking it for what he considers a greater goal. Ishmael has a debate with himself early in the novel about the propriety of his joining Queequeg in the worship of a pagan idol: "What is the will of God?—to do to my fellow man what I would have my fellow man to do to me. . . . Now, Queequeg is my fellow man. And what do I wish this Queequeg would do to me? Why, unite with me in my particular Presbyterian form of worship. Consequently, I must then unite with him in his; ergo, I must turn idolator" (p. 54). Ishmael is not serious here, for he does not go on truly to worship the idol. If he had worshipped it and turned "idolator," then his following the Golden Rule would have caused him to break a more fundamental commandment: "Thou shalt have no other Gods before me." He would then have given up the higher justice for the lower.

This fact has significant bearing on Ahab's later denial of Captain Gardiner's request which is made in terms of the Golden Rule: "Do to me as you would have me do to you in the like case" (p. 435). His decision not to help Captain Gardiner find his lost son—painful though it is to him—reveals his distance from ordinary standards and a lack of what we usually think of as human compassion. On the other hand, if he had done what Captain Gardiner asked and followed the Golden Rule, he would actually have done what Ishmael jokingly says he himself did: in the name of the lower justice, he would have violated the higher. Melville seemed to realize what Paul Tillich expressed a century later about the Golden Rule: "It is used even by Jesus. And it is certainly an expression of practical wisdom to do to people what one wants to have done by them! But it is not the criterion of justice."[8] It lends itself to subjective misuse. Following the rule of "practical wisdom" can sometimes lead away from true justice rather than to it.

8. Paul Tillich, *Love, Power, and Justice: Ontological Analyses and Ethical Applications* (New York: Oxford University Press, 1954), p. 79.

Therefore Ahab's actions with regard to Captain Gardiner are more ambivalent than they may appear. One of his own reasons for not helping Captain Gardiner is that he is pursing a form of justice that goes *beyond* the code of the Golden Rule.[9] As he conceives it, justice demands that he hunt the white whale, not Captain Gardiner's son, and the higher justice cannot be violated with impunity, for it is of divine origin. "God hunt as all," he cries to his crew, "if we do not hunt Moby Dick" (p. 146). It might well be argued that helping Captain Gardiner search for his lost child would surely not prevent Ahab from resuming his hunt for the white whale but would simply delay him briefly. Thus he could follow both the Golden Rule and what he conceives of as a greater code. The point is, however, that "higher" and "lower" forms of all concepts are not merely different degrees of the same things but are different in nature and mutually exclusive. That is, following the lower justice (or mathematics or anything else) *precludes* following the higher. The same person is psychologically incapable of doing both. Granting Captain Gardiner's request, therefore, would mean for Ahab that he had broken his allegiance to justice in the fullest sense. This hunger for rightness on the highest plane is involved in some of Ahab's seemingly most eccentric acts, such as his refusal to drop the ship's rods overboard during a storm and his smashing of the quadrant.

Consequently, the trauma that results from his lost leg is partly caused by his sensing that the whole event was shot through with implications of wrongness or imbalance. A whale, even a sperm whale, should not be as cunning and intelligent as this one that reaped away his leg. It simply is not *right;* "The time is out of joint," as Hamlet put it. Nor should a whale be as malignant as

9. Many critics fail to see it this way, however, and charge Ahab with having only base motivations. T. Walter Herbert, Jr., for example, states: "Ahab's violation of human decency, framed by Melville as a breach of the Golden Rule, is linked with the blasphemous arrogance by which he proposes to forgive himself. Melville invites us to measure Ahab's callousness: Ahab refuses an opportunity to relieve suffering caused by the whale, so as to pursue his revenge for an injury that cannot be repaired." *Moby-Dick and Calvinism: A World Dismantled* (New Brunswick: Rutgers University Press, 1977), p. 157.

this one seems to be. Nature, the witness to this horrible deed, should not have been cheery and pleasant after the attack, as if something happy had occurred. "Judge," says Ishmael (choosing precisely the right word) in his sympathetic description of what Ahab feels, "to what pitches of inflamed, distracted fury the minds of his [Moby Dick's] more desperate hunters were impelled, when amid the chips of chewed boats, and the sinking limbs of torn comrades, they swam out of the white curds of the whale's direful wrath into the serene, exasperating sunlight, that smiled on, as if at a birth or a bridal" (p. 159).

Ahab's desire for vengeance, therefore, does not in itself make him some kind of demon spitting in the face of God. It is partly because Ahab is deep and is aware of the cruciality of justice in any concept of an infinite presence that his victimization fills him with such utter woe. In her study of revenge in Shakespeare's plays, Sister Mary Bonaventure Mroz cites Saint Thomas's theory that "to every definite natural inclination there corresponds a special virtue," and she argues that behind the inclination to resent a deep injustice is the virtue of God-hunger.[10] Saint Augustine also recognized that a love of justice is the sign of a spiritual nature.

This aspect of Ahab, his God-hunger, is an extension of Melville himself.[11] Walter E. Bezanson's memorable description of Melville could apply equally well to Ahab: He "was a religious type. . . . The need to be twice-born was in his blood stream. The kinds of questions to which the great religions addressed them-

10. Sister Mary Bonaventure Mroz, *Divine Vengeance: A Study in the Philosophical Backgrounds of the Revenge Motif As It Appears in Shakespeare's Chronicle History Plays* (Washington: Catholic University of America Press, 1941), p. 4.

11. William Ellery Sedgwick states that "Ahab drew his being from Melville's knowledge of human nature, the best part of which was his knowledge of himself. Ahab was a projection of the strongest propensities in Melville's human make-up. His essential tragedy was an imaginative realization of a contingency which, being the man he was, Melville himself had to face." *Herman Melville: The Tragedy of Mind* (Cambridge: Harvard University Press, 1944), pp. 130–31. Sanford E. Marovitz puts succinctly Melville's unfulfilled God-hunger: "Melville was a man of faith who found nothing to put his faith in." "Old Man Ahab," in *Artful Thunder: Versions of the Romantic Tradition in American Literature*, ed. Robert J. DeMott and Sanford E. Marovitz (Kent: Kent State University Press, 1975), p. 159.

selves were precisely those . . . [his] temperament and training would not let him do without."[12] Ahab's crusade is not so much against God as against that which prevents him from finding God, that "mask" or "wall" that he must strike through.[13] For how else "can the prisoner reach outside except by thrusting through the wall?" (p. 144).

In "The Symphony" chapter, Ahab tells Starbuck that he has had "forty years of continual whaling! forty years of privation, and peril, and storm-time! forty years on the pitiless sea! for forty years has Ahab forsaken the peaceful land, for forty years to make war on the horrors of the deep!" (p. 443). He is speaking both literally and figuratively, for his entire adult life has been a hunt for whales and a search for meaning. His "intellectual and spiritual exasperations" through the years derive from his intuitive reading of events in his life. He is by nature a believer that all experience is pervaded with signs, manifestations, revelations. He feels that if he can just read aright what he observes, he will read aright some of the great mysteries that lie beyond. He is an inveterate epiphanist. He looks keenly for a signal of his own superiority to other men and to nature in his every experience. When a person with these proclivities receives the revelations that he does through his various misfortunes, he is bound to be thoroughly shaken. A great whale has taken away his leg. What can the event mean? It has attacked him and destroyed his balance. Like a flash of lightning the message has come, but it is too terrible to accept: there is no ultimate harmony, no justice. Be-

12. Walter E. Bezanson, Introduction to *Clarel: A Poem and Pilgrimage in the Holy Land* by Herman Melville (New York: Hendricks House, 1960), p. cviii.

13. Contrary views are readily available. William Braswell, for example, argues that "When Ahab strikes at Moby Dick . . . he does so in a mad desire for revenge on God. . . ." *Melville's Religious Thought: An Essay in Interpretation* (Durham: Duke University Press, 1943), p. 58. To Ahab, according to Merlin Bowen, Moby Dick is an "expression of the Divinity—conceivably even God Himself." *The Long Encounter: Self and Experience in the Writings of Herman Melville* (Chicago: University of Chicago Press, 1960), p. 146. Richard Chase is even more positive: "Moby-Dick is God incarnate in the whale." *Herman Melville: A Critical Study* (New York: Macmillan, 1949), p. 49. Ray B. Browne follows closely behind: "Moby-Dick the whale is God incarnate." *Melville's Drive to Humanism* (Lafayette: Purdue University Studies, 1971), p. 61.

cause this revelation violates an essential side of Ahab's nature, he fights back. He transfers the epiphany of chaos and imbalance arising from the attack of Moby Dick to the white whale itself and thereby incarnates and makes this revelation, his greatest enemy, assailable.

Ahab has undergone an actual experience of such pain and senselessness that it seriously threatens to make him into something he has not been. To be sure he has never been a pious and humble child of God. Elijah relates that he was irreverent enough to spit into a silver calabash and to fight before an altar in Santa. He has defied the world's methods of finding and worshipping God, but that does not mean that he has not sought God with his own methods, as we shall see in the next chapter. However, his belief in the purpose that exists behind (and perhaps in opposition to) all nature and all worldly events threatens to wane in the storm of his own dreadful experience, and his self-concept is brought into question as never before. Melville wrote Hawthorne in a letter that he admired him for saying "No! in thunder."[14] By "in" Melville meant *during* or *in the midst of,* and he used *thunder* as he frequently did to mean lightning. He was complimenting Hawthorne not for writing thunderous prose which expressed a rebellious *no,* but for a refusal to seek shelter when, figuratively, lightning is striking all around.[15] The lightning-rod salesmen of the world advise us to fear lightning, to run and hide from it, and to cringe in the knowledge of one's own impotency. It might strike you if you are not prudent and methodical in your precautions. The extraordinary few say *no* to the fear, and *no* to the

14. *The Letters of Herman Melville,* ed. Merrell R. Davis and William H. Gilman (New Haven: Yale University Press, 1960), p. 125.

15. Melville's comment is, of course, subject to more than one interpretation. Most biographers and critics of Melville seem to believe that what he meant was that he admired a person who thunders forth a powerful NO to, as Lewis Mumford puts it, "all the powers and dominions that lie beyond" the universe. *Herman Melville* (New York: Harcourt, Brace, 1929), p. 152. Considering his customary usage of the word *thunder,* however, to mean lightning and the implications of the story that most directly relate to his remark ("The Lightning-Rod Man"), it appears more likely that he was praising the person who retains his identity as seeker after meaning in the face of implications that there is no meaning.

73

message of purposelessness, and they continue to say no—almost impossible though it is—even after they are struck. So it is with Ahab, though he has to fight mightily.

His madness enables him to deny the implications of his victimization by the white whale. As Melville treats it, Ahab's madness is not the result of a mind that has snapped. It is not an unavoidable consequence of a traumatic experience; it is deliberately cultivated. Ahab actually *wills* his monomania, and though it controls him, he also uses it as his tool. He considers madness absolutely necessary to his quest and takes measures to insure its continuance. To Perth, the blacksmith, he says: "Thy shrunk voice sounds too calmly, sanely woefull to me. In no Paradise myself, I am impatient of all misery in others that is not mad. Thou should'st go mad, blacksmith; say, why dost thou not go mad? How can'st thou endure without being mad? Do the heavens yet hate thee, that thou can'st not go mad?" (p. 403). Later he tells Pip that he must not follow him around because he sees in Pip that which "I feel too curing to my malady." He cannot risk being among people who are either too sane in their woe or too tormented because they could well bring him out of his trance of monomania. To Pip he adds, "Like cures like; and for this hunt, my malady becomes my most desired health" (p. 436).

Ishmael understands perfectly this condition in which paradoxically the malady is the "most desired health," and in numerous places he defines and sympathetically explores it. Chapter 23, "The Lee Shore," is among other things an explanation of madness as imperative. The "tempestuous" storm Ishmael refers to is madness, and he is looking with both "sympathetic awe and fearfulness" at a person who willfully prefers it to sanity, the lee shore. He is describing the Ahab who shuns both Perth and Pip as "curing," when he writes of a storm-tossed ship: "But in that gale, the port, the land, is the ship's direst jeopardy; she must fly all hospitality; one touch of land, though it but graze the keel, would make her shudder through and through. With all her might she crowds all sail off shore; in so doing, fights 'gainst the very winds that fain would blow her homeward; seeks all the lashed sea's landlessness again; for refuge's sake forlornly rushing into peril; her only friend her bitterest foe!" (p. 97).

Ahab does not think of himself as mad in the ordinary sense of having lost his mind. "They think me mad—Starbuck does," he says to himself, "but I'm demoniac, I am madness maddened! That wild madness that's only calm to comprehend itself!" (p. 147). That is, he has not lost mental powers or had them permanently changed in nature; he has instead become "demoniac," possessed. A force that he himself created and that is both his ruler and his tool is in charge of his faculties, but they remain as strong and vital as they ever were. The personification of this force is Fedallah. The Parsee stands a "mystic watch" without intermission and constantly eyes Ahab, who is sometimes "awed," or "somehow, at least, in some wild way . . . affected" by the inscrutable stare (p. 438). At other times, Ahab seems "an independent lord; the Parsee but his slave" (p. 439). Some "potent spell" seems "secretly to join the twain," Ahab and Fedallah.

The sense of foreignness that results from reading about Fedallah aboard a Nantucket whaling ship parallels the foreignness of what the Parsee objectifies in Ahab's makeup. That is, Melville probably chose as strange and as out-of-place a creature as possible to portray Ahab's harpooneer because he wanted that character to serve as the projection of a phenomenon in Ahab's being that is equally alien to what is usually within human beings. What is usually there, as Ishmael explains it, is the mind and the soul. In moments of consciousness they work together, the mind "characterizing" the soul, the soul furnishing the mind with depth and substance. The mind sleeps at intervals, but the soul does not; consequently, during periods of sleep, the soul, as the normal condition, exists alone. In his probing into Ahab's makeup, Melville shows that Ahab is endowed with an abnormal third faculty, that internal entity that Fedallah externally objectifies—that "one supreme purpose" of Ahab. By willfully "yielding up all his thoughts and fancies to his one supreme purpose," Ahab has created a faculty of such vitality and independence that it, unlike the mind, never sleeps. So when Ahab retires to his cabin, the mind sleeps, the soul remains awake and thus confronts directly with supreme horror what should not be there, a wakeful, ever-present force, seen now clearly because in absence from the slumbering mind. Before the mind awakes, Ahab bursts forth from his hammock, the soul—not having the mind "to characterize" it—a tormented, formless spirit glaring from his eyes.

> In sleep, [the soul] being for the time dissociated from the characterizing mind, which at other times employed it for its outer vehicle or agent, it spontaneously sought escape from the scorching contiguity of the frantic thing, of which, for the time, it was no longer an integral. But as the mind does not exist unless leagued with the soul, therefore it must have been that, in Ahab's case, yielding up all his thoughts and fancies to his one supreme purpose; that purpose, by its own sheer inveteracy of will, forced itself against gods and devils into a kind of self-assumed, independent being of its own. Nay, could grimly live and burn, while the common vitality to which it was conjoined, fled horror-stricken from the unbidden and unfathered birth. Therefore, the tormented spirit that glared out of bodily eyes, when what seemed Ahab rushed from his room, was for the time but a vacated thing, a formless somnambulistic being, a ray of living light to be sure, but without an object to color. (p. 175)[16]

The internal force, a sleepwalker that never sleeps, this alien intruder that is associated with fire, is projected in Fedallah, whom Ahab willfully, though secretly, brought along on this voyage, a creature he uses and one whom he is used by, one that he values and is horrified by, a part of himself that he sometimes wants to run away from but, having come this far, cannot. In these rare moments, Ahab questions the nature of this force he has made his constant companion and ruler: "What is it, what nameless, inscrutable, unearthly thing is it; what cozening, hidden lord and master, and cruel, remorseless emperor commands me . . . ?" (pp. 444–45). As if in answer, he sees Fedallah's fixed eyes reflected in the water.

Though Ahab's "supreme purpose," as represented by Fedallah, is a rare and strange thing of almost supernatural powers, it is not a spirit or demon that has entered from the *outside*. It was created

16. See the analysis of this difficult passage in Paul Brodtkorb, Jr., *Ishmael's White World: A Phenomenological Reading of Moby Dick* (New Haven: Yale University Press, 1965), pp. 62–64. Brodtkorb feels that "unstated distinctions" are implied, and he charges Ishmael with making "too many abstract synonyms" and with leaving "loose ends" in his analysis of Ahab's mind.

from the inside and consequently is part of Ahab himself. As such, Fedallah plays the roles of foreseer and of both Ahab's ruler and victim. He is aware of Ahab's (and thus his own) fate from the beginning; his "low laugh from the hold" (p. 145) is really Ahab's own instinctive feeling that he is engaged in futility, though he will not allow himself to see this truth. That is, the Fedallah within recognizes it, laughs in the face of it, and urges Ahab on. But Fedallah is also aware that since Ahab will perish, so will he because he is a part of Ahab's makeup. Toward the end, Fedallah's knowledge of his own death is increasingly clear. When Moby Dick is first sighted, the "pale, death-glimmer" that comes into Fedallah's eyes is the result of his seeing his own death. When Moby Dick strikes Ahab's boat on the first day of the chase, Fedallah is unsurprised and simply gazes "with unastonished eyes" (p. 449). As Ahab struggles amid the ruins of his boat, "Fedallah incuriously and mildly eyed him" (p. 450). A stoicism colored ever so faintly with a tincture of sadness characterizes Fedallah in these last days.

The Ahab I have described thus far, a partial portrait, to be sure, can be summed up as follows. During his life he has constantly probed his experiences for the meanings they might convey about external reality. He has suffered greatly both physically and mentally. He encountered an unusual whale that took off his leg. This and other events were for him manifestations. They threatened to force upon him a message of universal disorder, disclaiming any Godly equilibrium behind the randomness of the world's happenings and proclaiming only a horrible one-leggedness. In such a spiritual crisis, a reader of signs like Ahab must either change his identity and stop reading, which he will not do, or make his own signs. And that is what Ahab is trying to do in hunting the white whale: he will himself *create* a manifestation, an epiphany of justice for which his heart profoundly aches. If fate will not give him an experience that will reveal the higher balance to him and his own superiority to the stolid world around him, then he will take matters into his own hands and make such an experience. Now Ahab may not articulate all this specifically to himself. He is not sure what Moby Dick means to him; he is uncertain whether it is "principal" or "agent," but by reaping away his leg, it has brought on a terrible trauma; so he hates it and finds it evil. It matters little to him what it is. By destroying it he will feel that reality is ordered, not chaotic. Instead, the white whale destroys him.

Ahab may thus appear as a God-seeking hero who does what he has to do to combat the force of nihilism threatening to engulf his mind and spirit, his defeat not negating his noble strength.[17] But there is more to the characterization of Ahab than his God-hunger and more to the white whale than its association with inscrutable reality. Another side of Ahab and another symbolic function of Moby Dick have to be examined now to fill out the picture, for what Melville is depicting finally in Ahab is not an epic hero warring with an external objective reality and going down in glorious defeat but a great and deep man who in battling Moby Dick is suicidally and blindly at war with himself. We have seen the source of Ahab's woe, the horror of one-leggedness to a man who would have two; now we must seek the source of his aggression.

Melville envisioned the white whale as an objectification of Ahab. Numerous references connect the two. What distinguishes Moby Dick from other sperm whales is not only "his uncommon bulk" but also a "peculiar snow-white wrinkled forehead, and a high pyramidical white hump" (p. 159). Ahab is associated with both the pyramid and the hump in Stubb's description of his strange dream in the "Queen Mab" chapter. Later Ahab dwells on his wrinkled brow, and tells the blacksmith: "It is unsmoothable; for though thou only see'st it here in my flesh, it has worked down into the bone of my skull—*that* is all wrinkles!" (p. 403). He confesses to Starbuck that he feels "humped" (p. 444). Numerous other details about Ahab and Moby Dick are described in similar terms. For example, while Ahab is viewing the doubloon,

17. Lewis Mumford holds this view. "In one sense," he writes, "Ahab achieves victory: he vanquishes in himself that which would retreat from Moby-Dick and acquiesce in his insensate energies and his brutal sway." He concludes: "There is no struggle so permanent and so humanly satisfactory as Ahab's struggle with the white whale. In that defeat, in that succession of defeats, is the only pledge of man's ultimate victory, and the only final preventive of emptiness, boredom, and suicide" (pp. 186, 190).

he says: "The firm tower, that is Ahab" (p. 359). Then only a few pages later, Captain Boomer refers to the tail of Moby Dick as a "Lima tower" (p. 366). Ahab feels that he is predestined; Moby Dick's head is "predestinating" (p. 468). Ahab is seeking retribution and vengeance; there is "retribution, swift vengeance" in Moby Dick's "whole aspect" (p. 468).[18] Once, Ahab seems on the verge of glimpsing that in trying to destroy the white whale he is really warring with himself. In a moment of anger Starbuck says to him: "Let Ahab beware of Ahab; beware of thyself, old man." When the mate leaves, Ahab repeats the warning to himself: "Ahab beware of Ahab—there's something there!" (p. 394).

When Melville writes of whales in *Moby-Dick,* he sometimes means the literal kind and sometimes the metaphoric kind, and often the figurative whale projects the deepest inner self. Though Ahab himself is unaware of it, the great whale he seeks to destroy is a projection of his complex inner being that consists of two powerful impulses. The side of Ahab that craves balance, justice, and epiphany of higher meaning views the white whale with horror and hatred because it sees in Moby Dick its opposite quality, also present in Ahab.

This second side of Ahab and the white whale can best be understood in the context of a motif that is so pervasive in *Moby-Dick,* so intimately a part of the very basics of the story, that its importance can easily be missed. Throughout the novel Ishmael tirelessly reiterates the *specialness* of his materials. Frequently he works toward a peak, each aspect of what he is describing becoming more special than the last. His various discussions of water is a good example. He moves from the four elements to water to oceans to the Pacific Ocean. Of the elements he says in the first chapter, water is special, for it provokes meditation. Among bodies of water, the vast oceans are special with their limitless expanses. Finally, the Pacific Ocean is a special ocean: "To any meditative Magian rover, this serene Pacific, once beheld, must ever after be the sea of his adoption. It rolls the midmost waters

18. Some of these similarities and others are pointed out in Sister Mary Ellen's article on "Duplicate Imagery in *Moby-Dick,*" *Modern Fiction Studies* 8 (1962): pp. 252–64, which also argues that the white whale represents an aspect of Ahab. Sister Mary Ellen's conclusions, however, are different from my own.

of the world, the Indian Ocean and the Atlantic being but its arms" (p. 399). Such series abound in the novel. Ishmael relates that sailors are a distinct breed from landsmen, but whalemen, as Captain Peleg insists, are unlike other seamen. The crew of the *Pequod* is a further extension. Whaling ships are also special: "Of all ships whaling vessels are the most exposed to accidents of all kinds" (p. 89). They touch land much less frequently than other ships and consequently carry a greater supply of materials. The *Pequod,* however, is special even among whaling ships. "You never saw such a rare old craft as this," says Ishmael of this strange vessel with whale bones everywhere and with a tiller made of the lower jaw of a sperm whale (p. 67). At every turn, Ishmael emphasizes the extraordinary. He himself has a special background for a sailor. He and Queequeg sleep in a special bed, an "almighty big" one (p. 27). This friendship is special; people stare at them because they are on "such confidential terms" (p. 58). Harpooneers are special, "a class unknown . . . in any other marine than the whale fleet" (p. 128). The three harpooneers aboard the *Pequod* reflect a further degree of specialness, and Queequeg is most special of all. And so it goes. Father Mapple is a distinctive preacher: "There were certain engrafted clerical peculiarities about him" (p. 42). He preaches from an extraordinary pulpit shaped like a ship. "Most young candidates for . . . whaling stop at . . . New Bedford," says Ishmael, but he goes to a special port, Nantucket, because it has a distinctive history of whaling. Ahab's mother was special, a crazy woman who gave her son a special name.

These and scores of other examples that would include many characters form a context of untypicality from which Ahab and the white whale emerge. Specialness surrounds them, but they are the most special of all. Creatures that swim in the sea are especially fascinating. Of these the whale is special: "the mightiest animated mass that has survived the flood" (p. 62). Among whales is a special kind, the sperm whale: "Not even at the present day has the original prestige of the Sperm Whale, as fearfully distinguished from all other species of the leviathan, died out of the minds of the whalemen as a body" (p. 157). And among these distinctive whales, there is one that is unique—Moby Dick, "the monstrousest parmacetty," says Captain Peleg, "that ever chipped a boat" (p. 69). What the white whale is to the animal kingdom, Ahab is to humanity. Melville builds his extraordinariness, his "Grand-lama-like exclusiveness" (p. 386), on blocks of specialness. Sea captains are in themselves special—men with total power over other men. Quaker whaling captains from Nantucket, however, are distinctive both among seamen and Quakers, for they "are fighting Quakers; they are Quakers with a vengeance" (p. 71). Standing alone among these is Ahab, "a man of greatly superior natural force, with a globular brain and a ponderous heart" who thinks "untraditionally and independently," a man that "makes one in a whole nation's census—a mighty pageant creature, formed for noble tragedies" (p. 71). He is, in Captain Peleg's words, "a grand, ungodly, god-like man" (p. 76).

No one is more aware of his specialness than Ahab himself. He is, in fact, preoccupied with it. When he views the doubloon nailed to the mast, he sees himself reflected in the noble symbols on the three mountain peaks: "The firm tower, that is Ahab; the volcano, that is Ahab; the courageous, the undaunted, and victorious fowl, that, too, is Ahab" (p. 359). He sets himself apart from all others: "Ahab stands alone among the millions of the peopled earth, nor gods nor men his neighbors!" (p. 452). The theomania that surfaces at times in Melville and is seen occasionally in Ishmael is a constant in Ahab's characterization.

In addition to representing Ahab's rage for meaning, the white whale projects his sense of specialness. Significantly, upon its first actual appearance in the novel, Moby Dick is described as a god: "Not Jove, not that great majesty Supreme! did surpass the glorified White Whale as he so *divinely* swam" (p. 447, italics mine). After withholding himself from full view, "the grand god revealed himself" (p. 448). Moby Dick is the image of the god that Ahab feels himself to be, though, again, he does not recognize the white whale as such.

At this point an important distinction must be established, that between gods and God. Both Ishmael and Ahab speak frequently of gods and God, and critics all too often fail to distinguish the difference. An insight into this distinction comes from "The Lightning-Rod Man," Melville's portrait in miniature of the massive Ahab. The narrator of that story constantly links the lightning of a thunderstorm with gods of ancient mythology, and he sarcastically calls the salesman of lightning rods "Jupiter Tonans," Roman god of lightning. The narrator implies that these random, meaningless bolts of destruction come from the gods; he refuses to believe that they emanate from God, the source of all that is opposite to randomness—order, balance, justice, and meaning. "The hairs of our heads are numbered, and the days of our lives," says the narrator. "In thunder as in sunshine, I stand at ease in the hands of my God. . . . The Deity will not, of purpose, make war on man's earth."[19] In *Moby-Dick,* as in "The Lightning-Rod Man," *gods* is a metaphorical term for all those powerful forces in life that conspire to destroy one's conviction that meaning and a higher justice do exist. Ahab does not "stand at ease in the hands" of God, to be sure, but one side of his nature is certainly drawn toward Him. It is not God but the fateful forces of life that he refers to as "ye great gods." He angrily defies them: "I laugh and hoot at ye, ye cricket-players, ye pugilists, ye deaf Burkes and blinded Bendigoes. I will not say as schoolboys do to bullies,—Take some one of your own size; don't pommel *me!* No, ye've knocked me down, and I am up again; but *ye* have run and hidden" (p. 147). Ahab cries out against the gods for two reasons, both of which are echoed in "The Lightning-Rod Man." The first is that they—as the forces behind the lightning—try to destroy belief in order and justice. The narrator of the story, who shows an inordinate interest in the theory of the returning stroke (that which goes from the earth to the sky), is echoing Ahab's desire to strike back at these gods who threaten to turn him into a nihilist. The second reason is that Ahab feels himself equal to any god and resents any attempt to diminish his stature. In "The Lightning-Rod Man," the narrator reacts with violence to the warning of the salesman that lightning will make of him "a heap of charred offal, like a haltered horse burnt in his stall; and all in one flash!"[20] Ahab would have been equally angered by this statement because of his passionate belief in his own specialness and

19. "The Lightning-Rod Man." in *The Complete Stories of Herman Melville,* ed. Jay Leyda (New York: Random House, 1949), p. 221.
20. Ibid., p. 220.

his outrage at any force, of whatever sort, that would reduce him to less than the titan he believes himself to be.

This side of Ahab that can be called his conviction of specialness may appear unrelated to the force of whiteness as Ishmael explains it in "The Whiteness of the Whale" chapter, but in reality, they are closely related. Whiteness is a threat that comes to Ahab from without, and his "fatal pride" is an inner quality, but the first is largely the result of the second. The terrifying vision of nothingness that assaults and annihilates any hope for cosmic substance and harmony and against which Ahab is heroically struggling is actually what a god (as distinguished from God) sees. In other words, Ahab's knowledge of his specialness has produced his vastations of nothingness. When Ishmael speaks of those travelers in Lapland who refuse to wear colored glasses to protect their eyes against the snow, he is really describing Ahab as he appears in "The Candles" chapter, refusing to use lightning rods as protection and looking straight into the lightning because he feels special. "And like wilful travellers in Lapland, who refuse to wear colored and coloring glasses upon their eyes, so the wretched infidel gazes himself blind at the monumental white shroud that wraps all the prospect around him" (p. 170). Melville's emphasis in this passage is not so much on the objective reality of nothingness underlying appearances of substance as upon the "wilful" quality of those who are *determined* to see whiteness and as a result, do see it, become blind, and believe thereafter in nothing. Consequently, the act of putting on sunglasses in snow or looking obliquely rather than directly at fire or lightning is not in this context an act of fear or cowardice but one in which the will brings about belief in a universal meaning. It is not merely a happy artistic accident that Moby Dick is white, for ultimately the freedom and self-sufficiency that constitute an exalted sense of specialness can end only in whiteness. That is to say, titanism as a self-concept pushes out all else from one's world.

Melville protested against his novel's being read as "a monstrous fable, or still worse and more detestable, a hideous and intolerable allegory" (p. 177), knowing full well that Ahab's pursuit of the white whale was a kind of allegory of mind.[21] In Ahab's quest he was depicting a great man acting against himself, for the white whale Ahab wishes to destroy incarnates the objectives of his life.[22] Yet toward this particular whale he directs the vengeful hatred of a king in ancient times for a brother turned disloyal. The difference is that Ahab does not realize that his traitorous enemy is a relative—indeed, closer even than a relative.[23] Except for brief moments of intuition, he is blind to what he is doing. Nowhere in literature is there a more tragic example of an extraordinary man of profound depths whose left hand is unaware of what the right one is doing. He is so powerfully and contradictorily constituted that self-understanding is vanquished from the mental field.

In developing Ahab's blindness, Melville creates an elaborate texture of irony based on a pattern of references to seeing and not seeing. Ishmael comments early in the novel that "no man can ever feel his own identity aright except his eyes be closed" (p. 55). Significantly, Ahab is practically sleepless; his eyes are open too much to see. Seeing is extremely important to this man involved in a blind quest. He offers a doubloon as reward for the first man who sees the white whale. He is the first to see it on all three occasions, but he does not see it for what it is. Consequently, the gold goes unclaimed. The novel is rife with references to sight. Fedallah is constantly gazing at Ahab. Ahab gazes in the ocean and sees Fedallah's eyes reflected there. Throughout all this looking, the paradox Ishmael stated holds true: when Ahab thinks he is seeing, he is closest to being blind, and when he is blind, he is closest to seeing, that is, to seeing the truth about himself. In

21. John Fentress Gardner states boldly that *Moby-Dick* is "a book where all is parable." It embodies "lessons Melville was teaching himself as an individual through the writing of this tragedy." *Melville's Vision of America: A New Interpretation of Moby Dick* (New York: Myrin Institute, 1977), pp. 37, 38.

22. John Freeman makes a brief but pertinent comment on this: "Ahab against the White Whale, like against like, man against himself." *Herman Melville* (New York: Macmillan, 1926), p. 118.

23. Newton Arvin expresses this relationship in terms of the "archetypal Parent; the father, yes, but the mother also, so far as she becomes a substitute for the father." *Herman Melville* (New York: Sloane, 1950), p. 173.

"The Candles" chapter, Ahab insists upon looking into the lightning and is temporarily blinded. He *"closes his eyes, his right hand pressed hard upon them."* According to Ishmael's paradoxical formula, the opportunity is now Ahab's to "feel his own identity aright," but he opens his eyes at the earliest possible moment. This crucial time of lightning flashing and Saint Elmo's fire burning atop the masts passes without Ahab's having truly seen into himself. He feels blinded again right after Moby Dick strikes the *Pequod*. As he witnesses this horrible spectacle, he smites his forehead and cries: "I grow blind, hands! stretch out before me that I may yet grope my way. Is't night?" (p. 467). It is night for Ahab, though with his eyes closed now he is near to the truth that the two secret sharers of his being are so incompatible that their conflict will destroy him. He soon sees again, however, and that is when the true darkness again surrounds him as it has all along. He complains of it, but he cannot alter his course: "So far gone am I in the dark side of earth, that its other side, the theoretic bright one, seems but uncertain twilight to me" (p. 433).

References to navigation in the novel function similarly to those of seeing. Ahab pilots his course with all the expertise that results from forty years of sailing experience. Night after night he pores over his old logbooks and yellowed sea charts, "for with the charts of all four oceans before him, Ahab was threading a maze of currents and eddies" (p. 171). He is adept at reading these lines on paper, intricate and confusing as they are to the uninitiated eye, but he cannot read the map of his inner self as marked out in the "lines upon his wrinkled brow" (p. 171). The "chart of his forehead," unlike the literal charts before him that he interprets expertly, reveals the true whereabouts of the white whale as within Ahab, but this chart is closed to him. He would have to have a mirror to see his own forehead-chart, but he rejects mirrors and anything or anyone—like Perth and Pip—when they begin to function as such.

Ahab consults his charts for the purpose of pinpointing the likely location of Moby Dick, and he proves himself a worthy navigator in the literal seas but not in the seas of self. For the closer he comes to what he hopes will be the peace and fulfillment of vengeance, the further away he moves from these desired states; the more on his course, the more off he is. Just as Ishmael establishes the paradox of not seeing though seeing, so he makes a central statement about navigation in the passage where he stares into the violent fire of the tryworks while he is at the helm, experiences an "unnatural hallucination of the night," becomes turned around, and heads his ship into the wind. He recovers just in time to right his own direction and that of the *Pequod*. Ishmael's narrow escape and his comments about darkness, the artificial fire, and fidelity to the true compass of self all bear directly on Ahab's experiences with the ship's compass and with Saint Elmo's fire late in the novel.

Chapter 124 ("The Needle") is an elaborate metaphorical treatment of Ahab's misnavigation brought on by his unawareness of the inner seas of his being. The symbol for what both sides of Ahab desire most is gold. It stands for the precious and the permanent which he yearns for; and it stands for the specialness that the other side of his nature aspires to. Yet he is never to find that gold, never to collect the doubloon that is the reward for truly *seeing* the white whale for what it is. As this chapter opens, Ahab is in the midst of one of those rare times when he appears on the verge of discovery, when the gold is almost at hand. Using one of many alchemistic images in the novel, Melville writes: "The sea was as a crucible of molten gold, that bubblingly leaps with light and heat" (p. 423). At this moment, however, Ahab discovers that he is heading in a direction opposite of what he had charted. On the night before, lightning has struck the ship and turned the compasses. He orders the helmsman to reverse course, and he makes a new needle that will show the correct way. "Thunder turned old Ahab's needles," he says, "but out of this bit of steel Ahab can make one of his own, that will point as true as any" (p. 425). As with seeing, however, navigation is paradoxical; when Ahab is on what he perceives to be his "true" course, he is moving outward and not navigating inwardly toward self-awareness. The closer he gets to Moby Dick literally, the further he is from seeing what it is in himself that Moby Dick projects.

So strong and different are the two sides of Ahab—that which reaches out hungrily for a greater reality with which to merge itself and that which feels itself raised high above the ordinary and jealously and fiercely attacks any threat to its individual identity—that he is like two people acting as one. Besides his artificial limb, the most distinctive aspect of Ahab's physical being is a great scar. On Ahab's first appearance in the novel, Ishmael describes it: "It resembled that perpendicular seam sometimes made in the straight, lofty trunk of a great tree, when the upper lightning tearingly darts down it, and without wrenching a single twig, peels and grooves out the bark from top to bottom." The theory of an old Gayhead Indian crew member that Ahab had not received this scar until he was forty "seemed inferentially negatived" by a "grey Manxman" with what appears "preternatural powers of discernment." He avers that "if ever Captain Ahab should be tranquilly laid out . . . whoever should do that last office for the dead, would find a birth-mark on him from crown to sole" (p. 110).[24] By this "perpendicular seam" of a "birth-mark," Melville suggests a bipartite Ahab, split down the middle of his being and that seam the outward manifestation of a partitioning blind that prevents one self from recognizing the other as its archenemy.

Consequently, Ahab has not one but two motivations for his every action, and they are always opposite in nature. What he thinks is a singleness of purpose is actually a double purpose, each act the result of his duality. In every instance his behavior is satisfactory not just to one self but to the other as well, each believing it is pursuing its own goal. All of the actions of Ahab the God-seeker discussed early in this chapter are also actions of Ahab the theomaniac. Ahab feels the phantom limb sensation because of his affinity for balance, an attribute of his religious proclivities. But equally important in this experience is his self-esteem, which has been profoundly violated by his amputation. He hungers for vengeance because of his need to be assured of the reality of justice, and it is true that a keen sensitivity to justice is a mark of the God-seeker. Yet, as Sister Mary Bonaventure Mroz wrote in a comment that earlier I quoted only partially, vengeance is revered by *both*

24. Opinions of critics vary greatly on how Ahab got this scar. Alan Lebowitz offers the notion that it "is the result of some long-past encounter with an oriental fire god." *Progress into Silence: A Study of Melville's Heroes* (Bloomington: Indiana University Press, 1970), p. 9.

those of spiritual and selfish natures. The God-seeker loves vengeance as an indication of divine order, and he yearns to be the instrument of it, the "avenger." There is in Ahab this desire to act as a tool of God and a servant of mankind to set things straight. On the other hand, the self-conceived demigod loves vengeance as proof of his own stature and invulnerability, and he, unlike the other type, wishes to be the *"one avenged."*[25] Ahab exhibits this drive and just as strongly as the other. All his actions are similarly derived from both of his disparate selves. He breaks the quadrant, it is true, because he wishes to rely only on the higher mathematics and not the mechanical way of the world, but he also does it because that other side of his nature resents any outside help and desires to assert complete self-sufficiency. His failure to follow the Golden Rule in his meeting with Captain Gardiner reflects his allegiance to deeper aims, but it also mirrors his conviction of his own specialness, his belief that other human lives are insignificant. In these and each of his other actions, his two selves reach the same decision in how to behave but for opposite reasons.

If one allegory can be illuminated by another, Ahab's duality and the result of it may be likened to what occurs in the following dream sequence. In a town of the American West in the last century, live two men unacquainted. One is black, the other white. The black man is aloof because of his self-assured greatness; he is convinced of his own superiority in every way, and he thinks of little else. The white man is bookish and spiritual in nature; he seems always searching for the truth and has intuitions of profoundly deep meaning. Into this town one day ride two men with white veil-like masks covering their entire faces so that they appear perfectly expressionless. For no apparent reason, one of them attacks the black and the other the white man. Both lie suffering for some time but finally heal. The black man feels that his pride has been wounded and his superiority challenged; so he determines to seek out and kill these two men, who are traveling as one. His self-image as demigod depends upon this act of vengeance. The other victim also decides to pursue the men, but his reason is far different. He has been deeply disturbed by being

25. Mroz, p. 3.

brutalized; he wonders how such things could be, and he feels he cannot rest until he makes sure justice is done. Though the black and the white man travel together as one in their pursuit, they have no time or inclination to think of each other, though whatever they do happens to be agreeable to both. They decide, for example, to throw away their compasses, but for different reasons. The black man feels that he is so superior that he can rely on his own talents of tracking and does not need the help of a mere gadget. His ignored companion decides that higher powers will guide him and that he will put faith in those instead of the compass. After much traveling they find the two masked men—still traveling as one. A furious gunfight ensues. When it is over, the black and the white man lie dead. The men in white masks stand over them a moment and then remove their masks. One is black and the other white. In fact, *their faces are identical to those of the two dead men.* In the fight, the black man behind the mask killed the white man, and the white masked man killed the black man. Here the dream ends. In *Moby-Dick* the white whale is a composite of the two Ahabs, self-conceived god and God-seeker, though masked in white.[26] Ahab's wound is self-inflicted in the sense that the two sides of him injured each other, and ultimately the two selves destroy each other.

The allegory does not negate the literal story, of course. Ahab does really encounter a great whale that chews off his leg. It is one of those events in life when externality happens perfectly to reflect internality. Ironically, Ahab, the reader of experiences for deeper meaning, will not read this one right. A true manifestation of his

---

26. Edward F. Edinger cites an instance where "a woman once dreamt of Melville's white whale connected with a black whale 'very much in the fashion of the Chinese T'ai-chi-t'u.' The white whale had a black eye and the black whale a white eye. For this dreamer, and likewise for Melville, the white whale Moby-Dick poses the archetypal problem of opposites. The Chinese T'ai-chi-t'u symbolizes the reciprocal relationship between two opposing principles. The white fish is Yang, the masculine principle of light, heaven, spirit, action. The black fish is Yin, the feminine principle of darkness, earth, matter, receptivity." *Melville's Moby-Dick: A Jungian Commentary* (New York: New Directions, 1978), pp. 79–80. Though Edinger's interpretation of the white whale does not precisely parallel my own, the dream he discusses above is fundamentally similar to the one I have described.

inner life situation occurs, but he will not see it as such. The reason he will not is that it is simply too horrible, too unacceptable for him to bear. Consequently his two selves act as one to create his monomania to insure continued blindness. Ahab's "torn body and gashed soul bled into one another; and so interfusing, made him mad" (p. 160). Actually he was, in a sense, mad before this, however, twice mad. One side is marked by theomania and the other by a mania for quintessence. A third form of madness takes its being from the other two, and this mental entity, the product of fusion, is both the tool and master of the other two, spurring them both onward and keeping them apart from each other and keeping each blind to the nature of the other.

The white whale is a mirror to this situation. Moby Dick has wounded Ahab, but Ahab has wounded Moby Dick—the harpoon is still in him. The great whale is a symbol of the truth seeker's aim; he swims in the sea of molten gold as the quintessence. Ahab is that seeker who pursues the answers to life's riddles. Moby Dick is also the symbol of the independence and strength of the demigod with which the other self of Ahab identifies. Ahab is vengeful; Moby Dick is vengeful. The same madness that characterizes the man is reflected in the whale. Moby Dick wants to destroy Ahab as much as Ahab wants to detroy Moby Dick. When the two selves of Ahab contemplate the white whale, each intuits only its opposite there and hates it. Theomania hates the mania for quintessence that in turn abhors theomania. The urge for God is incompatible with archpride. One is a drive to find one's indentity in a greater reality, whereas the other is a determination to retain individuality. No matter how hard Ahab strives to understand the great spiritual mysteries, to go outward and find God, he is doomed to frustration because of the other side of his nature. Similarly, no matter how much he feels and exerts his own specialness, he is destined to be struck-down. One side of Ahab will never let the other be what it wishes.

Ahab's Heresy

Chapter 4

The story of Ahab is one of self-warring. There are two Ahabs as there are two Ishmaels, but the two sides hidden within the single body of Ishmael recognize and understand each other. In Ahab, one self—that characterized by God-hunger—battles with a tendency within that self, a tendency toward what may be called atheism or nihilism. Concurrently, this same self is at war on another front with an enemy it does not even recognize, a hooded knight that turns out to be another aspect of Ahab's complex personality, the side that is godlike and so proud of its specialness that it hates the other side, the yearning for a higher God. The nature of the combatants and the great final battles of this self-war that occupy the foreground of *Moby-Dick* were the subjects of the previous chapter; what precipitated the breach to begin with that led to hostilities is the subject of this one.

If one factor can be said to be primarily responsible for the division of self that finally destroys Ahab, it is his preoccupation with the subject of evil. "Some deep men," Melville says in chapter 41 ("Moby-Dick"), are prone to "feel eating in them" the troublesome mystery of iniquity.[1] They simply cannot help prob-

---

1. *Moby-Dick*, ed. Harrison Hayford and Hershel Parker (New York: Norton, 1967). All references to *Moby Dick* are to this edition.

ing to the furthest possible extent the question of evil, its nature and especially its source. Where, they ask over and over, does this "intangible malignity" come from? With such deep and obsessive thinkers, several answers and subsequent courses of action based on those answers are possible.

After delving into the problem of evil to discover its source, some probers of this sort may conclude that it has no supernatural origins, that it is merely the absence of good, not, in its own right, a positive force at all. But to Ahab the evidences in his own experience of universal malignity have been far too great for him to be able to accept this answer. He reads signs, and the signs point to a real and powerful evil. Others may deny the presence of supernatural evil by denying the presence of *any* supernatural force: there is no devil because there is no God. The evil in the world, they may decide, derives from social injustices, from poor environmental conditions and conditioning, and from psychological abnormalities. But Ahab by his very nature is a God-seeker, and he engages in fierce combat with any tendency to blot out all supernatural forces.

Being as he is, unable to deny the reality of evil or its supernatural origins, Ahab in his pursuit of truth seems to have three options. First, he could recognize evil as being the overwhelming power of the universe and become its subject. Again, Ahab's God-hunger, his love of balance and justice, are too much a part of his nature to allow him to become a devil-worshipper. As a second possible course, he could follow the traditional way for a nineteenth-century American of religious bent and become an ardent Christian like Father Mapple, who recognizes the supernatural presence of evil but feels that God is stronger and allows evil to exist for purposes He alone understands but we in our limited finite minds cannot. No matter how hard they try to do this, however, some deep, questioning souls who are preoccupied with rightness and fair play cannot understand why God allows children to die in their cribs, innocent women to be violated, or whole populations to be wiped out by famine, earthquakes, tidal waves, or senseless wars. They are told by Christians that all is for the best, that God is on his throne, and that He sees every sparrow that falls. Such a person as Ahab cannot accept this orthodox

Christian God who is responsible for evil and who allows it to flourish. Nevertheless, Ahab must have some God; he will fight to have God.

The third option for Ahab is another way of thinking about evil and God, one that Melville knew about, one that he was strongly attracted to himself, and one that he has Ahab embrace as both the answer to his questions and the cause of his destruction—the ancient heresy of Gnosticism. Precisely how much Melville knew about this Christian heresy that arose in the first century, flourished in the second, and gradually died out, is impossible to determine. A few scattered references to the Gnostics do occur in his writings from each period of his career, but there is no direct evidence that he made any deep and systematic study of them. He did know at least the basic outlines of Gnostic beliefs, and this was enough to impress him profoundly because these fundamental concepts were startingly congenial to his own temperament. If he read no more on Gnosticism than in books he is known to have owned, he would have been supplied with all the basic tenets of the heresy.[2] He could not but be struck with how like himself those ancient thinkers were.

2. It is difficult not to assume, however, that he would have seen various other materials on the Gnostics, for the nineteenth century saw a great surge of interest in them. In tracing the rise and fall of Gnosticism, Hans Jonas writes: "The last of the major heresiologists to deal extensively with the Gnostic sects, Epiphanius of Salamis, wrote in the fourth century A.D. From then on, with the danger past and the polemical interest no longer alive, oblivion settled down on the whole subject, until the historical interest of the nineteenth century returned to it in the spirit of dispassionate inquiry." *The Gnostic Religion: The Message of the Alien God and the Beginnings of Christianity* (Boston: Beacon, 1958), pp. xiv–xv. The new interest that Jonas speaks of is evident in the periodicals of the time. The religiously oriented *Ladies' Repository* warned its readers against the seduction of the Gnostic vision in an article by George Waterman, Jr. ("Gnosticism," 3 [October 1843]: 292–93). Waterman charges the Gnostics with holding "the God of the Jews in supreme contempt—esteeming him as a malicious being, whom Jesus came to destroy. They supposed all sin to consist in matter" (p. 293). Even earlier in the century, a writer for the *Edinburgh Review* severely criticized George Waddington's *History of the Church from the Earliest Ages to the Reformation* (London, 1835) for its neglect of the Gnostics. In doing so, the reviewer gives a clear impression of the current fascination with Gnosticism: "At a period when some of the most gifted individuals on the Continent of

Two sets of reference books that he owned contain multiple entries on the Gnostics. In Pierre Bayle's *A General Dictionary, Historical and Critical,* which Melville obtained in 1849, he found discussions of Gnostics and related sects, including the Cainites, the Paulicians, the Marcionites, and the Manacheans. Millicent Bell has argued conclusively for Melville's fondness for Bayle and for the influence of the *Dictionary* on many aspects of *Moby-Dick.* Bell correctly perceives that "Melville must have discovered a state of mind remarkably like his own."[3] What she is referring to is the concern of both men for the question of evil. Whatever Bayle happens to be writing about, he likely will get around to the perplexing problem of evil. "Bayle was a man tossed between the will to believe and the compulsion to doubt. He denied that he was an atheist but, truly, one can say of him what Hawthorne was to say of Melville . . . : 'He can neither believe nor be comfortable in his unbelief.' "[4] Bayle chose to write several entries on the Gnostics because he was, in spite of his rejection of their solutions, obviously fascinated with them and attracted to their

---

Europe are turning their attention to the subject of the Gnostics, as one of the most interesting and important that can attract the notice of the historian, the philosopher, or the divine, and when philosophical societies are holding out prizes which bring forth such works as that by Professor Matter of Strasburg, such is the very different conclusion to which Mr. Waddington, in the simplicity of his heart, arrives. We are far indeed from undervaluing the advantages to be derived from an acquaintance with the Gnostics." Gnosticism, he continues, "presents to us the human mind in some of its most interesting attitudes,—mourning over the introduction of moral evil into the universe,—wasting itself in unavailing efforts to scale the inaccessible heights that carry up from the finite to the infinite—prying into the mysterious links that connect the will of the Omnipotent with the existence of the visible Universe,—and when the voice of the Eternal 'calls for "things that are not," ' vainly endeavoring to discover *how or whence* 'they come.' Even in their wildest excesses they exhibit the imperishable longings of the soul of man after the vast, the unknown, the infinite; they show us the extent—if they instructively teach us the limits also of the human faculties;—and in illustrating the vanity of the desire after perfect *gnosis,* they may convince us of the wisdom of resting in simple *faith* in the fundamental principles of natural and revealed religion." *Edinburgh Review* 62 (October 1835): 152–53.

3. Millicent Bell, "Pierre Bayle and *Moby-Dick,*" PMLA 66 (1951): 627.

4. Ibid., p. 629.

unorthodox handling of the thorny question of evil.[5] Melville was likewise.

Melville received more of an objective and systematic outline of the fundamentals of Gnosticism from his copy of Ephraim Chambers's *Cyclopaedia; or, An Universal Dictionary of Arts and Sciences* (1728). He acquired this two-volume reference work in 1846, a gift from his uncle Herman Gansevoort. It contains substantial entries not only on the general subject of "Gnosticks," but also on the individual sects, including the Valentinians, Simonians, Carpocratians, Nicolaitians, and others. No Gnostic outlook with which Melville furnished Ahab would need to have come from any source outside Chambers and Bayle, though it is likely that Melville did pick up knowledge of the subject here and there in his extensive reading elsewhere.

Biographers and critics have been uncharacteristically slow in recognizing both Melville's affinity for the Gnostics and his awareness of their beliefs. William Braswell perceptively but briefly pointed out Melville's reference to the Gnostics in *White-Jacket,* suggested that Melville "must have been stimulated by the heretical ideas of those early rivals of Christianity" as Pierre Bayle described them, and explicated a few of Ahab's speeches in Gnostic terms.[6] Braswell's groundbreaking work of 1943 was not really continued until much later and then only partially, although Millicent Bell did direct herself in 1951 to the single question of the Gnostic position on evil as described by Bayle. Building on Braswell's suggestion that Ahab reflects certain Gnostic ideas, Thomas Vargish published an article on the subject of Melville's interest in Gnosticism.[7] Vargish admirably outlines many of the intricacies of the heresy (more perhaps than Melville was actually acquainted with). In order to account for

5. See, for example, Bayle's entry on the Paulicians. He argues that the Paulician explanation for evil "would probably have made a greater progress still, had it been explained in a less gross manner," and he proceeds to debate at length the question of evil.

6. William Braswell, *Melville's Religious Thought: An Essay in Interpretation* (Durham: Duke University Press, 1943), pp. 52, 62–63.

7. Thomas Vargish, "Gnostic *Mythos* in *Moby-Dick,*" PMLA 81 (1966): 272–77.

Melville's knowledge of Gnosticism, Vargish conjectures that he must have read Andrews Norton's *The Evidences of the Genuineness of the Gospels,* published in 1844. If Melville had, indeed, read these three volumes, he would certainly have been something of an expert on the Gnostics, for they are the major target of Norton's inquiry. It is possible that he was acquainted with Norton's work, but there is no direct evidence that he was and some suggestion that he was not.[8] Nevertheless, the article remains a pioneering piece of scholarship that has not been followed up.[9] The purpose of this chapter is to do that, to argue (with Braswell, Bell, and Vargish) that Melville was acquainted with Gnostic beliefs, that he found them compelling, and that he used them in his creation of Ahab. In addition, I wish to suggest that Ahab's

8. In so establishing his argument, Vargish writes: "In *Moby-Dick* itself, Melville's single direct reference is to a Gnostic sect called the 'Ophites.' In Chapter xli, he pictures them worshipping their 'Statue-Devil' and *compares* [italics mine] them with Ahab who had personified all the 'subtle demonisms of life and thought' in the white whale. From Norton's *Evidences* we learn that . . . the Ophites took the part of the serpent and represented him as having given good counsel to Adam and Eve" (p. 273). Consequently, the Ophites were not truly worshipping evil, for they saw the serpent as a symbol of goodness, of, indeed, the Divine. If Melville had read Norton he would have known this, but he apparently did not. He does not "compare" Ahab with the Ophites, as Vargish indicated, but *contrasts* him with them. Ishmael says that Ahab saw in the white whale "that intangible malignity which has been from the beginning; to whose dominion even the modern Christians ascribe one-half of the worlds; that which the ancient Ophites of the east reverenced in their statue devil" (p. 160). Melville has the Ophites worshipping evil when they actually worshipped goodness, as Norton carefully explains. Ishmael continues, "Ahab did not fall down and worship it [evil] like them; but deliriously transferring its idea to the abhorred white whale, he pitted himself, all mutilated, against it." Melville had to be unaware of the true beliefs of the serpent-worshipping Ophites to have written this passage, and had he read Norton, as Vargish argues he had, he would never have made the contrast between Ahab and the Ophites. It is likely that he merely picked up somewhere in his reading the misleading information that the Ophites had worshipped serpents, did not realize that the Ophites were actually an unusual brand of Gnostics, and erroneously concluded that they were devil-worshippers.

9. William H. Shurr deals with the subject briefly but knowledgeably in *The Mystery of Iniquity: Melville as Poet, 1857–1891* (Lexington: University Press of Kentucky, 1972), pp. 164–66, 255.

destructive split, his war within, results from Ahab's heretical beliefs.

The most obvious characteristic of the Gnostics' behavior is also the most obvious aspect of Ahab's. The Gnostics believed that they were very special people, superior not only to the heathens and barbarians of the world but also to other Christians. In a fashion vaguely similar to Calvin's view of the Elect, they spoke of their own favored status. Ephraim Chambers wrote in his entry on the "Gnosticks" that they acted "as if they were the only Persons who had the true knowledge of Christianity: Accordingly, they look'd on all the other Christians as simple, ignorant, and barbarous Persons, who explained, and interpreted the Sacred Writings in too low, and literal a Signification."[10] The Gnostics could not have described themselves better than did Ishmael when he pointed to the differences between the ordinary masses and the "true princes of the empire," the "choice hidden handful of the Divine inert." These and many other expressions in *Moby-Dick* are so close to Gnostic belief and imagery that they could have been taken directly from the pages of the heresiarchs themselves.

The Gnostics believed they were the Elect because they felt that they had within them what Ahab refers to as royal essence ("queenly personality"): Ishmael's eloquent description of Ahab as a many-layered person is a description the Gnostics would have given of themselves, for they believed in a pristine, unfallen Adamic Man within, which they frequently described as a royal personage, a queen, a king, or the son of a king, held captive by the body and the world. Knowing that the Gnostics considered themselves by their very natures the most special and favored people on earth, Melville wrote passage after passage in *Moby-Dick* that startlingly reproduce the imagery they used. Ishmael says that if one could go down through the layers of being in Ahab, like the layers of civilizations uncovered in the Hotel de Cluny in Paris, one would come to a royal personage held there, a "captive king" (p. 161). The Gnostics considered themselves the

10. Ephraim Chambers, *Cyclopaedia; or An Universal Dictionary of Arts and Sciences* (London: Knapton, 1728), 1:165.

chosen because they were descended from the royal Godhead.[11] When they were not describing this divine spark or spiritual gift within them as a link in royal lineage they were using other similar images, such as uncorruptible gold in the midst of corruption.[12] The extent to which like temperaments and like thinking can produce ideas clothed in the same metaphors is to be seen in Melville's use of gold as the emblem of Ahab's self-concept. In the solid gold doubloon that he nails to the mainmast, Ahab sees his deepest and purest self, "nailed amidst all the rustiness and iron bolts and the verdigris of copper spikes, yet, untouchable and immaculate to any foulness" (p. 359). Though Starbuck, Stubb, and the others who gaze at the doubloon read a variety of meanings into it, Ahab sees there "his own mysterious self."

Ahab's specialness, which is projected in images of royalty and gold, makes him stand out in his own and in Ishmael's mind clearly above two other classes of men in *Moby-Dick*. Ahab believes that he has within him that which is "divinely inert," that is, a spiritual element that is of the same substance as God and is thus immune to the corrupting influences around it. Like gold, it cannot be oxidized. In his various estimates of his mates and seamen, he places most of them in a category well below himself. He refers to this class in general as "manufactured man." By this

---

11. In the Gnostic Acts of Thomas, the chosen are admonished to "Get up and sober up out of your sleep. . . . Remember that you are a king's son. You have come under a servile yoke. Think of your suit shot with gold." Werner Foerster, *Gnosis: A Selection of Gnostic Texts,* ed. R. McL. Wilson (Oxford: Clarendon, 1972), 1:357.

12. In his description of Gnostic beliefs, the second-century church father Irenaeus writes: "For even as gold, when submersed in filth, loses not on that account its beauty, but retains its own native qualities, the filth having no power to injure the gold, so they affirm that they cannot in any measure suffer hurt, or lose their spiritual substance, whatever the material actions in which they may be involved." *The Writings of Irenaeus,* trans. Alexander Roberts and W. H. Rambant (Edinburgh: Clark, 1868), 1:26. This is volume 5 in the *Ante-Nicene Christian Library: Translations of the Writings of the Fathers down to A.D. 325,* ed. Alexander Roberts and James Donaldson, 24 vols. (Edinburgh: Clark, 1867–72). Werner Foerster comments that "the totality of Gnosis can be comprehended in a single image. This is the image of 'gold in the mud.'" Introduction to *Gnosis,* 1:2.

he seems to mean that such men are more like machines—"androids" we would call them today—than like created human beings with an indwelling spirituality or soul. He applies the term *mechanical* to Stubb at one point (p. 452), and he uses the term later to describe most of his crew (p. 459).

Ishmael's thinking often parallels Ahab's in the matter of human categories. They are as one in their view of the ship's carpenter as an example of "mechanical" man. Ishmael compares him to an intricate tool, "one of those unreasoning but still highly useful . . . Sheffield contrivances" (p. 388). He is, Ishmael says, "a pure manipulator" (p. 388). Though he seemed not to possess a soul, he did have some sort of "cunning high-principle in him; this it was, that kept him a great part of the time soliloquizing; but only like an unreasoning wheel, which also hummingly soliloquizes" (p. 389). The point in using this pattern of imagery to refer to the ordinary mass of mankind is to convey the idea that unlike Ahab, who according to Elijah has enough soul "to make up for all deficiencies of that sort in other chaps" (p. 86),[13] the carpenter and those like him are "soulless," as, indeed, Ahab says of Stubb at one point (p. 452).

Ahab has a much higher regard for Starbuck, in whom he confides near the end that he feels like "Adam, staggering beneath the piled centuries since Paradise" (p. 444). Though Starbuck comes close to influencing Ahab to turn back, he cannot finally reach the old man, and Ahab remains in the isolation of his self-conceived "grand, Lama-like exclusiveness." To Ahab, Stubb and Starbuck represent the two types that are generally encountered in mankind. "Ye two are the opposite poles of one thing; Starbuck is Stubb reversed, and Stubb in Starbuck; and ye two are all mankind" (p. 452). Not *all* mankind, though, for Ahab and the few choice hidden handful like him represent a third type that stand above "the millions of the peopled earth, nor gods nor men . . . [their] neighbors!" (p. 452). In Ahab's mind Starbuck is higher than the "soulless" Stubb and the millions of mechan-

---

13. Elijah raises the significant question to Ishmael and Queequeg as to whether their souls will be in danger if they ship with Captain Ahab. He then conjectures that they may not even have souls to lose (p. 86).

ical-like people because Starbuck does have a soul. But Ahab realizes whenever he converses with Starbuck that his first mate lacks the depth of spiritual insight, the "specialness" that he himself possesses.

This hierarchical view of humankind, which Ahab and to a large measure Ishmael express, is precisely that espoused by the Gnostics. No belief of these early Christian heretics was better known than this or more frequently referred to in books Melville would have read. Chambers's *Cyclopaedia* includes the following information about the Gnostics: "On the like Principle they also distinguished three Sorts of Men; *Material, Animal,* and *Spiritual:* The first, who were Material, and incapable of Knowledge, inevitably perished. . . . The third, such as the *Gnosticks* themselves pretended to be, were all certainly saved: The Psychic, or Animal, who were the middle between the other two, were capable either of being saved, or damned according to their good, or evil Actions."[14] Earlier, Chambers refers to the favored third type as "Pneumatic," which means "spiritual."

Ahab's sense of superiority is the result of the same conviction that made the Gnostics feel special. He thinks that he is the only one aboard the *Pequod* who truly knows what is going on. He has been blessed with special insight, or so he believes. He is one of the few who has "the true Knowledge," as Chambers expressed the Gnostics' attitude toward themselves. That insight places him far above the masses of vulgar and stolid material men and even above psychics like Starbuck. In his entry on the Gnostics, Chambers explains that "the Word *Gnostic* is formed of the Latin *Gnosticus*" and from two Greek words, which mean "enlightened" and "I know."

Coming to know was for the Gnostics—as it was for Ahab—a form of initiation, and once initiated, the Gnostic felt above and apart from the unknowing masses. But this knowledge could not be gained from study. Gnosticism was not a philosophy but a form of intuitive conviction. The Gnostics' insights about good and evil and about God and mankind came not through the intellect, not through the ordinary processes of learning, but through

14. Chambers, 1:165.

something like a mystical experience, which they referred to as "the call." In a single moment one would be awakened and *know* one's true spiritual self.

Because of this mystical element in their beliefs, the Gnostics acquired the reputation, from the time of Simon Magus onward, as practitioners of magic. [15] Certain sects were noted for their creation of amulets, which they wore on their spiritual quests. [16] Chambers's *Cyclopaedia* claims for the Basilidians the invention of "certain Amulets, to which they attributed great Virtues." [17] Though he does not wear it or create it himself, Ahab seems to regard the doubloon in some magical way. Fascinated with the figures on it, its "cabalistics" (p. 359), he rubs it against his jacket before he nails it to the very center of the ship. While he is rubbing it, he produces a sound that is "strangely muffled and inarticulate" (p. 142). Indeed, Ahab is not only a believer in such things of the world of magic as Fedallah's riddle-prophecy, but he is something of a magician himself. [18] Melville probably read in

15. Evelyn Underhill comments on the Gnostics' "attempted fusion of the ideals of mysticism and magic." *Mysticism: A Study in the Nature and Development of Man's Spiritual Consciousness* (London: Metheun, 1911), p. 149. J. P. Arendzen states that "It is markedly peculiar to Gnosticism that it places the salvation of the soul merely in the possession of a quasi-intuitive knowledge of the mysteries of the universe and of magic formulae indicative of that knowledge." "Gnosticism," in *The Catholic Encyclopedia,* 1909.

16. Campbell Bonner points out that magical amulets were "intended to bring death or serious harm to an enemy." "Magical Amulets," *Harvard Theological Review* 39 (1946): 52. Herbert Loewe states that "amulets were regarded as potent charms to . . . assist the wearer to obtain his desire. The charms were usually written on parchment or *engraved on a precious metal*" (italics mine). *Encyclopaedia of Religion and Ethics,* ed. James Hastings (New York: Scribners, 1915), 7:626. For other discussions of the nature and uses of amulets and talismans see the following: Bonner, *Studies in Magical Amulets* (Ann Arbor: University of Michigan Press, 1950); C. W. King, *The Gnostics: Their Remains, Ancient and Mediaeval* (London: Nutt, 1887); and George Frederich Kunz, *The Magic of Jewels and Charms* (Philadelphia: Lippincott, 1915).

17. Chambers, 1:89.

18. Charles Olson discusses the distinction Melville makes between "goetic" and "theurgic" magic and refers to Ahab as "Conjur Man." *Call me Ishmael* (San Francisco: City Lights Books, 1947), pp. 53, 55–56. The distinction Olson alludes to occurs in a note Melville wrote in his copy of Shakespeare's plays: "—not the (black art) Goetic but Theurgic magic—seeks converse with the

his copy of Chambers the entry on the "Simonians," another sect of Gnostics who "made profession of Magic" and believed in the "Uses of Magic" as a means of enlisting the spiritual aid of certain supernatural forces or beings that were "the Mediators between God and man."[19] Ahab's control over his crew in "The Quarter-Deck" (chapter 36) is little less than magical. They are "magnet-

---

Intelligence, Power, the Angel." Douglas Robillard suggests that Edward Bulwer-Lytton's *The Last Days of Pompeii* (1834) may have furnished Melville with the terms *Goetic* and *Theurgic*. "A Possible Source for Melville's Goetic and Theurgic Magic," *Melville Society Extracts*, no. 49 (1982): 5–6. Richard Cavendish explains the nature of the higher magic—that practiced by Gnostics: "There is a useful rough distinction between high magic and low magic. High magic is an attempt to gain so consummate an understanding and mastery of oneself and the environment as to transcend all human limitations and become superhuman or divine." *A History of Magic* (New York: Taplinger, 1977), p. 12. According to A. E. Waite, "the central doctrine of the high theurgic faith . . . was that by means of certain invocations, performed solemnly by . . . mentally illuminated men, it was possible to come into direct communication with those invisible powers which fill the measureless distance between man and God." *The Magical Writings of Thomas Vaughan* (London: Redway, 1888), p. xxi. In a sense, Ahab appears to be practicing a form of theurgy in his very pursuit of the white whale. In his revealing to Starbuck a "little lower layer," he speaks of the importance of "the living act, the undoubted deed" as a way of "thrusting through the wall" to some great and eternal truth (p. 144). E. R. Dodds comments on this form of theurgic practice and quotes Iamblichus: "Theurgic union is attained only by the efficacy of the unspeakable *acts* performed in the appropriate manner, acts which are beyond all comprehension, and by the potency of the unutterable symbols which are comprehended only by the gods. . . . Without intellectual effort on our part the tokens by their own virtue accomplish their proper work." *The Greeks and the Irrational* (Berkeley and Los Angeles: University of California Press, 1951), p. 287. Though theurgic magic is supposedly the door to truth, it leads more often to error. What begins as God-hunger can end in personal fragmentation. Joseph Ennemoser recognized this truth: "To this white magic belongs the power of working miracles, of perceiving and using the signatures of natural things, of foretelling the future, and of uniting the spirit fully with God through love, and thereby becoming an immediate partaker in the being and the word of God. . . . It is difficult to arrive, however, at this beautiful idea of magic in the highest degree, since there requires for it a genuine holiness; and where pious minds strive honestly after it, yet they easily stray . . . and thence lose themselves in . . . frantic darkness." *The History of Magic*, trans. William Howitt (London: Bohn, 1854), 2:219–20.

19. Chambers, 1:79.

ically" attracted to their strange captain, and "the three mates quailed before his strong, sustained, and mystic aspect" (p. 146). Ahab arranges the crew in a kind of magical circle and performs a ritualistic ceremony replete with overtones of magic. Later in the novel, he declares himself "lord over the level loadstone" and repairs the compass needle. The crew members stare in "servile wonder," and "with fascinated eyes they awaited whatever magic might follow" (p. 425).

Ahab's belief in and practice of magic, however, is merely a single aspect, and not a major one at that, of his Gnostic tendencies as Melville understood Gnosticism from his reading in such volumes as Chambers and Bayle. Of more significance is Ahab's "Knowledge"—in the Gnostic sense—of the Creator. In the chapter entitled "The Candles," Ahab observes Fedallah, a Zoroastrian,[20] kneeling before the phenomenon of Saint Elmo's fire,

20. Fedallah has been frequently depicted by critics as a kind of fanatical religious figure, but it is probable that Melville was interested in him because of his indulgence in magic, prophecy, and superstitions and because of a vicious and treacherous nature thought popularly to be characteristic of the Parsees. To give one example of this widely held view, I quote a review of George Buist's *Annals of India for the Year 1848* (1849): "It is by this look, and by the character of which it is the expression, that the true Parsee shows that he traces back his origin to a northern country. More than a thousand years ago, faithful to a religion which for ages they had respected undisturbed, the Parsees, flying before Mohammedan persecution, left their native Persia, carrying with them their sacred, unextinguished fire. Guided by the bright emblem of their God, they found shelter on the western coast of India. Here they established themselves, and during succeeding centuries, preserving always traces of their ancient customs and faith, keeping as far as possible out of frequent quarrels and wars which have been the curse of the native races of India, taking no historical part in the affairs of the country . . . they have spread and prospered. . . . *The nobler qualities of character, those alone which give a people an honorable place in the history of the world, are almost as rare among them as among other Oriental races. . . . Whatever may have been the character of their religion in ancient times, it is now nothing better than a disjointed superstition . . . and possessing no moral influence over the lives of its professed adherents*" (italics mine). The review charges that Parsees appear mannerly but that this is actually "a suspicious suppleness," which is a "cover of falseness and deceit." It is far more likely that writings like this in current periodicals influenced the characterization of Fedallah than research into the heart of Zoroastrian religion. The review appears in the *North American Review* 73 (1851): 135–52.

and he indicates that he, too, once worshipped as does this "Persian" the Creator who manifests Himself through nature: "'Oh! thou clear spirit of clear fire, whom on these seas I as Persian once did worship, till in sacramental act so burned by thee, that to this hour I bear the scar; I now know thee, thou clear spirit, and I now know that thy right worship is defiance" (p. 416). Ahab is not saying that he is a converted Zoroastrian[21] but that the Creator he once worshipped—or tried to worship—was, like the one Fedallah is worshipping, a personal God that responds directly to mankind, one whose presence is manifested in nature and in the activities of the world. He no longer kneels before that God, however, because the Creator is responsible for the evils that have been visited upon him.[22] He has learned the nature of this personal, intervening God who takes part in the affairs of humankind, and he knows that in order to be true to a higher power, the "right" thing to do is defy the Creator. His blasphemy against the Creator is worship of the God—the real and true God—that is above the Creator.

It is clear from what he says, then, that Ahab has accepted fully the Gnostic belief that there is a Supreme God separate and

21. Vargish states that "Ahab once worshipped the fire as a Persian" (p. 276). For various other interpretations of the "Persian" passage, see Charles Child Walcutt, "The Fire Symbolism in *Moby-Dick*," *Modern Language Notes* 59 (1944): 304–10; Bell, "Pierre Bayle and *Moby-Dick*"; Dorothee Metlitsky Finkelstein, *Melville's Orienda* (New Haven: Yale University Press, 1961), pp. 236–39; and Mukhtar Ali Isani, "Zoroastrianism and the Fire Symbolism in *Moby-Dick*," *American Literature* 44 (1972): 385–97.

22. To Gnostics, the Demiurge was inextricably linked with fire, and fire, in turn, was associated with blindness. Hans Jonas writes: "To ignorance in the mental realm corresponds in the physical realm the fire, which like its archetype is not so much an element among elements, as a force active in all of them. . . . But what to the Stoics is thus the bearer of cosmic Reason, to the Valentinians is with the *same* omnipresence in all creation the embodiment of Ignorance. When Heraclitus speaks of 'the everliving fire,' they speak of fire as 'death and corruption' in all elements. Yet even they would agree that as far as *cosmic* 'life' so-called and *demiurgical* 'reason' so-called are concerned these are properly symbolized in fire, as indeed in many gnostic systems the Demiurge is expressly called the god of fire; but since that kind of 'life' and of 'reason' are in their true nature death and ignorance, the agreement in effect amounts to a subtle caricature of the Heraclitean-Stoic doctrine" (p. 198).

apart from the inferior Jehovah of the Biblical Old Testament who created the world and all in it except for the royal, divine spark that exists in some people, those favored true princes of the empire. That core of spirituality is a part of the highest God, not the Creator. In his entry on the Gnostic Cainites, Pierre Bayle describes this view of the Creator: "A Sect of Heretics which appeared in the second Century, and had this name by reason of their great respect for Cain." Cain, too, believed that the proper way of responding to the Creator was through defiance. Bayle continues: "These people had drawn their abominable dogms out of the sinks of the Gnostics, and were the spawn of Valentinus, of Nicolaus, and of Carpocrates. . . . They carried their boldness so far as to condemn the Law of Moses, and to regard the God of the Old Testament as a Being who had sown tares in the world, and subjected our nature to a thousand disasters; so that, to revenge themselves, they did the direct contrary of what he had prescribed."[23] Bayle is careful to point out, however, that the Gnostics did not believe that the Creator was purely evil but that He was merely a subordinate God and a somewhat careless and unperceptive one who was unaware that a Higher Power existed. They believed "in particular that the Jewish nation had been directed by a mischievous Being"[24] who was responsible for the evil in the world as practiced by still another subordinate supernatural being, Satan. The Supreme Power had no part in the creation of the world or man, but saw to it that part of Himself emanated into the fallen world, entered the Elect, and would be someday gathered and taken from the control of the Creator back to the true and highest God.[25] This is what the Gnostics "knew," and

23. Pierre Bayle, *A General Dictionary, Historical and Critical* (London: Bettenham, 1736), 4:19, 20.

24. Ibid., 4:20.

25. Versions of how man and the universe were created vary a good deal among the many sects of Gnostics. Often, the creation is the result of an unexplained fall or a fall motivated either by erotic feelings or by a spiritual desire to be more like the Supreme Being. The fallen one is generally a female entity, an aspect of the Most High. From this fallen female, Ialdabaoth, or the Creator, is formed, and he in turn makes man. Sometimes the fallen one is called Prunikos (Lust), sometimes Sophia (Wisdom). More often Sophia is the mother of Prunicos or Achamoth (Lover of Wisdom) and, with the consent of the Supreme

this is what Ahab knows when he states to the Creator: "Thou knowest not how came ye, hence callest thyself unbegotten; certainly knowest not thy beginning, hence callest thyself unbegun. I know that of me, which thou knowest not of thyself, oh, thou omnipotent. There is some unsuffusing thing beyond thee, thou clear spirit, to whom all they eternity is but time, all thy creativeness mechanical" (p. 417).[26]

One of the books of the Bible that Melville marked up most extensively in his copy was Isaiah,[27] which happened also to be the book of the Old Testament that the Gnostics used most often to show the limitations, the blindness, and the unjustified arrogance of Jehovah, the Creator, as opposed to the true Supreme Being. And it is to Jehovah's words as expressed in Isaiah that Ahab is directly responding in the above passage. Through Isaiah, Jehovah declares: "I am the Lord, and there is none else, there is no God beside me: I girded thee, though thou hast not known me. That they may know from the rising of the sun, and from the west, that *there is* none beside me. I *am* the Lord, and *there is* none else. I form the light, and create darkness: I make peace, and

---

Being, scatters the divine seed on the newly created earth into selected men—the pneumatics—without the Creator knowing about it.

26. What Ahab does not know, however, is the source within himself of the feminine principle. He recognizes that he is part of a royal lineage that goes back to the Unknown Father, the true God, that "unsuffusing thing" beyond the Demiurge, the Creator. But he says: "My sweet mother, I know not. Oh, cruel! what hast thou done with her? There lies my puzzle" (p. 417). Despite his Gnostic insight into the reality of a true God beyond Jehovah, therefore, Ahab still feels incomplete at this moment, though he goes on to say that the Demiurge's puzzle is greater than his own, for the Creator is *completely* ignorant of His heritage. Vargish feels that in this passage Ahab is invoking Sophia, whom he clearly recognizes as his Divine Mother, the "champion of the spiritual in man against the Creator of material evil." Vargish, p. 275. This seems to me unlikely since Ahab says he is ignorant altogether of the mother or feminine principle and confesses, "There lies my puzzle."

Braswell quotes this passage with the prefacing comment that "Ahab brings what seems to be a definitely Gnostic accusation against God when he [speaks] . . . to the symbolical corposants" (p. 62). Braswell feels, however, that the Gnostic theme in *Moby-Dick* "remains undeveloped" (p. 63).

27. Nathalia Wright, *Melville's Use of the Bible* (Durham: Duke University Press, 1949), p. 10.

create evil: I the Lord do all these *things*" (45:5–7). The Gnostics found here an inferior God, one who is unaware that there was a higher God and one who admits openly to the responsibility for evil in the world, for He says: "I make peace, and create evil." A true God, the highest God, could have no part in the creation of evil, they argued. Gnostic Ahab mocks the Jehovah of Isaiah, accuses Him of claiming that He is unique and unbegotten merely because He is blind that there is a power beyond Him "to whom all thy eternity is but time, all thy creativeness mechanical." The extent to which Ahab is defying the Creator in this passage is suggested by two other verses in the same chapter of Isaiah: "Woe unto him that striveth with his Maker! Let the potsherd *strive* with the potsherds of the earth. Shall the clay say to him that fashioned it, What makest thou? or thy work, He hath no hands? Woe to him that saith unto *his* father, What begettest thou or to the woman, what hast though brought forth?" (45:9–10). Consciously ignoring this warning, Ahab *is* striving with his maker, and he *is* asking him, "What makest thou?"—the forbidden question.[28] Moments like this in *Moby-Dick* have led many readers to assume that Ahab has taken up arms against God. It is again necessary to realize that in Ahab's view there is God and there are gods. The Creator, to whom he speaks defiance in "The Candles," is merely one of the gods, though He did make man and the earth. He is not truly lord over them, however, though He thinks He is. "There is one God" that is truly Lord, Ahab says of the Supreme Being (p. 394).

Ahab's view of the highest God reflects the Gnostic belief that He is not a personal god as is the Creator, for His only connection

28. Irenaeus states that Gnostics were instructed to address themselves boldly to the Demiurge in the following manner: "I am a son from the Father— the Father who had a pre-existence, and a son in Him who is pre-existent. . . . I derive being from Him who is pre-existent, and I come again to my own place whence I went forth. . . . I am a vessel more precious than the female [Achamoth] who formed you. If your mother is ignorant of her own descent, I know myself, and am aware whence I am." *Writings,* pp. 83–84. By this bold statement of divine identity and a direct show of power to the Demiurge and His companion gods, the Gnostics believed that they could escape enslavement by the seven heavens and throw the subordinate gods into a state of agitation and confusion.

with the world is through that piece of Himself that exists in some human beings, the pneumatics. These chosen few do not communicate directly with the Supreme Being, for He, unlike Jehovah, is unnamed, unknowable, unapproachable. The Elect sense his glory, power, and goodness only by sensing these qualities *in themselves*. In describing one of the chief Gnostics of the second century, Carpocrates, Chambers writes that "he own'd with them [the Gnostics], one sole Principle and Father of all Things, whose Name, as well as Nature, was unknown."[29] This unknown First Principle did not create the world, which is thoroughly corrupt. Matter, including man, was made by the Creator and his helper gods or angels, who are "vastly inferior to the first Principle."[30] Of this real and truly mysterious God, then, Ahab knows nothing except that it is "some unsuffusing thing beyond" the God of the Old Testament, the Jehovah that Jews and Christians worship, to whom all the Creator's "eternity is but time," all the Creator's "creativeness mechanical." This is the Most High God, given by the Gnostics several names to set Him apart from the God of Genesis: the Abyss, the uncreated, or "the Silence invisible and incomprehensible."[31] It is the unknown God that Melville spoke of in *Pierre* where he describes the attempt to find the true God through reason and philosophical inquiry: "That profound Silence, that only Voice of our God, where I before spoke of; from that divine thing without a name, those impostor philosophers pretend somehow to have got an answer; which is as absurd, as though they should say they had got water out of stone; for how can a man get a Voice out of Silence?"[32]

Once recognizing that this true God was not responsible for evil, which lies at the door of the Creator, Ahab could rebel against Jehovah as the father of all unfairness and as the somewhat blind author of corruption without violating his fundamentally

29. Chambers, vol. 1, entry on "Carpocratians."

30. Ibid.

31. Jean Doresse, *The Secret Books of the Egyptian Gnostics* (New York: Viking, 1960), p. 17.

32. *Pierre; or, The Ambiguities*, ed. Harrison Hayford et al. (Evanston and Chicago: Northwestern University Press and the Newberry Library, 1971), p. 208.

religious nature. Gnosticism was the only way for him to go. Now he could glory in his self-sufficiency and power without being irreverent, for the Gnostics believed that those qualities of the inner man derived from a spark of the Unknown God present in the Elect. *Gnosis* or Knowledge—of the nature of Isaiah's God, of his own nature as pneumatic, of the world as inferior and evil—freed him from the usual restrictions and laws imposed upon mankind by Jehovah and his host of subordinate gods to keep the human race subservient and ignorant of the truth.

These laws and restrictions are not merely those of Moses and the Old Testament but the seemingly unalterable system of nature itself, the planetary movements, the laws of reproduction, and all the rest.[33] Ahab—and the Gnostics—believed that man is caught in this vast machine. Jehovah, or Ialdaboath as He was sometimes called, "had forcibly taken possession of the seventh Heaven," as Chambers explained in the entry on the Nicholaitians. While orthodox Christians looked upon nature with wonder and awe as a mirror of God's harmony, the Gnostics saw it as a pernicious and degrading machine controlling and enslaving mankind. Beyond the seventh Heaven, the planetary system of which the earth is a part, is a higher Heaven, the Gnostics believed, what Chambers calls in the entry on Eon as the "Pleroma," and this is the true spiritual home of the pneumatics.[34] They must break through the Zodiac and go beyond. It is in this context of Gnostic freedom and destiny that Ahab breaks his quadrant, declares himself master of the loadstone, and speaks of striking the sun. And it is in this context that the "cabalistics" on the doubloon take an added significance. Though Melville was describing literally an actual coin of Ecuador, he chose one that also symbolizes generally the Gnostic view of man's entrapment

33. The "mud" of the Gnostic view, in which the gold is caught, is "that of the world: it is first of all the body, which with its sensual desires drags man down and holds the 'I' in thrall. . . . The hostility to the body is only part of a more far-reaching hostility to *the world*. The gnostic has no appreciation for the beauty of this earth, for him 'the whole world lies in wickedness,' and this because it is dominated not only by the power of sense but, beyond and including it, by the power of Fate" (Foerster, pp. 2–3).

34. Chambers, 1:318.

in nature and the proper reaction to this situation. "Arching over all" on the doubloon "was a segment of the partitioned zodiac . . . and the keystone sun entering the equinoctial point at Libra" (p. 359). This overarching span of the Zodiac seems to bear down upon the scene below it, to shut it in, dominate, and control it.[35] However, a volcano seems to be erupting below and on two other mountain peaks is a proud tower and "a crowing cock" (p. 359). These signs of defiance represent the Gnostic spirit of rebellion, and in them Ahab sees his deepest self.

But Ahab is not victorious; he is destroyed by divided and warring selves. The reasons for his defeat are precisely those that account for the demise of Gnosticism as a historical movement. The most basic of the reasons that Ahab in particular and the Gnostics in general could not survive is that Gnosticism does not satisfy the most fundamental needs of humankind. Through the centuries, orthodox Christianity proved more durable than Gnosticism and finally conquered. Gnosticism gave the elitist a few answers to troubling questions about evil and the nature of the true God, but it created psychological chaos—as it does in Ahab—simply because it was incompatible with basic human nature. Arthur Darby Nock has observed that Christianity was successful in its struggle with Gnosticism because of its "perfect because unconscious correspondence to the needs and aspirations of ordinary humanity."[36]

---

35. According to Werner Foerster, "Fate presented itself in that period above all in the world of the stars, especially in the seven planets which the ancients counted (Sun, Moon, Mercury, Venus, Mars, Jupiter, Saturn), but also in the twelve signs of the Zodiac; the 'seven' and the 'twelve' are therefore marked in a special way as the power of evil which enslaves mankind" (pp. 3–4). The soul, writes J. P. Arendzen, "had to pass the adverse influence of the god or gods of the Hebdomad before it could ascend to the only good God beyond. This account of the soul through the planetary spheres to the heaven beyond . . . began to be conceived as a struggle with adverse powers, and became the first and predominant idea in Gnosticism" (p. 593). R. M. [Robert] Grant comments that "Gnostics were ultimately devoted not to mythology but to freedom. Speculation and mythology were aspects of this freedom, which involved freedom from astral spirits, from the god of the Old Testament, from the tyranny of the creation, from Old Testament law or any law" (p. 12). *Gnosticism and Early Christianity* (New York: Columbia University Press, 1959).

Ahab is a heretic in the true sense of the word. Chambers's *Cyclopaedia* defines a "real Heretic" as "properly he who maintains a false Opinion out of a Spirit of Obstinacy." Yet he is not an infidel but one who professes to believe in God. What makes such a person a heretic is not what he does but what he believes that deviates from orthodoxy. "A man does not become a Heretic by doing a Thing condemned, or forbidden by the Gospel, and, of Consequence, repugnant to the Christian Faith; but by a stiff adherence to an Opinion opposite to some Article of the Christian Faith, whether it regard Speculation or Practice."[37] Ahab's probing, sensitive nature leads him to the troubling questions about evil and God; his personal misfortunes make him deeply resentful and rebellious; he becomes a heretic—he adopts with tenacity the beliefs of Gnosticism; these heretical notions play havoc with him psychologically; then all of this is manifested in his actions.

Melville's portrayal of Ahab reveals that he clearly recognized the Gnostic dilemma. Gnostic answers satisfy the intellectual hunger of those who cannot accept the seemingly illogical positions of Christianity. But orthodox Christianity is far more in tune with emotional and spiritual cravings.[38] Gnosticism may make more sense, but Christianity is better for the whole man. Gnosticism was created by the head; Christianity was created by the heart.

Father Mapple's sermon projects the reasons why he survives as a whole person and Ahab does not, why orthodox Christianity

36. Quoted in Elaine Pagels, *The Gnostic Gospels* (New York: Random House, 1979), p. 149. Accounting further for the survival of orthodox Christianity over Gnosticism, Pagels comments that "while the gnostic saw himself as 'one out of a thousand, two out of ten thousand,' the orthodox experienced himself as a member of the common human family, and as one member of a universal church" (p. 147).

37. Chambers, 1:241.

38. One reason for this is that orthodox Christianity sets out clear laws of conduct whereas by its nature Gnosticism seeks freedom from laws and leads to a lawlessness within. As Hans Jonas observes: "For all purposes of man's relation to existing reality, both the hidden God and the hidden pneuma [what Melville calls "the Captive King"] are nihilistic conceptions: no *nomos* emanates from them, that is, no law either for nature or for human conduct as a part of the natural order" (p. 271).

survived and Gnosticism did not. The God of Father Mapple is a father figure who personally takes a hand in the activities of His children and threatens to punish them when they disobey Him. He is not some unknown and unknowable force. He uses nature as an instrument to teach and chastise His children. He created nature (as well as man); therefore it is not an alien and repugnant realm to Him. The God that most closely corresponds with man's deepest spiritual needs is one that he can talk with, a personal God, the God of Father Mapple. We may not always understand Him—why he allows evil in the world, why he created imperfection—but children cannot always understand their earthly fathers either. Father Mapple says, and Christianity says, that we must simply love, accept, obey—not understand. These are the uncomplicated answers that have endured because they are among other things tailored to human nature. And herein abides one of the great ironies of Christian belief. Father Mapple teaches: "If we obey God, we must disobey ourselves; and it is in this disobeying ourselves, wherein the hardness of obeying God consists" (p. 45). In a superficial sense this is true. We must overcome temptations of the flesh in order to live a Christian life. But in a far more significant sense, Father Mapple is wrong, for Christianity is a system devised for obeying ourselves, our true, most fundamental selves that bring peace and health when not violated. Ahab the heretic violates his own nature by adopting Gnostic beliefs, and by disobeying himself he becomes divided, tormented, blinded.

What saved Melville himself from the same fate was his ability always to return to and act on this fundamental truth that any attitudes that violate the deepest aspects of human nature are psychologically destructive. I say "return to" this truth because he often strayed from it and, like Ahab, was tempted by many of the beliefs of Gnosticism. Indeed, his life was marked by a vacillation between the Gnostic ideas he shows Ahab succumbing to and others that are more in keeping with a healthy inner life. Two illustrations will reveal something of his personal affinities for Gnostic beliefs. He wrote to Hawthorne in November of 1851: "I feel that the Godhead is broken up like the bread at the Supper, and that we are the pieces."[39] This statement reflects one of the

39. *The Letters of Herman Melville,* ed. Merrell R. Davis and William H. Gilman (New Haven: Yale University Press, 1960), p. 142.

principal tenets of Gnosticism, that in the pneumatics of the world a segment of the true God exists which sets them apart from the masses as a chosen group. Melville seems to embrace the same position in his review of Hawthorne's *Mosses from an Old Manse.* Throughout, he sets up a distinction among men, especially writers. Hawthorne, he says over and over, is special and not to be understood by "the world" but only by those like himself who have the intuitive ability to recognize what lies under the surface: "You cannot come to know greatness by inspecting it; there is no glimpse to be caught of it, except by intuition; you need not ring it, you but touch it, and you find it is gold."[40] The Gnostics liked to refer to this specialness as the "gold in the mud." The gold that Melville was finding in Hawthorne—to be equated with the pieces of the Godhead he referred to in his letter—he was also finding in himself: "I cannot but be charmed by the coincidence; especially, when it shows such a parity of ideas . . . between a man like Hawthorne and a man like me."[41] Again he returns to the conviction that there exists an elect of writers; he calls them "men of genius" who together make up the "commanding mind."

These statements about his and Hawthorne's specialness do not in themselves prove that Melville was attracted specifically to Gnostic doctrines, but they do reveal the kind of mind that would be highly susceptible to such a set of beliefs. That Melville was, indeed, susceptible and that he fully realized the destructive powers of Gnosticism on the mind are evident in a number of his short stories. Several deal with narrators who are exposed to Gnostic insights and are driven to the brink of madness. The Gnostic view of God's chosen creatures existing in an evil and alien world is particularly evident in "Cock-A-Doodle-Doo!" Melville never created a more poignant statement of this theme. Nature is described in the story as a force foreign and abhorrent to the narrator: "It was a cool and misty, damp, disagreeable air. The country looked underdone, its raw juices squirting out all round."[42] He thrusts a stick in the "oozy sod" and notes that the

40. "Hawthorne and His Mosses," in *The Norton Anthology of American Literature,* 2d ed., ed. Nina Baym et al., 2 vols. (New York: Norton, 1985), 1:2164.
41. Ibid., p. 2173.
42. "Cock-A-Doodle-Doo! or, The Crowing of the Noble Cock Beneven-

"humped hills" resemble "brindle kine in the shivers." All in all, the imagery is calculated to arouse emotions of disgust with the natural world: "The woods were strewn with dry dead boughs, snapped off by the riotous winds of March. . . . Along the base of one long range of heights ran a lagging, fever-and-anguish river, over which was a duplicate stream of dripping mist, exactly corresponding in ever member. . . . It is a disagreeable and depressing world, but the world of mankind is no better. The narrator dwells on the chaos that characterizes man's activities, the ugliness of society matching that of nature. Revolts have been taking place, trains have been wrecked, steamers have blown up: "A miserable world! Who would take the trouble to make a fortune in it, when he knows not how long he can keep it, for the thousand villains and asses. . . ."[43] He sneers at "Great improvements of the age" and summarizes his overall attitude both toward the world of man and the realm of nature when he describes himself as in the act of climbing a hill in a bent and toiling posture, "as if I were in the act of butting . . . against the world."[44]

The narrator is a perfect candidate for a Gnostic call, and it comes in the form of a crowing cock, who brings him the message of his own specialness and his ultimate salvation; of the true God, who is not responsible for the pitiful state of society and the external world; and of the proper way for him to respond to his alien surroundings.[45] It is a message, delivered in a flashing in-

---

tano," in *The Complete Stories of Herman Melville,* ed. Jay Leyda (New York: Random House, 1949), p. 119.

43. Ibid., p. 121.

44. Ibid., p. 119.

45. The Gnostic concept of the call is described succinctly by Werner Foerster: "The central factor in Gnosis, the 'call,' reaches man neither in rational thought nor in an experience which eliminates thought. Man has a special manner of reception in his 'I.' He feels himself 'addressed' and answers the call. He *feels* that he is encountered by something which already lies within him, although admittedly entombed. It is nothing new, but rather the old which only needs to be called to mind. It is like a note sounded at a distance, which strikes an echoing chord in his heart. Here is the reason why the basic acceptance of Gnosis can and should take place in a single act" (p. 2).

The distinguished interpreter of Gnosticism Hans Jonas has observed that stant, of profound inspiration and hope. The problem is that it leads to such arch-arrogance that he is himself crowing like a cock.[46] By the end of the story he has lost his compassion for others and feels such contempt for everything in the world that he is totally unable to function in it. As is frequently the situation, Melville obviously admires the man's heroic revolt but recognizes what great price it costs. So frequently does Melville indulge in this kind of characterization that one is led to believe that whenever he was greatly tempted to embrace the Gnostic vision, he developed a hero who was destroyed by it. He often needed to remind himself that it was better to live among fools—without becoming one of them—than to alienate himself from them for a

---

"the first effect of the call is always described as 'awakening,' as in the gnostic versions of the story of Adam." The three elements that I have named as the content of the message the narrator of "Cock-A-Doodle-Doo!" receives are precisely those which, according to Jonas, make up the Gnostic call: "the *reminder* of the heavenly origin [of the one called] . . . ; the *promise* of redemption . . . ; and finally the practical *instruction* as to how to live henceforth in the world, in conformity with the newly won 'knowledge' and in preparation for the eventual ascent" (p. 81).

46. Irenaeus described Gnostics in the following manner: "But if anyone do yield himself up to them like a little sheep, and follows out their practice and their 'redemption,' such an one is puffed up to such an extent, that he thinks he is neither in heaven nor on earth, but that he has passed within the Pleroma; and having already embraced his angel, he walks with a strutting gait and a super-cilious countenance, possessing all the pompous air of a cock" (1:322). This is a perfect description of the narrator of "Cock-A-Doodle-Doo!" at the story's end. With his new sense of freedom and severe contempt for the world, he indulges himself fully in sensuous experience (overeating, drinking, and so forth) and thereby becomes a clear illustration of what the church fathers termed "liber-tine" Gnosticism, one of the two main branches. The other, which is its opposite, is asceticism, *withdrawal* from sensuous experience. Both, however, derive from the same fundamental view, as Hans Jonas points out: "Opposite as the two types of conduct are, they yet were in the gnostic case of the same root, and the same basic argument supports them both. The one repudiates allegiance to nature through excess, the other, through abstention. Both are lives outside the mundane norms. Freedom by abuse and freedom by non-use, equal in their indiscriminateness, are only alternative expressions of the same acosmism" (pp. 274–75). Irenaeus accused the libertine Gnostics of great excesses of all "kinds of forbidden deeds of which the Scriptures assure us that 'they who do such things shall not inherit the kingdom of God' " (1:26).

realm of what may be the truth but a truth that leads to psychological hell. He revealed this conviction in the brief poem "A Spirit Appeared to Me":

> A Spirit appeared to me, and said
> "Where now would you choose to dwell?
> In the Paradise of the Fool,
> Or in wise Solomon's hell?"—
>
> Never he asked me twice:
> "Give me the fool's Paradise."[47]

The Gnostic God, the unknown and unknowable, is so far removed from ordinary human emotions and activites that allegiance to Him—as opposed to Jehovah (or the Demiurge)—leads ultimately to severe self-ostracism, as the narrator of "The Lightning-Rod Man" illustrates. The God he worships has nothing to do with the war that is going on against mankind, which is suggested in the story by the battle imagery to describe rain, thunder, and lightning. This is a war without purpose waged by an inferior deity in which a "servant girl [is] struck at her bed-side with a rosary in her hand," struck by lightning sent by the very Demiurge she is worshipping.[48] The lightning-rod salesman is a priest of this inferior deity—the Jehovah of the Old Testament—who preaches fear and the strict obedience to a set of strict rules. Those likely to be struck down, the salesman explains, are "tall men," which means the extraordinary few who rebel against this capricious and blindly arrogant maker and ruler of earth ("*Mine* is the only true rod"). In the fashion of Ahab, the narrator of the story will not worship or tremble in fear of this god of other men. He believes in the "returning-stroke," in sending back lightning to the Demiurge. He throws himself "into the erectest, proudest

47. *Collected Poems of Herman Melville*, ed. Howard P. Vincent (Chicago: Hendricks House, 1947), p. 390. In *Moby-Dick*, Ishmael says that the "world hath not got hold of unchristian Solomon's wisdom yet," establishing the dichotomy that is in the poem between a fool's paradise and the hell Solomon can lead you to. Solomon's Ecclesiastes, says Ishmael, is the "truest of all books," but it is also "the fine hammered steel of woe. 'All is vanity.' All" (p. 355).

48. "The Lightning-Rod Man," in *Complete Stores*, p. 216.

posture" he can command while the preacher of fear and obedience to the author of lightning attempts to proselyte him. When in great anger and rebellion the narrator explains that he worships the only true God who has no part in the evil of the world and then bodily throws out his adversary, the salesman does not accuse him of being a religious fanatic but, in effect, a heretic with wrong notions about God.

It is not really the views of Gnosticism that Melville wants to espouse, however, in "The Lightning-Rod Man"; nor does he wish to emphasize the motivations, especially fear, that move ordinary men to worship Jehovah, though there may be great truth and nobility in the one and great shallowness and cowardice in the other. What he seems most to be interested in is the mind of the narrator, the course it has taken as a *result* of his Gnostic proclivities. As is true with the narrator of "Cock-A-Doodle-Doo!" rebellion has become a way of life with him. His ostensible enjoyment of the lightning is actually a manifestation of his fearless scorn of it and what it can do. In fact, his most obvious and most frequently displayed emotion is that which inevitably results from a Gnostic orientation—contempt. He is contemptuous of the storm and the force that produces it, of the salesman who tells him that he can be reduced to offal unless he bow down in trembling and obedience to the laws of this force, and of ordinary men, who do so. The story is a brief but poignant depiction of how the Gnostic differs from orthodox positions and how he becomes so proud and fearless in his contempt of all the world and the world's God (the Demiurge) that he ends up alienated and mentally twisted. Though the narrator seems amused at his visitor and plays a cat-and-mouse game with him, and though the story has itself been singled out for its humor, one cannot ignore the fact that there is something strikingly unusual about this narrator, something strange and disturbing in his baiting of the salesman, a quality of unhealthy glee that resembles Montresor's tone in Poe's "The Cask of Amontillado." In the end he says that he tried to warn others that the salesman was a false prophet, but they would not listen. It is he who remains the alienated heretic drowning in his flood of contempt. It is not that the salesman is right and he is wrong—he is presented as a more heroic and noble figure than the lightning-rod man—but that his truth leads to madness whereas the salesman's does not.

The same dilemma is the substance of several other stories: in them, a character cannot accept on the one hand the orthodox religious views of God, nature, and mankind because they violate his deepest sense of justice and contradict his own collective experience; but if he embraces a set of beliefs, heretical in nature, that gives him better answers to his questions, he faces destruction. The answers the world gives are wrong, but many of these characters cannot survive the alternative. Bartleby is a prime example of one caught in this dilemma. His self-imposed separation from ordinary human activities, his refusal to take heed of the needs of his body, and his determination to break off communication with the world all are characteristic of one large segment of the ancient Gnostics, those who practiced extreme asceticism.[49] The motive

49. Bartleby's world view seems parallel to what Hans Jonas calls the Gnostic "acosmic position" that "comes to express itself in a general morality of withdrawal, which develops its own code of negative 'virtues'" (p. 276). The principle involved was "not to complete but to reduce the world of the Creator and to make the least possible use of it" (p. 144). Jonas explains that "turned into a principle of practice, this conception engenders an extreme quietism which strives to reduce activity as such to what is absolutely necessary" (p. 232). Curiously, some understanding of why Bartleby acts as he does results from a study of the syndrome peculiar to (but not restricted to) some teenage girls, anorexia nervosa. Several of the underlying motives of those suffering from this form of starvation are surprisingly close to those of the acosmic Gnostics and, apparently, to those of Bartleby. A seventeenth-century physician, Richard Morton, is credited with first observing the disorder. He reported two cases of young women who developed an abhorrence of food and who withdrew from ordinary activities. In the nineteenth century, W. W. Gull observed the same syndrome, labeled it "anorexia," and attributed it to psychological causes. See Salvador Minuchin et al., *Psychosomatic Families: Anorexia Nervosa in Context* (Cambridge: Harvard University Press, 1978), pp. 11–12. What those suffering from this disorder have in common with Bartleby is evident in a statement Hilde Bruch has made concerning the motivation of anorectics: they are waging "a desperate fight against feeling enslaved and exploited. . . . They would rather starve than continue a life of accommodation." Besides manifesting a high degree of will in resisting appetite, such persons also develop "narcissistic self-absorption" and regress "to earlier levels of mental functioning." Hilde Bruch, "Psychological Antecedents of Anorexia Nervosa," in *Anorexia Nervosa,* ed. Robert A. Vigersky (New York: Raven Press, 1977), pp. 1, 2. These are clear characteristics of

behind their behavior was fundamentally the same as Bartleby's—
a desire for independence from the corruption that surrounded
them. Enveloped in matter, which is evil, the ascetic Gnostics
believed, as does Bartleby, that the most appropriate form of rebellion, the most effective way of insuring independence and purity, was to prefer not to; for earthly activity only leads away from
the true heaven.[50] Though I believe it has not been pointed out
before, a poem Melville wrote probably long after "Bartleby" is
closely related to it and suggests the scrivener's motivation for
withdrawal and starvation. "Fragments of a Lost Gnostic Poem of
the Twelfth Century"[51] reveals Melville's perceptive awareness of
the Gnostic mind:

Bartleby as well. Though known chiefly as a disorder growing out of modern
society, "in a strange way, anorexia still represents the triumph of the will over
bodily needs, bringing back centuries of learned argument on the dichotomy of
body and soul" (Minuchin, p. 232). What the anorectic has in common with
Bartleby, then, is that they both "consider self-denial and discipline the highest
virtue and condemn satisfying their needs and desires as shameful self-indulgence." Hilde Bruch, *The Golden Cage: The Enigma of Anorexia Nervosa* (Cambridge: Harvard University Press, 1978), p. x. No desire is more deeply felt in
the anorectic—and in Bartleby—than the desire to rebel against the forces that
enslave and to be free. They are all taking what Hilde Bruch calls the "misguided road to independence" (*Cage*, p. xii). Melville of course knew nothing of
this disorder from which a growing number of modern young women suffer, but
he did understand their profound drives that most of them consciously do not—
the will to prefer not to, the desire to defeat the world through denial of self,
drives that anorectics share with the ancient acosmic Gnostic.

50. Commenting on Gnostic asceticism, Hans Jonas writes: "The *asceticism*
thus prescribed is strictly speaking a matter not of ethics but of metaphysical
alignment. Much as the avoidance of worldly contamination was an aspect of it,
*its main aspect was to obstruct rather than promote the cause of the creator; or even, just to
spite him*" (p. 144, italics mine). Jonas quotes Hippolytus as saying that Marcion
"believes that he vexes the Demiurge by abstaining from what he made or
instituted" and Jerome as indicating that the "perpetual abstinence" from food
is "for the sake of destroying and condemning and abominating the works of the
creator" (p. 144).

51. Although Gnosticism flourished in the second century and began its
decline in the third, certain sects survived for centuries. In his excellent commentary on this poem, William H. Shurr suggests that Melville has in mind the
Paulicians, about whom Bayle wrote: "The Paulician movement was exceptionally long-lived, enduring from the fifth century well into the Middle Ages,
even though its advocates were constantly persecuted by the church" (p. 165).

Found a family, build a state,
The pledged event is still the same:
Matter in end will never abate
His ancient brutal claim.

*   *   *   *

Indolence is heaven's ally here,
And energy the child of hell:
The Good Man pouring from his pitcher clear,
But brims the poisoned well.[52]

Though the poem may seem to reflect a futile or nihilistic view, it is rather a statement of the Gnostic's belief in the evil of all matter, in the unimportance of worldly activities, and in a willful withdrawal as the best way to cope with the enslaving laws of nature and to remain in tune with the real God and higher heaven. "Bartleby" is the story of a man who believes this and acts upon it. The spectacle of his doing so is not that of a heroic victory—though there is this element present as in Ahab's destruction—but that of fearsome tragedy. Without being, by any means, didactic, "Bartleby" is another elaborate reminder by Melville to himself of where the seductive Gnostic vision, to which he was by temperament strongly drawn, could lead.

To dwell on the psychological ravages of the Gnostic vision is one way to avoid being seduced by it. Another way is quickly to close one's eyes and mind to it when it presents itself. Melville's narrator in the second part of his bipartite story "The Paradise of Bachelors and the Tartarus of Maids" does just that. What this man sees when he goes deep into the bowels of the earth is the Gnostic view of nature and mankind's horrible enslavement to the physical laws of the universe.[53] The paper machine that so shocks him that he almost faints is a symbol of universal nature. It is, to be sure, suggestive of the womb, as many readers have noticed, but the womb and the process of reproduction in general repre-

---

52. *Timoleon* (New York: Caxton Press, 1891), p. 40.

53. In Gnostic terms, this is *heimarmene*, universal Fate, "a concept taken over from astrology but now tinged with the gnostic anti-cosmic spirit. In its physical aspect this rule is the law of nature; in its psychical aspect, which includes for instance the institution and enforcement of the Mosaic Law, it aims at the enslavement of man." Jonas, p. 43.

sent in turn all of the physical laws by which pitiful mankind is ruled.[54] No tenet of Gnosticism is more different from orthodox Christian belief than this position on nature and natural laws. To the Gnostic, the world was an alien place, but the Christian goes to the "garden," as a popular hymn reads, and hears the "voice" therein of the true God.[55] This attitude toward nature is nowhere more clearly presented than in another Christian hymn, "This is My Father's World" (1901):

> This is my Father's world,
> And to my listening ears
> All nature sings, and round me rings
> The music of the spheres.
>
> This is my Father's world:
> I rest me in the thought
> Of rocks and trees, of skies and seas;
> His hand the wonders wrought.
>
> This is my Father's world:
> The birds their carols raise,
> The morning light, the lily white,
> Declare their Maker's praise.
>
> This is my Father's world:
> He shines in all that's fair;
> In the rustling grass I hear Him pass,
> He speaks to me everywhere.[56]

The narrator of "The Tartarus of Maids" encounters a different nature from this one—a cold and merciless world of horrible reg-

---

54. Hans Jonas writes that "a genuine and typical *gnostic* argument . . . [is] that the reproductive scheme is an ingenious archontic device for the indefinite retention of souls in the world" (p. 145).

55. According to R. M. Grant, "ultimately, the difference between Christian and Gnostic philosophical theology seems to lie in their attitudes toward the world. For any Gnostic the world is really hell. For Christians the world is one which God made, a world whose history he governs" (p. 150).

56. Maltbie D. Babcock, "This Is My Father's World," in *The Hymnbook* (Richmond: Presbyterian Church in the United States, 1965), hymn 101.

ularity in which emasculated mankind acts as handmaiden. Whether this Gnostic view of nature is the true one is a subordinate issue in the story. More significant is the fact that the narrator (called a "seedsman") is prone to see the external world in this way, to associate an actual place and a real paper factory with the overall realm of nature and its physical laws, and to be psychologically and physically imperiled *because* of the vision. His quick retreat back into the other nature, that of "This is My Father's World" (the paradise of the fool, though it may be), is all that saves him. He is fortunate, for many of those characters in Melville's fiction who are tempted by the Gnostic heresy succumb to its substantial magnetism and are destroyed. The dilemma rests in the question, "How can the truth lead to hell?" Ahab is Melville's carefully delineated answer. Noble though he is, Ahab exists in a living hell brought about through his envelopment in a set of convictions that pit one part of himself against the other without his even realizing it.

What I have attempted to show in this chapter is that Ahab's division of self, the nature of which was described in detail in chapter 3, is largely the result of his Gnostic orientation. Melville saw clearly that Gnosticism produces three devastating effects. First, and most important, it leads to the formation of two distinct and rivaling selves in a single personality—that which seeks to find and merge with God and that which arrogantly loves itself and leaves no room for God.[57] Second, it fails to satisfy in a God-seeker the deep hunger for a personal God whom one can go to directly for guidance, comfort, and rewards for faith. The Unknown Father that Ahab speaks of is a cold divine stranger, ill-suited to satisfy the cravings of the human heart.[58] Consequently,

---

57. This condition derives from the Gnostic desire to *be* God. This aim is set forth in a document both Gnostic and Hermetical in origins, the second-century *Poimandres:* "Such is the blissful goal of those who possess knowledge [*gnosis*]—to become God." *Gnosticism: A Source Book of Heretical Writings from the Early Christian Period,* ed. Robert M. Grant (New York: Harper, 1961), p. 217. "The potential divinity of man," points out Richard Cavendish, is the theme of both alchemy and Gnosticism. "If you do not make yourself equal to God," you cannot find God (p. 18).

58. The Gnostic Unknown God, according to Hans Jonas, is He "whose

the Gnostic is cut off, psychologically speaking, from one of the healthiest aspects of Christianity and experiences a sense of isolation. Third, this separation from a caring and controlling Creator is painful enough, but the Gnostic must face as well alienation from the realm of nature, for the world must be rejected as totally corrupt. No beauty is to be seen in nature, no higher harmony in its laws. With a sneer, the Gnostic must reject the appeals of rivers, trees, and flowers; the suggestion of order and rightness in the changes of the seasons; and all the natural affinity a human being feels for the lush supportive world around him because all of matter comes from the inferior Demiurge.

In a characteristically brilliant insight, Melville indicated in *Clarel* that modern Christianity has managed to get around the problem of evil, not by confronting the issue directly and accusing Jehovah, as did the Gnostics, but by gradually and subtly replacing Him with Jesus Christ as the Supreme Being. In that way the personal Savior is combined with the perfect God—innocent of all evil—and the best of two visions is fused without the ill effects that come from Gnosticism or the emptiness of unanswered questions that sometimes results from straight Christian doctrine. The strange usurpation, Melville says, has taken place without Christians even admitting it:

> 'Twas averred
> That, in old Gnostic pages blurred,
> Jehovah was construed to be
> Author of evil, yea, its god;
> And Christ divine His contrary:
> A god was held against a god,
> But Christ revered alone. Herefrom,
> Less frank: none say Jehovah's evil,
> None gainsay that He bears the rod;
> Scarce that; but there's dismission civil,
> And Jesus is the indulgent God.
>
> (III.v.39–45, 56–59)

acosmic essence negates all object-determinations as they derive from the mundane realm; whose transcendence transcends any sublimity posited by extension from the here, invalidates all symbols of him thus devised; who, in brief, strictly defies description" (p. 288).

Such is the quiet and unadmitted way in which Christians have absorbed a part of Gnosticism without suffering its consequences. The true Gnostic, however, must ultimately end up an alien to himself, to God, to the external world, and to his fellow man. This Melville clearly knew, as reflected in his portrayals of Ahab and other characters, and though he was mightily drawn to these bold, rebellious, free-thinking, arrogant ancients, he knew they beckoned him to self-destruction; so he made a conscious choice not to leave the "Paradise of the Fool" for "wise Solomon's hell." Hell is hell, no matter with whom you share it.

Surviving the Wreck

Chapter 5

On Wednesday, November 12, 1856, Nathaniel Hawthorne and his houseguest at Southport, England, Herman Melville, sat amid sand dunes that sheltered them from the brisk sea winds, smoked cigars, and talked. They had been together like this before, but not here, in a foreign country, and not for some years. Theirs was a strange friendship, nothing like that between Hawthorne and Franklin Pierce or Horatio Bridge or Henry Wadsworth Longfellow. Hawthorne always felt a little uneasy around Melville, partly because he was fifteen years Melville's senior but also because he realized that something about himself always seemed to encourage Melville to express his deepest and often most troubling sentiments. Back in Massachusetts—at Pittsfield and Lenox—Hawthorne could always count on Melville to forgo the small talk for matters that were to him of the profoundest importance.

Consequently, it was not surprising to Hawthorne that while they were sitting there with the strong wind whipping about the dunes, Melville should once again speak from the heart. Once again Hawthorne listened intently and contemplatively, not offering advice, not nodding his head in facile agreement, not disagreeing and challenging him to shallow and futile debate, but truly listening—like an ideal priest. No one before Hawthorne or after ever performed this same function for Melville. This meeting outside Liverpool, where Hawthorne was serving as the American Consul, famous as it is, still has more to teach about the relationship between these two men and, more especially, about the internal life of Herman Melville.

What has most caught the attention of biographers and critics is Hawthorne's comment that Melville could "neither believe, nor be comfortable in his unbelief," and that he was "too honest and courageous not to try to do one or the other."[1] Melville's depressed condition—Hawthorne said that he was "a little paler, and perhaps a little sadder" since they last met and that he was suffering from "a morbid state of mind"[2]—and Hawthorne's brilliant analysis of Melville's nature as a noble searcher for ultimate truth have tended to obscure other telling aspects of this celebrated visit, most notably, what it reveals about one of Melville's fundamental traits, his survival instinct. True, he told Hawthorne as they rested among the sand hills that he had "pretty much made up his mind to be annihilated." Hawthorne's thoughtful response in his journal to this often-quoted statement, however, says more about Melville than does Melville's own assessment of his mental state: *But still he does not seem to rest in that anticipation.*[3] Indeed, he did not.

Hawthorne's entry in his English notebooks recording Melville's visit runs for several pages, only a small part of which is given over to that memorable moment when Melville spoke of his "annihilation." Throughout, nothing is more pronounced than Hawthorne's deep respect for Melville. He does not characterize him as a man who has given up on life but as a deep and noble soul struggling with a problem: "He is a person of very gentlemanly instincts in every respect. . . . He has a very high and noble nature. . . . I do not know a more independent personage."[4] Melville did tell his old friend that he had just about given up, but Hawthorne sensed that he had not. The kind of total

1. Nathaniel Hawthorne, *The English Notebooks,* ed. Randall Stewart (New York: Modern Language Association of America, 1941), p. 433.
2. Ibid., p. 432.
3. Ibid.
4. Ibid., pp. 432, 433, 437.

surrender to despair that claims so many sensitive minds—and, sadly, was even to claim Hawthorne—was not in Melville. He was fully vulnerable to despair but not given to surrender. His will to survive was the actual motivation for his decision to take that journey in 1856. Hawthorne's way of putting it was that he did "not wonder" that Melville "found it necessary" to get away, necessary, that is, for survival. If he had really become emotionally reconciled to annihilation, he would have stayed in his room in Pittsfield.

Melville and Hawthorne were together for several days, talking, eating out, and sightseeing. They spent an entire Saturday in the historic town of Chester. Hawthorne's beautifully written account of what they did and what they saw that day is not the record of a man forced into the role of tour guide to a depressed friend who has lost all interest in life.[5] Even in those moments of depression, Melville manifested the unmistakable instinct for survival, that uncultivated and sometimes even unconscious drive to endure. In retrospect, Hawthorne's private record of Melville's visit is poignant testimony to the ironies of life. Though it was Melville who spoke of being annihilated, he lived on for another thirty-five years, perceptive and creative until the end. He died at seventy-two. Hawthorne, on the other hand, lived only seven and a half years longer, dying before he reached his sixtieth birthday. It is instructive to juxtapose Melville's comment to Hawthorne about annihilation to what he wrote his wife's half-brother six years later: "I begin to indulge in the pleasing idea that my life must needs be of some value. Probably I consume a certain amount of oxygen, which unconsumed might create some subtle disturbance in Nature. Be that as it may, I am going to try and stick to the conviction named above. For I have observed that such an idea, once well bedded in a man, is a wonderful conservator of health and almost a prophecy of long life. I once, like

---

5. Melville's keen interest in his sightseeing and his curiosity are reflected in several places in Hawthorne's account. For example, when they went into a small room of an ancient building in Chester, "Melville opened a cupboard and discovered a dozen or two of wine-bottles; but our guide told us that they were now empty, and never were meant for jollity, having held only sacramental wine" (p. 435).

other spoonies, cherished a loose sort of notion that I did not care to live very long. But I will frankly own that I have now no serious, no insuperable objections to a respectable longevity. I dont like the idea of being left out night after night in a cold church-yard."[6]

Even Melville's early novels deal centrally though not obstrusively with the issue of survival. *Typee* depicts its hero's survival of a three-month stay among South Sea natives, when he is forced to endure captivity (gentle though it is), illness, and anxiety over cannibalism. Here, as in his other early works, escaping is a recurrent motif. The reason his characters want desperately to escape is, simply, to survive. When conditions deteriorate and threaten the hero's physical safety or mental soundness, in other words, whenever the course that he is on seems to head him for grave danger of any sort, he changes courses. The pattern is one in which he escapes one kind of danger—enervation, boredom, depression—only to involve himself in another kind—an experience that is physically imperiling—then to escape that only to find himself again in danger. Continually, he escapes, the narrator of *Omoo* from the subtle but pernicious threat of "going native," Taji from the manifold physical and psychological dangers of the world of Mardi, Redburn from his mental shock of recognition that the past is no guide for the present and from the tempting but hollow lifestyle of Harry Bolton, and White-Jacket from all the excruciating trials that lead him to manhood and, physically, from a perilous fall into the sea from high atop a yardarm.

Ahab is the first of Melville's heroes not to survive. His death and that of all the others who go down with the *Pequod* cast over *Moby-Dick* a dark shadow of violence and destruction the effects of which are evident in the way the novel is often perceived. Remaining most vividly in the minds of generations of readers are perils and disasters, scenes that have been pictured endlessly by a host of illustrators of the book in images of whales with massive flukes and tremendous jaws destroying ships and boats and kill-

6. Melville to Samuel Savage Shaw, December 10, 1862. *The Letters of Herman Melville,* ed. Merrell R. Davis and William H. Gilman (New Haven: Yale University Press, 1960), p. 216.

ing sailors. Nevertheless, an important fact about the plot of *Moby-Dick* is that Ishmael survives. When he states in the epilogue that "one did survive the wreck," he is focusing upon what has been throughout the novel a persistent and vitalizing aspect of his character, present frequently as an undercurrent in his narration. Above all else, *Moby-Dick* is a story of survival; it is the deepest and most complex fictive expression of one of Melville's most compelling drives.

The presence of this basic inner force is the best explanation for his keen interest in Owen Chase and Agatha Hatch Robertson. When he first read Owen Chase's *The Wreck of the Whaleship* Essex (1821), borrowed from Chase's son while Melville was aboard the *Acushnet* in 1841, he found it a "wondrous story" which, he wrote, "had a surprising effect upon me."[7] Ten years later his father-in-law presented him with a copy. The influence of Chase's slim volume on *Moby-Dick* has been widely recognized because it was a great sperm whale "with tenfold fury and vengeance in his aspect" that battered the *Essex*.[8] It is natural that this most dramatic and unusual moment in Chase's narrative should be seized upon by Melville scholars as the very germ of Melville's plot in *Moby-Dick*.[9] In actuality, Chase does not dwell on the strangeness or the suggestiveness of the whale's action; he devotes little space to its ramming the ship, that event coming early in the account. Most of the book deals with the frantic attempt of the officers and crew to survive ninety days on the open sea in flimsy, leaky whaleboats with inadequate food and water. Of the original twenty-one men aboard the *Essex*, eight reached safety, their survival brought about by what must be civilized man's most desperate act of self-preservation—cannibalism.

7. Melville's manuscript notes inserted in his copy of Chase's *Narrative*. These notes are included in *Moby-Dick*, ed. Harrison Hayford and Hershel Parker (New York: Norton, 1967), pp. 597–601, and in Thomas Farel Heffernan, *Stove By A Whale: Owen Chase and the* Essex (Middletown, Conn.: Wesleyan University Press, 1981), pp. 184–209.

8. *The Wreck of the Whaleship* Essex: *A Narrative Account by Owen Chase, First Mate*, ed. Iola Haverstick and Betty Shepard (New York: Harcourt, 1965), p. 33.

9. Ibid., p. 118.

The destruction of the *Essex* by a sperm whale left an indelible impression upon Melville's mind. It was, indeed, for him a "wondrous story," but the "surprising effect" he speaks of derived not only from his contemplation of the whale's destructiveness and inscrutability but from his feeling of kinship with anyone who could survive such an ordeal as Chase experienced and remain stable and humane. During a gam of the *Acushnet* with another ship, Melville saw a man he took to be Owen Chase. Whatever Chase may have actually looked like, he remained in Melville's mind this person with an expressive face "of great uprightness & calm" reflecting "unostentatious courage."[10] The influence of Chase's narrative, with its painfully detailed record of suffering, its plainspoken rather than sensationalized treatment of such a repulsive subject as cannibalism, and its ultimate statement of what it means to be a survivor, goes far deeper into *Moby-Dick* than has been generally recognized.[11] It was not merely an adventure story for Melville, not just a tale from real life of the curious and unexplained; it was for him a seminal document, a philosophy of life.

The story of Agatha had no direct influence on *Moby-Dick* because Melville did not hear it until 1852, the year after the novel was published, but he responded to it with sharp interest because of the same instincts and affinities that he had already revealed in *Moby-Dick*. Consequently how he reacted to what the lawyer John Clifford (soon to be governor of Massachusetts) told him about Agatha Hatch Robertson bears significantly on his deepest urges. He wrote Hawthorne that what he had heard of Agatha from Clifford while they were visiting Nantucket together in the summer of 1852 was "enough to awaken the most lively interest in me."[12] He goes on to say that this was an inti-

10. *Moby-Dick,* ed. Harrison Hayford and Hershel Parker (New York: Norton, 1967), p. 598.

11. Two critics who cover in detail the influence of Chase's narrative on Melville's work both emphasize the ramming of the *Essex* by a whale rather than the nightmarish aftermath. See Henry F. Pommer, "Herman Melville and the Wake of the *Essex,*" *American Literature* 20 (1948–49): 290–304; and Howard P. Vincent, *The Trying-Out of Moby Dick* (Boston: Houghton Mifflin, 1949).

12. *Letters,* p. 154.

mately personal interest rather than a professional one. Clifford misunderstood his fascination and believed that Melville "proposed making literary use of the story." However, Melville confessed to Hawthorne: "My first spontaneous interest in it arose from very different considerations."[13] In fact, he sent all the material he had to Hawthorne—Clifford had followed up on their conversation on Nantucket by mailing to Melville at Pittsfield a copy of his journal entry that recorded the Agatha story—with the hope that Hawthorne would make "literary use" of it. Hawthorne was not interested.

This episode, like their later meeting in England, is one of the richest, most curious, and most revealing in the lives of the two authors. It raises numerous basic questions especially about Melville. Why did he become interested in the domestic situation of Agatha that most people would find only mildly curious rather than compelling? On the coast of Cape Cod, a stranger (a sailor) enters the life of a lonely woman, marries her, then deserts her. She waits for seventeen years for his return, having given birth to a daughter, but hears nothing. Then he turns up, tells her that he lives in Alexandria, Virginia, and brags of his prosperity. What he does not tell her is that he has married bigamously a second wife. He asks forgiveness for his desertion, is tender to his daughter by Agatha, supplies them with a little money, and takes off again without announcing his destination. Then the second wife dies and he marries a third, a Mrs. Irvin, but he does not live long after that. In trying to settle his estate, the son of Mrs. Irvin discovers a letter that Agatha's daughter has written to her father, and a legal tangle develops when the daughter is informed that her father is dead and she makes a claim for part of his estate. The story has the basic ingredients for a modern television soap opera, but to Melville it had "much of pathos, & . . . much of depth."[14] Why? And why, if he considered the story so provocative, did he turn his notes over to Hawthorne? Why did Hawthorne refuse to create a novel or a short story from it? Why did not Melville himself make literary

13. Ibid.
14. Ibid.

use of the material after he requested it back from Hawthorne, claiming that he wished to use it after all?

The answers to these questions lie deep within the natures of the two men. Melville probably found the history of Agatha Hatch Robertson curiously fascinating because of her survival of painful victimization. In his suggestions to Hawthorne about how the story should unfold, he stresses Agatha's role in saving Robertson's life and his subsequent betrayal of her. The story, he said, should "open with the wreck" of the ship on which Robertson serves. "Agatha," he writes, "should be active during the wreck, & should, in some way, be made the saviour of young Robinson [sic]. . . . He should be ministered to by Agatha at the house during the illness ensuing upon his injuries from the wreck."[15] The wreck from which Agatha saves her future husband is the beginning of a more prosperous life for him, a man Melville saw as exhibiting traits of the world in general. Not demonic or scheming, he was merely weak and insensitive. Melville thought that it would be a mistake to make him a great villain. "I do not at all suppose," he noted, "that his desertion of his wife was a premeditated thing. . . . No: he was a weak man & his temptations . . . were strong. The whole sin stole upon him insensibly."[16] In him Melville saw the stolidity of the world that can victimize without realizing or caring. The wreck of his ship was the beginning of Agatha's great trial. She survived the wreck of her life that began with Robertson's appearance, but how she managed it Melville did not know or, at least, did not say in his letter to Hawthorne. Perhaps he wanted Hawthorne to tell him, to work it out for him. After all, this kind of psychological drama was right up Hawthorne's alley. He wrote Hawthorne that the incident reminded him of the husband who deserts his wife for twenty years in "Wakefield."

In the notes that Clifford sent Melville, one passage no doubt struck him with great force. Agatha suspected that her husband had married a second time when she received gifts from him after he visited her and her daughter, and he actually announced to her

15. Ibid., p. 156.
16. Ibid., p. 155.

his intentions later when he was about to marry Mrs. Irvin, his third wife. Agatha refused to expose him, however. Clifford said that he came to understand her reasons and to admire her for her decision: "The only good it could have done to expose him would have been to drive Robertson away and forever disgrace him & it would certainly have made Mrs. Irvin & her children wretched for the rest of their days—'I had no wish,' said . . . [Agatha], 'to make either of them unhappy, notwithstanding all I had suffered on his account.'" To Clifford, this "was . . . a most striking instance of long-continued & uncomplaining submission to wrong and anguish on the part of a wife, which made her in my eyes a heroine."[17] Melville may or may not have shared this exact view of her, but he was magnetically attracted to the sequence of events in her life involving sacrifice, commitment, betrayal, and victimization. He must have turned over and over in his mind the questions, "Why did not Agatha become angry and bitter?" "Why did she not seek sweet vengeance on this person who caused the wreck of her life?"

By 1852, when he heard the story of Agatha and when, that summer, the reviews of *Pierre* began to come in (one of the earliest, in the Boston *Post,* called it "the craziest fiction extant" and found it full of "utter trash"), Melville was facing wreckage in his own life. His sacrifice, his commitment to writing and to "the great art of telling the truth" had not brought him recognition and fulfillment but a sense of victimization and betrayal. He could, consequently, identify with Agatha, but the important thing is that she survived. He wanted to know how she did it so that he could see if there was for him some lesson to be learned there. He knew the psychological dangers of anger and bitterness; he had already worked out in detail the ravages of revenge. So he wanted to avoid these wreckers of the mind *if* the method of doing so did not kill off certain vital aspects of his being. His interest in Agatha, therefore, derived I believe from his survival instinct, just as did his interest in the wreck of the *Essex,* one of his sources for *Moby-Dick.*

To say that *Moby-Dick* is a novel of survival, however, is not to

17. Ibid., p. 160.

say that it is some kind of tribute to the human spirit. It is not a story of man's ultimate and complete victory over the forces that would destroy him. It could not stand as a triumphant illustration of William Faulkner's uplifting declaration in his Nobel Prize acceptance speech that "man will not merely endure: he will prevail . . . because he has a soul, a spirit capable of compassion and sacrifice and endurance."[18] Ishmael's survival is not meant to inspire hope for the human race but *awe,* awe that this particular person, complex, moody, and brilliant, could live through the wreck of the *Pequod* and its aftermath or through—to put it another way—the tidal-wave challenges that threaten his body and mind.

Yet, live through them he does, always with the instinct of survival working within him. It is not as if he loves life so well that he cannot tolerate the thought of giving it up. Quite the contrary. He is melancholy, even subject to deep depression (the "hypos" he calls this state of mind); he feels keenly the "damp, drizzly November" in his soul (p. 12); and he even contemplates suicide. At times he, like the author who created him, believes temporarily that he has become reconciled to his own "annihilation." But like Melville, Ishmael always takes steps to avoid it. His going to sea, he says at the very beginning of the story, is for him an act of survival. It is his "substitute for pistol and ball." Cato may throw "himself upon his sword," but Ishmael "quietly take[s] to the ship" (p. 12). His doing so it not another form of suicide but an act of self-preservation taken in such a desperate moment as when others might kill themselves. Throughout, his narrative is punctuated both with indirect admonitions and with direct warnings about multifold dangers to survival. Narcissus, he says, plunged into the fountain and was drowned. "Heed it well," he warns Pantheistic visionaries, lest they "drop through the transparent air into the summer sea" (p. 140). Later he cautions: "Look not too long in the face of the fire, O man! Never dream with thy hand on the helm! Turn not thy back to the compass" (p. 354). Nearly all of these warnings grow out of Ishmael's own narrow escapes, after which he is moved to advise others about surviving.

18. *The Faulkner Reader* (New York: Random House, 1954), p. 4.

Death and destruction are almost constantly on Ishmael's mind. Where others would look at harpoons and lances as tools of the trade of whaling, Ishmael sees them as implements of death. Whereas others would view the weapons of a heathen culture that decorate the walls of the Spouter Inn as fascinating curiosities, he shudders as he gazes at them and wonders "what monstrous cannibal and savage could ever have gone a death-harvesting with such a hacking, horrifying implement" (p. 21). The bartender, who stands in an area made to resemble the head of a right whale, seems to him to be in the "jaws of swift destruction" (p. 21). Such references to the dangers of the whaling life serve to enhance the element of adventure in *Moby-Dick* and to create suspense and excitement about things to come, but there are so many of them and they occur so frequently and at times when an ordinary person (much less an ordinary whaleman) would not think of peril and death that they serve as well to reveal in Ishmael an unusual sensitivity to all the dangers around him, a sensitivity that is the complement to his survival instinct. He senses one kind of peril or another wherever he looks, and he states clearly the extent of these threats and his intentions with regard to them when he says early in the novel, "It is quite as much as I can do to take care of myself" (p. 14). Though the immediate context is comedy, his cry when Queequeg first crawls into bed with him is a serious expression of an intuitive determination: "Save me!" (p. 31).

Once the depth of Ishmael's survival impulse is understood, its manifestations are apparent in passages where it otherwise might have gone unnoticed. For example, he is deeply struck with Father Mapple's sermon, which presents the Christian message of unquestioning acceptance and obedience; it offers a stark alternative to Ahab's Gnosticism. But in the particular way that Father Mapple presents the example of Jonah, he is appealing not so much to the need of God in his particular congregation as to their sense of self-preservation. He uses Jonah to tell them what they must do if they wish to survive. The story of Jonah and the whale has nothing to do with heaven or hell, glorious mansions above or burning brimstone below; it focuses upon *this* life and the choice of surviving the perils that threaten us or being consumed by them. I suggested earlier that chapter 23 ("The Lee Shore") is Ishmael's sympathetic exploration of the subject of madness as imperative. What he is saying in that chapter is that there are times when a sudden shift to reasonableness and common sense, to the well-ordered and peaceful shores of life, can bring destruction and that the law of survival demands at least a temporary rejection of those attractive shores. Thus that chapter is fundamentally about survival under terrifying pressures. Even Ishmael's contemplation of the whale becomes a message of survival. Already in Melville's day the question of the whale's extinction was being raised. Old whaling grounds were no longer as thickly populated as they once were; and the great bison of the American West, once so numerous that the herds seemed endless, was now in its near extinction pointed to as an example of what could happen to whales. In chapter 105, Ishmael faces this issue of the whale's survival. His response is more emotional than logical: he simply will not accept the extinction of the whale in the near future or the far future. The whale, he concludes in a defiant outburst that ends the chapter, will survive eternally: "He swam the seas before the continents broke water; he once swam over the site of the Tuileries, and Windsor Castle, and the Kremlin. In Noah's flood he despised Noah's Ark; and if ever the world is to be again flooded, like the Netherlands, to kill off its rats, then the eternal whale will still survive, and rearing upon the topmost crest of the equatorial flood, spout his frothed defiance to the skies" (pp. 384–85).

Ishmael, then, is a man with a highly sensitized, ever-alert, built-in danger-detector operating on the electric current of his survival instinct. The ending of *Moby-Dick* with its widespread destruction has the unmistakable ring of tragedy, it is true, and even the epilogue strikes a melancholy note in the way Ishmael describes his being fished from the sea: *"It was the devious-cruising* Rachel, *that in her retracing search after her missing children, only found another orphan"* (p. 470). The sense of rootlessness and loneliness in Ishmael is strong here, but reverberating as well through the epilogue are the powerful words: *"One did survive the wreck."* It is important thematically that *only* Ishmael and, sadly, no one else lives through the ordeal, but it is equally significant that Ishmael *does* survive. An orphan, on the one hand, is a sad spectacle because mother and father are dead and the child has been left alone, but on the other hand, and on the positive side, an orphan is a survivor, the one who gets through the accident, the epidemic, the war, or other perils, alive. Ishmael's epilogue, therefore, should not be read merely as the final melancholy note in a tragic symphony but also as his quiet but proud announcement of survival with dignity.

Ishmael is thus by nature a survivor, sharing traits of character with other survivors of the world who live through physical trials and the aftermaths and who hold themselves together (if sometimes barely) through psychological crises. What some of these shared traits are can be seen in modern studies of the survivor as a type. In the twentieth century a considerable body of literature has emerged that deals with the survivors of Soviet work camps, Nazi death camps, and even lunatic asylums. Sociologists, historians, and psychologists who have devoted themselves to this subject have concluded that in the broadest terms survivors appear to have in common three traits. Though Melville of course could have no knowledge of Siberian political prisoners or of the Holocaust ordeal, he had enough insight into human nature and into himself to depict in the survivor of *Moby-Dick* these same precise qualities.

Those who manage to survive great physical or psychological trials tend to possess a high degree of self-knowledge, to know who and what they are. More self-sustaining, and often introspective, than the usual person, they become defiant more easily and abhor perhaps more than anything else the thought of losing their identity. According to Terrence Des Pres, who closely examined those who lived through death camps and remained sane and human, " 'Recalcitrance' splendidly describes survivors in their stubborn refusal to be completely shaped by their environment. . . . Stripped of everything, prisoners maintained moral identity by holding some inward space of self untouchable." Survivors are those, he adds, "who make radical adjustments in order to live; but at the same time, and also in order to live, they strive to keep themselves *fundamentally* unchanged by the pressures to which they respond.[19] They "struggle fiercely for an existence apart, for an integrity absolutely unbreachable. That is the basis

19. Terrence Des Pres, *The Survivor: An Anatomy of Life in the Death Camps* (New York: Oxford University Press, 1976), p. 202.

of dignity, of personality, of the egoism which fuels creation and discovery, and finally of the sense of individual 'rights.' "[20] No one ever saw this more clearly than Melville. Bruno Bettelheim has suggested that it requires "well-developed self-respect, and great inner security for such an individual not to soon lose interest in himself, and become ready to give up living, particularly when the circumstances of his life are extremely disagreeable and destructive."[21]

The second common denominator of survivors is their possession of an inexplicable wish to live, a wish whose origin is not clear but so deep in some that it exists even when the *will* to live has eroded. It is what Bruno Bettelheim saw as the "life drive" in some prisoners of the Nazis. One had to have this "strong life" tendency, he writes, to survive the terrible ordeal.[22] In another context, William Seabrook spoke of his knowledge that alcohol was destroying him and some deep-seated desire beyond will that made him want to escape from it by being placed by force in an institution: "I think there was an intuitive element of survival-wish in it, too. . . . I knew that I had lost my will with relation to alcohol. I knew that there was only left to me the wish—which is entirely different from the will—to be saved. . . . I knew I was drinking myself to death, that I couldn't stop—and that I wanted to be stopped—by force."[23]

The third characteristic in this composite portrait of the survivor is a compulsion to tell others, sometimes directly, sometimes indirectly, but to bear witness. Ishmael is bearing witness in his narrative, and in his, at times, Ancient-Mariner-like intensity and insistence upon being believed, he is reflecting this quality modern researchers have come to associate with the survivor. Many of the accounts that we have of the Soviet and German concentration camps and of the horrors of man-made and natural disasters were written by survivors themselves. "To bear witneess," writes Des Pres, "is the goal of their struggle."[24] Viktor

---

20. Ibid., p. 203.
21. Bruno Bettelheim, *Surviving and Other Essays* (New York: Knopf, 1979), p. 107.
22. Ibid.
23. William Seabrook, *Asylum* (New York: Harcourt, 1935), p. ix.
24. Des Pres, p. 31.

E. Frankl tells of the strange action of Jews who were finally liberated from German death camps: "When one of the prisoners was invited out by a friendly farmer in the neighborhood, he . . . began to talk, often for hours. . . . Hearing him talk, one got the impression that he *had* to talk, that his desire to speak was irresistible."[25]

Ultimately, of course, there are no survivors since death is inevitable. As is often the situation with survivors of catastrophes, Ishmael's remaining alive after all others aboard his ship are dead is largely a matter of good luck. He happens to be thrown from his whaleboat just at the right time to escape the destruction. Survival in the fullest sense, therefore, is not merely a matter of getting through a life-threatening ordeal alive. Many who do that owe their lives purely to chance. A true survivor by type will not *always* survive, but he is that person whose death when it finally comes will be brought on by causes entirely beyond his control. Death will be superimposed upon him; he will not contribute to it. Ishmael is a survivor in this broader and more meaningful use of the term. He remains alive physically, but he also survives the test of the mental and spiritual ordeal.

In this sense, what Ishmael survives is, in a word, Ahab, not just Ahab's directing of the ship and its crew into the jaws of destruction but Ahab personally, his great magnetism, the temptation to be his disciple. Ishmael is strongly drawn to Ahab even before he actually sees him: "I felt a sympathy and a sorrow for him, but for I don't know what. . . . And yet I also felt a strange awe of him; but that sort of awe, which I cannot at all describe, was not exactly awe; I do not know what it was. But I felt it; and it did not disincline me towards him" (p. 77). His first view of Ahab affects him, he says, "powerfully" (p. 110). What Ahab says of the white whale is also true of himself as far as Ishmael is concerned: "He's all a magnet!" (p. 368). When Ahab enlists his crew to join him in his vengeful search, Ishmael says that "a wild, mystical, sympathetical feeling was in me; Ahab's quenchless feud seemed mine" (p. 155). It is from this compelling magnetism that Ishmael must escape if he is to survive.

25. Viktor E. Frankl, *Man's Search for Meaning: An Introduction to Logotherapy* (Boston: Beacon, 1962), p. 89.

He does so, but the Ishmael who has lived through the destruction of the *Pequod* to tell about it sounds remarkably like Ahab on many occasions. When Ishmael is speaking on certain subjects, it could just as easily be Ahab.[26] For example, the contempt that Ahab shows for the ship's carpenter and for the type of person he so clearly represents is wholly shared by Ishmael. In fact, he appears to be Ahab's spokesman when he says: "For nothing was this man more remarkable than for a certain impersonal stolidity as it were; impersonal, I say; for it so shaded off into the surrounding infinite of things, that it seemed one with the general stolidity discernible in the whole visible world, which while pauselessly active in uncounted modes, still eternally holds its peace, and ignores you, though you dig foundations for cathedrals" (p. 388). In the next chapter, Ahab toys with the carpenter and reflects the same attitude toward him. And it is Ishmael, after all, who makes the distinction between the "dead level of the mass" and "the choice hidden handful of the Divine Inert" (p. 129). As I suggested in chapter 2, Ishmael, like his creator Melville, sometimes is as much a theomaniac as is the maddened Ahab. Unquestionably, Ahab represented a side of them both. Like Ahab, Ishmael discriminates between what the narrator of "I and My Chimney" calls the higher and the lower mathematics. Men try to understand the whale by looking at its skeleton, Ishmael states. But he knows this earthly mathematics is "vain and foolish" (p. 378). He does not trouble himself with "odd inches" when measuring the whale (p. 376), such trivia being the stuff of lower mathematics. Ahab is thinking the same way when he breaks his quadrant and complains about "mortal inter-indebtedness which will not do away with ledgers" (p. 392).

Melville connected Ahab to the white whale by a series of descriptions; he links Ishmael to Ahab similarly through attitudes

26. In an excellent essay, "Old Man Ahab," Sanford E. Marovitz comments: "Ishmael's meditations often set the stage for Ahab's and harmonize with them. The two men are not as different as they often appear to be; both are brooders, both are fatalistic, and strangely, both do a good deal of pondering over the questions and conditions of senescence" (pp. 143–44 in *Artful Thunder: Versions of the Romantic Tradition in American Literature,* ed. Robert J. DeMott and Sanford E. Marovitz [Kent: Kent State University Press, 1975]).

and echoes in their comments. That they share the same idea about fate is shown in "the Mat-maker" chapter, where Ishmael describes the warp as "necessity," the controlling shape that is fixed and "not to be swerved from" (p. 185). This passage follows Ahab's statement a few chapters earlier: "Swerve me? The path to my fixed purpose is laid with iron rails, whereon my soul is grooved to run" (p. 147). Ishmael feels that his going on this whaling voyage "formed part of the grand programme of Providence that was drawn up a long time ago" (pp. 15–16), and Ahab declares, "This whole act's immutably decreed. 'Twas rehearsed . . . a billion years before this ocean rolled. . . . I am the Fates' lieutenant" (p. 459). Early in the novel, Ishmael says that "the Fates put me down for this . . . whaling voyage" (p. 16). In chapter 69, Ishmael observes sea birds eating a dead whale and says: "Oh, horrible vulturism of earth! from which not the mightiest whale is free" (p. 262). Then in chapter 132, Ahab comments on this same vulturism in nature: "Look! see yon Albicore! who put it into him to chase and fang that flying-fish?" (p. 445). Both stand in horror at this natural phenomenon. Finally, Ishmael admits to being a "savage, owning no allegiance but to the King of the Cannibals; and ready at any moment to rebel against him" (p. 232). The king of the cannibals is perhaps the man that Ishmael does indeed swear allegiance to, his captain, for Ahab refers to himself as "cannibal old me" (p. 444).

Ishmael's psychological survival is partly the result of his being, in a metaphorical sense, a cannibal, from his rebelling against his "King," and from his "eating" of him. The reason Ishmael sounds at times so much like Ahab is that the narrator has assimilated his former king without having surrendered his own essential identity.[27] Indeed, Ahab is referred to as "King" in

27. The idea of assimilating into one's own being the strong qualities of those eaten is explored in detail by Sir James George Frazer in *The Golden Bough,* 3d ed. (London: Macmillan, 1955), where he examines cannibalism and head-hunting among primitive tribes. A native of Borneo explained that through cannibalism "those who were once our enemies, hereby became our guardians, our friends, our benefactors" (5:295). Even in more civilized societies, myths abound involving this same principle, including one with which Melville was familiar, that of Orpheus. This was among scores of cults and religions where

chapter 34 (p. 131). Melville's fascination and familiarity with cannibalism are assurances that he understood the most basic myth associated with its ritualistic practice: the survivor and consumer of flesh of his enemy or former king becomes imbued with the strengths and virtues of the dead; they live on in the survivor now made subject to his own dominant traits. Two strong recurrent patterns of reference tie together Ahab, whales, Queequeg, and Ishmael, as if they are all parts or projections of the same complex mind in something like an elaborate psychological parable. They are allusions to cannibals or cannibalism and to kingship. Ishmael and Ahab both refer to themselves as cannibals; Ishmael speaks of eating a piece of raw whale in cannibalistic terms (it tasted like Louis Le Gros); Queequeg is from a cannibalistic tribe and peddles heads. Ahab is "King"; and Queequeg is the son of a king and perhaps even king himself since it has been years since he has seen his father. The whale is referred to as king of the seas.

These two interrelated sustained motifs make for a structure upon which Melville builds his theory of survivorship. He himself survived psychologically in the same way as did Ishmael—by calling forth from the depths of his innermost being aspects of himself that could destroy him unless they were allowed to come forth, be recognized, and then to be destroyed, not completely destroyed, though, their attractive and life-giving features retained and made creative. "But Ahab, my Captain," says Ishmael speaking in the present, "still moves before me in all his Nan-

---

the eating of the king (especially one of divine origins) insured acquisition of noble qualities. In Orphism, Zagreus, the son of Zeus by Persephone, was slain by the Titans and eaten. Somehow, the heart was preserved and carried back to Zeus, who ate it and destroyed the Titans with lightning. From their ashes arose the human race, noble on the one hand because the Titans had eaten Zagreus but ignoble on the other because it sprang from the Titans. In one of his famous visions seminars, C. G. Jung responded to a student who spoke of this myth of the assimilation of kingly power on the part of the Titans who ate Zagreus: "That really started from the totemic meals, where the totem animal was eaten, and in the course of thousands of years, it degenerated into the idea of eating the God in more ordinary form. Then at later stages it developed into the idea of killing and eating the king." C. G. Jung, *The Visions Seminars* (Zurich: Spring Publications, 1976), book 1, p. 168.

tucket grimness and shagginess" (p. 130). Ishmael is stronger for having lived through the ordeal of Ahab. Queequeg is not such a threat to him; he did not need to dredge up the savage in himself in order to make it impotent but in order to give it a greater part in his existence. That he does so, that he "eats" Queequeg in the same symbolic sense that he does Ahab, is suggested by his cannibalistic tendencies and his strange comment at the conclusion of chapter 102 that he has become so tattooed over his body that there are few blank spaces remaining, which means, if we take him literally, that he has truly become savage in appearance and has taken on the aspect of Queequeg. He is speaking metaphorically, however, as he is when he talks of comparing whale meat to that of King Louis. What Queequeg represents to him has become a more immediate and accessible aspect of himself than it was when hidden away. It was frightening to meet this part of himself face to face, but he proved to be no enemy. Ishmael the narrator is more like him in his total personality than when he was a school teacher.

Ahab was different. Ishmael-Melville took a profound risk in meeting him face to face. He was magnetic, powerful in his rebellion and his heroism. But Ishmael possessed two qualities that he knew to be vital for surviving, qualities that Ahab lacked: a high degree of self-understanding, which included a knowledge of what was necessary for survival, and an intellectual and emotional tie to the ordinary world, to commonality, which he, unlike Ahab, never relinquished.[28] He could take off and then put back on the rose-colored glasses. He could be both sub-sub-librarian and pale usher, and while either, he retained full knowledge of the presence and need of the other. Ahab hated his other side without even realizing that that was what it was.

28. This is Ishmael's true reason for insisting upon being a common sailor rather than an officer. "No, when I go to sea," he says, "I go as a simple sailor, right before the mast, plumb down into the forecastle, aloft there to the royal mast-head" (p. 14). Now it is a mistake to interpret this passage as evidence of Ishmael's love of the common man, as proof of his democratic proclivities. He finds living in the forecastle painful, not pleasant; he does it because he knows that he must retain his tie with the ordinary world in order to survive psychologically.

The voice of the narrator Ishmael must be one of the strangest in all of literature. It undergoes such drastic swings in tone, such shifts in emotions, that he seems to be many people, a composite. And so he is. The Ishmael that we hear speaking in *Moby-Dick* is essentially the sensitive school teacher given to depression who took to the sea, but living on within him and heard through his mouth are others, most notably Ahab and Queequeg. In one sense, there is only one survivor of the wreck of the *Pequod,* but in another there are several because transmogrified they live on in Ishmael. In *Mardi,* Melville wrote admiringly of an imaginary author, Lombardo, whom he conceived to be like himself. "Lombardo," he says, "wrote right on; and so doing, got deeper and deeper into himself."[29] In *Moby-Dick* Melville got deeper and deeper within himself. His profoundest reason for writing was to do that, and by expressing in art what lay within him, he survived. Some twenty years before his death, he acquired a copy of William R. Alger's *The Solitudes of Nature and of Man; or, The Loneliness of Human Life* (1867), and he underscored in it the following: "[Beethoven] says, 'I was nigh taking my life with my own hands. But Art held me back. I could not leave the world until I had revealed what lay within me.'"[30]

In biographical and critical studies of Melville and his work, the subject of surviving has become covered over with discussions of his psychological difficulties and their projections into what he wrote. Somehow, he has come down to us as one of American literature's leading candidates for suicide. It seems almost unfair of him not to have obliged by killing himself, if not through sword or pistol and ball, then at least through psychosomatic illness, alcoholism, or some other form of self-destruction leading to an early death. Those who find his long life and continued creative alertness incongruous with all of his emotional suffering posit a theory that he was, indeed, a suicide but not in the generally understood way. Henry A. Murray argues that Melville in

29. *Mardi and A Voyage Thither,* ed. Harrison Hayford et al. (Evanston and Chicago: Northwestern University Press and the Newberry Library, 1970), p. 595.

30. Jay Leyda, *The Melville Log: A Documentary Life of Herman Melville, 1819–1891* (New York: Harcourt, Brace, 1951), 2:721.

five categories established by the Suicide Prevention Foundation was like 220 patients at veterans hospitals who had killed themselves. These patients had "(1) more crying spells, (2) more fist fights and violent episodes, (3) more severe depressions, and (4) more periods of withdrawal and mutism. Furthermore, (5) they escaped from the hospital more often."[31] In depicting Melville as a suicidal type, Murray makes up his own "equivalents" to correspond to such things as crying spells, fist fights, and escapes from the hospital, applies them to Melville, and concludes that he killed himself all right but in terms of his becoming "a burnt-out crater, dead inside as well as outside."[32]

This determination to find some way to categorize Melville as a suicide is also reflected in the work of other scholars. Edwin S. Shneidman agrees with Murray that Melville before his literal physical cessation of life committed suicide in his "human spirit."[33] Shneidman's method is to document Melville's interest in death as reflected in his works (he offers charts showing how much death there is in the fiction), to point out that after the early writings Melville "met with a barrage of annihilating criticism," and then to conclude that because of this criticism he killed off vital aspects of his being: "Melville was partially dead during much of his own life."[34] Survivors, genuine survivors, those who withstand great ordeals, the Owen Chases and Agathas, those who lived through the torture of concentration camps and death marches, often found it necessary to change, to give up certain sensibilities, to become deadened in certain ways. Survival in the best sense does not preclude these internal shifts but demands them as long as what is relinquished does not affect the core, the essential self. *That,* Herman Melville did not violate. He remains to my mind not our classic suicidal temperament, though he was given to the

31. Henry A. Murray, "Dead to the World: The Passions of Herman Melville," in *Essays in Self-Destruction,* ed. Edwin S. Shneidman (New York: Science House, 1967), p. 12.

32. Ibid., p. 27.

33. Edwin S. Shneidman, *Deaths of Man* (New York: Quadrangle, 1973), p. 163. An earlier version of Shneidman's chapter on Melville was published as "The Deaths of Herman Melville," in *Melville and Hawthorne in the Berkshires,* ed. Howard P. Vincent (Kent: Kent State University Press, 1968), pp. 118–43.

34. Ibid., p. 177.

deeper melancholy at times and even to hopelessness, but our most admirable survivor. He told Hawthorne that he had made up his mind to be annihilated, but something within him would not allow that course of action. What his heart and soul said throughout his life was what Edward Buca, a Polish prisoner in one of the horrible Soviet labor camps, said to an astonished fellow prisoner: "I've decided to survive this hell."[35]

35. Edward Buca, *Vorkuta,* trans. Michael Lisinski and Kennedy Wills (London: Constable, 1976), p. 135.

The Wonderful Work
on Physiognomy: PIERRE

Chapter 6

Melville had hardly caught his breath from the rigors of completing *Moby-Dick* before he was at work on his next novel, *Pierre; or, The Ambiguities*. From the time when he wrote Sophia Hawthorne about his new work, *Pierre* has been perceived in stark contrast to *Moby-Dick*. "But, My Dear Lady," he stated, "I shall not again send you a bowl of salt water. The next chalice I shall commend, will be a rural bowl of milk."[1] Salt-sea and mild milk are oceans apart, and though critics have spoken vaguely for generations about Melville's "trilogy"—*Mardi, Moby-Dick,* and *Pierre*—in practice they have often treated *Pierre* as a striking and profoundly disappointing departure from its immediate predecessor. Its setting for the first time is not the sea, and the first-person point of view utilized in Melville's first five novels has been replaced by a third-person narrator. Other obvious differences abound to give the appearance of something radically different, but this is a misleading impression.[2]

---

1. *The Letters of Herman Melville,* ed. Merrell R. Davis and William H. Gilman (New Haven: Yale University Press, 1960), p. 146.
2. See, for example, Richard Chase, who writes that "The mood and texture

Because of the drastic shifts in setting, point of view, character types, style, and structure, *Pierre* may well be the most underrated of Melville's novels, for the differences in technique invite *contrast* with *Moby-Dick* and lead away from the most fundamental fact of all about the book: in the deepest sense it is a companion piece to *Moby-Dick*. The mode of expression is different, but what is being expressed is the same. Melville did not, as one critic has conjectured, "somewhere in the months between *Moby-Dick* and *Pierre*" discover some new truths he was trying to present.[3] The concerns that engaged Melville's mind during the composition of *Moby-Dick* did not suddenly change as he wrote on quickly through his next book.[4] *Pierre* has a tighter structure than *Moby-Dick* and appears to have been wrought with the intention of making it more like a traditional novel, but paradoxically it is less independent as a work of art. One can understand *Moby-Dick* without *Pierre*, but *Moby-Dick* offers an invaluable context for an understanding of *Pierre*. The rural bowl of milk is a highly disguised offering of more salt water, so disguised, in fact, that it resists detection when examined merely on its own stated terms.

Seen traditionally as Melville's failed attempt to write a romantic novel of the sort popular in the mid-nineteenth century, *Pierre* is actually one of his boldest experiments in fiction, an expression of the same interests and insights in a radically different form from that which he had just given them. The novel poses a rare and peculiar problem to critics trying to judge it as a work of art. Standing alone, it pales in contrast to the story of the great whale; as a companion piece, an unidentical twin, to *Moby-Dick*, it not

---

of the two novels are as different as light and dark." *Herman Melville: A Critical Study* (New York: Macmillan, 1949), p. 103. "In *Pierre*," writes F. O. Matthiessen, "Melville conceived a tragedy the opposite of Ahab's." *American Renaissance: Art and Expression in the Age of Emerson and Whitman* (New York: Oxford University Press, 1941), p. 467.

3. Robert Milder, "Melville's 'Intentions' in *Pierre*," *Studies in the Novel* 6 (1974): 189.

4. As John Bernstein correctly points out, "Intellectually and philosophically, *Pierre* covers much the same ground as *Moby-Dick*, posing the same questions and arriving at the same conclusions as does the earlier book." *Pacifism and Rebellion in the Writings of Herman Melville* (The Hague: Mouton, 1964), p. 126.

only takes on new meaning but appears in a new light as a work of art.[5]

In both novels Melville was attempting to understand his own inner sea and to survive its wild storms. Water, of course, is almost omnipresent in *Moby-Dick*. Melville's fascination with the actual, outer seas of the earth arose in part from his metaphorical association of the surface of water with the surfaces of human existence. He was aware of several types of water-gazers—those who in staring dreamily at the water were gradually carried outside themselves into a dangerous illusory state; those who saw nothing and felt nothing; those who considered the water a facade that covered over all of the multifold truths about life and the nature of their fellow human beings; and those, like himself, who considered the surface of the water not a transcendental gateway, or a blank page, or a covering for the secrets of the universe but a mirror reflecting back the features of oneself, a tool for self-recognition rather than for mystically going beyond self or for interpreting life's hieroglyphics. What is going on on the surface of the water in *Moby-Dick,* then, is a reflection of what was going on within the self of Melville.

Though water plays little part in *Pierre,* "the sea is the sea" (p. 303),[6] the surface of life, represented in the novel, that is, is best understood as Melville's mirror, not the face that objective universal truth wears. The distinction is fundamental, for if one believes that Melville thought of the surface of *Pierre*—essentially the characters and their actions—as the outward manifestation of life's secrets, the book appears in an entirely different light from

5. Melville was to continue this experimentation on into his writing of short fiction with the composition of bipartite stories, two seemingly separate tales that are closely related. Some of these Melville himself clearly designated as companion pieces by publishing them together: "The Two Temples," "Poor Man's Pudding and Rich Man's Crumbs," and "The Paradise of Bachelors and the Tartarus of Maids." Others, however, such as "Bartleby, the Scrivener" and "Cock-A-Doodle-Doo!," "The Bell-Tower" and "Benito Cereno," were published individually, and because they are so different in subject and technique, they went long unrecognized as companion stories.

6. *Pierre; or, The Ambiguities,* ed. Harrison Hayford et al. (Evanston and Chicago: Northwestern University Press and the Newberry Library, 1971). References to *Pierre* are to this edition.

that which results from the premise that the surface of the novel mirrors his own inner concerns. In order to illustrate the error of those who think that they can find the answers to life's deepest mysteries by examining the surface, Melville has made his hero, Pierre Glendinning, who is referred to as a victim of civilization, philosophy, and ideal virtue (p. 302), in actuality, and in a more immediate sense, one whose destruction can be traced in part to his affinity for the principles of physiognomy and the notorious theories of John Caspar Lavater, a devoted advocate of the belief that the highest reality is accessible through a right reading of the surface that lightly covers it.

Lavater is referred to indirectly early in *Pierre* when Aunt Dorothea is trying to explain why Pierre's father did not want his Cousin Ralph to paint his portrait: "But Cousin Ralph had a foolish fancy about it. He used to tell me, that being in your father's room some few days after the last scene I described, he noticed there a very wonderful work on Physiognomy, as they call it, in which the strangest and shadowiest rules were laid down for detecting people's innermost secrets by studying their faces. And so, foolish cousin Ralph always flattered himself, that the reason your father did not want his portrait taken was, because he was secretly in love with the French young lady, and did not want his secret published into a portrait; since the wonderful work on Physiognomy had, as it were, indirectly warned him against running that risk" (p. 79).

The "wonderful work on Physiognomy" that Pierre's father read and believed in so thoroughly that he would not allow his portrait to be painted lest it give away his inner secrets was almost certainly *Essays on Physiognomy* by John Caspar Lavater (1741–1801). It is a strange and wonderful work, indeed, just the sort to appeal to Melville's curiosity if not to his convictions. Lavater was a Swiss-born theologian and Protestant pastor who devoted his life to the optimistic premise that the reality of God and the spiritual world can be concretely determined from external features. Highly influential during his lifetime, his *Essays on Physiognomy* continued to attract followers throughout the nineteenth century. Published in 1772, it was translated into English in the 1790s and became one of the most discussed books of the time. Its early editions in English were elaborately printed in handsome multivolumes of quarto size, full of illustrations. Soon, however, less expensive one-volume translations were available, and the work's fame spread rapidly.

The basic difference between physiognomy, as espoused by Lavater, and the other prominent pseudoscience of the day, phrenology (whose greatest exponents were Franz Joseph Gall and Johann Spurzheim), is that the one was fundamentally related to philosophy—a way of seeking ultimate reality—whereas the other was akin to modern psychology—a way of relating human actions to functions of the brain. The one was largely subjective and even mystical; the other was materialistic.[7] Lavater held that by understanding man, one could come closer to understanding God. His missionary zeal to find a way to get into man, then, was more than scientific motivation: it was a holy quest. And when he developed his theories of physiognomy, he thought the way had been found. He explained the essence of his theories as follows: "Taking it in its most extensive sense, I use the word physiognomy to signify the exterior, or superficies of man, in motion or at rest, whether viewed in the original or by portrait. Physiognomony, or, as more shortly written Physiognomy, is the science or knowledge of the correspondence between the external and internal man, the visible superficies and the invisible contents. . . . Whoever forms a right judgment of the character of man, from those first impressions which are made by his exterior, is naturally a physiognomist."[8] Lavater argued that there were many "advantages" in the practice of physiognomy, uppermost of which was its sharpening the physiognomist's sense of beauty and virtue at the same time that it in-

7. "Lavater had meant simply that the features were expressive of the soul. But Gall reversed the premises of physiognomy in a peculiarly materialistic fashion: character and intellect, he maintained, were simply the sum of the combined functions of the organs of the brain. Character *was* the brain." John D. Davies, *Phrenology, Fad and Science: A Nineteenth-Century American Crusade* (New Haven: Yale University Press, 1955), p. 7. See also Madeleine B. Stern, *Heads and Headlines: The Phrenological Fowlers* (Norman: University of Oklahoma Press, 1971).

8. John Caspar Lavater, *Essays on Physiognomy, Designed to Promote the Knowledge and the Love of Mankind,* trans. Thomas Holcroft, 13th ed. (London: William Tegg, 1867), pp. 11–12.

creased his abhorrence of the base and imperfect: "As this physiognomonical sensation is ever combined with a lively perception of what is beautiful, and what deformed; of what is perfect and what imperfect . . . how important, how extensive, must be the advantages of physiognomy! How does my heart glow at the supposition that so high a sense of the sublime and beautiful, so deep an abhorrence of the base and deformed, shall be excited; that *all the charms of virtue shall actuate the man who examines physiognomonically;* and that he who, at present, has a sense of those charms, shall, then, so powerfully, so delightfully, so variously, so incessantly, be impelled to a still higher improvement of his nature" (italics mine).[9] To be a physiognomist, then, was to be child of virtue and truth and an enemy of injustice and imperfection.

Melville's knowledge of Lavater derived from both his reading of *Essays on Physiognomy* and from his reading about Lavater in other works. In his checklist of *Melville's Reading,* Merton M. Sealts, Jr., records that Melville purchased in London an unidentified edition of Lavater's book on November 21, 1849.[10] During this same trip to England, Melville bought a month or so later a copy of the *Auto-Biography* of Goethe, a man who had known Lavater intimately, helped him with the composition of *Physiognomy,* and recounted the details of their friendship in the volume Melville obtained in London.[11] The view of Lavater that Melville received from Goethe was that of a man not deep or learned but gifted with intelligence who felt the need always to *act,* and to act in the name of highest truth and virtue.[12] Because he believed, said Goethe, that "our inward moral nature is incorporated in outward conditions, whether we belong to a family, a class, a

9. Ibid., p. 43.

10. Merton M. Sealts, Jr., *Melville's Reading: A Check-List of Books Owned and Borrowed* (Madison: University of Wisconsin Press, 1966), p. 74.

11. Ibid., p. 62.

12. "He was not born for contemplation," writes Goethe. "He felt himself rather . . . impelled to activity, to action; and I have never known any one who was more unceasingly active than Lavater." *The Auto-Biography of Goethe, Truth and Poetry: From My Own Life,* trans. John Oxenford and A. J. W. Morrison, 2 vols. (London: Bohn, 1848–1849), 2:10.

guild, a city, or a state, he was obliged, in his desire to influence others, to come into contact with all these external things and to set them in motion." As a consequence, he became entangled: "Hence arose many a collision, many an entanglement."[13] Goethe found Lavater's "pressing incitements to action" stimulating to his own more "contemplative nature," but he became convinced that Lavater was "neither Thinker nor Poet" but an impulsive compiler who maintained supreme self-confidence. "Utterly unable to take a comprehensive and methodical view, he nevertheless formed an unerring judgment of individual cases."[14] In his estimate of *Essays on Physiognomy,* Goethe accuses Lavater of finding what he considered evidence to prove what he already believed rather than drawing conclusions from hard evidence. "His mental bias," writes Goethe, "led him rather to heap up cases of experience, than to draw from them any clear and sober principle. For this reason he never could come to results, though I often pressed him for them. What in later life he confided as such to his friends, were none to me; for they consisted of nothing more than a collection of certain lines and features, nay, warts and freckles, with which he had seen certain moral, and frequently immoral, peculiarities associated."[15] His evidence for subjectively drawn conclusions was not true evidence. He was "incessant" in his "demand for a realization of the ideal," but he remained convinced that he was dealing reasonably and practically with life. "Accordingly, he never could detect the error in his mode of thinking and acting."[16] Goethe's portrait of Lavater, therefore, is that of a "noble and good man" pursuing with frenzied energy what he considered right and true but ultimately failing partly because his zeal was fanatical and error-based and partly because despite all of his analysis of others, he did not fully perceive the confusion within his own being.

Though Goethe was not one of his literary heroes, Melville must have found his delineation of Lavater poignantly meaningful, for it parallels to an amazing degree the outline of Pierre's

13. Ibid.
14. Ibid., 2:14, 140.
15. Ibid., 2:141.
16. Ibid., 2:138.

character—his lack of a full and deep education, his unbounded energy, his impulsiveness, his predilection for "entanglements," his idealism, his proneness to accepting impressions as facts, and his lack of self-knowledge. From his reading of *Essays on Physiognomy* and Goethe's autobiography, however, Melville conceived not the basic idea of Pierre—he needed to go no further than his own inner self for that—but the notion of making Pierre akin to the physiognomists. In physiognomy Melville discovered a metaphor for his protagonist's blindness, a way of expressing his error of perception.

That Melville considered physiognomy a totally erroneous mode of looking at life is clear from the numerous references to it and its sister science, phrenology, in his works. His interest predates his purchase of Lavater and Goethe by at least two years, for in his third article on Zachary Taylor, he commented satirically that the face of the great man was a "physiognomical phenomenon, which Lavater would have crossed the Atlantic to contemplate."[17] Other references occur in several places including *Mardi, White-Jacket,* and *The Confidence-Man.* But it is in *Moby-Dick* that he most clearly represents his view. Ishmael begins chapter 79, "The Prairie,"[18] with the comment that Lavater and others never examined a whale externally in order to read what it is internally:

> To scan the lines of his face, or feel the bumps on the head of this Leviathan; this is a thing which no Physiognomist or Phrenologist has yet undertaken. Such an enterprise would seem almost as hopeful as for Lavater to have scrutinized the wrinkles on the Rock of Gibraltar or for Gall to have mounted a ladder and manipulated the Dome of the Pantheon. Still, in that famous work of his, Lavater not only treats of the various faces of men, but also attentively studies the faces of horses, birds, serpents, and fish; and dwells in detail upon the modifications of expression discernible there-

17. Quoted in Tyrus Hillway, "Melville's Use of Two Pseudo-Sciences," *Modern Language Notes* 64 (1949): 146.

18. For a discussion of the chapter that follows "The Prairie," chapter 80, "The Nut," which deals more with phrenology than physiognomy, see Harold Aspiz, "Phrenologizing the Whale," *Nineteenth-Century Fiction* 23 (1968): 18–27.

in. . . . Therefore, though I am but ill qualified for a pioneer, in the application of these two semi-sciences to the whale, I will do my endeavor.[19]

Then Ishmael proceeds, with irony in his voice, to regard the head of the sperm whale "physiognomically," to take a "physiognomical voyage" around "his vast head" to find "the most imposing physiognomical view to be had of the Sperm Whale."[20] In looking at the head "in profile, you plainly perceive that horizontal, semi-crescentic depression in the forehead's middle, which, in man, is Lavater's mark of genius."[21] By the end of the chapter, Ishmael's satirical mask drops, and he comments directly upon the folly of physiognomy: "Champollion deciphered the wrinkled granite hieroglyphics. But there is no Champollion to decipher the Egypt on every man's and every being's face. Physiognomy, like every other human science, is but a passing fable."[22] Melville's thoughts on Lavater and on physiognomy thus had been expressed strongly before he began writing *Pierre*.[23] *Moby-Dick*

19. *Moby-Dick,* ed. Harrison Hayford and Hershel Parker (New York: Norton, 1967) p. 291.

20. Ibid.

21. Ibid., p. 292. In his autobiography, Goethe blames Lavater for a widespread misuse of the term *genius*. Once, he writes, "genius was ascribed to the poet alone. But another world seemed all at once to rise up; genius was looked for in the physician, in the general, in the statesman, and before long, in all men, who thought to make themselves eminent either in theory or practice. . . . Lavater, by his views of Physiognomy, was compelled to assume a more general distribution of mental gifts by nature; the word *genius* became a universal symbol, and because men heard it uttered so often, they thought that what was meant by it, was habitually at hand. But then, since every one felt himself justified in demanding genius of others, he finally believed that he also must possess it himself. . . . In this way the word *genius* had suffered so much from misrepresentation, that it was almost desired to banish it entirely from the German language" (2:141, 142). That Melville joined Goethe in deploring such free use of *genius* is clear from his satiric treatment of journal editors and vanity publishers who courted Pierre when he was a juvenile poet and addressed him as a celebrated genius (p. 253).

22. *Moby-Dick*, p. 292.

23. Howard P. Vincent tentatively suggests that "Lavater's remarks on foreheads stimulated Melville into writing 'The Prairie.'" *The Trying-Out of Moby-Dick* (Boston: Houghton Mifflin, 1949), p. 267.

depicts a great and noble sea captain who was given to the reading of signs. From the physiognomy of life he thought that he could decipher its secrets. Therefore, "The Prairie" is a commentary not only on the inscrutability of life and on the futility of deludedly believing that by knowing how to interpret the features of its surface you learn eternal truth, but also on Ahab himself, who is in a sense like Lavater as he derives deep and settled meanings from appearances and happenings.

Pierre is Ahab's twin in this endeavor. Furthermore, echoes of Lavater are pervasive in the novel, and the science of physiognomy serves as the basic metaphor to reveal Pierre's particular kind of blindness. Melville appears to have had Lavater in mind when he created the portrait motif as a way of revealing his hero's deepest cast of mind, for in the way Pierre responds to portraits he shows his kinship to the tenets of physiognomy. In *Essays on Physiognomy,* Melville read that the trained reader of faces can learn more from looking at portraits than from their actual subjects: "Could we indeed seize the fleeting transitions of nature, or had she her moments of stability, it would then be much more advantageous to comtemplate nature than her likeness; but, this being impossible, and since likewise few people will suffer themselves to be observed sufficiently to deserve the name of observation, it is to me indisputable that a better knowledge of man may be obtained from portraits than from nature, she being thus uncertain, thus fugitive."[24]

Melville would have been naturally skeptical that great human secrets could accurately be deduced from portraits. He read in Goethe's autobiography that Lavater himself failed in his repeated attempts to have portraits represent his theories. "He called on all the world," writes Goethe, "to send him drawings and outlines, and especially representations of Christ. . . . He had ordered of a painter in Frankfort, who was not without talent, the profiles of several well known persons." But what Lavater hoped to receive from such portraits, he never did. "The opposition into which he fell both with painters and with individuals showed itself at once. The former could never work for him faithfully and sufficiently;

24. Lavater, p. 172.

the latter, whatever excellences they might have, came always too far short of the idea which he entertained of humanity and of men to prevent his being somewhat repelled by the special characteristics which constitute the personality of the individual."[25] Thus Lavater's trust in portraiture became the subject for a double joke: he could neither read, as he believed he could, man's deepest and most complex nature from a portrait nor could he have portraits painted that would accurately show forth certain aspects of human nature he wanted to illustrate. His great book on physiognomy, Goethe commented, "sadly shows us how in the commonest matter of experience so sharp-sighted a man, may go groping about him." The poor man expended vast sums in hiring "every artist and botcher living" to produce drawings and engravings for his book, representations that even he "is obliged in his work to say after each one that it is more or less a failure" in projecting what he wanted it to.[26]

In an intelligent, sharp-sighted, and in some ways brilliant young man, Melville has created such a one who goes "groping about him." Though Pierre is not writing an optimistic book on physiognomy in which portraiture plays a great part, he does attempt to write a book, and in his life he exhibits the same misguided belief in his infallible ability to read character and meaning from the surface of canvas and oil. Though Pierre's interpretations of paintings change as his mood becomes darker, his certainty that he is reading them right at that moment remains constant. In his early happiness, he receives evidence that his faith in life is not unwarranted by viewing "a fine joyous painting, in the good-fellow, Flemish style," which is so hung that it can be swung out to be seen better (p. 17). It is for him an airy veil through which he perceives life's bounties and beauties. Similarly, the portrait of his grandfather is "truly wonderful in its effects" upon young Pierre. He interprets from it "majestic sweetness." He reads there "a glorious gospel framed and hung upon the wall, and declaring to all people, as from the Mount, that man is a noble, god-like being, full of choicest juices; made up of

25. Goethe, 2:8, 9.
26. Ibid., 2:140.

strength and beauty" (p. 30). Here is a strong echo of the idealism of John Caspar Lavater.

The two portraits to which Pierre devotes most of his attention are those of his father, the chair and the drawing-room portraits, the one painted secretly by Cousin Ralph against the wishes of its Lavater-reading subject and the other commissioned and sat for by the now middle-aged and happily married man. Pierre's mother dislikes the earlier painting in favor of that of the loving husband she knew, but Pierre considers them as a diptych, as two representations of one ideal man, seen first in youth and then in middle age and both projecting the wonderful qualities of each age of man. In the sitting form Pierre sees the restless excitement, the vitality, the wonder, and the freedom of young manhood. In the standing form he perceives the contentment, the security, the strength, the understanding of life, and the responsiveness of mature manhood. All qualities are favorable, though some are more mysterious to Pierre than others, and all are associated with his idealized father, who embodies in the diptych all that Pierre reverences and strives for. When Pierre looks at the chair portrait, it admonishes him not to believe that the other painting is all of his father: "Consider in thy mind, Pierre, whether we two paintings may not make only one" (p. 83). Naturally, the chair portrait favors youth, the other middle age: "I am thy father as he more truly was" (p. 83), the one tells Pierre, while the more expansive face belies that message by reminding the young viewer of the father he actually remembers. Perhaps because he is young himself, Pierre spends more time pondering the chair portrait, but no matter which one he is studying, he is like Lavater, a "spiritual artist" (to use Melville's term), who can paint transcendental truths while using noble faces for his models. Melville may indeed have had in mind Lavater's preference for the portrait over the subject itself when he writes of that "spiritual artist" who even "in the presence of the original . . . will rather choose to draw" from the "ideal faces" of portraits "than from the fleshy face, however brilliant and fine" (p. 72).[27]

27. In book 17, "Young America in Literature," Melville speaks satirically of a few persons who approached Pierre in his days as a young poet who "did not even seem to remember that the portrait of any man generally receives, and indeed is entitled to more reverence than the original man himself" (p. 253).

Even the founder of physiognomy with his unlimited love of mankind and his faith in unbounded divine grace and with his unshakable conviction that, as Goethe put it, "the sensible corresponds throughout with the spiritual, and is not only an evidence of it, but indeed its representative"[28]—even Lavater believed in the powers of darkness, and he found those, too, through the practice of physiognomy. Pierre continues to perceive in the same manner as Lavater when he begins to see in portraits what is no longer the paragon of virtue but is now the essence of ignobility. When he hears Isabel's story and then confronts the chair portrait, he is just as certain that he sees lust, deception, and self-ishness as he was previously when he perceived in his father the opposite qualities. Consequently, he first turns the portrait to the wall to close the window on what he conceives as reality—now too hard and stark to bear—then packs it away in a trunk, then finally burns it.

How Pierre responds to the various portraits in the book reveals his growing bitterness and skepticism. Late in the novel when he, Isabel, and Lucy visit a painting exhibition, Pierre's subjective view of the world is what he sees as he stares at the pictures: "All the walls of the world seemed thickly hung with the empty and impotent scope of pictures, grandly outlined, but miserably filled" (p. 350). Isabel is astonished at the resemblance between herself and that of "a stranger's head, by an unknown hand," the best of the paintings. The unreliability of physiognomy as a way of reaching ultimate truth is suggested by the fact that as Pierre studies the same face in the painting, "his far-interior emotions" cause him to perceive it differently from the way Isabel sees it: "For though both were intensely excited by one object, yet their two minds and memories were thereby directed to entirely different comtemplations; while still each . . . might have vaguely supposed the other occupied by one and the same contemplation" (p. 352).

The portrait of the stranger, Pierre believes, is the cover for a vaster truth than he has known before. As he looks at it, he is reminded of the chair portrait, all the emotions and supposed revelations that bombarded him when he last viewed it and

28. Goethe, 2:137.

burned it return to him. Now, however, he perceives new dimensions of what he thinks is reality. The chair portrait had seemed to reveal to him the imperfections of his father and had started him on the one hand upon a pessimistic and woeful train of thought, but it had launched him on the other hand into a glorious holy crusade that he exaltingly undertook, moved as he was by the certainty that he was being directed by a far greater and nobler force within him than he had ever felt before. When he views the portrait of the stranger who resembles his father, he no longer sees a glorious side to his painful destiny. Now his cynical vision has broadened to include Isabel, and he comes to doubt her and the validity of his self-sacrifice.

The final portrait that Pierre sees is an incomplete sketch. Just before he goes out to murder Glen Stanly, he enters Lucy's chamber and finds her at her easel. "Holding a crust of bread, she was lightly brushing the portrait-paper, to efface some ill-considered stroke. The floor was scattered with the bread-crumbs and charcoal-dust; he looked behind the easel, and saw his own portrait, in the skeleton" (p. 357). Pierre's world has crumbled; all that remains of it are bread crumbs and charcoal dust. He is like Ahab in his final days, of whom Starbuck says: "Of all this fiery life of thine, what will at length remain but one little heap of ashes."[29] Lucy has drawn merely a simple outline in charcoal of Pierre's face, but as always he reads portraits as a physiognomist. What he sees represented in Lucy's drawing is the very nadir of his ever more pessimistic world view. If the Flemish painting in his mother's house reaffirms for him the fulness of life, this sketch reveals to him its emptiness, for he sees it "in the skeleton," a *memento mori*.

Throughout the novel, Pierre conceives of human faces in precisely the same manner as he does those in portraits. The face of Lucy Tartan emerges from the early pages, a countenance perfectly constituted to illustrate Lavater's convictions about beautiful and modest women, and she is described with the same gushing sentimentality that must have amused Melville when he read *Essays on Physiognomy.* "What better can temper manly

29. *Moby-Dick,* p. 412.

rudeness, or strengthen and support the weakness of man," writes Lavater. "What so soon can assuage the rapid blaze of wrath; what more charm masculine power; what so quickly dissipate peevishness and ill temper; what so well can wile away the insipid tedious hours of life, as the near and affectionate look of a noble beautiful woman?"[30] It is in viewing such pure and beautiful women, he says, that he finds his practice of physiognomy most rewarding, for their faces do but serve as masks behind which can be seen the perfection of God: "Can there be a more noble or important practice than that of a physiognomonical sensation for beauties so captivating, so excellent, as these?"[31] He admits that some attractive women are deceitful, but he argues that their malice, their arrogance, and their wantonness are immediately detectable to the physiognomist. "The obviousness of these, and many other characteristics, will preserve him who can see from the dangerous charms of their shameless bosoms!"[32]

As Melville describes her in the opening section, Lucy seems contrived to fit Lavater's conception of "a noble spotless maiden." Such a woman, according to Lavater is "all innocence, and all soul; all love, and of love all worthy, which must as suddenly be felt as she manifestly feels." Visible "in her large arched forehead [is] all the capacity of the immeasurable intelligence which wisdom can communicate." Her "compressed, but not frowning, eyebrows speak an unexplored mine of understanding," and "her gentle-outlined or sharpened nose" reveals to the physiognomist "refined taste, with sympathetic goodness of heart, which flows through the clear teeth, over her pure and efficient lips." She is humble; "mildness" is "in each motion of her mouth, dignified wisdom in each tone of her voice." Her eyes, which are "neither too open, nor too close, but looking straight forward, or gently turned, speak the soul that seeks a sisterly embrace." Indeed, she is "superior to all the powers of description." All the "glories of her angelic form" are "imbibed like the mild and golden rays of an autumnal evening sun."[33]

30. Lavater, p. 397.
31. Ibid., p. 398.
32. Ibid.
33. Ibid., p. 399.

Lucy is also "superior to all the powers of description," and one despairs of depicting her fully: "How, if with paper and with pencil I went out into the starry night to inventorize the heavens? Who shall tell stars as teaspoons? Who shall put down the charms of Lucy Tartan upon paper?" (p. 25). And just as Lavater, in feeling the power of the idealized female form, cries out "What! man,—having this sensation, which God has bestowed, wouldst thou violate the sanctuary of God?"[34]—so Pierre exclaims, "*I* to wed this heavenly fleece? Methinks one husbandly embrace would break her airy zone, and she exhale upward to that heaven whence she hath hither come, condensed to mortal sight" (p. 58). When Melville writes that "youths like Pierre Glendinning, seldom fall in love with any but a beauty" (p. 23), he is not so much praising his good taste in women as he is underscoring Pierre's tendency to follow Lavater's principles of physiognomy.

Had he not possessed this proclivity, he might have questioned more seriously Isabel's claim to be his half sister. Once he has seen her beautiful face, it haunts him. In it he sees that which he immediately accepts as genuine and loving. Though in its sadness the face of Isabel embodies a different kind of beauty from that of Lucy, he sees no less there and finds its attraction so compelling that his intuition seems to say to him: "Pierre, have no reserves; no minutest possible doubt" (p. 112). For Pierre, her face tells all that she truly is. Among those "strangest and shadowiest rules" that are "laid down for detecting people's innermost secrets" in the "wonderful work on Physiognomy" that Aunt Dorothea describes to Pierre are several that instruct the reader on first impressions. Melville would have found them dangerous guidelines for behavior, but Pierre seems to have been schooled in them insofar as his instantaneous convictions about Isabel's nature are concerned. In "General Rule III," Lavater indicates that people can be trusted who in spite of stress and shifts in mood seem always directed by the same inner being. Let that person, he advises, "be to thee sacred."[35] Observing Isabel's strange and changeable behavior, Pierre believes that it all results from the same mysterious but genuine, beautiful, cohesive, and noble self;

34. Ibid.
35. Ibid., p. 462.

and looking at her face he can see no trace of cunning or vanity. Consequently, for a time she does become for him "sacred." In closely watching her he seems to apply another principle of Lavater's "General Rule IV": "Observe the moments, rapid as lightning, of complete surprise. He who in these moments can preserve the lineaments of his countenance favourable and noble: he who then discovers no fatal trait; no trait of malignant joy, envy, or cold-contemning pride, has a physiognomy and a character capable of abiding every proof to which mortal and sinful man can be subjected."[36]

When Pierre gives his confidence, he gives it quickly and fully, basing his certainty upon his ability to read appearance. He joins his life unhesitatingly to that of a total stranger, Isabel, just as he earlier links it with the two colts that pull the Glendinning phaeton. He trusts them not to harm him when he moves among their legs because they appear to him as "sort of family cousins" (p. 21). His actual danger and the fallacy of his confidence based on appearances are suggested by the fact that his real family cousin, Glen Stanly, becomes his mortal enemy. The colts do not appear to be "vain or arrogant." With their "redundant manes and mighty paces," they remain "full of good-humor too, and kind as kittens" (pp. 21, 22). Beautiful and noble in appearance, they are high-spirited and obedient in temperament. What possible reason, then, would there be for not placing complete trust in them? Pierre finds no such reason, for he thinks like a physiognomist not only with regard to humankind but also the animal kingdom. In this he again follows Lavater, who devotes a section of his book to noble as opposed to ignoble horses.[37] In considering the actions of beasts as well as humans, both Lavater and Pierre appear to be unaware of the factor of unpredictability.

Physiognomically speaking, the face of Plotinus Plinlimmon

36. Ibid.
37. Ibid., pp. 218–22. Melville's description of Pierre's two colts fits Lavater's analysis of the "swan-necked" type: "This kind is cheerful, tractable, and high-spirited. They are very sensible of pain. . . . Flattery greatly excites their joy, and they will express their pride of heart, by parading and prancing.—I dare venture to wager that a man with a swan-neck, or, what is much more determinate, with a smooth, projecting profile, and flaxen hair, would have similar sensibility and pride" (pp. 220–21).

offers a great challenge to Pierre. Whereas his reading of Lucy's countenance in his days of happiness matched exactly his conviction of life's beauty and promise, and his interpretation of Isabel's face fit in precisely with his longing for a lovely and dependent sister at the time he discovered her, Plinlimmon's cheerful, wrinkle-free expression, his bright blue eyes, and general mildness all contrast sharply with Pierre's then dominant emotions. Since what he is feeling—depression, emptiness, rebellion, woe—does not at all correspond with Plinlimmon's physiognomy, the difference being immeasurable, Pierre cannot interpret it at all. The man seems to be wearing some kind of disguise; he is "inscrutable." He appears in his impenetrableness to be leering at Pierre and mocking him for his self-sacrificing mission on behalf of another. As long as a face does not violate Pierre's emotional needs or states, he reads that countenance in accord with these factors. Melville points up the subjective basis for Pierre's reading of faces when he raises the question of whether Isabel would have been so readily accepted if she had not been beautiful: "How, if accosted in some squalid lane, a humped, and crippled, hideous girl should have snatched his garment's hem, with—'Save me, Pierre—love me, own me, brother; I am thy sister!'" (p. 107). Though Melville does not answer the question directly, he strongly implies that she would have been rejected, seen in a far different light by Pierre. What the physiognomist sees in an actual face or in a portrait is likely to be what is within him rather than something within the person he views or the subject of the portrait. Those "very special emotions, called forth by some one or more individual paintings," Melville writes, do not arise because of something intrinsic within the paintings but often because of "accidental congeniality, which occasions this wonderful emotion" (p. 350). Thus it is merely "accidental congeniality" that produces "an accumulated impression of power" when Pierre and Isabel study the portrait of an unknown stranger (p. 351).

The difference between Pierre's Lavater-like reading of portraits, faces, and other aspects of the surface and Melville's mode of perception is the same as that between Ahab's interpretative vision and Ishmael's. Ahab believes that "all visible objects" are covers masking the universal truth—whatever that may be—behind them. Ishmael echoes Melville's position that when the seeker thinks he has penetrated the surface by discovering a deeper reality from interpreting appearances, he probably has found only what has been within himself. The distinction is that between those who view the surface of life as a thin cover or veil, to be broken through or removed with the right approach—Lavater was such a person—and those, like Melville, who consider the surface as a reflector, mirroring back rather than masking.

It should be no surprise, then, that Pierre does not seem to like mirrors. Even during his happiest times early in the novel, he is temporarily saddened when he peers into his looking glass and realizes that he is "companioned by no surnamed male Glendinning, but the duplicate one reflected to him in the mirror" (p. 8). When he goes at Lucy's request to bring back a portfolio from her chamber, a mirror causes him momentary but intense distress: "Now, crossing the magic silence of the empty chamber, he caught the snow-white bed reflected in the toilet-glass. This rooted him. For one swift instant, he seemed to see in that one glance the two separate beds—the one real and the reflected one—and an unbidden, most miserable presentiment thereupon stole into him" (p. 39). He does not understand the reason for this brief misery, but a mirror occasions it. Shortly before opening Isabel's letter, he again glances into a mirror, again with unpleasant results. He "started at a figure in the opposite mirror. It bore the outline of Pierre, but now strangely filled with features transformed, and unfamiliar to him; feverish eagerness, fear, and nameless forebodings of ill! He threw himself into a chair, and for a time vainly struggled with the incomprehensible power that possessed him" (p. 62). After his decision to accept Isabel has been made, he reevaluates his mother in unfavorable terms, thinking that she has been using him for a mirror: "In me she thinks she seeth her own curled and haughty beauty; before my glass she stands,—pride's priestess—and to her mirrored image, not to me, she offers up her offerings of kisses" (p. 90). Since mirrors cause him great discomfort, he detests the thought of being used as one.

Wherever references to mirrors occur in connection with Pierre, they consistently are part of an unfavorable context. During the anxious time before he first visits Isabel, a lake and its surroundings project the gloom he feels within him. It is a "wet and misty eve." The "scattered, shivering pasture elms" appear to be "standing in a world inhospitable, yet rooted by inscrutable sense of duty to their place." In the midst of this oppressive scene is the lake, "one sheet of blankness and of dumbness" that reflects but the "duplicate, stirless sky above" (p. 109). Since he repeatedly is depressed or shocked by mirrors, Pierre finally avoids them entirely: "For dreading some insupportably dark revealments in his glass, he had of late wholly abstained from appealing to it" (p. 347).

A mirror is abhorrent to Pierre because it is a metaphor for that mode of perception in opposition to his own. The difference between the two is that the one is that way of seeing practiced by a person whose conviction is that his own inner being is endlessly complex, fascinating, and dangerous if not properly understood and managed, whereas the other is that practiced by a person who is less interested in understanding his own motivations and his inner voices than he is in uncovering transcendental truths outside himself. Melville felt that the latter led away from self-knowledge, the indispensable factor of survival. Nothing, for Melville, is more challenging than his own inner self. A mirror to such a person would not be offensive or shocking because *all* of life's surfaces would in a sense be mirrors. Even great books are mirrors. Pierre erroneously considers them otherwise: "He did not see, that even when thus combined, all [great books were] . . . but one small mite, compared to the latent infiniteness and inexhaustibility in himself; that all the great books in the world are but the mutilated shadowings-forth of invisible and eternally unembodied images in the soul; so that they are but the mirrors, distortedly reflecting to us our own things; and never mind what the mirror may be, if we would see the object, we must look at the object itself, and not at its reflection" (p. 284).

The real object is within, and all things without, including books, but mirror that inner self, which therefore is Melville's proper study—himself. It should be, he implies, the territory in which all men explore the unknown. The fascination and awe with which he regards his varied inner terrain are suggested in one of the most revealing passages in *Pierre*:

> But, as to the resolute traveler in Switzerland, the Alps do never in one wide and comprehensive sweep, instantaneously reveal their full awfulness of amplitude—their overawing extent of peak crowded on peak, and spur sloping on spur, and chain jammed behind chain, and all their wonderful battalionings of might; so hath heaven wisely ordained, that on first entering into the Switzerland of his soul, man shall not at once perceive its tremendous immensity; lest illy prepared for such an encounter, his spirit should sink and perish on the lowermost snows. Only by judicious degrees, appointed of God, does man come at last to gain his Mont Blanc and take an overtopping view of these Alps. (p. 284)

But even then the full self is not known, for less than "the tithe" has been shown to him. "Far over the invisible Atlantic, the Rocky Mountains and the Andes are yet unbeheld" (p. 284). It is a frightening and dangerous world, full of unsuspected perils. To be lost in that vast inner realm, to be "fairly afloat" without knowledge of where one is or what lies beyond, "better might one be pushed off into the material spaces beyond the uttermost orbit of our sun" (p. 284). Therefore self-knowledge is the one imperative.

In Pierre, as in Ahab, Melville has created a character much like himself but drastically different in not, above all, attempting to gain, as Melville did, more and more knowledge of his inner world. "Pierre, though strangely and very newly alive to many before unregarded wonders in the general world," still persists in looking outward for truth rather than inward. He does not, perhaps cannot, see the world as a mere mirror. He has not fished internally, "for who dreams to find fish in a well?" His fishing is in the external world: "The running stream of the outer world, there doubtless," he thinks, "swim the golden perch and the pickerel" (p. 284). The water image here is still another suggestion of the two modes of perception. Pierre sees the stream as cover for the choicest prizes of his quest—the golden perch and the pickerel. Melville perceives the stream as a reflection of his inner well—and *there* are the truly great fish.

Pierre is exceptional; his terrain of self is complex, awe-inspiring, and perilous. Finally it is his ignorance of that inner realm that destroys him because it is ultimately the only real and meaningful world. He has been trying to cope with the wrong world. The outer world is but emptiness. In what is probably one of the most often misinterpreted passages in the novel, Melville *contrasts,* rather than compares as similar, the outer world in which we live and act with the internal country which he has previously described as full and varied. Externality, he says, is like an "old mummy" that "lies buried in cloth on cloth." Even after we spend a lifetime unwrapping it, we find nothing there but a dried corpse. There is no lasting reward for digging deeper and deeper into anything external to ourselves, but such is Pierre's activity. "Because Pierre began to see through the first superficiality of the world," his having removed the outer wrapping of the mummy, "he fondly weens he has come to the unlayered substance." But there is no such real substance to be found externally. "Far as any geologist has yet gone down into the world, it is found to consist of nothing but surface stratified on surface. To its axis, the world being nothing but superinduced superficies. By vast pains we mine into the pyramid; by horrible gropings we come to the central room; with joy we espy the sarcophagus; but we lift the lid—and no body is there!" (p. 285). Melville is not denying here the existence of meaning and substance in life as many readers suppose. He is denying that they can be found by what he calls in *Billy Budd* "knowledge of the world." He sees as ultimately futile any search for truth that is pursued in the world rather than in the inner self of the individual quester. The exclamation that ends the passage quoted above has done much to mislead readers. In concluding his comment on the empty sarcophagus within the pyramid—which represents the world as opposed to the internal realm—he exclaims: "Appallingly vacant as vast is the soul of a man!" (p. 285). The entire context for this remark demands that we read it not as "the soul of a man is appallingly vacant as it is vast." Such a reading goes diametrically in opposition to the consistent argument that precedes the remark since Melville has just finished showing that the world is emptiness and the inner being fullness. Therefore, what Melville actually seems to mean is that the world is as vacant in its confined essence as the soul is vast.[38]

Because they misunderstood in which of these two places was to be found the only real meaning, those who ironically devoted themselves to seeing and to reading appearances, the physiognomists of the world, Melville counted as the truly blind. Pierre, who actually begins to have severe troubles with his eyes near the end of the novel, is to be numbered among them. By that time it is clear how erroneous his vision has been from the beginning. Physiognomists were prone not only to read into a person's character something which really was not there but also to miss traits that were present. Struck with Lucy's beauty of face and modesty of behavior, Pierre attributes to her qualities that she does not possess. He sees her as angelic, as the fragile exemplar of all that is pure. She is for him an incarnation of the spirit. To the end, Lucy remains in his sight "transparently immaculate, without shadow of flaw or vein" (p. 317). No one, of course, could be as flawless as Pierre makes Lucy in his blind idealization of her. She is a flesh-and-blood woman, imperfect by nature of her flesh. How little Pierre really knows her is indicated by his perplexity when she joins him in New York. Though he has known her for a long time, her action did not "fail to amaze him." At the same time that he was giving her too much credit, he was giving her too little. By seeing her as pure as a lamb, she becomes to his mind weak as a lamb. Thus any display of womanly strength in her leaves him baffled.

Pierre's reading of Isabel involves him in errors of the same nature: because of his own ill-understood motives, he sees in her more than is there and at the same time less. He reads her as an embodiment of the profoundest mysteries, as a noble victim of the world's deepest injustices, as patience and unselfishness personified. Whatever the actual facts of her past, she proves during the

---

38. Edgar A. Dryden's reading of this passage is representative of those who feel that Melville is describing the soul as empty: "Both soul and world consist of 'surface stratified on surface,' and the 'unlayered substance' in each case is emptiness—infinite, uncreated nothingness." *Melville's Thematics of Form: The Great Art of Telling the Truth* (Baltimore: Johns Hopkins University Press, 1968), p. 120.

course of the novel that Pierre's early estimate of her is distorted in her favor. He failed to see her jealousy, her possessiveness, her mental instability. He does not even consider the possibility that she was as a child confined to an asylum because she was emotionally disturbed. Late in the novel, she warns him that she carries a deadly poison in a vial around her neck, and she threatens to commit suicide if he ever changes toward her. In fact, she does attempt suicide by trying to jump into the water when she, Lucy, and Pierre take their excursion near the end. Pierre misinterprets a lonely, suicidal girl who is looking leechlike for a person to attach herself to as a warm and virtuous soul-mate incapable of duplicity. The young enthusiast, who intuitively seemed to hear the whispered words of John Caspar Lavater that "all the charms of virtue shall actuate the man who examines physiognomically," by doing just that (examining physiognomically) actually becomes "the fool of Virtue" (p. 358).

Perhaps the clearest evidence of this is his misperception of his father first as a kind of deity then as a deceptive rake. The chair portrait is actually a mirror reflection of Pierre himself. He is his father's son: he inherited all of his sire's proclivities, including a faith in the prinicples set out in "the wonderful work of Physiognomy" that Aunt Dorothea describes. But Melville did not write *Pierre* merely to expose the fallacies of Lavater's *Essays on Physiognomy*. Lavater, his famous book, and his followers constituted for Melville a synecdoche, a segment of that vast body of misperceivers of the world, which he centers on to represent the whole class. They were consistently on the wrong track, Melville believed, because they were seeking truth in the wrong realm. He was convinced that it lay within, not without, and he never strayed far away from a concern with what was going on inside himself. This obsession led him to view all of external reality not as a mask covering ultimate truth but as just a reflection of his vast inner world. It also made him aware of his tendency to interpret other people's character in terms of his private needs and emotional states, although he frequently had to remind himself that he had this characteristic.

Since the people around him often represented to him manifestations of his inner being, he tended to create characters in his fiction that were projections of sides of himself or of fundamental qualities in a central character or both. Like *Moby-Dick, Pierre* is such a work; its nature as a work of art derived from Melville's nonphysiognomical perception of the world as mirror. The cast of supporting characters in *Pierre* play two parts, one as incarnation of the central character's interior drives and one as participants in the realistic level of the plot.[39] Isabel, for example, is on the latter level a disturbed young woman who may be Pierre's half sister, but she is also clearly something that has been dredged up from within Pierre, some "before unexperienced and wholly inexplicable element" (p. 88). At one point Melville writes that Pierre "almost could have prayed Isabel back into the wonder-world from which she had so slidingly emerged" (p. 129). From *Moby-Dick* we know that the "wonder-world" is the inner realm of self. Lucy, Glen Stanly, and others perform a similar double function. Melville as a writer of fiction was thus a kind of reverse-physiognomist. He believed that what one saw in the face of another revealed truth about the viewer.[40] If Lucy and Isabel do not seem adequately lifelike for characters in a novel, if their thoughts and motivations appear either somewhat obscure or simplistic, if their human complexity is insufficiently realized, it is because they are

39. Setting serves similar functions. The wild and unexplored inner self of Pierre, now in upheaval, is suggested by the description of a landscape: "On both sides, in the remoter distance, and also far beyond the mild lake's further shore, rose the long, mysterious mountain masses; shaggy with pines and hemlocks, mystical with nameless, vapory exhalations, and in that dim air black with dread and gloom. At their base, profoundest forests lay entranced, and from their far owl-haunted depths of caves and rotted leaves, and unused and unregarded inland overgrowth of decaying wood—for smallest sticks of which, in other climes many a pauper was that moment perishing; from out the infinite inhumanities of those profoundest forests, came a moaning, muttering, roaring, intermitted, changeful sound: rain-shakings of the palsied trees, slidings of rocks undermined, final crashings of long-riven boughs, and devilish gibberish of the forest-ghosts" (pp. 109–10). The city similarly projects Pierre. See James Polk, "Melville and the Idea of the City," *University of Toronto Quarterly* 41 (1972): 277–92.

40. In his appreciative article, E. L. Grant Watson commented that Melville "is as courageous an explorer into the secrets of the soul as any man who has ever written." This is probably true but the territory he explored most was just one soul—his own. "Melville's *Pierre,*" *New England Quarterly,* 3 (1930): 208.

less interesting to Melville in their one role as realistic characters than they are in their other as projections of certain sides of Pierre. Once their second, and more fundamental, role is understood, however, once the aspects of Pierre's inner self are discovered, all the characters take on added dimensions, and the depth of Melville's art is revealed.

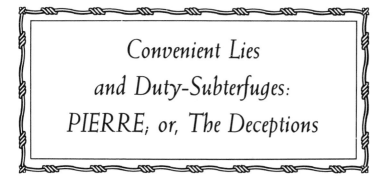

Convenient Lies
and Duty-Subterfuges:
PIERRE; or, The Deceptions

Chapter 7

D uring those halcyon days at his ancestral estate of Saddle-
Meadows, Pierre Glendinning is asked by the Urquhartian
Club for the Immediate Extension of the Limits of all Knowledge,
both Human and Divine to give a lecture on the topic of human
destiny. The Chairman of the Committee on Lectures assures him
that the Club will take excellent care of him and make the town of
Zadockprattsville highly agreeable to him, the distinguished author of the poem "The Tropical Summer." Melville recounts this
episode in a tone of humorous irony that characterizes the entire
chapter on "Young America in Literature," where he attacks the
absurdity and shallowness of dilettantish writers, lecturers, and all
those who wax enthusiastic at "Lyceums, Young Men's Associations, and other Literary and Scientific Societies" (p. 251). Though
lightly treated, this is one of the most suggestive occurrences in the
novel, for the subject Pierre is asked to lecture on, destiny or fate,
occupies, as it does in *Moby-Dick,* a central position.

Whatever else may be ambiguous, it is clear that fate is against
Pierre. In the early pages of the novel, Melville hints that it is
Pierre's destiny to be brought down from his "noble pedestal" and

unhappily to lose his "fine footing." Twice within two pages, Melville ominously prophesies: "we shall see if Fate hath not just a little bit of a small word or two to say in this world" (p. 12). As problems mount, Melville occasionally pauses to philosophize about the role of fate in Pierre's life: "Eternally inexorable and unconcerned is Fate, a mere heartless trader in men's joys and woes" (p. 105). Pierre becomes involved in "such an inextricable twist of Fate, that the three dextrous maids themselves could hardly disentangle him" (p. 175). Melville mentions the three goddesses of destiny again later when he describes Pierre's presentiment about his madness and destruction: "How then shall you escape the fateful conclusion, that you are helplessly held in the six hands of the Sisters?" (p. 287).

In *Moby-Dick*, Ishmael argues that life is controlled by a combination of free will, fate, and chance. Ahab, however, sees himself as fate's lieutenant, his course set on iron rails. Pierre appears similarly obsessed with the force of fate in life, and he receives strong support from Isabel. Her story is pervaded with references to fate. She says that though she is persuaded that fate dispenses its "own secrets" and in its "own good time," she believes "that in some cases Fate drops us one little hint . . . so that we of ourselves may come to the grand secret in reserve" (p. 152). Clear evidence that Isabel is Pierre's half sister is lacking; she bases her case upon "hints." To the dispassionate and logical mind, her claim is flimsy, but it rings true to Pierre because he yearns for a sister and because it is made in the name of fate, a concept strongly appealing to him. She tells him that when he walked into the room where she and others were sewing, "Fate was in that moment" (p. 158). The more she stresses this conclusion, the more Pierre feels compelled to accept her. "But Fate will be Fate," she tells him, "and it was fated" (p. 159).

Isabel's comment that "Fate will be Fate" is similar to Melville's statement later in the novel that "the sea is the sea": though Pierre knows he is drowning in it, he cannot alter his fate (p. 303). He believes that he has been victimized by some overwhelming and inexplicable external force, that he has become "the fool of Fate" (p. 358). In his early trouble, he wishes that "Fate had made him a blacksmith, and not a gentleman, a Glendinning, and a genius" (p. 260). Pierre's attitude toward fate is symptomatic of the self-deception that ultimately brings on his destruction. Thus it is a mistake to take his conviction about fate as a position Melville as narrator is assuming. Melville shows in the novel that fate is, indeed, inexorable and irresistible, but it is in what makes up fate that he reveals Pierre's self-deception. Fate is not principally an external force but an internal one. Pierre could not know this because of his inherent lack of self-knowledge, but had he been able to do so, he could have avoided his madness and youthful death. Over and over throughout the novel, Melville plays off Pierre's assumption that fate is an ambiguous external ruler of our lives against the poignant truth that Pierre is his own fate, that the unconscious aspects of self move him toward his destruction. Like Ahab, he is a victim of self. He realizes at the end that he has made hasty decisions and that he has seen life in a deceptive light, but he does not truly know himself even then.

When Melville writes that our lives do not depend on ourselves but on fate, he seems to be giving credence to Pierre's conviction that fate is external. Much that we do, he says, "illustrates the necessitarian dependence of our lives, and their subordination, not to ourselves, but to Fate" (p. 276). The context of this sentence, however, makes it clear that he is contrasting conscious motivations ("ourselves") with unconscious ones ("Fate") and stressing the dominant power of the latter. "So in youth," he says, "do we unconsciously act" in accordance with the deepest aspects of character rather than from consciously articulated motivations, a fact that proves our dependence upon these internal forces that constitute our fate. The second time Melville predicts that the story of Pierre will show that fate has "a word or two to say in this world," he adds: "we shall see whether this wee scrap of latinity be very far out of the way—*Nemo contra Deum nisi Deus ipse*" (p. 14). The source for this Latin proverb is Goethe's autobiography, which Melville purchased in 1849 and which, as we have seen, supplied him with information about Lavater.[1] In the passage

1. Henry A. Murray points out the source in his notes to the Hendricks House edition of *Pierre* (New York, 1949), pp. 437–38.

where Goethe quotes the proverb, he is speaking not of God but of exceptional men, those of extraordinary stature. The element that gives them power and raises them above the common, Goethe calls "the Demonical." It is "a power which, if it be not opposed to the moral order of the world, nevertheless does often so cross it that one may be regarded as the warp, and the other as the woof."[2] Despite his temperamental differences with Goethe, Melville must have been struck with this fascinating analysis of the extraordinary person, for it parallels in several ways his own concept of "the choice hidden handful of the Divine Inert." Goethe observes that "such persons are not always the most eminent men, either morally or intellectually," but "a tremendous energy seems to be seated in them, and they exercise a wonderful power." Though "the more enlightened portion of mankind" may point to them as "deceived if not deceivers," they plot their own courses and go right ahead. "Seldom if ever do the great men of an age find their equals among their contemporaries." Only a tremendous force, explains Goethe, can overcome them, "and it is from observation of this fact that the strange, but most striking, proverb must have risen: *Nemo contra Deum nisi Deus ipse.*"[3]

Thus in the context of his discussion of extraordinary men, Goethe seems to be saying that no one overcomes a godlike being but that being himself just as "No one goes against God but God Himself." It is with this thought of a strong and unusual man containing within himself his own destiny that Melville follows up his comment on Pierre and fate with the Latin proverb that he read in Goethe's autobiography. What is within Pierre, far more than what is without, creates his particular destiny, though he himself never fully understands this. Consequently, when he refers to "the uttermost bounds and possibilities of Fate" (p. 113), feels that "the thews of a Titan were forestallingly cut by the scissors of Fate" (p. 339), goes out to meet his "fate" in the person of Glen Stanly, or thinks of himself as a "Fool of Fate," a sharp and

2. *The Auto-Biography of Goethe, Truth and Poetry: From My Own Life,* trans. John Oxenford and A. J. W. Morrison, 2 vols. (London: Bohn, 1848–49), 2:158.

3. Ibid., p. 159.

powerful irony results, for those uttermost bounds are within himself, as are the terrible scissors. Saying that he is the fool of fate, therefore, is merely another way of saying that he is the fool of himself. Significantly, he feels inadequate to deliver a lecture to the club in Zadockprattsville on the subject of human destiny and refuses the invitation. Fate is one of several areas where this vigorous and extraordinary young genius abides in blindness.

The irony of Pierre's view of fate is heightened by Melville's several allusions to the three sisters of fate, personifications in classical myth of the external forces of human destiny. Pierre's view of fate is, indeed, close to that expressed in Greek mythology, but the personifications of fateful forces in his own life are not Clotho, Lachesis, and Atropos but Mary, Lucy, and Isabel, and they are manifestations not of external governing powers but of dominant aspects of his own inner being, the forces *within* that decide his fate. Thus the women who influence Pierre's character and actions so deeply—his mother, his fiancée, and his would-be half sister—may recall the Sisters of Destiny, but they are among other things suggestions of what is within him.[4]

One of the essential functions of the early pages of the novel is to reveal in Pierre, even before the appearance of one claiming to be his half sister and the resultant upheaval in his life, strong sides of his character that in interacting largely create his fate. The first is pride. He is proud of his noble ancestry, of his long and distinguished family history. He is proud of his mother. In fact, "all the associations of Saddle-Meadows were full of pride to Pierre" (p. 6). The "glow of family pride" (p. 32) is frequently on his face. With one so fortunately endowed, it would seem almost perverse if he were not proud; therefore, in this respect he does not appear extreme in the early part of the novel as Melville recounts the pleasure he takes in being a Glendinning. It is through the characterization of his mother that Melville hints at what will later be seen in Pierre as an Ahab-like haughtiness, a pride of immense proportion that is not based so much on family

4. Richard Chase makes fundamentally the same point: "The characters from whom Pierre gradually separates himself represent emotive qualities in himself." *Herman Melville: A Critical Study* (New York: Macmillan, 1949), p. 121.

status as on the unshakable conviction of personal superiority. Mary Glendinning's scorn of the commonplace, disgust with the morally and spiritually weak, and pleasure in her own independence and superiority project a side of Pierre present but dormant in the early section. Pierre comes to recognize that pride is his mother's all-consuming emotion, but he does not see that she is a manifestation of what is within himself. When she is injured and insulted by Pierre's violation of what she considers her parental right, she becomes a vengeful, raving denouncer of the world and ends in madness, precisely the fate of Pierre. He realizes that his mother would never accept Isabel but would forever consider her an enemy: "High-up, and towering, and all-forbidding before Pierre grew the before unthought of wonderful edifice of his mother's immense pride;—her pride of birth, her pride of affluence, her pride of purity" (p. 89). She is "pride's priestess—and to her mirrored image, not to me, she offers up her offerings of kisses" (p. 90). What Pierre fails to see is that in a sense she is *his* mirrored image.

The second fundamental characteristic of the Pierre of Saddle-Meadows days, stressed but, again, somewhat disguised as to its full dimensions in the early pages, is his vigorous animal nature and, in particular, his strong appetites. He bounds through the opening section of the novel radiating robustness:

> But when we consider that though Pierre's hands were small, and his ruffles white, yet his arm was by no means dainty, and his complexion inclined to brown; and that he generally rose with the sun, and could not sleep without riding his twenty, or walking his twelve miles a day, or felling a fair-sized hemlock in the forest, or boxing, or fencing, or boating, or performing some other gymnastical feat; when we consider these athletic habitudes of Pierre, and the great fullness of brawn and muscle they built round about him; all of which manly brawn and muscle, three times a day loudly clamored for attention; we shall very soon perceive that to have a bountiful appetite, was not only no vulgar reproach, but a right royal grace and honor to Pierre; attesting him a man and a gentleman; for a thoroughly developed gentleman is always robust and healthy; and Robustness and Health are great trenchermen. (pp. 16–17)

His love of food is obvious in the scene with his mother at the breakfast table. "He always had an excellent appetite," Melville writes, "and especially for his breakfast." The point of Melville's mentioning twice that Pierre's having been born and raised in the country is deeply tied up with his fate is to stress his strong physical development, for the vast and beautiful estate of his ancestors provided him with the greenest pasture in which a young stallion can reach vigorous maturity: Nature "blew her wind-clarion from the blue hills, and Pierre neighed out . . . as at the trumpet-blast, a war-horse paws himself into a lyric of foam" (p. 14). But on the heels of this statement and the comment that "the country was a glorious benediction to young Pierre," Melville suggestively follows up with his ominous prediction about fate having "a bit of a word or two to say" and with the proverb, "*Nemo contra Deum nisi Deus ipse.*"

Pierre's much-emphasized youth, his vigorous animal nature (like that of a high-spirited horse with which he is compared), and his appetites are thus components of his fate. In the opening pages his great appetite for food is stressed; that he has developed a strong physical appetite of another kind—a sexual appetite—comes out later, forcing itself to the surface. He will not allow himself to think with lustful anticipation of a normal sexual relationship with Lucy. "*I* to wed this heavenly fleece?" he remarks. "Methinks one husbandly embrace would break her airy zone. . . . I am of heavy earth, and she of airy light. By heaven, but marriage is an impious thing!" (p. 58). Instead of regarding the sexual aspect of marriage as a natural fulfillment of a natural appetite, he considers it a violation and is deeply saddened by the thought of it. "I am Pluto stealing Proserpine," he gravely tells himself, "and every accepted lover is" (p. 59). Lodged within this idealistic and modest young man are powerful drives, one showing itself at Saddle-Meadows merely as an understandable and justified pride in family heritage, the other manifesting itself during this period as boyish "Robustness and Health," those "great trenchermen."

A third dominant force within Pierre is also early in the foreground, and like the other two this fateful quality is disguised as a simple virtue, more amusing and harmless than deep and dangerous. In him is a profound hunger for God, but in the introductory analysis of his background and character, it is treated as a shallow emotion, a kind of necessary accouterment for all young gentlemen of fine breeding passed on from generation to generation: "It had been a maxim with the father of Pierre, that all gentlemanhood was vain; all claims to it preposterous and absurd, unless the primeval gentleness and golden humanities of religion had been so thoroughly wrought into the complete texture of the character, that he who pronounced himself gentleman, could also rightfully assume the meek, but kingly style of Christian" (p. 6). Consequently, "at the age of sixteen, Pierre partook with his mother of the Holy Sacraments" and became "girded with Religion's silken sash" (p. 7).

That Pierre's religious impulse is deeper than that of a mere superimposed cultural style, however, is evident from his early worship of his father, who in Pierre's young mind is confused with God.[5] His mother fosters this confusion when she speaks of her late husband and God in such a way as to fuse them in Pierre's mind: "God bless you, my dear son!—always think of *him* and you can never err; yes, always think of your dear perfect father, Pierre" (p. 19, italics mine). Until he hears Isabel's story, he thinks of his father with such reverence as to reveal his need for spiritual fulfillment. In his heart he creates "a shrine" to which he goes "by many tableted steps of remembrance" and "around which" he hangs "fresh wreaths of a sweet and holy affection." And "in this shrine, in this niche of this pillar, stood the perfect marble form of his departed father; without blemish, unclouded, snow-white, and serene." Pierre goes to the shrine and pours out "the fullness of all young life's most reverential thoughts and beliefs. Not to God had Pierre ever gone in his heart, unless by ascending the steps of that shrine, and so making it the vestibule of his abstractest religion" (p. 68).

5. "His father," writes E. L. Grant Watson, "is in the image of God, and as God he had known him as the original source." "Melville's *Pierre*," *New England Quarterly* 3 (1930): 203. George C. Homans remarks that "Pierre's father . . . is the Deity." "The Dark Angel: The Tragedy of Herman Melville," *New England Quarterly* 5 (1932): 727. For similar comments, see Willard Thorp, ed., *Herman Melville, Representative Selections* (New York: American Book Co., 1938), p. lxxx, and Chase, pp. 106–7.

Pierre is carried swiftly to his destiny by the workings of these three inexorable drives—a need to preserve intact his prideful individuality, strong human urges, and strong religious yearnings. In the early section of the book, they can all be detected but only faintly because the crisis that is to rush them to the fore and bring them into conflict has not yet occurred and because Melville's ironic method somewhat obscures them. With perverse artistry, Melville seems to have been experimenting with irony in a curious attempt to discover its absolute bounds. In his analysis of Pierre's character in this first section of the novel, he appears to have come close to those limits, beyond which there is no communication. Irony here functions not only to reveal and enlighten but, as an aspect of the pervasive theme of deception, to cover up and mislead. For example, Melville's obvious irony in his treatment of Pierre as a rather foolish young romantic leads one in the direction of believing the early section a satire on current bestselling novels of no substance. But that is merely the top level of irony, and it amounts to a red herring. Many readers look no further but follow its trail as it leads away from the brilliant and complex network of irony that remains.

Sustained irony results not only from the fact that Pierre views fate as an external force while it is largely internal—his deep inner drives charting his destiny—but also from the fact that he perceives ambiguity to be the nature of externality while in truth it arises more from his inability to recognize his own profoundest impulses. He is ever ready to attribute what happens to him to universal fate and what he does not understand to universal ambiguity. Melville experienced the same temptation frequently in his personal life, and he wrote *Pierre* partly to keep his own thinking straight. Indeed, he presents Pierre's views with such compelling arguments that he has perpetrated the same deception upon countless readers that Pierre did upon himself. In much writing about the novel, it is clear that critics have taken Pierre's concept of ambiguity to be Melville's as well.[6] The confusion is under-

6. According to William Braswell, the novel's basic subject is the "'unravelable inscrutableness' of life." "The Satirical Temper of Melville's *Pierre*," *American Literature* 7 (1936): 436. In "Imagery, Myth, and Melville's *Pierre*,"

standable, for the book is shot through with uncertainties of all sorts. What was Pierre's father actually like? What is the truth of Isabel's past? Is she really Pierre's half sister? Did Pierre's father sit for the portrait that turns up in a gallery near the end of the novel? Do Pierre and Isabel literally commit incest? Contributing to the overall impression of ambiguity are such questions involving character and plot, questions that an ostensibly omniscient narrator chooses not to answer directly or clearly.

In addition to leaving certain key answers shadowy, Melville stresses with frequency Pierre's interpretation of events, people, and surroundings as mysterious. That the book is to emphasize strongly the subject of mystery is suggested in the very first paragraph where Melville describes the setting for Pierre's initial appearance: "All Nature, as if suddenly become conscious of her own profound mystery, and feeling no refuge from it but silence, sinks into this wonderful and indescribable repose" (p. 3). One of the things Pierre finds most attractive in the chair portrait of his father is its air of mystery, even though at times it makes him uncomfortable. In fact, the "essence" of his young sense of "romance" is "that very mystery" (p. 85). Had he not been so disposed, the face of Isabel as it appeared to him in the sewing room and later in his imagination might not have been so fascinating. He sees her as a "Mysterious girl" with "eyes of mournful mystery," and he is drawn toward her face partly because he finds it "inexplicable" (p. 41).

Though some answers do come to Pierre, they create for him new and even deeper ambiguities. After he reads Isabel's letter, he sees "all preceding ambiguities, all mysteries ripped open as if with a keen sword," but "on all sides, the physical world of solid objects now slidingly displaced itself from around him" (p. 85). With an inherent affinity for the mysterious, he had, before Isabel's appearance, been disappointed that the "visible world" had

---

American Literature 26 (1955), James Kissane states that "the ambiguity of truth itself" is "the theme of the novel" (p. 569). See also Mario L. D'Avanzo, "*Pierre* and the Wisdom of Keats's Melancholy," *Melville Society Extracts*, no. 16 (1973): 6; and Gerard M. Sweeney, *Melville's Use of Classical Mythology* (Amsterdam: Rodopi, 1975), p. 117.

"seemed but too common and prosaic to him; and but too intelligible," but now he feels "that all the world, and every misconceivedly common and prosaic thing in it" is "steeped a million fathoms in a mysteriousness wholly hopeless of solution" (p. 128). In his first interview with Isabel, he finds himself "entranced, lost, as one wandering bedazzled and amazed among innumerable dancing lights." To the "large-eyed girl of Mystery," he cries "Girl of all-bewildering mystery! . . . Speak to me." She does so with the melodious words:

> Mystery! Mystery!
> Mystery of Isabel!
> Mystery! Mystery!
> Isabel and Mystery!
> (p. 126)

As the second and fourth lines suggest, she is not only mysterious to Pierre; she has now become inextricably linked with his perception of mystery in general. For Pierre, to think of Isabel is to be engulfed in ambiguities and vice versa.

Fate and mystery are inseparable metaphysical companions in the Pierre who hears Isabel's account of her past. He feels a quick receptivity for her belief that fate brought her to him; and her mysterious behavior together with her frequent references to mystery so effectively strike the target in him that he is as "bewitched" and "enchanted" as if he were "caught and fast bound in some necromancer's garden" (p. 128). Both his concept of fate as a transcendental force and his affinity for mystery are by-products of his instinctive religious impulse. Since "he saw that human life doth truly come from that, which all men are agreed to call by the name of *God*," he is ready to believe that any aspect of life "partakes of the unravelable inscrutableness of God" (p. 141). Therefore, to probe skeptically into the mysteries of Isabel's past would be to Pierre like questioning the eternal mysteries of God. "In her life there was an unraveled plot; and he felt that unraveled it would eternally remain to him. No slightest hope or dream had he, that what was dark and mournful in her would ever be cleared up into some coming atmosphere of light and mirth" (p. 141). He will have it no other way. He does not truly *wish* to understand her fully because to do so would be to him like simplifying God. His respect for mystery, springing as it does from his religious impulse, prevents him from doubting and questioning: he "renounced all thought of ever having Isabel's dark-lantern illuminated to him. Her light was lidded, and the lid was locked" (p. 141).

Psychologically, a proclivity for seeing ambiguity wherever one looks is similar to an acute sensitivity to evil in the world. Both predilections can easily become preoccupations once an episode steeped in suggestions of one or the other jolts the psyche. Thus, after Pierre hears Isabel's mystery-saturated tale, he begins "to see mysteries interpierced with mysteries, and mysteries eluding mysteries," and he begins "to seem to see the mere imaginariness of the so supposed solidest principle of human association" (p. 142). In their second interview, Isabel repeats her performance of the chanted "Mystery! Mystery," and Pierre is lost in a "haze of ambiguities" (pp. 150–51). He does, however, ask a few questions about Isabel's strange guitar to which she responds in a manner perfectly calculated to appeal to his reverence for mystery. She indicates that she prefers not to seek definite answers or even to surmise: "Oh, Pierre, better, a million times, and far sweeter are mysteries than surmises: though the mystery be unfathomable, it is still the unfathomableness of fullness; but the surmise, that is but shallow and unmeaning emptiness" (p. 153). As Pierre looks out from his low dungeon at the end, he is still unable to understand the full meaning of what has happened to him. "It is ambiguous still," he remarks shortly before taking his life.

While Pierre believes that he is probing deeper and deeper into external reality and encountering its true nature—ambiguity— he is actually experiencing the bafflement that results from his incomprehension of inner forces. As Melville describes Pierre's perception of mystery, he is frequently careful to underscore the subjectivity of the experience. Pierre feels as he does about Isabel's face (as it appears to him in his imagination) because of what is within him and not because of some inherent quality in the face itself: "And so much the more that it was so subterranean in him, so much the more did he feel its weird inscrutableness" (pp. 48–49). Reality is within, not without, Melville warns as he continues to explain why Pierre found the image of Isabel compelling: "But his profound curiosity and interest in the matter—strange as it may seem—did not so much appear to be embodied in the mournful person of the olive girl" as in something within "his own soul." Within Pierre, "*there,*" Melville writes, "lurked the subtler secret." Then Melville reveals one of his most fundamental beliefs about the self as center and seat of truth and reality with externality as secondary and subordinate: "From without, no wonderful effect is wrought within ourselves, unless some interior, responding wonder meets it. That the starry vault shall surcharge the heart with all rapturous marvelings, is only because we ourselves are greater miracles, and superber trophies than all the stars in universal space" (p. 51). Though Pierre intuitively realizes that there is a "strange integral feeling" within him, and that Isabel's face has evoked a profound spell out of proportion with the usual expectation, the specific internal source of his response remains unknown to him. Later he again glimpses the complexity of his inner world, but he cannot clearly identify its components: "Is it possible," he questions, that "I and all mankind, beneath our garbs of common-placeness, conceal enigmas that the stars themselves, and perhaps the highest seraphim can not resolve?" (pp. 138–39).

What these components of Pierre's internal makeup are that restlessly disturb his outer peace is clear as Melville gives insights that Pierre does not share. Leading Pierre to his perception of universal ambiguity is the combination on the one hand of "enthusiastic Truth, and Earnestness," the desire to transcend oneself for a higher reality, and on the other hand of "Independence," the desire to break all ties that threaten to enslave one's individuality. A mind "fitted by nature" with these strong opposing sides, Melville writes, tends to see "all objects . . . in a dubious, uncertain, and refracting light" (p. 165). Only by identifying, giving recognition to, and then coping with these fiery armies within can destructive war be avoided. Like Ahab, however, Pierre feels the pain of battle but fails to see through the smoke raised by war just who the combatants are or what positions they occupy. His inner turmoil is responsible for his inability to see the point of the pamphlet he finds on his way to the city: "The more he read and re-read, the more his interest deepened, but still the more likewise did his failure to comprehend the writer increase. He seemed somehow to derive some general vague inkling concerning it, but the central conceit refused to become clear to him" (p. 209). To understand Plinlimmon's reasoning would be for Pierre to define his own problem, which he is not ready to confront: "For in this case, to comprehend, is himself to condemn himself" (p. 209).

Though often considered such, *Pierre* is not a book about life's maddening ambiguities. It depicts instead Pierre's misconception as to the source of ambiguity. The single overriding theme of the novel is deception. Pierre's perception of ambiguity as universal is an unconscious subterfuge functioning to prevent self-understanding. Melville clearly makes the connection between ambiguity and deception when he is discussing the nature of a smile: "a smile is the chosen vehicle for all ambiguities, Pierre. When we would deceive we smile; when we are hatching any nice little artifice, Pierre; only just a little gratifying our own sweet little appetites, Pierre; then watch us, and out comes the odd little smile" (p. 84). The subtitle of *Pierre* is *The Ambiguities,* but in view of Melville's treatment of the subject throughout the book, he means *The Deceptions.* Not only is Pierre involved in self-deception, but characters deceive each other aboundingly. Pierre deceives Lucy, his mother, and the world when he pretends to be married to Isabel, who may well be engaged in deception herself when she claims Pierre as her half brother. Pierre's father was possibly a deceiver. Glen Stanly deceives Pierre. And so forth. Melville's interest in physiognomy (and his wide-ranging treatment of this subject with its many ramifications) is closely related to the overall theme of deception. One of the most ironic events in the novel occurs when Pierre prays that he may be above the "convenient lies and duty-subterfuges" commonly a part of the world (p. 107), ironic because the deception that he hates is the very essence of his character.

To understand that character more fully (and the essential role that deception plays in it), it is necessary to examine closely each of the three phases that Pierre goes through. "Look for no invariableness in Pierre," Melville warns, "Nor does any canting showman here stand by to announce his phases as he revolves. Catch his phases as your insight may" (p. 337). Pierre's three distinct stages create the basic structure of the novel. Because there are only two general settings in the story—the country and the city—and because approximately half of the total pages is devoted to events that take place in each, critics have as a rule considered the structure of the novel to consist of only two parts, Pierre in the Saddle-Meadows environment and Pierre in New York, before he renounces his inheritance and after. It is important to challenge this widespread assumption because it may lead not only to an oversimplification of Pierre's character, especially as it is delineated before he departs Saddle-Meadows, but also to the probable misconception—also widespread—that Melville experienced a sudden and dramatic change of mind about Pierre and the nature of the novel he was writing after he completed the first half of it.[7] A fundamental understanding of *Pierre* begins with the

7. The most influential advocate of this speculative position is Leon Howard, who feels that Melville's return in January 1852 from a trip to New York marked the point where he changed the nature of *Pierre* from a "rural bowl of milk" to a drastically different kind of novel. According to Howard, Melville felt "under pressure" and "somewhat sorry for himself." *Herman Melville: A Biography* (Berkeley and Los Angeles: University of California Press, 1951), pp. 187–95. Surprisingly and unfortunately, Howard's theory has somehow taken on with time the appearance of fact, and numerous readers and critics now accept this account of the book's composition without question. For example, in his analysis of point of view in *Pierre*, Bert C. Bach begins with the assumption that Melville started out to write one kind of book and changed his mind. "Narrative Technique and Structure in *Pierre*," *American Transcendental Quarterly*, no. 7 (1970): 5–8. James Polk follows suit in his comment that *Pierre* was "originally designed to woo the sentimental popular audience." "Melville and the Idea of the City," *University of Toronto Quarterly* 41 (1972): 277–92. Hershel Parker's premise is that *Pierre* is a novel that "went wrong," and creating a thin but complex web of circumstantial evidence, he sets about trying to show why. His argument, a more elaborate version of Howard's, is that Melville wrote all of the Saddle-Meadows section with the intention of creating a "study of his hero's psychology." Then certain experiences in New York during his visit "profoundly altered his feelings about his career as a whole as well as the manuscript at hand." Having read adverse reviews of *Moby-Dick* and having failed to secure the contract he wished for *Pierre*, Melville returned to Pittsfield to write the last half of his novel in another mood. "Melville was diverted from the exploration of Pierre's psyche into a psychological analysis of his own literary career." The

knowledge that setting may be the most readily apparent basis for determining the author's own concept of the novel's structure, but it is not the most accurate and certainly not the most fruitful. Melville skillfully organized his narrative into three sections, not two, emphasizing in each different aspects of the same theme of deception, different facets of the same character, and different patterns of imagery and allusion.

Most of the details about Pierre in part one, from the novel's beginning up to the time he receives Isabel's letter toward the end of book 3, are carefully chosen to depict him in this phase as a romantic idealist. The two concepts that appear to be most in his mind and, consequently, in the foreground of the narration are love and beauty. Melville's indulgence in the sentimental clichés about love reflects not his belief but the state of mind of Pierre at this time, and whenever Melville waxes enthusiastic about love or young lovers, an undercurrent of irony flows with such force as to undermine the staged sincerity of the words. As he depicts the innocent, joy-laden courtship of Pierre and Lucy and defines the quality of young love, a discordant note is heard sounding through the harmony: "Love was first begot by Mirth and Peace, in Eden, when the world was young." Yet that Eden was short-

---

result was a much diminished book and a fragmented one, Parker believes. He strongly disagrees with Howard's opinion that the last half of the novel is more powerful than the first. "Why Pierre Went Wrong," *Studies in the Novel* 8 (1976): 7–23. See also Parker's "Contract: *Pierre*, by Herman Melville," *Proof* 5 (1977): 27–44, in which he makes the same assumptions. Parker's argument is based on a series of conjectures presented as historical fact. Even more disturbing, however, are his serious misreading and his striking underevaluation of this profound and skillfully organized novel. While one does not have to accept E. L. Grant Watson's appraisal of *Pierre* as "the greatest of Melville's books" (p. 232), he is undoubtedly more sensitive to what Melville achieved in this great novel than is Parker. Robert Milder's words in response to the Howard-Parker speculation ring true: "In *Pierre* . . . there is no evidence of . . . discontinuity, and the impending tragedy of its young hero is foreshadowed from the very start. . . . The conclusion to be drawn from all this is that Melville was in command of his material from the very start—in command of his plot, which did not change substantially as he labored on it, and in command of his complex and ironic attitude toward Pierre, which also did not change. The book Melville published . . . is the book he set out to write." "Melville's 'Intentions' in *Pierre*," *Studies in the Novel* 6 (1974): 192–93.

lived, and sin and grief soon took the place of bliss. In nearly every sentence of overblown praise of romantic love, Melville has erected a stately pleasure dome, and then amid this beauty and laughter, created a sense of impending disaster through ancestral voices prophesying war. "The man oppressed with cares, he can not love," he continues. "The man of gloom finds not the god. So, as youth, for the most part, has no cares, and knows no gloom, therefore, ever since time did begin, youth belongs to love. Love may end in grief and age, and pain and need, and all other modes of human mournfulness, but love begins in joy. Love's first sigh is never breathed, till after love hath laughed. Love laughs first, and then sighs after." Pierre's admiration for Christ's Sermon on the Mount is ironically pertinent here, for Melville's linking of romantic love with laughter seems calculated to call up Jesus's admonition: "Woe unto you that laugh now! for ye shall mourn and weep" (Luke 6:25). The kind of love that Pierre is enjoying is thus both temporary and deceptive. "Love has not hands," Melville continues, "but cymbals" (p. 33). Again a strong biblical echo resounds: Paul reminded others and himself, in what is possibly the most profound definition of love ("charity") ever offered, that unless the deeper and truer love is experienced, he is nothing—a mere "tinkling cymbal" (1 Corinthians 13:1).[8]

Romantic love proves deceptive for Pierre because it seems profound but is shallow, seems eternal but is brief, and—most significant of all—seems to lead to deep truths of existence but in actuality obscures them. Throughout the novel, Melville deftly refers to Pierre's physical vision as a reverse measure of his metaphysical vision. That is, the more experienced he becomes in life's grave realities and the more his initial joy and optimism are supplanted by woe and pessimism, the more his physical eyesight fades. It is appropriate, therefore, that in this first section, where he is deceived by the illusions of romantic love, eyes should be emphasized: "No Cornwall miner ever sunk so deep a shaft be-

8. The words of Pierre, reflecting naive ebullience, should be juxtaposed to the words he later places in the mouth of his fictional creation, Vivia. The music of heroism, he says, is "but from a sounding brass and a tinkling cymbal!" (p. 302).

neath the sea, as Love will sink beneath the floatings of the eyes. Love sees ten million fathoms down, till dazzled by the floor of pearls. The eye is Love's own magic glass, where all things that are not of earth, glide in supernatural light. . . . . Love's eyes are holy things; therein the mysteries of life are lodged; looking in each other's eyes, lovers see the ultimate secret of the worlds" (p. 33). In this state of pseudo-insight, where he is misled by romantic love into believing that he is looking into the nature of things, Pierre "seemed a youthful Magian, and almost a mountebank together" (p. 35). The first he is to himself only; the second he is in truth.

Love, Melville implies, is a disguise. To be in love is to practice a kind of physiognomy of the emotions. From feeling romantic love, one becomes falsely confident of being able to interpret life. Melville's conviction was that the only real and substantial form of love is self-love, which meant for him the sympathetic understanding and acceptance on equal terms of all sides of oneself no matter how different each is from the other. It is a hard-won love totally impossible without deep self-knowledge and a natural bent toward compassion. In Pierre's failure to obtain enough of this kind of love, he differs fundamentally from his creator.

In the first part of the novel, beauty is romantic love's twin deception. It betrays the eye as love does the heart. Everything around Pierre at Saddle-Meadows is beautiful; consequently, he is misled into believing that he exists in the midst of truth as well. "Thou art young, and beautiful," Lucy tells him (p. 36). His mother "had never yearned for admiration; because that was her birthright by the eternal privilege of beauty; she had always possessed it" (p. 15). Lucy is beautiful to the point of uniqueness: "the world will never see another Lucy Tartan" (pp. 23–24). If Melville's elaborate and overblown digression in praise of beautiful women seems a "rather irregular sort of writing," it is because it undercuts itself, the deceptiveness of beauty and the absurdity of accepting it on face value apparent even in the exaggerated words of praise. "A true gentleman in Kentucky would cheerfully die for a beautiful woman in Hindostan," he writes, "though he never saw her. Yea, count down his heart in death-drops for her; and go to Pluto, that she might go to Paradise. He would turn Turk before he would disown an allegiance hereditary to all gentlemen, from the hour their Grand Master, Adam, first knelt to Eve" (p. 24). Though of a different kind, Isabel's beauty is striking, a "wonderful loveliness" (p. 46). Her face "bewilderingly allured" Pierre "by its nameless beauty" (p. 49).

Not only is Pierre himself beautiful in an ideal Greek-like way and surrounded by the great beauty in all those closest to him, but he also exists in a setting of unrelieved natural beauty. In several descriptions the loveliness of the Saddle-Meadows environment is emphasized. Lucy and Pierre sit on a bank "gazing far, and far away; over many a grove and lake; corn-crested uplands, and Herd's-grass lowlands; and long-stretching swales of vividest green, betokening where the greenest bounty of this earth seeks its winding channels" (p. 35). No doubt much of the strangeness that early reviewers attributed to *Pierre,* a strangeness that those reading the novel for the first time still experience, results from the contrast between a setting early in the book saturated with dreamy beauty and a later setting marked by depressing ugliness. The ever-present beauty that is almost oppressive in part one takes on the effect of a smiling mask that but covers woe. Melville warns that this is the function of images of beauty when he writes near the beginning, "Pierre little foresaw that this world hath a secret deeper than beauty" (p. 7).

In this stage of Pierre's life, beauty and love merge into a single glorious emotion. "All things that are sweet to see," he believes, "all these things were made by Love." Ugliness and love he considers alien to each other: "Love made not the Arctic zones," and as love comes in, so does beauty. Love provides the beautiful "orange blossoms and lilies of the valley" so that "men and maids should love and marry." The beautiful world and beautiful women are in Pierre's eyes as one: "So on all sides Love allures; can contain himself what youth who views the wonders of the beauteous woman-world?" (p. 34). Pierre feels that he "pressed the wide beauty of the world in his embracing arms; for all his world resolved itself into his heart's best love for Lucy" (p. 39). Pierre thus dismisses the specters of ugliness and evil, for in his world of romantic idealism, there is room only for love and beauty. As he watches a glorious sunset, it seems to say to him: "I go down in beauty to rise in joy; Love reigns throughout all worlds that sunsets visit; it is a foolish ghost story; there is no such thing as misery. Would Love, which is omnipotent, have misery in his domain? Would the god of sunlight decree gloom?" (p. 60). It is the eternal question of how God could allow evil to exist in the world he created. At this stage of his life, Pierre answers the question by simply denying the existence of evil. Later he will answer it differently.

Melville's point in linking love and beauty in part one and then in showing them to be determinant in all else that Pierre believes is to call up Keats's dictum that " 'Beauty is truth, truth beauty,'—that is all / Ye know on earth, and all ye need to know." But beauty is *not* truth, Melville insists in this book, which is not only antiromantic in the way usually described—as satire on the current best-selling sentimental novels—but also in its implied objection to the Romantic poets. When Melville has Pierre cry out in the early pages, "And now for the urn" (p. 15), he is thinking of more than just coffee. John Caspar Lavater, the high priest of physiognomy, had no better ally in his crusade to prove the validity of appearance than John Keats, who declared in his "Ode on a Grecian Urn" that "Beauty is truth," and no more forceful enemy than Melville, who shows the destructive result of believing too firmly in the connection. Melville does not mention that Pierre has read Keats; the words of that poet do not come to him in crucial moments as do those of Dante and Shakespeare. Melville does not want to make his hero a young John Keats by having him think precisely the same way, but it is clear that Keats is in Melville's mind when he writes that "as the glory of the rose endures but for a day, so the full bloom of girlish airiness and bewitchingness, passes from the earth almost as soon." Though Pierre does not experience "utmost sadness" in "pondering on the inevitable evanescence of all earthly loveliness; which makes the sweetest things of life only food for ever-devouring and omnivorous melancholy," his thought is "somehow akin to it" (p. 58), akin, that is, to Keats's in his "Ode on Melancholy." Suggestions of Keats's urn are present in the description of Mary Glendinning—"She evenly glowed like a vase" that "seems to

shine by the very virtue of the exquisite marble itself" (p. 15)—
and in the opening paragraphs of the novel, where a scene of a
"trance-like" sylvan repose and silence recall the pastoral setting
of "Ode on a Grecian Urn." Picturing the human component in
this dreamy tableau, Melville assumes the stance of a Romantic
poet: "The verdant trance lay far and wide; and through it nothing came but the brindled kine, dreamily wandering to their
pastures, followed, not driven, by ruddy-cheeked, white-footed
boys" (p. 3).

The first section of *Pierre* in particular embodies among other
things Melville's recollection of his own early interest in the English Romantic poets and his covert denunciation of their influence. Though he does not reveal openly until much later in the
novel that his hero aspires to authorship, he hints strongly in the
early pages that Pierre is an immature poet of the Romantic ilk.
He possesses a "fond ideality" (p. 8) and "romantic merits" (p.
16). As he composes an elaborate poetic conceit involving his
horses, Lucy comments that the animals respond to his "lyrics"
(p. 23). When he thinks of Lucy, "improvisations burst from
him, in quick Golden Verses" (p. 35). If his thought at times is
akin to Keats's, his muscular body and small hands resemble
those of Byron.[9] The country life that he leads is of all existences
"the most poetical and philosophical," and "numerous bards have
ennobled it by many fine titles" (p. 13), the most celebrated of
whom was William Wordsworth whose ideal sweetheart was also
called Lucy.[10]

Like some of the Romantic poets, Pierre is drawn toward the
ideals and artistry of ancient Greece, and in keeping with that
bent, Melville frequently alludes to the classical world. Several

9. Henry A. Murray makes this connection in his notes to *Pierre*, p. 438.
Melville may have taken the name of Isabel from Keats's "Isabella, or the Pot of
Basil."

10. Maxine Moore feels that "Melville wrote *Pierre; or, The Ambiguities* as a
parody on the life and work of Wordsworth." "Melville's Pierre and Wordsworth: Intimations of Immorality," *New Letters* 39 (1973): 89. According to
Michael Davitt Bell, Melville modeled Pierre's father on Wordsworth and thus
"the influences on Pierre's early life are Wordsworthian." "The Glendinning
Heritage: Melville's Literary Borrowings in *Pierre*," *Studies in Romanticism* 12
(1973): 751.

critics have noted the "Arcadian imagery" in the first section.[11] Consciously or unconsciously, Pierre has patterned his life on the classical Greek ideal. He makes every effort to acquire what C. M. Bowra calls "that quality of balance and completeness which we call classical."[12] He keeps his body strong and muscular, and in this period of his life values as did the Greeks poetry before prose.[13] We learn later in the novel that he wrote on subjects like "The Tropical Summer," "The Weather: A Thought," and "Life: An Impromptu," the kinds of topics congenial to the ancient Greeks.[14] His mother holds Socrates up to him as a model of moderation. He refers to himself as "Pluto stealing Proserpine" (p. 59), and he thinks of the "primeval pine-tree" that he likes to sit under as "this Eolean pine" (p. 41). Melville supplies other such allusions to make this section distinctive for its pervasive Greek flavor. Lucy's "hair was Danae's" (p. 24), and she and Pierre are "the two Platonic particles" that "after roaming in quest of each other, from the time of Saturn and Ops till now," finally come together (p. 27). The "ruffled roll" that Pierre spots on Lucy's bed is more dear to him than a "precious parchment of the Greek" (p. 39). When he hears Isabel cry out during the sewing episode, it is a "Delphic shriek."

Pierre's perception of his environment as a kind of Arcadia, however, is, like love and beauty, deceptive, and his attempt to mold himself into a "gentleman" (a term synonymous with "Greek of the classical age") ends in failure because he does not possess the indispensable ingredient for the Greek ideal of balance—self-knowledge—and by temperament he cannot abide by the highest dictum of classical Greece, "nothing in excess." The role of music in the novel is to suggest where Pierre departs from the Greek ideal he is trying to follow. Music is a form of beauty that can lead one away from the recognition of self and the highest reality found there and toward confusion and destruction. As

11. For example, see Mary E. Dichmann, "Absolutism in Melville's *Pierre*," *PMLA* 67 (1952): 702–15; and Charles Moorman, "Melville's *Pierre* and the Fortunate Fall," *American Literature* 25 (1953): 13–30.

12. C. M. Bowra, *Classical Greece* (New York: Time, 1965), p. 14.

13. Ibid.

14. Ibid., p. 15.

C. M. Bowra explains: "But a taste for beauty must not be over-indulged; the Greek rule that everything in life must be enjoyed in moderation applied even here. Socrates warned that 'when a man allows music to play upon him and to pour into his soul through the funnel of his ears those sweet and soft and melancholy airs . . . he becomes a feeble warrior.'"[15] As Pierre succumbs to the music of Isabel, as he listens to her melancholy chants and the sounds of her inexplicable guitar, he becomes lost to that Arcadian world of ideal love and beauty in which, by virtue of his innermost being, he was always an alien without knowing it.

In the second section of *Pierre,* which picks up at the end of book 3 with Isabel's letter and concludes with Plinlimmon's pamphlet at the end of book 14, love and beauty disappear from the foreground in favor of "truth." Pierre is now determined to follow what he considers the truth at the cost of all else. Having abandoned his Greek world, in which beauty and truth were one, he becomes an "enthusiast" for truth alone. Melville uses the word several times to describe Pierre (sometimes capitalizing it); consequently, it becomes clear that in calling his hero an "Enthusiast," he means to suggest more than merely Pierre's youthful zeal. An enthusiast is "one who is (really or seemingly) possessed by a god; one who is under the influence of prophetic frenzy." In ecclesiastical history the word designates "a sect of heretics of the fourth century, who pretended to special revelations."[16] According to Wilhelm Moeller, the Enthusiasts followed "the precept of renunciation of the world and surrender of goods and absolute poverty."[17] Both Epiphanius and Theodoret wrote of the Enthusiasts' belief in personal revelations through dreams and visions.

Melville may or may not have known that there were heretics who actually were called Enthusiasts, but he was certainly aware of a related heretical sect, the Gnostics (as *Moby-Dick* clearly attests), and in the second section of *Pierre,* Gnosticism offers the most fruitful context for understanding what is going on within

15. Ibid., p. 20.
16. *Oxford English Dictionary.*
17. Wilhelm Moeller, *History of the Christian Church, A.D. 1–600,* trans. Andrew Rutherfurd (London: George Allen, 1912), p. 362.

the hero. Melville was familiar with the tenets of Gnosticism, but Pierre is not. That is, Melville has created a character who comes to accept the same fundamental beliefs and attitudes as those of a group of second-century Christian heretics called Gnostics without realizing that others in the far past have shared precisely his own new convictions. Ironically, Pierre believes that he is discovering truths previously unrevealed when actually he is following a well-worn path of heresy, which leads him as it did Ahab to mental chaos. After *Moby-Dick,* Melville did not lose his fascination with Gnosticism but created in Pierre another victim of the heresy, one who ironically believes his insights are unique.

Pierre is a prime candidate for Gnosticism because of four factors in his life, the four prerequisites for conversion to this way of perceiving and believing: (1) A deep yearning for God—a religious impulse; (2) individualism, a drive toward independence—a prideful impulse; (3) a strong and tenacious physical nature with pronounced appetites; (4) a profound disappointment in God, usually brought on by an occurrence that appears to connect the God that one has been worshipping with injustice, personal injury, and evil. In part one of the novel, Pierre is shown to possess the three traits of character, though he does not seem aware of the depth of the first two. The three flow like parallel streams within him, never merging, never out of their bounds, never one with a greater volume or current than the others, but all in a sort of quiet harmony of peaceful coexistence. Then an event occurs, traumatically shaking Pierre's faith in his "father," who has been long associated in his mind with the traditional Heavenly Father. Isabel's letter and the subsequent interviews are described in terms of an inexplicable lightning bolt: "we see the cloud, and feel its bolt; but meteorology only idly essays a critical scrutiny as to how that cloud became charged, and how this bolt so stuns" (p. 67). If lightning strikes and causes pain, if it kills off an old way of thinking, it also brings brilliant light—though short-lived. Thus it is a perfect metaphor for the emotional upheaval and the concurrent illumination that marks the initiation into a Gnostic mode of thought. Melville used it in *Moby-Dick* to suggest both Ahab's early injury, his being struck in such a way as to cause a new woeful preoccupation with the concept of evil, and at the same time his eye-opening introduction to Gnostic convictions. When Isabel suddenly appears from nowhere, she is "a before unexperienced and wholly inexplicable element, which like electricity suddenly received into any sultry atmosphere of the dark, in all directions splits itself into nimble lances of purifying light" (p. 88). While Pierre contemplates Isabel's letter, there is within him an "electrical storm," and he begins to receive "electric insight" as well as painful injury from the knowledge that his father was not perfect. Throughout both interviews of Pierre and Isabel, lightning is Melville's useful metaphorical tool.

The three phases of Pierre's life can be traced through the courses of the three streams of his makeup. Flowing apart from each other and peacefully in the young romantic idealist of traditional Christian upbringing, who aspires to the balance and order of classical Greece and who cherishes love and beauty, they are suddenly forced violently together by Isabel's lightning-like revelations and then follow the common riverbed of Gnostic-like conviction, which seems ready-made to accommodate all three and incorporate them because of its depth and breadth and its ostensibly bold and straight direction over and through the ugly terrain of the world. At this stage, Pierre thinks, as does Ahab, that he is united within and that his soul will run "over unsounded gorges, through the rifled hearts of mountains, under torrents' beds, unerringly."[18] The problem is that the Gnostic way is not the unifier it appears to be. As Melville says in *Moby-Dick,* when "hostile currents meet," they do not gently and quickly merge.[19] "One river will flow into and then along with another," he explains, "without at all blending with it for a time."[20] Such is exactly the situation with Pierre. In the second phase of his life where he seemingly has found a singleness of purpose, the three hostile currents of his being do not flow as one river with a single strong current of life-giving waters but remain as separate and distinct streams. Furthermore, they appear to become jealously aware of

18. *Moby-Dick,* ed. Harrison Hayford and Hershel Parker (New York: Norton, 1967), p. 147.
19. Ibid., p. 296.
20. Ibid., p. 342.

each other's presence as they were not in the earlier and happier phase of Pierre's existence when they occupied their own individual channels. The Gnostic period of Pierre's thinking is thus to be temporary. In the final stage, as shown in the third part of the novel, the hostile currents, as if in danger of being completely mingled and of losing their individual identities as rivers, cease to flow onward but turn violently upon each other and in their chaotic warring finally create a fierce maelstrom like the one that destroys all remaining life in *Moby-Dick*. Ironically and terribly, Pierre feels these earth-shaking disturbances in his inner terrain, but he is never enough of a geologist of self to understand truly what is happening to him.

In many ways, his life is similar to that of the man traditionally credited with the founding of the Gnostic heresy, Simon Magus, a Samaritan of the second century who is mentioned in the biblical book of Acts (8:9–24) and who is described in the writings of such Church Fathers as Irenaeus and Justinus. At least twice in the novel, Melville refers to Pierre as "Magian" (pp. 35, 51). An energetic and zealous man of strong appetites, Simon was enamored of mystery, but he was also consumed with his own arch specialness. His search to understand the source of evil in the world led him, like later Gnostics, to conclude that Jehovah is a flawed divinity and that there is a higher God. By the young Orthodox Church he was branded a fraud. One account of his death relates that at a time of intense pressure on him, with cries of "impostor" ringing in his ears, he—in a sense—committed suicide by having himself buried alive in a tomb.[21] Irenaeus attributed to Simon a work called *The Great Revelation*. The most striking aspect of his life was his relationship with a woman who because of her reputation contributed greatly to his downfall. Somehow a woman named Helena came into his life and managed to convince him that she was in a spiritual way deeply related to him. She had endured great hardship and had been forced into prostitution. When he discovered her, he felt divinely inspired "to rescue her first and free her from her bonds," as Irenaeus

---

21. Jean Doresse, *The Secret Books of the Egyptian Gnostics* (New York: Viking, 1960), p. 17.

writes, and then to speak and write the truth of what he had learned through her.[22] She was not a soiled ordinary woman to him, but his spiritual relative, the Sophia of the Gnostics. From the Church Fathers onward, Simon's relationship with this woman has been described with a smirk, as if he were a lecherous confidence man. Even Hans Jonas, one of the most knowledge-able and reliable historians of Gnosticism, calls Simon's claims for Helena a "piece of showmanship" and comments on the "pictur-esqueness and effrontery of the exhibition."[23] Nevertheless, Jonas and almost all other authorities on Gnosticism take him seriously, acknowledging that the "Fathers of the Church regarded Simon Magus as the father of all heresy."[24] His relationship with Helena is sadder than it is humorous, more suggestive of human frailty than of shame. Though deceived, Simon was chasing truth; if he had physical relations with the woman he reverenced, as many writers appear to believe, he did so because his strong natural appetites could not be forever resisted.

Anyone familiar with even the broad outlines of Gnosticism and its peculiar and fascinating history, as Melville unquestion-ably was, would know of Simon Magus and the mysterious woman that he was drawn to both spiritually and physically, a woman he believed to be of the same divine parentage as himself. It would not be surprising, then, if Melville had in mind the Gnostic Simon when he plotted the events in the strange career of his Gnostic Pierre. The greater similarity, however, is in the mo-tivations of the two men. In *The Recognitions* of Clement, Simon is quoted as having said to the Apostle Peter: "The unreasoning populace will assent to you, and embrace you as one teaching those things which are commonly received among them; and will curse me, as professing things new and unheard of."[25] Hans Jonas

22. Quoted in Robert M. Grant, ed., *Gnosticism: A Source Book of Heretical Writings from the Early Christian Period* (New York: Harper, 1961), p. 25.

23. Hans Jonas, *The Gnostic Religion: The Message of the Alien God and the Beginnings of Christianity* (Boston: Beacon Press, 1958), p. 104.

24. Ibid., p. 103.

25. *Ante-Nicene Christian Library: Translations of the Writings of the Fathers down to A.D. 325,* ed. Alexander Roberts and James Donaldson, vol. 3 (Edin-burgh: T. and T. Clark, 1867), p. 217.

is undoubtedly correct in identifying the "new and unheard of" in Simon's reputed statement as "the revolt against the world and its god in the name of an absolute spiritual freedom."[26] That was Simon's burning drive, and it is Pierre's as well.

The second part of *Pierre* begins, appropriately, with what is considered in Gnosticism as the awakening to truth, the "call." That the call comes in the form of Isabel's letter is also appropriate since in Gnostic writings, a letter is sometimes the metaphor used.[27] In the various writings of the heresiarchs themselves and in the writings about their beliefs that Melville probably had read, the call is commonly described as involving three characteristics: awakening from a slumber or dream, light, and shock— all included in Pierre's response to Isabel's letter. The call was presumed to be "gnosis" (knowledge) of the highest God responded to by the Godly impulse within. Isabel's seemingly supernatural communication with Pierre is a tolling bell to which his yearning heart answers. In fact, she tells Pierre that "I have nearly always gone by the name of Bell" (p. 148). But she stresses that she was merely the instrument of the call. "God called thee, Pierre," she says, "not poor Bell" (p. 159). As Melville describes the appeal of Isabel's revelations, the Gnostic context is apparent: "The deep voice of the being of Isabel called to him from out the immense distances of sky and air, and there seemed no veto of the earth that could forbid her heavenly claim" (p. 173).[28] The mysterious messenger who carries Isabel's letter is first seen as a light in the surrounding darkness. Pierre "somehow felt a nameless

---

26. Jonas, p. 110.

27. The Gnostic "Hymn of the Pearl," for example, is an account of a letter that goes out from heaven to awaken a member of the elect who is exiled and asleep in the world: "Like a messenger was the letter which the King had sealed with his right hand. . . . I awoke and arose from my slumber . . . and directed my steps that I might come to the light of our home. The letter who had awakened me I found before me on the way." Quoted in Jonas, p. 75.

28. Though he does not recognize the specifically Gnostic flavor of this passage, Joel Porte comments on its religious overtones: "The religious terminology which Pierre habitually uses with regard to Isabel . . . is the sure sign of both his damnation and his delusion." *The Romance in America: Studies in Cooper, Poe, Hawthorne, Melville, and James* (Middletown, Conn.: Wesleyan University Press, 1969), p. 174.

presentiment that the light must be seeking him" (61). In a characteristically Gnostic manner, Pierre feels amid the light that bursts in on him—often in the form of lightning—that he is now undeceived: "Henceforth I will see the hidden things; and live right out in my own hidden life!—Now I feel that nothing but Truth can move me so. This letter is not a forgery" (p. 66).[29]

With the call, Pierre awakes from his dream world of romantic idealism, an awakening underscored by his literal sleeplessness in the second section of the novel. Others sleep around him, but he finds that he cannot go back to that long and comfortable restfulness that he now feels was lotus-induced stupor. "In the profoundly silent heart of a house full of sleeping serving-men and maids, Pierre now sat in his chamber" (p. 168). Though the Gnostics believed that the call was their personal revelation of truth—truth about their own divine nature, the truth about Jehovah (or the "Demiurge"), the truth about a higher Unknown God, the truth about the world—they often did not receive immediate release and joy from it as other kinds of mystics experience from their transcendental moments. The shock and anxiety that follow Pierre's epiphany may appear inconsistent with his concurrent feelings of enlightenment, reverence, and self-confidence, but the strange combination is frequently characteristic of the Gnostic response to the call. Hans Jonas describes this reaction as a "tone of lamentation" that comes from "the earthbound soul terrified at the prospect of having to depart and clinging desperately to the things of this world."[30]

Pierre's various attitudes and emotions through part two of the novel have a decided Gnostic cast. He takes on, for example, a new self-reliance because he believes that he has discovered divinity within himself. With his new mission before him—to follow Truth at the cost of his worldly ease—he finds "support in himself." He feels "that deep in him lurked a divine uniden-

29. Charles Moorman remarks that "Isabel is like the serpent as it appears as a messenger in more complete versions of the Fall" (p. 26), but he does not mention that the most elaborate version of the Fortunate Fall is that included in Gnostic myth. The Ophites and Cainites in particular held the serpent in reverence as the awakening messenger of the great Unknown God.

30. Jonas, p. 87.

tifiableness, that owned no earthly kith or kin" (p. 89). This is the inner spark of God, the Gnostic "pneuma" that is held captive in the body and is silent before the call. In one place, Pierre calls it his "heart." Men, he says, are "jailers of themselves. . . . The heart! the heart! 'tis God's anointed; let me pursue the heart!" (p. 91). He now senses that he is "charged with the fire of all divineness" (p. 107), and he will do only what his "deepest angel dictates" (p. 65). In following these dictates of the Godly light within, the Gnostic believed that he must renounce the world as evil and alien. Pierre's attitudes toward society and nature undergo sharp reversals after he receives Isabel's letter: "the before undistrusted moral beauty of the world is forever fled" and "all brightness hath gone from thy hills" (p. 65). Society to Pierre has now become suddenly marked by, as he tells the Reverend Mr. Falsgrave, "detestable uncharitableness and heartlessness" (p. 163). He must give up material possessions, his view of the physical world as his Father's world, and his love of external beauty. "Now I see," he exclaims, "that in his beauty a man is snared, and made stone-blind. . . . Welcome then be Ugliness and Poverty and Infamy, and all ye other crafty ministers of Truth, that beneath the hoods and rags of beggars hide yet the belts and crowns of kings" (p. 90).

With his denunciation of his Father's world must come his denunciation of his Father as he has previously conceived him. His "sacred father is no more a saint" (p. 65). Long confused in his mind with his actual parent, the Creator now pays the price for the mortal father's sin. God, or the traditional Jehovah, becomes for Pierre the "Infinite Haughtiness," his mother's God and creator (p. 90). When he cries that henceforth "Pierre hath no paternity, and no past," he is severing his ties of love and devotion not only with his physical father but also with the God of love and beauty and goodness that he previously worshipped. Taking the place of the Demiurge is the Unknown God, the "*great* God" (p. 155, italics mine) that awakes him from his sleep and sends the call through Isabel. This is the Gnostic God of Silence, as Simon Magus called it. Now he knows that "All profound things, and emotions of things are preceded and attended by Silence" and that "Silence is the only Voice of our God" (p. 204). The concept of God represented here is decidedly Gnostic. What Pierre comes to believe in part two of the novel is not that there is no God but that there is more than one and that men have generally misconceived the nature of the highest God, who is not the God of the Old Testament—the Demiurge—but an Unknown God, so holy and powerful, so far removed from soiled mankind and corrupt matter, that human beings can sense his presence only through that spark of divinity, the pneuma, that exists in the Elect. It is not only absurd but blasphemous, the Gnostic believed, to assert that the all highest and purest divinity would stoop to have intercourse in any form with base mankind. Such is the meaning of Melville's comment on the falseness of men's claims to having heard the direct voice of God. "That profound Silence, that only Voice of our God, which I before spoke of; from that divine thing without a name, those impostor philosophers pretend somehow to have got an answer which is as absurd, as though they should say they had got water out of stone; for how can a man get a Voice out of Silence" (p. 208). Having initiated the single communication of the call, which is responded to by man's inner divinity, God then is heard from no more in this life.

Pierre enters into this Gnostic world because of the way his inner makeup responds to this disillusionment. He is an idealist who wants a sister, a craving that is really a manifestation of his God-hunger. Time after time Melville suggests that Isabel is as much a projection of some inner drive in Pierre as she is an actual character. She "seemed half unearthly"; her voice is from a "far interior" (p. 118). She writes Pierre, "hitherto my existence has been utterly unknown to thee" (p. 63), but she has nevertheless existed and, in one sense, within Pierre. She tells him that she "never knew a mortal mother" and does not seem "of woman born" (p. 114). As Pierre remembers Lucy, "for an instant, he almost could have prayed Isabel back into the wonder-world from which she had so slidingly emerged" (p. 129). He perceives her as he does because she has, indeed, come from his own inner wonder-world. She embodies his Gnostically oriented need for union with God. As such, she is described as possessed by an "intense and indescribable longing" (p. 174); it was her "longing heart," she tells Pierre, that "called thee to me" (p. 189). Her strongest drive is toward union with a greater force. She yearns "for the feeling of myself, as of some plant, absorbing life without seeking it, and existing without individual sensation. I feel that there can be no perfect peace in individualness" (p. 119).

It is clear almost from the moment when Isabel appears that if Pierre devotes himself to her, she will not share him. She wants exclusive rights over his whole being. He might have been able to give himself over had not his pride begun to develop strongly and concurrently at the moment of the call, being fed by the precise Gnostic convictions that compelled him to seek the higher truth, reject the flawed God, and denounce materialism and the world. From the moment when he discovered Isabel, he became convinced that he was superior to the masses. Like a Gnostic who has been awakened to the pneuma within, he feels that he is one of the "chosen souls" (p. 137). Again reflecting Pierre's own stage of thought, Melville describes the differences between the pneumatics and the hylics (or ordinary men): "all the world does never gregariously advance to Truth, but only here and there some of its individuals do; and by advancing, leave the rest behind; cutting themselves forever adrift from their sympathy, and making themselves always liable to be regarded with distrust, dislike, and often, downright—though, ofttimes, concealed—fear and hate" (p. 166). Knowing the truth makes one feel superior, even God-like: "Pierre was now this vulnerable God" (p. 181). Released from slavery to a corrupt world and a deceptive Creator, he now feels "untrammeledly his ever-present self!—free to do his own self-will" (p. 199).

The Gnostic dilemma is thus repeated in Pierre. In his Gnostic way of thinking, his desire to lose identity in God and his wonderfully rewarding conviction of his specialness and superiority find a common ground congenial to both but only temporarily, and even then these two sides of Pierre will not completely become one. Pierre's quoting of lines from Dante, "descriptive of the two mutually absorbing shapes in the Inferno," suggest precisely his inner condition:

> Ah! how dost thou change,
> Agnello! See! thou art not double now,

Nor only one!
(p. 85)

Gnostic convictions are as deceptive for Pierre as were his ideals of love and beauty. He finds no more healing self-knowledge as a Gnostic than he did as a Greek. His Gnostic thinking makes all that he has lived by before seem invalid and perverse, but it in turn leads to error and destruction. Seen through his new-found "Truth," the "most immemorially admitted maxims of men begin to slide and fluctuate, and finally become wholly inverted; the very heavens themselves being not innocent of producing this confounding effect, since it is mostly in the heavens themselves that these wonderful mirages are exhibited" (p. 165).

Toward the end of the second section of the novel, Pierre's wonderful Gnostic mirages begin to fade just as did his Arcadic existence before the end of part one when disturbing thoughts of the face he had seen intrude on his happiness. That is, he begins to experience brief moments, a "temporary mood" now and then, in which he is not so positive of the truth as he has been. These moods foreshadow his mental state throughout much of part three of the book: "his thoughts were very dark and wild; for a space there was rebellion and horrid anarchy and infidelity in his soul." He even "propounded the possibility of the mere moonshine of all his self-renouncing Enthusiasm" (p. 205). The stage is thus set, as it was toward the end of part one, for the appearance of another seminal document in Pierre's life, Plinlimmon's pamphlet. It marks, as did Isabel's letter to him, the end of one phase of his life and the beginning of another. As Isabel's letter refutes the truth of what Pierre holds to be most dear in his early days, the pamphlet refutes his Gnostic-like attitude. The positioning of the pamphlet in *Pierre,* then, is of great significance.

In spirit the pamphlet is strongly anti-Gnostic. The starting place for all Gnostic beliefs is that human beings with the divine spark are alien to the world and should remain so and that the true and highest Unknown God could have had no part in the creation and subsequent running of this corrupt earth. The pamphlet calls it an "infidel idea" that "whatever other worlds God may be Lord of, he is not the Lord of this; for else this world would seem to give the lie to Him; so utterly repugnant seem its ways to the instinctively known ways of Heaven. But it is not, and can not be so; nor will he who regards this chronometrical conceit aright, ever more be conscious of that horrible idea. For he will then see, or seem to see, that this world's seeming incompatibility with God, absolutely results from its meridianal correspondence with him" (p. 213). The message of the pamphlet is threefold: (1) align oneself virtuously with earthly surroundings; (2) understand all sides of oneself (3) practice moderation in all things. It expresses, in essence, the Greek ideal while attacking, by implication, Gnostic hatred of the world and extremes in behavior.

Melville suggests his intentions in this regard through the first name that he chose for Plinlimmon. The Neoplatonist Plotinus, greatly admired by Pierre Bayle (whose account in his *Dictionary* Melville probably read), was famous for his anti-Gnosticism. His widely read treatise "Against Those That Affirm the Creator of the Cosmos and the Cosmos Itself to Be Evil" (usually called "Against the Gnostics") is a document that bears directly on Plotinus Plinlimmon's pamphlet, for both say essentially the same thing, namely that it is an error of the greatest magnitude to think oneself uniquely special and to seek God without regard for rational self-knowledge and respect for the natural world. The Gnostic says simply, look not at the corrupt world and its ways but "Look to God." This is "not helpful," Plotinus writes, "without some instruction as to what this looking imports; one can 'look' and still . . . be the slave of impulse."[31] He finds the Gnostics guilty of acting in the name of truth but exercising a dangerous individualism. We cannot, he stresses, cut ourselves off from the world: "This world must be the starting-point of the pursuit."[32] He is especially impatient of Gnostic arrogance, a sense of specialness that breeds an attitude of superiority: "We must recognize that other men have attained the heights of goodness."[33] Had Pierre read this Plotinus rather that the other one,

31. Grace H. Turnbull, ed., *The Essence of Plotinus* (New York: Oxford University Press, 1934), p. 66–67.
32. Ibid., p. 66.
33. Ibid., p. 68.

he would have received just about the same basic message, though probably he would have understood it no more clearly.

Plotinus's name on the pamphlet suggests not only its anti-Gnostic position but also its pro-Hellenic stance. Its title is "EI" (If), the word that appeared over Apollo's tomb at Delphi. Melville's source for the title is probably one of Plutarch's essays in the *Morals*, "The Word EI, Engraven over Apollo's Temple at Delphi."[34] Describing Apollo's temple, Plutarch points out two maxims that were inscribed there, the same admonitions that run through Plotinus's "Against the Gnostics" and Plinlimmon's "EI": "Know thyself" and "Nothing in extremes."[35] He discusses at length the wisdom of these Grecian ideals. Plutarch's conception of the self as multifaceted would have found ready acceptance from Melville. "Each of us," Plutarch wrote is "made up out of an infinite number of different things in conditions of existence—a motley assemblage of articles of all sorts and gleanings."[36] Knowing thyself is not easy, then, but the alternative is a destructive confusion of mind and motives. The penultimate sentence of the essay expresses this notion in a way that throws light directly on Pierre: "But, to say the truth, those who have mixed up things relating to gods with those relating to daemons, have brought themselves chiefly into trouble."[37] The pamphlet is thus an "excellently illustrated re-statement" of Pierre's "problem" (p. 210), namely his impulsiveness where there should be moderation, his angry determination to defy the world, where he should exercise benign expedience, and his blindness to his own deepest motives, where there should be intimate self-understanding. It is, in other words, a document whose function it is to reveal the nature and the extent of Pierre's self-deception.

34. Henry A. Murray writes: "After this note was written, my friend Professor M. M. Sealts kindly referred me to what must have been Melville's source for the title (*EI*) as well as for one or two ideas in harmony with the argument of the pamphlet—Plutarch's *Moralia*" (pp. 474–75). Murray does not indicate what the "one or two ideas" may be.

35. Plutarch, *Essays and Miscellanies*, in *The Complete Works of Plutarch*, vol. 4 (New York: Kelmscott Society, 1909), p. 511.

36. Ibid., p. 526.

37. Ibid., p. 528.

Whereas deception is an undercurrent in parts one and two of the novel, it comes to occupy Pierre's mind in the third section (which begins with book 15) as Love and Beauty did in the first and Truth in the second. No longer motivated mainly by his feelings of love and his adoration of beauty, no longer certain that his acts of renunciation have been divinely inspired, he now is shaken and propelled by the awareness of his victimization. Deception, therefore, is both the underlying theme, as it has been all along, and also the subject almost constantly on Pierre's mind (as it has not been before). A wish to draw special attention to it may well have been Melville's reason for including in this final segment three chapters that could have been in part one: book 15, dealing with Pierre's past relationship with Glen Stanly; book 17, "Young America in Literature"; and book 18, "Pierre, as a Juvenile Author, Reconsidered." Melville explains that there are two principal methods of writing: "By the one mode, all contemporaneous circumstances, facts, and events must be set down contemporaneously; by the other, they are only to be set down as the general stream of the narrative shall dictate; for matters which are kindred in time, may be irrelative in themselves" (p. 244). Though he claims that he follows neither, with the three chapters mentioned above he has clearly chosen to violate chronology for theme (the "stream of the narrative"). Deception, or as Melville puts it, "equivocalness," lies at the heart of Glen's relationship with Pierre. Long jealous of Pierre, Glen becomes secretly injured when Lucy does not show interest in him but becomes engaged to his cousin. He does not reveal his displeasure and envy, however, but conceals them under a cape of friendship and generosity: "For the deeper that some men feel a secret and poignant feeling, the higher they pile the belying surfaces. The friendly deportment of Glen then was to be considered as in direct proportion to his hoarded hate" (pp. 224–25). His motive in offering Pierre and Lucy his house is "the intense desire to disguise from the wide world . . . the fact that . . . Pierre had so victoriously supplanted him" (p. 225). After Pierre leaves Lucy and his mother wills Saddle-Meadows to Glen, the situation is drastically altered. Pierre realizes the extent of Glen's deception, and he is so embittered and enraged by it that he commits murder.

The other two chapters that are out of place in terms of setting and chronology fit perfectly into the last section thematically, for they emphasize the extent to which Pierre has been deceived in the past—this time by flattering editors, publishers, and lecture societies—within the present situation of his awakening angrily and sardonically to his general victimization. He has been variously deceived, he knows it, and he is deeply injured by the injustices perpetrated against him. This is the context for the final act of *Pierre*. Though Melville ran the risk of being charged with springing new and vital information about his hero so late in the novel that it appears an amateurish afterthought, he gained a poignant context for Pierre's growing preoccupation with deception and injustice. He writes precisely as he pleases, as he boldly stated (p. 244), and in doing so he may alienate some who do not really see what his pleasure is.

In this final section, Pierre exists within a bog of deceptions—his new awareness of his previous illusions, the surrounding sham of the trancendental "apostles," the lies he hears everywhere, even from his own mouth. He cannot avoid deception even when he goes out for a stroll, for he encounters inferior paintings passed off as masterpieces. It is no wonder, then, that he comes to question the validity of nearly everything in his life. Finally he takes a sort of perverse pleasure in entertaining suspicions of deception, even in regard to Isabel: "How did he know that Isabel was his sister?" (p. 353). He now considers her story "nebulous," and he realizes that it might have been "forged" (p. 354). These "bewildering meditations" of Pierre run up "like clasping waves upon the strand of the most latent secrecies of his soul" (p. 353).

This world of deceptiveness is for Pierre nothing less than hell. Charlie Milthorpe suggests far more than he imagines when he says to Pierre: "You are in the Inferno dream yet" (p. 318). Indeed, he is. In fact, *Pierre* is a kind of reversed *Divine Comedy*.[38]

---

38. Nathalia Wright points out that "parallels exist between the structure and some of the scenes and action of the novel and the poem," but she posits that the *opening section* of *Pierre* is Melville's version of hell. *"Pierre:* Herman Melville's *Inferno," American Literature* 32 (1960): 167. My argument that Pierre's principal conflict is with elements within himself runs somewhat counter to most of the critical commentary on Melville's use of Dante, which as a rule asserts that

Both works have three structural parts, both have paradises, purgatories, and hells. In *The Divine Comedy,* Beatrice meets Dante in purgatory and leads him into paradise. In Melville's novel, Isabel meets Pierre in the purgatorial middle section and leads him into hell. In the *Inferno,* the lower region of hell is dreadfully cold, and those condemned to it are the deceivers of the world. To be cold and suffer in a world of fraudulence is exactly Pierre's fate in the final section of the novel.

Pierre is more sensitive than ordinary people to deception, more profoundly offended by it, because he is by nature so attuned to what is open, right, just. In this he is a younger version of Ahab. His violent reactions to deception and to charges that he is a deceiver come from the same aspect of his being that makes him forsake everything to acknowledge and protect Isabel, that motivates him to help Dolly Ulver in her great troubles, and that causes him to shock the Reverend Mr. Falsgrave with his questions about right and justice. His love of justice and his abhorrence of deception are in turn manifestations of his basic spiritual impulse, his reaching out for a transcendent God. By striking out against Glen Stanly, he is committing what is for him a Godly act, not a criminal one. Glen is for him the incarnation of Deception as Moby Dick is for Ahab the incarnation of Evil. Pierre's emotional development follows the same course as Ahab's. Lightning strikes him in the form of Isabel's letter, making him aware

---

Pierre's battle is with the external force of evil. G. Giovannini states that Melville alludes to Dante's *Inferno* in order to play up Pierre's naivete and to stress "the ubiquity and universality of evil." "Melville's *Pierre* and Dante's *Inferno,*" *PMLA* 64 (1949): 71. See also Giovannini's "Melville and Dante," *PMLA* 65 (1950): 329; and J. Chesley Mathews, "Melville and Dante," *PMLA* 64 (1949): 1238. In "Flaxman, Dante, and Melville's *Pierre,*" *Bulletin of the New York Public Library* 64 (1960), Howard H. Schless also argues that the influence of Dante can be seen in Melville's depiction of an innocent's encounter with evil (p. 76). Pierre is unusually sensitive, as is Ahab, to what he perceives as evil, and, indeed, his turn to a Gnostic mode of thought is his way of trying to deal with the source of this malignant power while retaining his belief in a divine force. Furthermore, he later sees Glen Stanly as the embodiment of all evil and wishes to destroy him for that reason. This highly subjective perception of evil, however, is a far cry from its depiction in Dante. Dante's Inferno is not within himself; Pierre's is.

of deception; he vows to live for truth no matter what traditions he must break; then he is struck again, this time by the living image of disguised evil—Glen Stanly. At that point he declares war on Glen and all deception and fights his battles until his destruction. Pierre's encounter with Glen at a party, where he receives insult and deep injury emotionally, is equivalent to Ahab's encounter with the white whale when he is maimed. Seeking what is his through kinship and through a previous promise, Pierre finds only deception and rejection. "I do not know him," Glen lies. "It is an entire mistake; why don't the servants take him out, and the music go on?" He then turns his back on Pierre to address a young woman on the subject of a statue in the Louvre, the Fighting Gladiator. At this, Pierre jumps forward as if to attack: "'Fighting Gladiator it is!' yelled Pierre, leaping toward him like Spartacus. . . ." He is restrained, however, and is powerless to strike back. "This is very extraordinary," coolly remarks Glen, "remarkable case of combined imposture and insanity" (p. 239). His rage does border on insanity just as does Ahab's after Moby Dick reaps away his leg. It is a rage that will boil in Pierre throughout the final section of the novel until he faces Glen again with the vengeful eye of a justice-lover victimized by injustice, a deceit-hater victimized by deception, a God-seeker frustrated in his seeking.

In his reasons for killing Glen, Pierre's complex inner turmoil is revealed. "Deep, deep, and still deep and deeper must we go," writes Melville as a prelude to his description of Pierre's hatred of Glen, "if we would find out the heart of a man" (pp. 288–89). Glen has deceived Pierre and has committed a grave injustice. These acts violate one of Pierre's most basic impulses, that which draws him toward the Godly and away from wrong. But Pierre also hates Glen because of a second strong trait of character, his pride. Glen has offended that deep and powerful sense of worth in Pierre, given an affront to it as no one else ever has. He treated him not only as a stranger but as a deranged beggar, giving him money as he had him thrown from his residence. Pierre's desire for vengeance grows within him as his sense of superiority emerges more and more in the final part of the novel. Thus, deception becomes the common object of abhorrence by both that side of Pierre that reaches out for transcendent truth and that side that feels it needs nothing beyond itself. What was shown in the early pages as youthful pride of family becomes a theomania similar to Ahab's. He believes that he has been shown such truth that is known only by those high above ordinary mankind. "The demigods," he says, "trample on trash, and Virtue and Vice are trash" (p. 273). He no longer feels bound by the standard of behavior of the masses.

As this conviction of his own specialness grows in him, he is more and more isolated, and the more isolated, the colder he appears to be. In his early days, he was "closely folded by the world, as the husk folds the tenderest fruit." Then he is "born from the world-husk," but for a while he "still clamors for the support of . . . the world" and the traditional God. His progress is toward independence. "When at Saddle-Meadows, Pierre had wavered and trembled in those first wretched hours ensuing upon the receipt of Isabel's letter; then humanity had let go the hand of Pierre." This was the point where he moved into a Gnostic denunciation of the world and the Creator in favor of a more fundamental truth and a higher god, the Gnostic God. He was then "willing that humanity should desert him, so long as he thought he felt a far higher support." But his Gnostic attitudes resulted not in inner peace but brought on a third stage: "Then, ere long, he began to feel the utter loss of that other support, too; ay, even the paternal gods themselves did now desert Pierre" (p. 296). He has now a boiling sense of outrage, bitterness, an appetite for revenge, and a burning zeal to show his independence and his superiority by writing a book so profound and original that it will shock and transform the world.

The layers of clothing that Pierre takes on in his cold chamber represent the ever-increasing distance that he puts between himself and humanity. One of the most memorable images of the novel is Pierre "in his own solitary closet" (p. 297), no longer warmed by human contact but wrapped in old clothing and shivering as he pours forth his anger on paper. His room has a "permanent chill"; the water in his wash bowl "thickened with incipient ice" (p. 298). This "warm lad that once sung to the world of the Tropical Summer," has become an isolate, "shivering thus day after day in his wrappers and cloaks" (p. 306). His solitude and his coldness function to reveal the extent to which he has divorced himself from others as he has concurrently developed a strong sense of independence and a conviction that he is actually god-like. Melville sums up this condition when he describes Pierre's relationship with Isabel and Lucy: "On either hand clung to by a girl who would have laid down her life for him; Pierre, nevertheless, in his deepest, highest part, was utterly without sympathy from anything divine, human, brute, or vegetable. One in a city of hundreds of thousands of human beings, Pierre was solitary as at the Pole" (p. 338). He feels himself "gifted with loftiness" but victimized. Still, "like a demigod [he] bore up" (p. 339). His sense of God-like superiority is manifested in the scorn and contempt with which he regards the critics who will read his book. He considers them all "infinitesimal" from his "pyramidical" loftiness (p. 339). The extent to which he has come to feel apart from and superior to ordinary humankind is indicated in his thoughts as he takes a cold evening walk: "Pierre felt a dark, triumphant joy; that while others had crawled in fear to their kennels, he alone defied the storm-admiral, whose most vindictive peltings of hail-stones,—striking his iron-framed fiery furnace of a body,—melted into soft dew, and so, harmlessly trickled from off him" (p. 340). The changing route of these walks attests again to his increasing separation from everyday life and common humanity, for he moves gradually further and further away from the main streets until finally "nothing but the utter night-desolation of the obscurest warehousing lanes would content him, or be at all sufferable to him" (p. 341).

Pierre's inexorable movement toward darkness is also suggested by his failing eyesight and his vertigo. There appears to be a proportionate relationship between the growth of his righteous ire and sense of Godliness on the one hand and his increasing blindness and dizziness on the other. In one of his rebellious evening walks, he finds himself lost in darkness: "He knew not where he was; he did not have any ordinary life-feeling at all. He could not see; though instinctively putting his hand to his eyes, he seemed to feel that the lids were open. Then he was sensible of a combined blindness, and vertigo, and staggering . . . and knew no more for the time. When he came to himself he found that he was lying crosswise in the gutter, dabbled with mud and slime" (p. 341). In a book whose terrain is mountainous irony, the Himalayan peak is in this situation of a character who has come to be super-sensitive to deception, who feels profoundly victimized, who abhors deception in others but who is tragically deceived about himself. His physical blindness but duplicates his blindness to his inner situation.

He is not aware, for example, of his most fundamental reason for killing Glen. Melville develops that motivation in his complex characterization of Pierre. His hatred of Glen is self-hatred, and the murder is in a sense Pierre's true suicide. Melville's purpose in making Glen look so much like Pierre is to have him play the part of a mirror image.[39] When Pierre calls up Glen's face in his mind or actually encounters him, the rage he experiences is actually directed against himself. In abhorring deception in Glen, he is expressing hatred for the deception he senses within himself, and in reacting with repugnance to Glen's arrogance, he is showing his antipathy for the sense of superiority he feels. "As Pierre conjured up this phantom of Glen transformed into the seeming semblance of himself," Melville writes, "an infinite quenchless rage and malice possessed him. Many commingled emotions combined to provoke this storm. But chief of all was something strangely akin to that indefinable detestation which one feels for any impostor who has dared to assume one's own name and aspect . . . an emotion greatly intensified if this impostor . . . by the freak of nature . . . be almost the personal duplicate of the man whose identity he assumes" (p. 289). What Melville calls "that indefinable detestation" is the same complex emotion that Ahab feels when he thinks of the white whale. Moby Dick projects two warring sides of Ahab, each of which recognizes in the great whale the incarnation of that opposite and intolerable side. One aspect of his being is thus trying to kill off

39. Richard Chase comments: "Etymologically, we perceive, Pierre Glendinning and Glendinning Stanly are the same name, since 'Stanly' comes from a Germanic word for 'stone' and 'Pierre' comes from a Greek word meaning the same" (p. 121). Chase calls Glen, Pierre's "alter ego" (p. 121).

the other strong impulse. Pierre's desire for a sister is a manifestation of his yearning to lose his separateness, to merge with a purer reality. The natural enemy of this urge is his determination to break all ties and to be completely free in his lofty superiority, to be a demigod. When Pierre fires at Glen, he shouts: "For thy one blow, take here two deaths!" (p. 359). He probably means that Glen will die and that he will have to die, too, for the act of murder. But the underlying implication of his remark is that two deaths are immediately taking place; Pierre's fierce individualism and his spirituality are killing each other: "Spatterings of his own kindred blood were upon the pavement; his own hand had extinguished his house" (p. 360).

Pierre has a second "duplicate," however, one which is even more closely comparable than Glen to the white whale in *Moby-Dick*—the Mount of Titans. Melville's description of this great mountain is a masterpiece of rich suggestiveness, almost every detail applying poignantly to Pierre's inner terrain as well as to the actual elevation of two thousand feet near his ancestral home. Stone and mountain imagery pervades the novel (even the name of the hero means "stone").[40] Wherever such references occur, they serve metaphorically to project Melville's vision of the "wonder-world" within. Mountains are used in book 21, for example, to suggest the vastness of and the difficult accessibility to "the soul of a man" (p. 285). This "Switzerland of his soul" is depicted as an alpine region of "tremendous immensity" that includes the Alps, the Rocky Mountains, the Andes and much more besides, an area that one has to find his way in, for "better might one be pushed off into the material spaces beyond the uttermost orbit of our sun" than to be blind and lost in the wild and mountainous world of self (p. 284). Frequently such imagery is characterized by ruggedness, desolation, and ruin. A foreshadowing of Pierre's destruction is offered early in the novel when Melville comments upon his hero's being "unadmonished" by the "foreboding and

---

40. For discussions of this pattern, see Saburo Yamaya, "The Stone Image in Melville's *Pierre*," *Studies in English Literature* (Japan), 34 (1957): 31–57; Richard F. Fleck, "Stone Imagery in Melville's *Pierre*," *Research Studies* 42 (1974): 127–30; and Carol Colclough Strickland, "Coherence and Ambivalence in Melville's *Pierre*," *American Literature* 48 (1976): 302–11.

prophetic lesson taught, not less by Palmyra's quarries, than by Palmyra's ruins" (p. 8). Both what is above and below are equally strewn with crumbling desolation. The "capital" that should have been carved out below ground was left in chaos and destruction just as will be the mind of Pierre Glendinning. In his lack of self-knowledge, Pierre takes no more warning from Palmyra than he does from the Memnon Stone. The two are connected not only through stone imagery but through the legend of Solomon, whom Melville believed to be the profound author of Ecclesiastes ("the fine hammered steel of woe"). Palmyra was a Syrian city supposedly built by Solomon. The letters carved on the Memnon Stone are interpreted by a white-haired acquaintance of Pierre's as Solomon's initials. Though Pierre seems unaware of Palmyra's message and amused by the old man's interpretation, Melville uses Solomon as a foil to Pierre's self-deception. Ironically, Pierre sometimes calls the Memnon Stone the Terror Stone as well he might, for it, like the example of Palmyra, manifests the terrors of the inner world with its "giddy height" and "ponderous in-scrutableness" (p. 134). Yet Pierre is unaware of this metaphorical meaning of the great structure. He feels that he is very familiar with it, and without actually knowing what he is doing, he puts it to a test. When Pierre crawls under the Memnon Stone and addresses it, he is unknowingly going within himself and chal-lenging that dark and complex psyche to destroy him if he is not taking the right course. If he is blind in all his assumptions about life and himself, he is saying, then "Mute Massiveness, fall on me!" (p. 134). That is precisely what happens though not at the moment of Pierre's invocation. The massiveness of his internal world cracks and tumbles upon him because in his ignorance of his real makeup he detects only muteness from self. The descrip-tion of Pierre in jail near the end recalls this passage in which he senses the "Massive Muteness" of the Memnon Stone; it reveals that the terrible and inscrutable self has answered Pierre's chal-lenge: "That sundown, Pierre stood solitary in a low dungeon of the city prison. The cumbersome stone ceiling almost rested on his brow; so that the long tiers of massive cell-galleries above seemed partly piled on him" (p. 360). Surrounded by stone and attended by a jailer who remarks "Kill 'em both with one stone,"

Pierre is at last a "deluge-wreck" crushed by the huge rocks that always threaten the traveler who cannot properly chart the inner wilds.

His moment under the Terror Stone is consequently one of the most ironic in the novel, for Pierre—having spent so little time within himself and thus having not discerned his true situation— emerges from his brief visit with a false sense of security: "and slowly Pierre crawled forth, and stood haughtily upon his feet, as he owed thanks to none, and went his moody way" (p. 135). That Melville meant to suggest Pierre's very center of being by the Memnon Stone is evidenced by its implied similarity to the Omphalos at Delphi, a great stone on which mysterious letters were carved. It was located on a spot the Greeks believed to be the very center of the world, the "navel" of all existence. The Memnon Stone is "shaped something like a lengthened egg" (p. 132). The temple of Apollo at Delphi contained "an egg-shaped stone which was situated in the innermost sanctuary of the temple. . . . Classical legend asserted that it marked the 'navel' (Omphalos) or centre of the Earth."[41] The location of the Memnon Stone "deep into the woods" (p. 131), its strange letters carved thereon, its shape, and its incrutableness all connect it with the Apollonian Omphalos, though this similarity has apparently gone unnoticed in critical writings on *Pierre*.

Whenever Melville speaks of mountains, rocks, stones, or marble, then, he is probably referring to Pierre's inner landscape. The hard and rugged terrain of self, he writes, must be understood and made use of creatively: "These are immense quarries of fine marble; but how to get it out; how to chisel it; how to construct any temple?" One must "get tools to use in the quarry" and must "thoroughly study architecture. Now the quarry-discoverer is long before the stone-cutter; and the stone-cutter is long before the architect; and the architect is long before the temple; for the temple is the crown of the world" (p. 257). Pierre did not prove to be a stone-cutter. Probably the most succinct explanation of his destruction is his vision that comes when he is in a trance, actu-

41. H. W. Parke, *A History of the Delphic Oracle* (Oxford: Basil Blackwell, 1939), p. 9.

ally a rare moment when he experiences a glimpse into self. In book 25 he sees in this "state of semi-unconsciousness," a rock on a slope of the Mount of Titans that resembles "a form defiant." It appears to be Enceladus "the most potent of all the giants, writhing from out the imprisoning earth" and "turning his unconquerable front toward that majestic mount eternally in vain assailed by him" (p. 345). This was an actual rock that had, like the Memnon Stone, interested Pierre in his youth though "its latent significance had never fully and intelligibly smitten him" (p. 345). He had once tried with other boys to uncover the total rock that so resembled the legendary armless giant, but in vain. In his imagination this rock figure comes alive and batters "at the precipice's unresounding wall." Armless, he wreaks "his immitigable hate" on the mountain by turning his "vast trunk into a battering-ram" to pound again and again "against the invulnerable steep." As Pierre cries out "Enceladus," he sees on the giant's "armless trunk," his "own duplicate face and features" magnified (p. 346).

The dream is far more telling than Pierre realizes. He sees himself as a kind of superior being victimized but fighting back against the world's and heaven's deceptions. What he does not see is that he is both the "sky-assaulting" rock figure of Enceladus and the assaulted Mount of Titans. He battles himself when he attacks the mountain as Ahab does when he attacks Moby Dick. Melville suggests Pierre's change from a joyous youth who takes delight in life to a defiant rebel of unusual stature when he comments that the name of the mountain was changed from "The Delectable Mountain" to the "Mount of Titans": "For as if indeed the immemorial mount would fain adapt itself to its so recent name, some people said that it had insensibly changed its pervading aspect" (p. 342). Its pervading aspect upon close examination is frightening, for through the rents among the leaves, one glimpses with horror "dark-dripping rocks, and mysterious mouths of wolfish caves" (p. 343). Once in close and clear view, the great slope is a nightmarish, wreck-strewn land of "scarred rocks" that "shot up, protruded, stretched" and repelled (p. 344). Here some "unquenchable quarrel" seems to have taken place, for it is a "battle-ground" where forces contended with "barbarous disdain" (p. 344). Less than a score of pages before the end of the novel, this startling imagery projects symbolically Pierre's final condition, that terrible state that Melville described as "the woe that is madness": "Stark desolation; ruin, merciless and ceaseless; chills and gloom,—all here lived a hidden life, curtained by that cunning purpleness, which, from the piazza of the manor house, so beautifully invested the mountain once called Delectable, but now styled Titanic" (p. 344).

In addition to manifesting Pierre's private battleground, the Mount of Titans mirrors as well the opposing forces in this war. In its unusual elevation, its reaching toward the sky, it is an apt symbol for Pierre's spiritual nature, his desire to rise above the earth's values to unite with a transcendent realm. At the same time, it is equally appropriate as a representation of specialness, for what is more above the ordinary, more above the dead level of the masses, as Melville called them, than such a proud peak? The God-seeking Pierre-Enceladus throws himself against this peak of pride because arrogant individualism is the foe of the spiritual impulse. The proud demigod Pierre-Enceladus wages war with what he sees in the mountain: a compulsion to merge with the heavens, a drive which threatens to destroy individuality by uniting it with universal oneness. Each side of Pierre-Enceladus sees the opposite quality in the mountain and abhors it. Exactly as was the situation with Ahab, the forces of the internal world are at war with each other without the conscious Pierre knowing clearly what is going on.

It is an inner civil war.[42] To develop this idea, Melville created an intricate pattern of imagery having to do with soldiers, battles, and wars. Culminating with Pierre's actually taking up arms against his enemy toward the end, this motif runs the entire length of the novel. Echoes of past battles reverberate through the early pages where Pierre's military heritage is emphasized. On the very site of his ancestral meadows "an Indian battle had been fought" in which his paternal great-grandfather was killed after

---

42. A fairly widespread interpretation argues that Pierre's main war is with society and its conventions. See, for example, Nicholas Canaday, Jr., "Melville's *Pierre*: At War with Social Convention," *Papers on Language and Literature* 5 (1969): 51–62.

heroically cheering on his troops (p. 5). Only a day's walk away is the battleground where his grandfather fought in the Revolutionary War. As if sensing that he will himself be involved in a kind of internal strife, Pierre in his boyhood "read the History of the Revolutionary War" (p. 13), and he tells his Aunt Dorothea that he knows "all about" the French Revolution (p. 75). He takes great interest in the exploits of his grandfather, who significantly has the same name as he. Pierre is likened to a "war-horse" (p. 14), and at the end of book 1, Melville describes him as being of "double revolutionary descent," for "on both sides" he had a legacy of revolutionary warriors (p. 20). His mother speaks far more than she realizes when she explains, "This is his inheritance" (p. 20). Playfully, he and Lucy use war metaphors in their teasing remarks. When she asks if there are any of their friends watching them, he replies that there are "sharp-shooters behind every clap-board" (p. 23). As his mood grows more somber and he begins to have dark presentiments, he says: "I feel I should find cause for deadly feuds with things invisible" (p. 41), and after he receives Isabel's letter, he is described as feeling "two antagonistic agencies within him" (p. 63). He "invaded" the privacy of Mr. Falsgrave and "made war" on him" (p. 166). Melville also uses the metaphor of battle to chastise that person who in his "miraculous vanity" believes that he has all the answers to life's infinite questions: "Sudden onsets of new truth will assail him, and overturn him as the Tartars did China; for there is no China Wall that man can build in his soul, which shall permanently stay the irruptions of those barbarous hordes which Truth ever nourishes in the loins of her frozen, yet teeming North; so that the Empire of Human Knowledge can never be lasting in any one dynasty, since Truth still gives new Emperors to the earth" (p. 167). Pursuing the same idea, Melville later writes: "All round and round does the world lie as in a sharp-shooter's ambush, to pick off the beautiful illusions of youth, by the pitiless cracking rifles of the realities of age" (p. 218). Even before Pierre leaps "like Spartacus" at Glen, their relationship, though friendly, is described in terms of war. In trying to outdo Pierre in courtesy, Glen "like Napoleon, now seemed bent upon gaining the battle by throwing all his regiments upon one point of attack, and gaining that point at all hazards" (p. 220). Even Pierre's excitement when he first receives money for some poems is expressed in language of battle. He finds the experience more stimulating than "drums and the fife" or "the trumpets of Sparta" (p. 261).

Within this context of war, the purpose of another recurrent metaphorical pattern that may appear curious—if not whimsical—becomes clear. Often in conjunction with references to Pierre's military heritage are many allusions to his "noble," "majestic," or "royal" lineage. In what seems a lighthearted digression in book 1, Melville spends several pages arguing that "the monarchical world" is inaccurate if it assumes that America has no aristocratic families: "in this matter we will—not superciliously, but in fair spirit—compare pedigrees with England, and strange as it may seem at the first blush, not without some claim to equality" (p. 9). He traces English peerage, mentioning names like "Richmond, and St. Albans, and Grafton, and Portland." But he finds that in many instances such English pedigree does not go back very far. George III, he points out, "manufactured" over five hundred peers. This is not so much to devalue the English nobility as to claim for America old and distinguished families with lands and tenants comparable to their English counterparts. That he is indulging in more than patriotic boasting is suggested by the remark that opens his next chapter. The reason that he has been "asserting the great genealogical and real-estate dignity of some families in America," he says, is that "in so doing we poetically establish the richly aristocratic condition of Master Pierre Glendinning." Why he should wish to do that, he intimates, will come out in the narrative that follows. "And to the observant reader the sequel will not fail to show, how important is this circumstance, considered with reference to the singularly developed character and most singular life-career of our hero" (p. 12). Early in the novel, therefore, Melville spends considerable time clothing his hero with the garb of nobility—if not royalty—and then mysteriously challenges his reader to figure out why Pierre should be compared with English kings and dukes. He will say only that such a comparison is extremely important in understanding this "singular" character with a "singular life-career," and he warns that he did not spend all that time in the previous chapter placing Pierre in a frame of nobility for petty reasons. Let not "any man dream," he admonishes, "that the last chapter was merely intended for a foolish bravado, and not with a solid purpose in view" (p. 12).

That purpose may have been simply to make Pierre a kind of American heir-to-a-throne figure in order to dramatize, as the story goes on, his fall from such a great height. But the numerous allusions to English nobility and the royal line throughout the novel suggest that Melville has a more complex intention. He compares "lordships" and their estates "in the heart of a republic" to those "in the reign of the Plantagenets" (p. 11), and he speaks of Pierre's "grand John of Gaunt sire" (p. 271). The Plantagenets ruled England from the middle of the twelfth century to late in the fifteenth. John of Gaunt was founder of the royal house of Lancaster and the great-grandfather of Henry VI, who ruled England—or tried to—during the most notorious civil strife in British history, the Wars of the Roses, a thirty-year conflict (1455–85) between the houses of Lancaster and York. Melville makes Pierre figuratively a descendant of John of Guant, refers to him frequently as of noble birth, and depicts him in a condition of war (especially a civil or revolutionary war) in order to create subtly and brilliantly an associational background for Pierre's psychological turmoil. Shakespeare's view of the Wars of the Roses, as presented in such plays as *Henry VI* and *Richard III,* prevailed throughout most of the nineteenth century, though the modern interpretation of this period is vastly different.[43] Melville, with Shakespeare, would have immediately thought of the Wars of the Roses when seeking for the example *par excellence* of the tragic civil strife. Early historians viewed this breakup of order and law within a great realm with nothing short of horror. It was the natural and perfect choice for Melville, therefore, as the historical analogue to his hero's terrible and destructive mental wars. In the

43. Detailed coverage of this period of English civil strife from a twentieth-century standpoint is afforded by R. B. Mowat, *The Wars of the Roses, 1377–1471* (London: Crosby Lockwood, 1914); and J. R. Lander, *The Wars of the Roses* (London: Secker and Warburg, 1965). A less detailed but excellent overview is Charles Ross, *The Wars of the Roses: A Concise History* (London: Thames and Hudson, 1976).

very first scene of the novel, he associates battle with a flower. Pierre sees on Lucy's white pillow a red flower. Shaking a shrub, "he dislodged the flower, and conspicuously fastened it in his bosom." In parting, he shouts to Lucy, "under these colors I march." She replies, "Bravissimo! oh, my only recruit!" (p. 4). The house of Lancaster, at least in traditional lore, marched under the symbol of the red rose, the house of York under the white.

The colors red and white appear here and there throughout the novel, and flowers are sometimes associated with Pierre, Lucy, and Isabel. "You shall one day be lord of the manor," Pierre's mother tells him. "I anticipate," she continues, "a rare display of rural red and white" (p. 45). Lucy's complexion glows "like rosy snow," and Pierre thinks of her in connection with "the glory of the rose" (p. 58). Young women admirers send Pierre their autograph albums, "not omitting to drop a little attar-of-rose in the palm of the domestic who carried them" (p. 250). Sitting alone in his room at the Apostles, Pierre is "like a flower" whose "bloom is gone" (p. 271). When the references to flowers, roses in particular, are understood as part of the context of war, a passage such as Melville's definition of love, which has been roundly condemned for being sentimental and overblown, becomes pointedly effective because of its biting irony. Love may be "a volume bound in rose-leaves" (p. 34), but when roses are associated with bloody civil strife, that is more ominous than sentimental. If that connection is not enough to undercut his swooning concept of love, Melville much later in the novel shows hypocritical Glen Stanly writing to Pierre his testament of love. The language is so similar as to make it a clear comment on the earlier passage where Melville exclaimed not only that love is a book bound in rose leaves but that it is "printed with peach-juice on the leaves of lilies." Glen selects "his rosiest sheet, and with scented ink, and a pen of gold, indited a most burnished and redolent letter . . . a really magnificent testimonial to his love" (p. 220). Pierre's, then, is the "hard bed of War" (p. 270). He fights his own Wars of the Roses, kin against kin, usurpation the motive. Each side wants to be king, to rule this internal land swept by confusion, lawlessness, and destruction.

A civil war always involves more than the two opposing sets of ideals in open conflict. The "human" elements—ambition, greed, jealousy, and so forth—usually lurk in the shadows of both camps and leap when the time is right. Because Pierre is human, a young man of strong physical makeup, neither his compelling drive to lose his individuality in a higher undefiled force nor his proud determination to preserve the inviolable integrity of that individuality—the warring ideals within him—is pure, for both are tainted and influenced by a characteristic which becomes a major aspect of his fate, namely his sexual appetite. Pierre's repressed sexuality and the theme of incest are strong currents in the novel. Though Melville's fondness for sexual puns and for phallic symbols is well known, it has gone unnoted insofar as I can determine that *Pierre* begins with a kind of sardonic sexual joke. Melville's dedication to Mount Greylock seems flippant, or even silly, unless one gets the joke—which is that he is dedicating his work of art to his male organ.[44] Then it seems shocking and perverse until one gets the point—which is that the indomitable male sex drive is to play a fateful role in this work of art. Melville's stance resembles that of the narrator who searches for and finally finds a "noble cock" in "Cock-A-Doodle-Doo!" The narrator of that short story refers to the crowing cock, a symbol of masculinity, as "princely" and "imperial."[45] The narrator of "I and My Chimney" thinks of his great chimney in a similar vein, and believes it to have great "majesty."[46] Melville uses the word "majesty" six times in his brief dedicatory preface in *Pierre*. "The majestic mountain, Greylock," he says, is his "immediate sovereign lord and king." This "central majesty," he explains, "presides" over an "amphitheater" and gives forth "bounteous and

44. Greylock, however, is more than one of Melville's numerous phallic images. It represents Herman Melville in totality, his tendency toward seeing himself as a vastly superior man and his never-relinquished spiritual impulse. Of utmost importance in distinguishing Melville from his fictive hero who possesses basically the same qualities is the fact that Melville recognizes what Greylock reflects in himself whereas Pierre fails to see his innermost traits manifested in the Mount of Titans.

45. *The Complete Stories of Herman Melville*, ed. Jay Leyda (New York: Random House, 1949), p. 129.

46. Ibid., p. 381.

unstinted fertilizations," for which Melville kneels devoutly and offers up his gratitude, "whether thereto, The Most Excellent Purple Majesty of Greylock benignantly incline his hoary crown or no." When Hawthorne visited the area in 1838, he described Greylock as follows: "It does not ascend into a peak, but heaves up a round ball, and has supporting ridges on each side."[47]

In dedicating *Pierre* to such a sexually suggestive image, Melville is doing what his hero fails to do: he is giving full recognition to one of the strongest human impulses. If that urge is not identified for what it is, if it is repressed or if its great power is attributed to another motive, it will invade other drives and work secretly and destructively in exerting itself. Melville pursued this theme elsewhere, most notably in poems like "After the Pleasure Party" and "The Ambuscade."[48] Pierre believes at first that his reasons for being attracted to Isabel are noble and virtuous. He will not admit that he is sexually drawn to her until this hunger, mingling itself with his higher aspirations, has forced itself upon him and created profound confusion in his soul.

Pierre's story is, in a sense, a serious version of a comic anecdote mentioned in Plinlimmon's pamphlet. Only a perfect person, comments the author of the pamphlet, can live a life "entirely without folly or sin." Christ was able to do it, but with the rest of us, "the absolute effort to live in this world" in accord with the highest and purest ideals is "apt to involve" us in "strange, *unique* follies and sins, unimagined before. It is the story of the Ephesian matron, allegorized" (p. 213). Despite his determination to reverence Isabel as a sister, Pierre desires her as a wife, and that desire, "strange, *unique*" to him, "unimagined before," conflicts with both his desire for God and his desire to be God and thus confounds him. The story of the Ephesian matron is related in *The Satyricon* of Petronius Arbiter. It concerns a young wife of Ephesus who led a life of such exemplary virtue that she acquired

47. Quoted in Luther Stearns Mansfield, "Melville and Hawthorne in the Berkshires," in *Melville and Hawthorne in the Berkshires,* ed. Howard P. Vincent (Kent: Kent State University Press, 1968), p. 7.
48. See William H. Shurr's informative commentary on this recurrent theme. *The Mystery of Iniquity: Melville as Poet, 1857–1891* (Lexington: University Press of Kentucky, 1972), p. 196.

a widespread reputation for her saintliness. When her husband died, she would not be consoled but followed the corpse of her loved one into the vault. There she remained for five days and nights without eating, tearing her hair in grief and weeping until she was dangerously weak. Her admiring friends and acquaintances, seeing that she would not be persuaded to tend to her own human needs, finally left her. In the meantime, a soldier was stationed nearby to guard the bodies of recently crucified criminals so that relatives could not remove them from the crosses and bury them. Being a curious soul and bored with his job, he wandered over to the tomb from which he saw a light and heard sobs. He entered the vault, observed the disconsolate widow, and immediately proceeded to comfort her and offer her part of his supper of food and wine. Though she at first refused him, he was persistent, and finally she broke her fast and began to listen to his kind words of sympathy and practical philosophy about the living having to go on with their lives. After sharing his meal, she succumbed to his embraces. He came back to the vault the next night and the next, bringing meals and spending the night with her in passionate amours. Seeing that the soldier was away from his post, a relative of one of the crucified criminals removed the body from the cross and took it away for burial. The soldier sadly informed the Ephesian matron of this development and, since the punishment for deserting one's post was death, asked her to see that he receive a decent burial. "Upon which she order'd her Husband's Body to be taken out of the Coffin, and fixt to the Cross, in the room of that which was wanting."[49] The soldier gladly performed the switch. He was saved, and, presumably, they were free to continue their affair of lust.

The story of the Ephesian matron has universal appeal because of the timeless theme of hypocrisy. The widow had hidden her passionate nature under a guise of otherworldliness and denied its existence even to herself until the right moment arrived and it burst forth like fiery sparks from a volcano. From that moment on, she could not fulfill her self-concept because it was based on

49. *The Satyricon of T. Petronius Arbiter* (Burnaby's translation of 1694), ed. C. K. Scott Moncrieff (London: Simpkin Marshall, n. d.), pp. 169–70.

false self-assessment. Pierre similarly lives a life of almost spotless virtue and then devotes himself to carrying out a selfless mission until his own volcano erupts. The words of Plutarch in his essay on "EI" again reverberate: "Those who have mixed up things relating to gods with those relating to daemons, have brought themselves chiefly into trouble."[50] Though Melville never indicates directly that Pierre and Isabel indulge in sexual intercourse, it is clear that Pierre has a sexual awakening that shakes him deeply. There can be no doubt that in their intimate moments, he stops thinking of her as a sister and is driven by lust. "His arms embraced her tighter," Melville writes at one point. "His whole frame was invisibly trembling. Then suddenly in a low tone of wonderful intensity he breathed: 'Isabel! Isabel!' " (p. 272). After moments like this, Pierre's movement toward madness is accelerated because the guilt he feels after experiencing intense lust (whether or not he actually acts upon it) violates both his virtuous religious impulse and his growing sense of superiority that tells him he needs no one but himself.[51]

The subject of incest, however, has wide ramifications that go far beyond the destructive guilt that Pierre feels when he has been physically drawn to one who could be his half sister. Late in the novel, Pierre, Lucy, and Isabel encounter in the gallery they visit a copy of "that sweetest, most touching, but most awful of all feminine heads—The Cenci of Guido" (p. 351). Melville finds it "awful" because of the implied contrast between the beautiful face and the horrible crimes that surround it: "With blue eyes and fair complexion, the Cenci's hair is golden—physically, there-

50. Plutarch, p. 528.

51. Critics are divided on the question of whether or not Melville meant to convey the impression that Isabel and Pierre actually engage in sexual intercourse. Impressive arguments are offered on both sides. For a sampling of those who say that the evidence points in the direction of consummation, see Richard Chase, *Herman Melville: A Critical Study;* John Bernstein, *Pacifism and Rebellion in the Writings of Herman Melville* (The Hague: Mouton, 1964); and Floyd C. Watkins, "Melville's Plotinus Plinlimmon and Pierre," in *Reality and Myth,* ed. William E. Walker and Robert L. Welker (Nashville: Vanderbilt University Press, 1964), pp. 39–51. Among those who are convinced that the relationship between Pierre and Isabel definitely does not include sexual intercourse is Nicholas Canaday, Jr., who cites Henry A. Murray as being of like mind.

fore, all is in strict, natural keeping; which, nevertheless, still the more intensifies the suggested fanciful anomaly of so sweetly and seraphically *blonde* a being, being double-hooded, as it were, by the black crepe of the two most horrible crimes (of one of which she is the object, and of the other the agent) possible to civilized humanity—incest and parricide" (p. 351). The daughter of a sixteenth-century Italian nobleman, Beatrice Cenci was a popular subject for nineteenth-century artists and was immortalized in prose, poetry, and painting. Forced to commit incest with her father and kept a virtual prisoner, she plotted revenge with the help of her brothers and a lover. The count, her father, was first drugged, then killed. Beatrice and the others involved were imprisoned and put to death. In Shelley's five-act drama (1820), Beatrice comes to feel that she is divinely directed to exact retributive justice, and as her desire for vengeance burns within her, she develops into a megalomaniac.

The details of Beatrice Cenci's story do not parallel those in the lives of Isabel and Pierre. Beatrice committed incest with her father; Isabel may or may not have committed incest, but if she did, it was with her half brother. Beatrice committed parricide, Isabel suicide. Melville is not as interested in literal parallels here as in metaphorical ones; he is not as concerned with the literal act of incest as he is with the concept of incest as metaphor.[52] In this more imaginative sense, the Cenci legend is highly relevant to Pierre's situation and illumines Isabel's role in the novel. By the time Melville introduces the Cenci portrait into the story it matters little whether Pierre is Isabel's half brother or whether they have shared the same bed. They have an even more fundamental relationship, and incest has taken place on an even more intimate level. Pierre was from the beginning attracted to Isabel physically. His strong sexual urge secretly infiltrated both of the basic impulses of his being—his desire to lose his own individuality in merger with a "sister" and his powerful self-esteem—and united

---

52. Brook Thomas, "The Writer's Procreative Urge in *Pierre*: Fictional Freedom or Convoluted Incest?" *Studies in the Novel* 11 (1979): 416–30, expresses a similar idea, but argues that the incest theme reflects Melville's attitude toward writing.

them in a kind of temporary wedlock that could not last because of the opposing natures of the impulses. In this way, Pierre made Isabel. What the real-life Isabel is remains largely unknown, but that is less important than what she is to Pierre. The Isabel of his mind was conceived through the union of two members of the same psychological household that should never have been allowed intimacy and intercourse because their encounter, brief though it was, put their relationship on a new footing of hate. Isabel is thus the child of incest, and Pierre is her father.[53] He created her in the same way that Simon Magus created Helena, and after conceiving her, he then felt lust for her, the incestuous desire of a father for his daughter. These circumstances produce chaos in Pierre's internal world, and Isabel, both his "daughter" and the object of his lust, becomes a poison to him. In fact, it is the drug that Isabel carries around her neck that kills Pierre.

Melville prepares for that final scene carefully, for Isabel's role as poisoner is intimated throughout the novel. Even before his first interview with her, Pierre feels her toxic influence. He tries to drive from his mind the face that he saw in the sewing group, for "it seemed to have in it a germ of somewhat which, if not quickly extirpated, might insidiously poison and embitter his whole life" (p. 53). Isabel herself recognizes her noxious effect on Pierre and offers at one time to "let thee go, lest some poison I know not of distill upon thee from me" (p. 191). Isabel's poison acts quickly, not only upon Pierre but also upon his mother, who becomes infected with bitter rage that leads to madness and death when she hears of Pierre's marriage. She calls herself a "pride-poisoned woman" (p. 194), and exhibits a "venom" (p. 200) in her makeup that was not there until Isabel's influence entered her life. The vial that Isabel carries is the concrete image of her destructive influence on Pierre. Melville first reveals the existence of this vial late in the novel, when Pierre draws back and Isabel puts her hand on her bosom, "as if resolutely feeling of something deadly there concealed" (p. 332). Literally, she feels the vial, but

---

53. Edgar A. Dryden observes that "for both Isabel and Lucy, Pierre seems capable of fulfilling all the traditional familial roles." "The Entangled Text: Melville's *Pierre* and the Problem of Reading," *Boundary* 2, 7 (1979): 151.

her poison is suffused throughout her being. Her venomous words in the end kill Lucy as Pierre recognizes. "In thy breasts," he cries to her, "life for infants lodgeth not, but death-milk for thee and me!" (p. 360). "The drug," then, is Isabel herself.

As the child of an incestuous union, metaphorically speaking, Isabel inherits the dominant quality of each "parent." She is prideful, selfish, and jealous by nature, much like Pierre's mother and, consequently, much like a side of Pierre himself. On the other hand, she has been visited since early childhood with an "intense and indescribable longing" (p. 174), the counterpart of Pierre's desire for a sister (which is in turn a manifestation of his desire for God). This side of her nature is represented as a flower, the amaranth, which Melville appropriately depicts as springing from the soil on the Mount of Titans, appropriate because that mountain is a metaphor for Pierre. It is a flower that if allowed to go unchecked in its wild growth becomes a threat to the balanced vegetation of the mountain. "The small white flower, it is our bane," the tenants of the mountain complain. "The aspiring amaranth, every year it climbs and adds new terraces to its sway! The immortal amaranth . . ." (p. 343). It is suggestive, Melville says, of "the ever-encroaching appetite for God" (p. 345).

In Isabel are the warring factions of Pierre's own mind. She manifests, therefore, his tendency toward self-destruction. In contrast, Lucy is the objectification of that psychological quality that brings a measure of peace to battling enemies in the mind. She is the catnip of the Mount of Titans, "that dear farm-house herb" that faithfully remains "though all that's human forsake the place" (p. 344).[54] It is the symbol of man's "household peace" (p. 345). The catnip, with its healing properties, is a suitable metaphor for Lucy because she is constantly associated with sweetness and health whereas Isabel is linked with poison and self-destruction. The "sweet aromaticness" of the herb recalls Lucy's use of scents in her room. Isabel brings Pierre bitterness; Lucy offers him strawberries. Her "errand" to the mansion, she says early in

---

54. Carol Colclough Strickland discusses the amaranth and catnip as symbols for Isabel and Lucy but arrives at conclusions about their roles somewhat different from my own.

the novel, is to bring strawberries to Pierre, who "is so wonderfully fond of them" (p. 57). Henry A. Murray suggests that in this episode Melville may have been thinking of the notion once widely held that strawberries remain pure even when surrounded and threatened by poisons of all kinds.[55] Lucy's deep sense of caring that motivates her to go to Pierre even after he has rejected her and to remain with him despite his deplorable state, her willingness to accept Isabel as she is without questions and without rancor, her desire simply to make a flourishing household by contributing to it and by loving all its members—these qualities may strain her believability as a character, but they make her a superb projection of that psychological element so essential to survival in Melville's way of thinking, namely self-love.[56] In this complex psychological allegory, Lucy is the mediating principle that strives for health and peace by understanding all the factions, loving them all, and without trying to exterminate any of them, bringing them into a kind of balance that is necessary for survival. She is the peacemaker that ends self-war.[57] Melville's own Lucy-principle was successful, and he survived long, through many storms. Pierre's Lucy was not able to save him; the instinct of self-love, which is to say understanding and acceptance of all the basic sides of one's self, could not prevail over forces carrying him to madness and destruction.[58]

Like *Moby-Dick, Pierre* is very much a book about survival,

55. Murray, p. 450.

56. Her letter to Pierre stands in sharp contrast to Isabel's. Lucy's letter is the opposite of a "call." Instead of beckoning Pierre to come forward, it notifies him that she is coming to him in love and patient understanding.

57. Others have found Lucy a less positive character. Charles Moorman, for example, writes that "Lucy may very well represent a sort of sterility when she is considered in relation to Isabel" (p. 23). Moorman finds Isabel to stand for "life-fertility" and Lucy for "death-sterility" (p. 24).

58. Lucy does prove to be surprisingly strong, however. Pierre's mother is fond of Lucy because the strong-willed Mary feels, erroneously, that the younger woman is weak and will not compete with her for control over Pierre. Early in the novel Melville indicates that Mrs. Glendinning "very widely and immeasurably erred" in her estimate of Lucy (p. 59). Had she realized Lucy's real strength, Pierre's mother would have rejected her (as she did Isabel) in order to be the controlling force in Pierre's life.

though death is in the foreground. Lucy's is a voice of health and life in *Pierre,* but it is drowned out by the trumpets of the hero's warring factions. Nevertheless, Melville pauses at intervals to express various strategies for survival. He is especially concerned with methods of avoiding confusion and madness. "If a frontier man be seized by wild Indians," he writes, "and carried far and deep into the wilderness, and there held a captive . . . then the wisest thing for that man is to exclude from his memory . . . those beloved objects now forever reft from him." If he dwells upon his separation from them, "the same man shall, in the end, become as an idiot" (p. 307). The "wild Indians" here are forces of one's own mind over which control has been lost. It is infinitely better not to reach that point of captivity, however. In order to avoid such a situation, Melville advises against straying too far on wild and unknown trails. "The example of many minds forever lost, like undiscoverable Arctic explorers, amid those treacherous regions, warns us entirely away from them; and we learn that it is not for man to follow the trail of truth too far, since by so doing he entirely loses the directing compass of his mind; for arrived at the Pole, to whose barrenness only it points, there, the needle indifferently respects all points of the horizon alike" (p. 165). By the "trail of truth," Melville means truth external to man, the profound mysteries which by his limited nature man is not equipped completely to solve. He does not mean truth about one's self, self-knowledge and understanding, which one should pursue, in preference to any other trail that leads away from self into a barren labyrinth.

Self-knowledge, then, is the first principle of survival, and fundamental to it is knowing that things of the body should not be confused with things of the soul. "Feed all things," Melville writes, "with food convenient for them,—that is, if the food be procurable. The food of thy soul is light and space; feed it then on light and space. But the food of thy body is champagne and oysters; feed it then on champagne and oysters" (p. 299). If one does not, the flesh will work its way through subterfuge and violence: "For there is no faith . . . and no philosophy, that a mortal man can possibly evoke, which will stand the final test of . . . Life and Passion upon him. . . . Amidst his gray philosophizings, Life breaks upon a man like a morning" (p. 289).

All of these wise admonitions find their way into Plinlimmon's pamphlet, which is essentially a handbook of survival whose principles, as far as they go, parallel Melville's own convictions.[59] The story of the Ephesian matron alluded to in the pamphlet makes precisely the same point that Melville makes in his advice to feed the body what it needs. Whenever the pamphlet refers to "virtuous expediency" or "practical results," it is dealing with survival. Its overall message is exactly that expressed in Ecclesiastes: "Be not righteous over much; neither make thyself over wise; why shouldest thou destroy thyself? Be not over much wicked, neither be thou foolish: why shouldest thou die before thy time?" (7:16–17). In his Bible, Melville changed "destroy thyself" in verse 16 to "be desolate," a marking Jay Leyda believes to have been made in 1850.[60] The theme that pervades the pamphlet is that which resounds throughout *Pierre*: "Know thyself; avoid extremes."

This is not to say, however, that the pamphlet and the man whose ideas it expresses, Plotinus Plinlimmon, serve as vehicles for Melville's exact views on survival. There are common denominators to be sure: an emphasis upon surviving in a materialistic world alien to spirituality and idealism, the futility of pursuing any truth but self-understanding, the necessity of avoiding obsessional behavior. These are Melville's convictions as well as Plinlimmon's. Why, then, is Plinlimmon himself not presented in a more favorable light? It is clear that Melville agrees with the basic ideas of the pamphlet, yet he writes of the man who holds those ideas as a person in whom "there was still something" that "repelled" (p. 290). Unquestionably, Plinlimmon is a survivor.[61] He has maintained "the directing compass of his

59. Not infrequently, however, readers interpret the pamphlet as Melville's satire on views he abhorred. See, for example, Brian Higgins, "Plinlimmon and the Pamphlet Again," *Studies in the Novel* 4 (1972): 27–38. The pamphlet seems to me no more satirical than is Father Mapple's sermon in *Moby-Dick*. In fact, the two serve much the same function as commentaries on survival but not presenting exactly or completely Melville's own thoughts on the subject.

60. Jay Leyda, *The Melville Log: A Documentary Life of Herman Melville, 1819–1891* (New York: Harcourt, Brace, 1951), 1:370.

61. One of the most eloquent defenses of Plinlimmon and the pamphlet is offered by Floyd C. Watkins, who makes the observation that, after all, Plinlim-

mind." Melville describes him as "a very plain, composed, manly figure, with a countenance rather pale if any thing, but quite clear and without wrinkle" (p. 289). He mirrors "a cheerful content," not delight or happiness, but a kind of pleasant acquiescence. He exercises an unusual degree of self-awareness; consequently, to others he appears "inscrutable." Paradoxically, those who possess great self-knowledge seem to the world unfathomable whereas those who are pulled this way and that way by impulses they do not understand are likely to appear transparent and thus to be gravely misunderstood.[62] An example of how Plinlimmon puzzles the world is seen in an episode involving a certain "foreign scholar, a rich nobleman," who admiringly sends Plinlimmon a set of books embodying man's quest for answers to the eternal riddles. Plinlimmon leaves the bundle of volumes unopened and tells the count, "missent." Instead of sending him books, he complains, the count should have offered him "a few jugs of choice Curaçoa" (p. 291). Bewildered, the scholar-nobleman replies that he thought the society which Plinlimmon heads opposed drinking. "Dear Count," says his host, "so they do; but Mohammed hath his own dispensation." The count indicates that he sees the point, but he does not, as Plinlimmon realizes: "I am afraid you do not see, dear Count," he calmly states, "and instantly before the eyes of the Count, the inscrutable atmosphere eddied and eddied roundabout this Plotinus Plinlimmon" (p. 291).

Melville is Plinlimmon's ally in this episode; he has given the strange philosopher words that he might have spoken himself.[63]

---

mon "survives and endures" (p. 50) and that "the reader must see that some expediency and reconciliation are necessary for sanity and existence" (p. 51).

62. That Plinlimmon is out of the ordinary is suggested by Melville's including in his discussion of his background a detail that is usually the mark of an extraordinary person—he seems to have no past. "Whence he came," Melville writes, "no one could tell. . . . He seemed to have no family or blood ties of any sort" (p. 290).

63. For an opposing view, see Nathalia Wright, who argues that "Plinlimmon is doubly a hypocrite and impostor, since he does not practice total abstinence as the Apostles are supposed to do." In addition, he is an "evil counsellor, especially in his lectures, like the one Pierre read on his way to the city" (p. 176).

Plinlimmon rejects the books for the reason Melville expresses just a few pages earlier: "All the great books in the world are but the mutilated shadowings-forth of invisible and eternally unembodied images in the soul. . . . If we would see the object, we must look at the object itself, and not at its reflection" (p. 284). Plinlimmon looks for truth within himself, not within books. And he understands, as does Melville, that the body needs its champagne and oysters (or in this episode, Curaçoa).[64] He is a striking foil to Pierre because he truly *sees;* Melville depicts him constantly staring through a window at Pierre, who is deeply disturbed by this face of repose because his own inner world is in turmoil. Still, there remains something negative about Plinlimmon. "That something," Melville writes, "may best be characterized as non-Benevolence. Non-Benevolence seems the best word, for it was neither Malice nor Ill-will; but something passive" (p. 290). In manifesting this quality, Plinlimmon diverges from Melville. Constantly Melville had to remind himself to pull back from benevolent involvement. Sometimes he waited too long and was injured. His devotion to Hawthorne is perhaps the best example of that. Plinlimmon, on the other hand, is cold and aloof even though he shares with Melville certain fundamental attitudes. He is named for a mountain in Wales that contrasts sharply with that which Melville uses to represent himself, Greylock, and also with that which is a metaphor for Pierre, the Mount of Titans. To be sure, the actual Plynlimon in Wales is a mountain and consequently embodies symbolically the aspects of the inner being that both Melville and Pierre possess. Despite this, there is an unattractiveness about Mount Plynlimon that moved Melville to select it for his use. Tudor Edwards describes Plynlimon as "the centre of a bog-overlaid shale plateau," which is "remote and austere," even "desolate."[65] Later in his book on

---

64. In this self-love, he possesses a strong component of what Lucy represents in *Pierre*. Indeed, he is linked to Lucy through several references. She is of Welsh background; his surname is Welsh. She has striking blue eyes; his blue eyes are emphasized. She preaches to Pierre to avoid extremes; he espouses the same view.

65. Tudor Edwards, *The Face of Wales* (London: B. T. Batsford, 1950), p. 3.

Wales, Edwards refers to the mountain as "sodden" and "tantalisingly elusive."[66]

The basic difference between Plotinus Plinlimmon and Melville is that they do not act on their self-knowledge in the same way. They have chosen dissimilar courses for survival, though they share the secret for not losing one's directing compass of mind. Plinlimmon is an exemplar of the Greek ideal—the Golden Mean. Melville associates him with the classical Greek world by indicating that in his eye "the gay immortal youth Apollo, seemed enshrined; while on that ivory-throned brow, old Saturn cross-legged sat" (p. 290).[67] For many of his "apostles," he is, indeed, a sort of Apollonian oracle. They cling to his every word as if it were divinely inspired. He seems, too, to speak a deep and prophetic message to Pierre, a message that the youth cannot fully interpret. "Look, look," his countenance appears to say to Pierre. "Look within yourself for truth; know yourself well and then chart your course in accord with that knowledge." Plinlimmon has gone beneath his own Memnon Stone, dwelled at the center, the Omphalos, much longer than did Pierre in his momentary incursion. It is no coincidence that his name, Plinlimmon, is close in sound to "Memnon," the designation Pierre gives to the natural phenomenon that represents the center-self.

In Plinlimmon, Melville has depicted an alternate mode of survival from his own.[68] Having acquired intimate knowledge of his own nature, of different impulses that coexist in his inner

66. Ibid., p. 56. William Van O'Connor identifies (as did Henry A. Murray earlier) the source of Plinlimmon's surname as the mountain in Wales, but, strangely, he describes Mount Plynlimon as a towering and inspiring site of beauty and glory. "Plotinus Plinlimmon and the Principle of Name Giving," in *The Grotesque: An American Genre and Other Essays* (Carbondale: Southern Illinois University Press, 1962), pp. 92–97.

67. The association is deepened by Melville's comment that on Plinlimmon's "ivory-throned brow, old Saturn cross-legged sat" (p. 290). Saturn, or Cronus, was ruler during the Golden Age of which Hesiod writes. No work was necessary during this period (Plinlimmon does no work) of easy abundance.

68. John J. Gross sees Plinlimmon as projecting the *only* "alternative to a world in which absolute idealism, ending in despair and final destruction, fails to create community among men." "The Face of Plinlimmon and the 'Failures' of the Fifties," *Emerson Society Quarterly,* no. 28 (1962): 8.

world, and having come to the point of being able to attribute accurately certain motivations and desires to their actual sources, Plinlimmon contrasts sharply with Pierre, but he is also a foil to Melville, who did not choose the route of the Golden Mean. Their difference lies in the ways they exert discipline and control over their internal forces. Plinlimmon retains his directing compass of mind by understanding his conflicting emotions and then by meshing them, as it were. He removes from each its potential for moving him to extremes of thought or behavior by bringing it into a relation of compromise with the other sides of his being. He forms, then, a kind of synthesis from opposing components of mind. That Melville was highly sensitive to the perils of self-ignorance and self-deception is apparent in his portrayal of Pierre. That he was also aware that there is more than one way to act on self-knowledge is seen in his depiction of Plotinus Plinlimmon. Tyranically, Plinlimmon forces the subjects of his inner realm into a peace of compromise, treating them sympathetically and caring for them, but taking away any weapons that might lead to insurrection. Consequently, his is a world of survival and "cheerful content," but it is also "passive" and "non-benevolent." A certain vitalizing energy is missing, and those swings of emotion that may terrify but nevertheless make one intense and bring on moments of sudden inspiration are disciplined into calm, steady, and moderate states of consciousness. Melville's reaction to Plinlimmon's way of surviving is indicated in his comment that from the pamphlet he derives an understanding of the problem of survival but does not receive a solution that fits his own needs. From it, he says, "I confess, that I myself can derive no conclusion which permanently satisfies those peculiar motions in my soul." For *him,* he stresses, the pamphlet is "the excellently illustrated re-statement of a problem" rather than a chart of the course he would himself follow to survival (p. 210).

Melville's way is that which he projected through Ishmael and through various other characters in his works, not the following of a steady middle course between extremes, but an oscillation involving those extremes. His is a more stormy realm than Plinlimmon's. He, too, knows well those warlords that exist there and what their particular needs are, but he does not force them into the same degree of subjugation. He even allows this one and then that to hold sway for a limited time over the kingdom, but not for long, lest the power gain permanent control over the whole land. Thus it is a precarious balance. The strong, separate, and jealous rulers of states are kept from destructive civil war only by the love that a wise king has for each of them and the shrewd understanding that he has of their every move. Though a less cheerful and contented land than Plinlimmon's, it is a more vital one because when his time comes, each powerful chieftain can express himself and shake the kingdom. Each realizes, however, the strength of the king and remains silent when commanded to do so.

Pierre and Ahab are both captive kings, overcome and ruled by their subjects whom they never adequately understood. That essential self-knowledge must precede any course of action. Melville's life-long struggle was to gain it and retain it. His intense pursuit is reflected in his treatment of a character like Pierre, in whom Melville embodies his own fundamental traits as if to get them down on paper and thus to analyze them closely and understand them. But understanding what is within him is just half the plan; he must also imagine vividly what will happen if he ceases his constant vigilance of self. Writing becomes for him not only a way of knowing but also a way of warning. To create Pierre's terrible plight is in effect an act of survival on Melville's part. Biographers and critics have frequently commented on certain similarities between Melville's own habits when he was composing and those he describes as Pierre's. In questioning the wisdom of Pierre's obsession with his writing, he shows genuine concern for his own health: "Here surely is a wonderful stillness of eight hours and a half, repeated day after day. In the heart of such silence, surely something is at work. Is it creation, or destruction? Builds Pierre the noble world of a new book? or does the Pale Haggardness unbuild the lungs and the life in him?— Unutterable, that a man should be thus!" (p. 304). Melville is here gazing with horror over a precipice in his own life, marking it well so that somehow he can avoid it. Instead of allowing himself to be totally controlled by feelings of bitterness, anger, and scorn, he gives those destructive emotions to his vicarious creation who goes mad for him and dies for him. Almost certainly his account of Pierre's contempt for nearly everyone but especially for those who bestow literary fame (or who prevent a writer from receiving it) is an exaggerated version of his own tendencies, but instead of justifying Pierre's scorn, he recognizes it as a surrender of self to wild and destructive emotions. Pierre, he adds, has become "a doorless and shutterless house for the four loosened winds of heaven to howl through" (p. 339). Such analyses and admissions involving his temptations help prevent him from carrying through on them.[69]

This fact—namely, that Melville was writing to such a great degree for his own sake in *Pierre*—accounts for many of the peculiarities in point of view. He created a character like himself to be destroyed in place of himself and whose story is to be told by himself. The problems inherent in such a plan are infinite, but perhaps the most fundamental one he faced was how to keep himself, as the narrator, from expressing great sympathy and pity for Pierre. The temptation was powerful because Pierre shadows forth Melville. Yet, he had to avoid such an emotional entanglement with his hero; to identify too closely with him would be to minimize Pierre's deplorable self-deception. Pierre is not a survivor; Melville is. That difference could never be forgotten lest Pierre's value to Melville in his plan of survival diminish to nothingness. It was not forgotten, and Melville exhibits a startling lack of sympathy for his suffering young hero throughout most of the book. The methods that he uses to do so, however, create a bizarre effect. He expresses Pierre's views on life early in the novel as if they were his own, but he does it in such an exaggerated manner as to make those ideas appear inanely idealistic. "Oh,

69. Because many of Melville's characters arrive at no answers to the dilemmas of life, some biographers and critics have assumed that Melville himself found all problems and no solutions. "Melville presents moral and spiritual problems," writes Tyrus Hillway; "he rarely solves them." "Pierre, the Fool of Virtue," *American Literature* 21 (1949): 201. Such a position rightly takes issue with those scores of critics who have seen Melville as moralist, Christian or otherwise, but it may lead to the assumption that Melville could not work out for himself a viable strategy of survival. By the very act of presenting those moral and spiritual problems of imaginary beings, he was finding a way for himself to live.

praised be the beauty of this earth," he intones in a symphony of silliness, "the beauty, and the bloom, and the mirthfulness thereof" (p. 32). This statement and a hundred others like it, together with the anachronistic use of *thee* and *thou*, create a curious artificiality that has puzzled and repelled readers since the novel appeared. Surely Melville recognized the stilted unnaturalness of the words Pierre speaks when he hears of Dolly Ulver's plight: "'Curses, wasp-like, cohere on that villain, Ned, and sting him to his death!' cried Pierre, smit by this most piteous tale. 'What can be done for her, sweet Isabel; can Pierre do aught?'" (p. 155). Melville would not himself indulge in outbursts in praise of Nature or Beauty or Love, speak like a Quaker, or create curses that could have come from the shallowest nineteenth-century melodramas. He is doing more than satirizing romantic novels: he is putting necessary distance between himself and his character.[70]

Other methods are used as the novel goes on. He mocks Pierre; he analyzes him with calculated objectivity; he even lectures him on the error of his ways. All these aspects of tone and point of view enable Melville to refrain from embracing this imaginary version of himself with both arms. He must maintain distance in order to experience difference; his survival as narrator of this particular intricate and complex tale depends upon his remaining apart and aloof from Pierre. The task is arduous, the task of writing about a character as admirable and as well-meaning as Pierre (who starts off in life so well and ends up so sadly) without committing oneself emotionally to him. Melville succeeds, however. He survives as narrator and proves for the first time that he does not need to create a fictional figure as he did in each of his six

70. One of the recurrent complaints about *Pierre*, however, is that Melville was too *close* to his hero. The novel is a "fiasco," claims Newton Arvin, and one reason for its failure is that Melville "could not remove himself far enough from it [his material] to be its master rather than its victim." *Herman Melville* (New York: William Sloane, 1950), pp. 226, 227. Murray Krieger argues similarly: "The distance between Melville and Pierre . . . frequently comes close to vanishing altogether." "Melville's 'Enthusiast': The Perversion of Innocence," in *The Tragic Vision: Variations on a Theme in Literary Interpretation* (New York: Holt, Rinehart and Winston, 1960), p. 196.

preceding novels to perform that function. But his survival of this severe psychological and aesthetic test involves him in such multifold stances that point of view has become one of the most controversial issues involving the novel.[71]

That Melville's motivation for writing *Pierre* was largely to purge himself emotionally and to keep himself alert to the necessity of firm self-control should not be surprising considering the state of the art of psychiatry in his day. After expressing to his mother the inexplicable shock with which he first witnessed Isabel's face, Pierre calms her with this remark: "If you know aught of the physical and sanitary authors, you must be aware, that the only treatment for such a case . . . is for all persons to ignore it in the subject. So no more of this foolishness. Talking about it only makes me feel very unpleasantly silly, and there is no knowing that it may not bring it back upon me" (p. 48). The "physical and sanitary authors" of today would urge Pierre to talk about his wild feelings so that he himself could understand them better. Talking out such aberrant emotions in Melville's day, however, was thought to encourage, not prevent, madness. Pierre's assumption thus fits squarely into what Melville knew to be the prevalent opinion of contemporary psychologists. More important, it suggests that he felt that talking about his disturbances with others was not an option in his quest for self-knowledge. Consequently his writing became his mode of expressing, understanding, and controlling self. If he had tried to give vent orally to the anxieties that are hidden in the pages of *Pierre,* he would have met with the theories that lay behind all the study of madness in his day. Patients in mental institutions were urged not to talk about their troubles but to forget them. They were encouraged to rest, to get away from the things causing them pain. The homes for the disturbed were called "asylums." In 1846, John

71. See, for example, Raymond J. Nelson, "The Art of Herman Melville: The Author of *Pierre*," *Yale Review* 59 (1969): 197–214; and Karl F. Knight, "The Implied Author in Melville's *Pierre*," *Studies in American Fiction* 7 (1979): 163–74. Nelson argues that *Pierre* is the novel that Pierre is writing—that Pierre's is the narrative voice in the book. Knight agrees that the narrator is not Melville but believes him to be an implied author who is the real subject of Melville's satire.

Barlow wrote in *On Man's Power over Himself to Prevent or Control Insanity* that were the thoughts that agitate a man's mind "all expressed and indulged, they would be as wild, and perhaps as frightful in their consequences as those of any madman."[72] At the same time that one was warned not to articulate disturbing thoughts, he was expected to understand and control his mind, "What is now fashionably termed *monomania*," wrote Barlow, "is more often owing to a want of moral control over the mind than to any unsoundness of the intellectual faculties."[73] Echoing some of the most prominent physicians of his day, Barlow goes so far as to say that "the difference between sanity and insanity consists in the degree of self-control exercised."[74] The contradiction inherent in a theory that on the one hand prohibits a probing into and a free expression of the matters that most disturb the mind and on the other hand prescribes control of the mind through understanding self-discipline must have struck Melville with great poignancy. He knew that he must probe, understand, and express *in order to* exercise control. But he also realized that there was only one medium open to him because of current attitudes about mental health—his art.

But Pierre is also an author of sorts and he, too, is writing a novel that expresses his own deepest emotions. "It is much to our purpose," Melville comments, that "he seems to have directly plagiarized from his own experiences, to fill out the mood of his apparent author-hero, Vivia" (p. 302). Yet the art of fictional creation does not provide Pierre with a route toward survival. The more he writes, the more bitter he becomes and the more chaotic internally. "I hate the world," Vivia raves, "and could trample all lungs of mankind as grapes" (p. 303).[75] From the various parts of Pierre's manuscript that he quotes, Melville remarks that the young author is reflecting in his writing what is "black and ter-

72. John Barlow, *On Man's Power over Himself to Prevent or Control Insanity* (Philadelphia: Lea and Blanchard, 1846), p. 36.

73. Ibid., p. 37.

74. Ibid., p. 36.

75. Melville may have chosen the name Vivia because of its suggestion of vivification, the process of giving life to. Through Vivia, Pierre is giving life to the Demigod urge in him.

rific in his soul" (p. 303). Expressing one's most profound and disturbing thoughts in fiction, then, does not guarantee survival. In Pierre's case, it hurries him toward madness and destruction.

Since there are so many details of Pierre's background that parallel Melville's, it is tempting to see Melville as using his hero in the same way that Pierre is using Vivia—as a thinly disguised version of the author proclaiming his deepest convictions. To a large extent this is true. Melville narrates a story about a character much like him named Pierre, who in turn is composing a novel about a character named Vivia, who is much like him. Melville survives his act of creation, however, whereas Pierre does not. The reason is as fundamental as any principle embodied in the book: Melville begins from a base of self-knowledge to create a character who is like himself in every other way except in the possession of this essential ingredient. Then he builds distance between himself and his character by stressing in numerous ways Pierre's fatal self-deception. That distance enables him to view his character not as what he is but what he could possibly become. In contrast, Pierre merely perpetuates his own self-blindness through Vivia. He does not analyze himself by separating out for examination the complex strands of mind in his hero and then by working out imaginatively the disastrous consequences of convenient lies and duty-subterfuges, but pours all of his rage and self-pity and newly gained insight about the nature of the world unfiltered into Vivia. Pierre, then, was for Melville not only an example of how not to live internally but also of how not to write.

Poverty and Liberty:
ISRAEL POTTER

Chapter 8

I *srael Potter: His Fifty Years of Exile* emerges from one of the most productive periods of Melville's life, the years of his short fiction. During this time in between the publication of *Pierre* in 1852 and *The Confidence-Man* in 1857, he composed that impressive body of sixteen short stories and sketches published principally in two prominent magazines, *Putnam's Monthly* and *Harper's New Monthly*. *Israel Potter* is the only novel to come from this period, and even it was first published serially—his only novel to appear in that form—in *Putnam's* (July 1854–March 1855). It is not surprising, then, that in subject and method it appears more akin to the short fiction than to *Moby-Dick* and *Pierre*, the two novels that immediately preceded it. The raving and rebelling hero is gone; profundity becomes effectively camouflaged behind an illusion of vapidity. And a chief concern of the novel is one which Melville came back to time and again in his short stories— poverty. He depicted it in "Cock-a-Doodle-Doo!," "The Two Temples," "Poor Man's Pudding and Rich Man's Crumbs," "The Paradise of Bachelors and the Tartarus of Maids," "Jimmy Rose," and elsewhere in these stories of the fifties.

244

Like "Benito Cereno," which was composed during the same general period,[1] *Israel Potter* is based upon the life of a real person and to some extent follows a written source. The *Life and Remarkable Adventures of Israel R. Potter* was published in Providence in 1824. Somewhere Melville picked up "a tattered copy" of this 108-page pamphlet "forlornly published on sleazy gray paper" (p. vii) and read it several years before he wrote his own version of Potter's life.[2] As early as 1849 he was thinking about writing the story. On December 18, 1849, he recorded in his European journal that he had spent a rainy day browsing in London bookshops and had purchased a map of London (as the city was in the eighteenth century). "I want to use it," he wrote, "in case I serve up the Revolutionary narrative of the beggar."[3] In one brief phrase—"the Revolutionary narrative of the beggar"—Melville revealed wherein lay his interest—a search for liberty through revolution that ends in poverty. The *Life and Remarkable Adventures,* supposedly composed by Potter himself but, as Melville realized, written by another (now known to be Henry Trumbull), breaks into halves, the first dealing with Potter as a youthful adventurer, as combat soldier, as captive, and as escapee; and the second with Potter as victim of destitution. The final half of the book is one long journey through hardship with scenes that haunt the mind and disturb its peace: Potter in debtors' prison, a widow with five children having to eat roasted dog, a dead woman in her simple coffin surrounded by her children crying from hunger as much as from grief, a dead man in whose stomach is found (during the

---

1. See Merton M. Sealts, Jr., "The Chronology of Melville's Short Fiction, 1853–1856," *Harvard Library Bulletin* 28 (1980): 391–403, reprinted in *Pursuing Melville, 1940–1980: Chapters and Essays by Merton M. Sealts, Jr.* (Madison: University of Wisconsin Press, 1982), pp. 221–31; and Alma A. MacDougall, "The Chronology of *The Confidence-Man* and 'Benito Cereno': Redating Two 1855 Curtis and Melville Letters," *Melville Society Extracts,* no. 53 (1983): 3–6.

2. Herman Melville, *Israel Potter: His Fifty Years of Exile,* ed. Harrison Hayford et al. (Evanston and Chicago: Northwestern University Press and the Newberry Library, 1982). All references to *Israel Potter* are to this edition.

3. *Journal of a Visit to London and the Continent by Herman Melville, 1849–1850,* ed. Eleanor Melville Metcalf (Cambridge: Harvard University Press, 1948), p. 75.

autopsy) absolutely nothing except some grass that he ate in desperation, and so forth. During a time when poverty was much on Melville's mind and the subject of his pen, it is no wonder that he was drawn to this tale of great woe.

In his short fiction, Melville depicts characters reacting in one of two ways when they find themselves in a state of deprivation. Some, like Bartleby, the narrator of "Cock-A-Doodle-Doo!," and Merrymusk, defy the power of poverty to encroach upon their inner lives and destroy their independence. Almost perversely they seem to welcome the challenge of poverty because it furnishes them with the opportunity to overcome the external physical world. Because they lose touch with that world, such characters, heroic as they may be, are not survivors. Others, like the pathetic Coulters in "Poor Man's Pudding and Rich Man's Crumbs," become victims of poverty in a double sense. The wolf devours not only their bodies but their spirits as well. Though they may continue to live on, managing somehow to exist even in the poorest circumstances, they die internally. So one way or the other, poverty was for Melville destructive; his goal was to avoid it.

When Melville read the *Life and Remarkable Adventures,* he envisioned a man who survived fifty years of exile and hardship but who died, in a sense, long before he died. In Israel Potter, Melville saw a person who became exiled from himself, who lost touch with his inner world, and who reached the end of his life as a man without a country, *any* country. In his old age, England is still an alien realm to him; America is indifferent and will not recognize his claim to a pension. More important, he has no inner country, no wonder-world from which understanding and psychic energy flow forth. Trumbull's Potter is pathetic, his tribulations moving, but he is a mere vapor, a shadow rather than a fleshed-out, three-dimensional character. Genre and mediocre artistry may have combined to produce such an effect, but Melville looked deeper and realized the ultimate truth of the portrait. Though Melville's version of Potter's life is different in a great many respects from Trumbull's, it preserves the final impression of the hero's lack of substance.[4]

4. For a differing view, see Robert M. Farnsworth, who refers to Potter as a

Indeed, Melville's departures from his basic source underscore his concept of Israel Potter as a man who became a ghost long before his actual demise and reveal his interest in the process that brought this about rather than in the events of his hero's life after it happened. Though Melville claims in his dedication that he simply "retouched" the *Life and Remarkable Adventures,* he followed closely only about the first half of his source, which he included in merely five of the twenty-six chapters of his novel. Beginning with chapter 2 and continuing on until Israel meets Benjamin Franklin at the beginning of chapter 7, Melville with a few exceptions echoes the first fifty pages or so of the *Life and Remarkable Adventures.* After that, he puts his major source aside in favor of other materials, notably Robert C. Sands's compiled *Life and Correspondence of John Paul Jones* (1830), James Fenimore Cooper's *History of the Navy of the United States of America* (1839), and Ethan Allen's *A Narrative of Colonel Ethan Allen's Captivity* (1779).[5] His own imaginative contributions, however, dominate the novel after he departs from Trumbull. With all his changes, Melville was nevertheless truthful in his claim of "general fidelity to the main drift of the original narrative" (p. viii), for he makes Israel Potter a cypher just as did Trumbull. He simply goes about it with all the cunning, brilliance, and artistic skill that Trumbull, a writer of "lives" and captivity narratives, lacked.[6] He uses a few of the details from the second half of Trumbull, but he does not follow him into a lengthy and relentless depiction of Israel's London years. Trumbull emphasizes Potter's physical destitution. Melville focuses upon the poverty of the inner man. Consequently, he does not include scenes like those involving the

---

"Titan." *Israel Potter:* Pathetic Comedy," *Bulletin of the New York Public Library* 65 (1961): 125–32.

5. Walter E. Bezanson's "Historical Note" to the Northwestern-Newberry edition of *Israel Potter* is a comprehensive treatment of background and sources. See also Roger P. McCutcheon, "The Technique of Melville's *Israel Potter,*" *South Atlantic Quarterly* 27 (1928): 161–74. R. D. Madison points out that Melville did not use the first edition of Cooper's *History of the Navy* but a later one (1840, 1846, or 1853). *Melville Society Extracts,* no. 47 (1981): 9–10.

6. In addition to writing the *Life and Remarkable Adventures of Israel R. Potter,* Trumbull was the author of the *Life and Adventures of Colonel Daniel Boone* (Providence, 1824) and the *Life and Adventures of Robert, the Hermit of Massachusetts* (Providence, 1829).

roasted dog or the loss of every piece of the Potters' pitiful furniture. Instead, he quickly summarizes Israel's tribulations of four decades in London in one brief chapter (chapter 25).

Israel Potter has been called an historical novel, and in a sense it is because of the background details of the Revolutionary War and its aftermath in England and because such historical figures as Benjamin Franklin, John Paul Jones, and Ethan Allen are characters in the plot.[7] For Melville, however, the book was essentially biography, an *inside* biography. He probably never wrote a more deceptive or mischievous statement than the first sentence of the novel's dedication in which he accurately identifies his primary concern as biographical but then disclaims any personal connection with the subject or any benefit to be derived from writing about him: "Biography, in its purer form, confined to the ended lives of the true and brave, may be held the fairest meed of human virtue—one given and received in entire disinterestedness—since neither can the biographer hope for acknowledgment from the subject, nor the subject at all avail himself of the biographical distinction conferred" (p. vii). Not "entire disinterestedness" but entire self-interest was behind Melville's writing about this obscure soldier of the American Revolution. He was, again, practicing preventive medicine, delineating in art the characteristics of another kind of nonsurvivor in order to know himself better and to insure his own inner plentitude.

Israel Potter has also been designated a picaresque novel, and to some extent it is because it is episodic in nature with a central figure getting in and out of various predicaments.[8] It is more closely akin, however, to that form of the presentation of a life that could be termed a "progress," in which the hero is headed toward a definite place and in which he has to proceed through various other places in order to get there. The destination and the various stops on the way have allegorical or metaphorical significance. John Bunyan's *Pilgrim's Progress* is of course the best known

7. Melville produced, according to William Ellery Sedgwick, "what is in all truth a brilliant historical novel." *Herman Melville: The Tragedy of Mind* (Cambridge: Harvard University Press, 1944), pp. 179–80.

8. See, for example, Jane Mushabac, *Melville's Humor: A Critical Study* (Hamden, Conn.: Archon Books, 1981), pp. 123–24.

example. The outcome for Israel, however, as he proceeds on his journey through these symbolic places is vastly different. He moves in the wrong direction. Instead of exploring his own inner world, he goes outward and away from self-understanding; instead of traveling toward life and meaning, he journeys toward emptiness and death. In his yearning for freedom, he passes through three great cities, Boston, Paris, and London, each of which represents an aspect of liberty that is illusive, deceptive, and destructive. On the way to London, he has numerous opportunities for the self-revelation that brings psychic wealth, but he continues always toward that place of inner as well as outer poverty.[9]

Though Melville made several changes in his use of the first half of Trumbull's *Life and Remarkable Adventures,* probably the most significant was his shifting of Israel's birthplace from Cranston, Rhode Island, to the Berkshire Mountains of Massachusetts. Critics of the novel have made little of this curious departure from fact and source,[10] but it sets the stage for Melville's depiction of Israel as a man who in search of liberty moves away from the liberating power of self-knowledge. Melville changed Israel's place of birth because symbolically the lowlands of the Narragansett Basin in Rhode Island were out of keeping with his concept of the inner realm as a wild mountainous terrain. In *Pierre* he describes this world as "the Switzerland of his soul," and speaks of its "tremendous immensity." Through great effort and "by judicious degrees," one may at last "gain his Mont Blanc and take an overtopping view of these Alps," but he never explores all, for he realizes that "the Rocky Mountains and the Andes are yet unbeheld."[11] Chapter 1,

9. Arnold Rampersad, *Melville's Israel Potter: A Pilgrimage and a Progress* (Bowling Green, Ohio: Bowling Green University Popular Press, 1969), discusses the "progression" structure of *Israel Potter* and contrasts Israel's journey toward London with that of Christian in *Pilgrim's Progress* toward the Celestial City. See particularly pp. 74–84.

10. Leon Howard, for example, explains it this way: "He made Israel a native of the Berkshires in order to open the book with a more general description of his own neighborhood than he had used in 'Cock-A-Doodle-Doo!'" *Herman Melville: A Biography* (Berkeley and Los Angeles: University of California Press, 1951), p. 214.

11. *Pierre; or, the Ambiguities,* ed. Harrison Hayford et al. (Evanston and

"The Birthplace of Israel," describes the same vast and wondrous world. It is for that person "who is not to be frightened by any amount of loneliness, or to be deterred by the roughest roads or the highest hills." Here one will find "singular scenery," which "owing to the ruggedness of the soil and its lying out of the track of all public conveyances, remains almost as unknown to the general tourist as the interior of Bohemia." Indeed, climbing these mountains, "you have the continual sensation of being upon some terrace in the moon. The feeling of the plain or the valley is never yours; scarcely the feeling of the earth" (p. 3). As you traverse this sublime landscape of the wonder-world, "you seem to be Boótes driving in heaven" (p. 4). It is a realm both of unspeakable grandeur and awesome solitude. At certain times, "the beauty of every thing around you populates the loneliness of your way. You would not have the country more settled if you could" (p. 5). But at other seasons, the footing is treacherous, traveling hazardous. The "wild, unfrequented roads" become "inaccessible and impassable" (p. 6).

The purpose of chapter 1, which has been highly praised as a masterpiece in miniature for its stylistic grace and beauty,[12] is to present an image of "the Switzerland of the soul," Israel's proper sphere that he should have explored and loved, the world in which he should have centered his existence. In the ominous ending of the chapter, Melville contrasts this lofty and magnificent landscape of self with the place of Israel's ultimate destination. In his "progress," he will travel "three thousand miles across the sea," often in a state of self-ignorance or "bewilderments," until he wanders "forlorn in the coal-fogs of London." Far from the bright and "sparkling Housatonic," with its life-giving waters, he is destined "to linger out the best part of his life," in a sort of death-in-life, "a pauper upon the grimy banks of the Thames" (p. 6). Cranston, near the Providence River, was too similar in terrain to London on the Thames to afford the degree of contrast Melville

---

Chicago: Northwestern University Press and the Newberry Library, 1971), p. 284.

12. See Warner Berthoff, *The Example of Melville* (Princeton: Princeton University Press, 1962), pp. 69–76; and Arnold Rampersad, p. 91.

desired as he suggested Israel's movement away from the lofty sublimity of the inner self to the marshy hellishness of an existence without deep self-understanding. Though he violated fact, chapter 1 of *Israel Potter* is, indeed, a masterpiece in miniature, not just for its superb style but also for its rich metaphorical depiction of the land his hero loses.

What lures Israel from that magnificent land is the attraction of liberty. Even before he travels to Boston to confront the British, he is moved by love of independence and abhorrence of tyranny to depart his birthplace. "It appears," writes Melville, "that he began his wanderings very early; moreover, that ere, on just principles throwing off the yoke of his king, Israel, on equally excusable grounds, emancipated himself from his sire" (p. 7). In other words, his reason for leaving home and his reason for becoming an American soldier were the same, the prospect of freedom that is associated with the spirit of Boston and Bunker Hill during the Revolution. His father was the oppressor on the one hand, George III on the other hand. Unable to tolerate "the tyranny of his father," he begins his search for liberty (p. 8). Before enlisting in the army, he becomes, ironically, a surveyor of new lands. Having never truly surveyed his own inner terrain, he is engaged to survey a territory—the exterior world—where he will remain always an alien. Later, on his way to Canada, he trades with the Indians and proves to be a successful businessman, again motivated by the same spirit that pervaded the Continental army at Bunker Hill: "In this way was bred that fearless self-reliance and independence which conducted our forefathers to national freedom" (p. 9). In fact, almost everything he does before he makes his way to Boston is both a preparation for Bunker Hill and a result of the same drive that he felt there. Even when he is a harpooner aboard a whaleship, he is "preparing himself for the Bunker Hill rifle" (p. 10). With his innate resentment of external controls, it was natural that Israel should become an avid patriot when his country sought its independence.

Certain changes that Melville made indicate that he wished to portray Israel as even more patriotic than he appears to be in Trumbull. For example, through a slip that Trumbull himself made in calling Sir John Millet "Mr. Millet," Melville must have hit upon the idea of having Israel refer to the generous English lord in this way. To call him "Sir John" would be a symbolic act for Israel contraverting all that as an American he has been fighting for. So he stubbornly refuses to extend the respect and courtesy.[13] Sir John comments that if all Israel's countrymen are as unshakable and patriotic as he, "it's no use fighting them" (p. 26). Melville also increases Israel's devotion to his country by adding a detail not in his source to the interview Potter has with King George III. The king asks Israel to join the British army, and "had it not been for the peculiar disinterested fidelity of our adventurer's patriotism, he would have soon sported the red coat; and perhaps under the immediate patronage of his royal friend, been advanced in time to no mean rank in the army of Britain" (p. 32). Thus, Israel's patriotism continues to direct him along the path to poverty even when he has a chance to turn off into a road that may lead to personal advancement. He would have had to give up his country, but by doing so, he might have gained a greater reward, a devotion through close familiarity and understanding to the most secreted aspects of himself. It is far better, Melville would say, to be a mercenary genuinely in tune with himself than an avid patriot who identifies with his country but fails to search out honestly his own wondrous and complex facets of being. During Israel's meeting with Squire Woodcock, Horne Tooke, and James Bridges, these gentlemen applaud "his generous patriotism in so patiently enduring adversity" (p. 35). Though the Potter of Trumbull's version speaks of his love of country and even his willingness to die for it, Melville's Israel is more consistently, consciously, and actively a patriot.

In intensifying this aspect of his hero's personality, Melville was not himself indulging in patriotism, for *Israel Potter* is not a novel that sings the praises of his country and the American character. It is instead a novel that speaks of the folly of chauvinism. Nor is this a new subject with Melville; he lashed out with biting satire in *Mardi* at his fellow countrymen's unwarranted pride in America. Leon Howard points out that "rhetorical chauvinism" was "one of the dominant characteristics of American politics at

13. Rampersad comments that Melville makes certain changes and thereby "dramatises Israel's instinctive patriotism" (p. 38).

this particular time," and he describes Melville's response: "The American willingness to invite an armed conflict with the mother country, which was particularly common among the Democrats, he considered both absurd and intolerable. The United States had gained its independence and won the War of 1812 less by its own strength than by the force of circumstances, he insisted." Melville was convinced, for example, "that the British were defeated during the Revolution by the geography of America rather than by its people."[14] Howard argues that Melville had been "feeling and repressing" a strong impatience with boastful patriotism "ever since he had returned from the South Seas."[15]

It is in this context of Melville's distrust of shrill patriotism that his dedicatory preface to *Israel Potter* should be read. Though purporting to be respectful and appreciative, it is sarcastic and mischievously obscene. Melville's intent is closely akin to his purpose in dedicating *Pierre* to a mountain. One dedication reads: "To Greylock's Most Excellent Majesty." The other reads: "To His Highness the Bunker-Hill Monument." Both take the position of a humble writer-subject dedicating his work to an exalted royal patron. On one level, both books are dedicated to Melville himself with a phallic symbol serving synecdochically to represent him. In this sardonic private joke, the sort of which Melville was inordinately fond, he envisions his country's most impressive national monument of the time, with a base of thirty square feet and a height of 221 feet, as his own masculine giver of life, his own "Great Biographer." He is to celebrate his own creativeness, his fire, and his force that comes from an understanding of what is within himself, and he is to do it by writing of one of those small and "anonymous privates," Israel Potter, who did not possess that power.[16] Without explaining what he meant, Alfred Kazin concluded that *Israel Potter* "is thus a very personal and positive novel about masculine force."[17] And so it is, Melville's *own* masculine

---

14. Howard, p. 124.

15. Ibid.

16. Melville was aware that *privates* is a word often used to designate the external genitals. He plays upon the term by using "private" and "privacy" in two other places in his brief dedication.

17. Alfred Kazin, Introduction to *Israel Potter: His Fifty Years of Exile* (New York: Warner Books, 1974), p. 10.

force, represented phallically with Rabelaisian hyperbole in the book's dedication.

That is not the only sense in which Melville is using the Bunker Hill monument, however. On another level, he is actually writing of the monument, but with a sarcasm that approaches bitterness. In this second way in which he views the structure, the difference between the ideal it supposedly commemorates and the reality it abrasively calls forth is to him profoundly disturbing. Every American of Melville's generation was intimately aware not only of the existence of the great monument but also, through Daniel Webster's famous speech dedicating it, of what it was intended to represent. Though it was not actually completed until 1843, the cornerstone was laid on June 17, 1825, with the great General Lafayette present. In his *History of the Seige of Boston* (1849), Richard Frothingham, Jr., described this moment in history that every American schoolchild was to know about for scores of years to follow: "This celebration was unequalled in magnificence by anything of the kind that had been seen in New England. The morning proved propitious. The air was cool, the sky was clear, and timely showers the previous day had brightened the vesture of nature into its loveliest hue. Delighted thousands flocked into Boston to bear a part in the proceedings, or to witness the spectacle."[18] In detail Frothingham depicts the procession of officials and veterans, a good many of whom had actually fought at Bunker Hill. It was, he adds, "a touching spectacle. . . . Glistening eyes constituted their answer to the enthusiastic cheers of the grateful multitudes who lined their pathway and cheered their progress."[19] How different Israel Potter's "progress" was and how different his reception from America. Melville recognized that the patriotic fervor that characterized the dedication of the Bunker Hill Monument was more show than substance.

Daniel Webster, more than any other single person, is linked to the construction and idealistic purpose of the monument. He

18. Richard Frothingham, Jr., *History of the Siege of Boston, and of the Battles of Lexington, Concord, and Bunker Hill. Also, an Account of the Bunker Hill Monument* (Boston: Charles C. Little and James Brown, 1849), p. 344.

19. Ibid.

was in the small original group of men who expressed interest in such a memorial and who organized a public meeting to discuss the project. On the document where the first subscribers pledged money, his name appears first.[20] When a committee was formed to decide on the nature of the structure, he presided.[21] And, most memorably, it was he who spoke to that multitude gathered in "a spacious amphitheatre on the northern declivity of the hill," an address which became, through McGuffey and other educators, the most admired and reprinted dedicatory oration of the nineteenth century.[22] Frothingham animatedly recounts the emotional peak of Webster's classic address: "It was at the close of a dedicatory passage on the monument that he uttered the words, 'Let it rise till it meet the sun in its coming; let the earliest light of the morning gild it, and parting day linger and play on its summit.'"[23]

These ringing words of Webster's may well have been in Melville's mind when he closed his own dedication to the monument with the wish, acridly stated, that the summer sun "may shine . . . brightly on your brow," as brightly "as each winter snow shall lightly rest on the grave of Israel Potter" (p. viii). It is inconceivable that Melville was not at one time or the other in his early life exposed to Webster's paragon of dedications.[24] In his edition of Webster's speeches (1854), B. F. Tefft commented that before Webster "was called upon to deliver the address at the laying of the cornerstone of the Bunker Hill Monument," it had been rare "to require such services on such occasions; but the manner in which he that day discharged his duty not only covered his own name with undying luster, but brought the practice into such repute, that nothing can now be erected, from a schoolhouse to a cathedral, without its being consecrated by a public dedication."[25] Up until the time that Tefft wrote these words,

20. Ibid., p. 341.
21. Ibid., p. 343.
22. Ibid., pp. 344–45.
23. Ibid., p. 345.
24. Bezanson comments that it "was a school classic for a century" (p. 186).
25. B. F. Tefft, *The Speeches of Daniel Webster, and His Master-Pieces* (Philadelphia: Porter and Coates, 1854), p. 156.

however (the same year that *Israel Potter* began to appear in *Putnam's*), no one had "surpassed, or equaled, or very nearly approached the great model" of Daniel Webster.[26]

If, as is highly likely, Melville was familiar with Webster's famous speech, he could not fail to marvel at the irony and incongruity that fairly erupt when the oration is juxtaposed to Trumbull's *Life and Remarkable Adventures of Israel R. Potter.* The idealism of the one is made a lie of by the reality of the other. They read almost as if they were meant to be linked, as if they were one of Melville's contrasting bipartite stories like "The Paradise of Bachelors and the Tartarus of Maids." "Here is what patriotism offers you," says the one. "Here is what you get from it, " says the other. Poverty—both in his internal and his external existences—is what Potter got. What Webster promised was liberty and progress. The word *liberty* pervaded Webster's oratorical hymn to patriotism. He desired the Bunker Hill Monument to remind every American of the "liberty and the glory of his country."[27] The United States, he claimed, had taken the lead and had offered its example in the search for freedom, for "unaccustomed sounds of liberty . . . have reached us from" abroad.[28] While Israel Potter was starving in London, Webster was addressing other veterans of Bunker Hill and exclaiming how fortunate they were to see so much happiness. God, he said, "has allowed you to behold and to partake the reward of your patriotic toils." He thanked them "in the name of liberty" and reminded them that they had lived into a wonderful period in which "on the light of liberty you saw arise the light of peace."[29] He spoke eloquently of "transports of patriotism and liberty," of the "great public principles of liberty," of "the electric spark of liberty," and of changes beneficial "to human liberty."[30] From the perspective of 1854–55, when America was already deeply divided over the issue of slavery, Webster's optimistic prediction that major wars would

26. Ibid.
27. Ibid., p. 161.
28. Ibid., p. 162.
29. Ibid., p. 163.
30. Ibid., pp. 164, 169, 172.

cease to be fought and that peace and liberty would reign in the country must have appeared unsound, and his thesis that patriotic love of liberty leads to happiness must have seemed to some who had also read of Israel Potter foolishly unrealistic as well. Certainly Melville would have thought so.

As Melville saw it, the great paradox of patriotism is that the more one is devoted to what Daniel Webster called in his oration at Bunker Hill "the spirit of national independence," the more difficult it is to reach self-understanding and thus to enjoy the liberation that results. Ironically, the end of fervid patriotism is personal bondage, not liberty. Israel is proud to reject the idea of royalty. He even says to George III, "I have no king" (p. 31), but in a sense he does. What the Bunker Hill Monument represents—the spirit of '76, "Give me liberty or give me death"—becomes as much of a ruling force over Israel's life as any king could be. Consequently, Melville refers to the monument in royal terms, as "His Highness" and "Your Highness." What happens to Israel occurs because he was seeking an elusive form of liberty, and he was encouraged in this futile search by the revolutionary contagion that spread through America. At least part of the blame for his lack of fulfillment, his poverty of being, goes to that ideal or spirit that the Bunker Hill Monument commemorates. When Melville writes that he feels justified "to lay this performance at the feet of your Highness," he seems to mean that his version of Potter's life is a worthy gift to this symbol of his country, but he is actually charging that America's patriotic fervor, the obsession with national liberty, is partly responsible for what happens in the life he is about to relate. All that Israel and others like him received as "requital," Melville says to the monument, was "the solid reward of your granite" (p. viii). Though he never truly realizes the impoverishing effect his insistence upon personal freedom has had upon him or how his patriotism has made him miss opportunities to know himself better, Israel voices Melville's position precisely when he cries out in frustration: "Ah! what a true patriot gets for serving his country!" (p. 81). Just what he "gets" is metaphorically depicted in the final chapter when he returns to his native country on July 4, 1826, and lands in Boston: "Hustled by the riotous crowd near Faneuil Hall,[31] the old man narrowly escaped being run over by a patriotic triumphal car in the procession, flying a broidered banner" with these words:

BUNKER-HILL.
1775.
GLORY TO THE HEROES THAT FOUGHT!
(p. 167)

To say that Israel is victimized by the spirit of national liberty that almost runs over him in Boston is not to suggest that it is totally responsible for the emptiness and wretchedness that come to characterize his existence. Chauvinism is but one blind, one barrier, that can stand in the way of that self-knowledge that is the true parent of wisdom. Israel is attracted to every lure of liberty that comes his way. Though he is prevented by circumstances and by Benjamin Franklin from pursuing it, he is greatly drawn to the freedom of self-indulgence that is represented by Paris.[32] At first, however, he does not realize what Paris is offering him—pampering and pleasure for a price. The first offer is made by a man standing "just under the equestrian statue of Henry IV" (p. 37). The man wishes merely to improve Israel's appearance by polishing his boots so that he will be more in keeping with the dandified air of Paris, but Israel misunderstands and kicks the bootblack's box over. Even though Israel does not immediately feel the temptation of that form of liberty inherent in libertinism, he has nevertheless arrived in his "progress" at that place which represents it. The reference to the statue of Henry IV of France is telling in this context, for that great monarch of the sixteenth century was legendary for his amorous exploits. With numerous mistresses and countless indiscretions, he

31. Frothingham reports that Faneuil Hall had been the site for a great dinner held on the evening of Webster's famous dedication of the monument (p. 352).

32. Melville refers to the "voluptuaries" of Paris, which he calls "the showiest of capitals" (p. 48).

has come down to us as a brave and effective king but one far too self-indulgent to avoid a reputation for personal folly.[33]

Dr. Franklin keeps a tight grip on Israel, but not so tight as to prevent the young American from manifesting his appetite for the Parisian good life. He asks Franklin's permission to dine in one of the city's cafés or restaurants but is instead invited to eat at the doctor's table, a plain and sparse one where he is disappointed that there is no drink stronger than water. "Squire Woodcock gave me perry," he says, "and the other gentleman at White Waltham gave me port, and some other friends have given me brandy" (p. 44). Franklin points out that "plain water is a very good drink for plain men," but Israel wants to broaden his horizons of pleasure beyond simplicity and plainness. He thinks that he may have found the opportunity to do so when he discovers in his room on the marble mantle several articles including a bottle of otard, a glass tumbler, some sugar, a container of cologne, flowers, and a few other items. He is about to enjoy these new pleasures when Dr. Franklin interrupts and removes every "senseless luxury." Israel's response—"Oh, you better take the whole furniture. . . . Here, I'll help you drag out the bedstead"—has both the flavor of amusement and the biting sarcasm that comes from sharp disappointment. He sits "gloomily" after his sage friend departs. Had not his provincial background deprived him of worldly knowledge, he might well have undergone his initiation into the rites of libertinism with the appearance of a pretty young chambermaid, but he does not grasp the purpose of her visit though he is not insensitive to her charms. When Franklin explains that she is a prostitute as well as a maid and offers to prevent her visiting him further, Israel protests but to no avail. Again, "the man of wisdom" saves Israel from Paris ("another strange custom of Paris," he calls the chambermaid-prostitute vocation), but the point is that it is against Israel's wishes, for he feels that he is being robbed rather than saved (p. 53). He wishes to free himself, to experience Parisian sensuousness. He wants "something extraordinary" to turn up, such as a man coming in

33. When he was fifty-five, for example, he lusted after a fifteen-year-old girl and schemed (unsuccessfully) to have her.

and giving him "ten thousand pounds" (p. 53). He does not see the prostitute, as does Dr. Franklin, as "an artful Ammonite" (p. 53). In the Old Testament, the Ammonites, a Semitic race and neighbors of the Israelites, are depicted as bad for Israel, corruptors of their morals, tempters who try to lure them away from their true relationship with God and each other.[34] Franklin views the chambermaid as embodying the temptation of a form of liberty, self-indulgence, which will come between Israel and a true understanding of himself. She will divert him from self-revelation, not direct him toward it.

It is not that Benjamin Franklin is prudishly opposed to all the pleasures that Paris offers. Melville knew that the popular American sage enjoyed his stay in France and lived anything but the life of a straitlaced pinchpenny. Melville's Franklin protects Israel from Paris not because he himself finds it destructive but because he wisely realizes that it is dangerous to this particular young man who has not found himself, has not established his identity.[35] This is a wise and deep Benjamin Franklin far removed from the shallow materialist that many critics of *Israel Potter* detect in the novel. A typical view is that "Franklin is the embodiment of the purely materialist values that Melville repeatedly portrays as standing in the way of America's professed political, social, and religious ideals."[36] Such an assessment probably owes much to the notorious pejorative delineation of the historical Franklin by D. H. Lawrence.[37] Lewis Leary evaluates Melville's Franklin in much the same way. "Franklin," he states, "represents almost everything which Melville found reprehensible among the plausi-

34. Nehemiah 13:23–31 and 1 Kings 11:1–8.

35. Michael Paul Rogin depicts Franklin as a hypocrite who "is denying Israel his birthright": "Poor Richard's strictures against enjoyment in his *Almanack* do not apply to its author." *Subversive Genealogy: The Politics and Art of Herman Melville* (New York: Knopf, 1983), p. 226.

36. Joyce Sparer Adler, *War in Melville's Imagination* (New York: New York University Press, 1981), p. 81.

37. For Lawrence, Franklin was the "pattern American," an "automaton," a "dry, moral, utilitarian little democrat," who "has done more to ruin the old Europe than any Russian nihilist." "Benjamin Franklin," in *Studies in Classic American Literature* (New York: Thomas Seltzer, 1923), p. 31.

ble, respectable, successful David Harums who in Philadelphia, New York, and Boston paced with sedate confidence toward the Gilded Age."[38] Another critic feels that in *Israel Potter,* Franklin's "is the portrait of a pedantic, parsimonious, mundane and entirely soulless American."[39] Upon Melville's Franklin has been heaped the scorn of generations of readers influenced by the twentieth-century fashion of condemning the real Franklin as the father of much that has gone wrong with America.[40]

This view of Benjamin Franklin (as Melville portrayed him) errs on at least two counts: it distorts his character in the direction of shallowness, and it greatly overemphasizes his materialistic bent. The very first image of Franklin in *Israel Potter,* which is pervaded with suggestions of the occult, undercuts any notion that Melville perceived him as a kind of utilitarian simpleton. He is "wrapped in a rich dressing-gown" that is "curiously embroidered with algebraic figures like a conjuror's robe, and with a skull-cap of black satin on his hive of a head." He is "seated at a huge claw-footed old table, round as the zodiac" (p. 38).[41] Even the walls of his apartment have "a necromantic look" (p. 38). The suggestion that Franklin is somehow a resident of realms beyond the mundane and ordinary runs through much of Melville's description of him. He has not been dulled by old age but sharpened, and "it seemed as if supernatural lore must needs pertain to this gravely ruddy personage" (p. 39). Even the area in which he has chosen to live, the Latin Quarter of Paris, is "monastic and theurgic" (p. 47). He is practical but not in a superficial

38. Lewis Leary, Introduction to *His Fifty Years of Exile (Israel Potter)* (New York: Sagamore Press, 1957), p. xi.

39. Rampersad, p. 94.

40. On Melville's portrayal of Franklin, see also Lewis Mumford, *Herman Melville* (New York: Harcourt, Brace, 1929), p. 242, and Kazin, pp. 8, 9. William Ellery Sedgwick finds Melville's characterization of Franklin "sympathetic and yet ironical" (p. 180). Jane Mushabac sees the depiction as "just amiable affectionate ribbing" (p. 130).

41. Charts with strange "geometrical diagrams" decorate his walls (p. 39). Franklin was fond of creating from numbers what he called "magic squares." See his letter to Peter Collinson in *A Benjamin Franklin Reader,* ed. Nathan G. Goodman (New York: Thomas Y. Crowell, 1945), pp. 775–78.

sense. Melville associates him with a few other extraordinary minds, "practical magians in linsey woolsey" (p. 47).

Indeed, Melville goes to considerable lengths to contradict the idea that Franklin's "pastoral simplicity" of speech and manners reflects an uncomplicated and shallow personality. Something of "primeval orientalness" exists in him; his exterior is a wall, a facade. He is like the biblical Jacob, for under "Arcadian unaffectedness" is depth and complexity. His style of writing is, like his clothing and manner, "neat, trim" with "nothing superfluous, nothing deficient," but—again like his external appearance— that simplicity and lucidity are deceptive. He, Jacob, and "Hobbes of Malmsbury" form a trio, "three labyrinth-minded, but plain-spoken Broadbrims" (p. 46). At dinner with Israel, Franklin uses over and over the word *plain*. He urges his guest to "be a plain man, and stick to plain things" (p. 45). Franklin's speech on plainness serves ironically to point up his complexity; it echoes Melville's memorable comment in *Moby-Dick:* "My dear sir, in this world it is not so easy to settle these plain things. I have ever found your plain things the knottiest of all."[42] The more Franklin emphasizes his plainness, the more his inscrutable "primeval orientalism" and his "labyrinth-mindedness" emerge. Below his plainness, he is one of "the knottiest of all."

Significantly, Israel does not perceive what lies under Franklin's paternal and benevolent, if somewhat overly protective, advice to him. Melville makes it clear that the perception of Franklin as a magian is his own, not that of Israel, who "lost the complete effect of all this" (p. 39). When Israel enters Franklin's world, he resembles a child who has not yet fully learned to walk. As he attempted to negotiate "this slippery floor, his unaccustomed feet slid about very strangely, as if walking on ice, so that he came very near falling" (p. 40). Nevertheless, Israel does suspect that there is more to Dr. Franklin than meets the eye, though he detects only a vague slyness. "I rather think," Israel muses, "he's one of those old gentlemen who say a vast deal of sense, but hint a world more. Depend upon it, he's sly, sly, sly" (p. 54). So he is,

42. *Moby-Dick,* ed. Harrison Hayford and Hershel Parker (New York: Norton, 1967), p. 312.

Melville agrees, but with a depth and complexity that Israel cannot grasp. "Very little indeed of the sage's multifariousness," Melville writes, "will be portrayed in a simple narrative like the present. This casual private intercourse with Israel, but served to manifest him in his far lesser lights. . . . Seeking here to depict him in his less exalted habitudes, the narrator feels more as if he were playing with one of the sage's worsted hose, than reverentially handling the honored hat which once oracularly sat upon his brow" (p. 48).

Melville's Benjamin Franklin, though no poet, has traveled much in the realms of gold, surveying his wild inner terrain so that it is no longer unknown and untraversed. Through self-examination he has learned far more about himself than most of humankind, and he takes his place in Melville's fiction among other true survivors. Franklin's degree of self-exploration is metaphorically projected in a large map that hangs on his wall. It represents the "New World," which is to say, symbolically, the inner world that may be largely unknown to others but not to the old sage himself. The map contains "vast empty spaces in the middle, with the word D E S E R T diffusely printed there, so as to span five-and-twenty degrees of longitude with only two syllables,—which printed word however bore a vigorous pen-mark, in the Doctor's hand, drawn straight through it, as if in summary repeal of it" (p. 38). The area in Franklin that some may consider arid and sterile is actually cool and productive; what may appear a Sahara is a Switzerland of the soul where the aging survivor frequently goes to leave the heated and empty outer world around him. This contrast between desert heat without and self-contained coolness within is further developed as Israel approaches Franklin, who is rapt in his meditations: "The weather was warm; like some old West India hogshead on the wharf, the whole chamber buzzed with flies. But the sapient inmate sat still and cool in the midst. Absorbed in some other world of his occupations and thoughts, these insects, like daily cark and care, did not seem one whit to annoy him. . . . There he sat, quite motionless among those restless flies." Internally, he is "serene, cool and ripe" (p. 39). That Melville is writing admiringly rather than satirically is clear if a relevant passage from *Moby-Dick* is recalled as context: "It does seem to me, that herein we see the rare virtue of a strong individual vitality, and the rare virtue of thick walls, and the rare virtue of interior spaciousness. Oh, man! admire and model thyself after the whale! . . . Do thou, too, live in this world without being of it. Be cool at the equator. . . . Retain, O man! in all seasons a temperature of thine own."[43]

Melville's Franklin has never denounced the world and withdrawn from it. He lives very much in it, as he must do in order to survive mentally as well as physically. But at the same time, he has a "strong individual vitality" that supplies him with psychic energy and an "interior spaciousness" that furnishes him with a cool retreat when he needs it, free from the buzzing, trivial, insectlike society of the masses. Melville's understanding of the complicated Franklin was wider and deeper than that of those who admire the famous American merely for his useful inventions, his practical discoveries, and his unselfish service to his country and certainly more accurate than that of Franklin's detractors who fail to grasp the man's genius and multidimensions. Melville seemed to know not only the Franklin who preached thrift but also the one whose underlying recurrent message was genuine survival, the one who said "9 Men in 10 are suicides."[44] This is the Franklin who had no delusions about the nature of ordinary life and society. "He that best understands the World," he said in one of his almanacs, "least likes it."[45] But this is also the man of wisdom who realized that such dislike had to be controlled and mitigated by communication with that world and service to it.

For Franklin, wealth, self-knowledge, and survival were synonymous. This is apparent to any alert and sensitive reader of his most famous work, "The Way to Wealth." Melville doubtlessly perceived it as it truly is—a deceptively simple statement setting forth guidelines for survival and self-esteem that come from the tapping of inner resources. En route to London in 1757, Franklin

43. Ibid., p. 261.
44. *The Complete Poor Richard Almanacks,* ed. Whitfield J. Bell, Jr., vol. 1 (Barre, Mass.: Imprint Society, 1970), p. xxi.
45. Ibid.

wrote "The Way to Wealth" as a kind of preface to his 1758 *Poor Richard's Almanack.* Ostensibly a speech that Richard Saunders (Franklin's pseudonym) had heard at a country sale, delivered by one Father Abraham, it is a collection of one hundred maxims that Franklin had either borrowed from other sources or invented over the years since *Poor Richard's Almanack* had begun appearing in 1733. Arriving at the sale before opening time, Richard hears the crowd complaining of heavy taxes being imposed upon them. *"Won't these heavy Taxes,"* they ask Father Abraham, *"quite ruin the Country?"*[46] The "plain clean old Man" proves to be programmed with Poor Richard's maxims, for he gives one after another, frequently inserting, "as *Poor Richard* says." His address to the crowd, however, is not merely a compendium of random sayings but a tightly organized argument on a single profound theme. The taxes imposed upon them from the outside, explains Father Abraham, are not nearly so heavy and enervating as those that they impose upon themselves. "We are taxed," he tells them, "twice as much by our *Idleness,* three times as much by our *Pride,* and four times as much by our *Folly,* and from these Taxes the Commissioners cannot ease or deliver us by allowing an Abatement."[47] The point that he wishes to make is that this form of self-taxation is going on without most of them even realizing it. They do not know themselves well enough to recognize their idleness, pride, and folly for what it is. Everything that he says is spoken with the purpose of creating in them some understanding of their unconscious motivations and of showing them a way of moving from the poverty of self-ignorance to the wealth of self-esteem, from the bondage of taxation to the freedom of abatement.

The most fundamental truth of all and the very first saying that Father Abraham reminds them of is that "God helps them that help themselves," which means several things, the most basic of which is that God helps those who *understand* themselves, self-

46. "The Way to Wealth," in *Benjamin Franklin, Representative Selections,* ed. Frank Luther Mott and Chester E. Jorgenson (New York: American Book Co., 1936), p. 281.

47. Ibid.

knowledge coming before any other real and lasting assistance is possible. He then divides his advice into three sections, each offering a solution to one of the three faults mentioned earlier. In place of idleness, he recommends industry; for pride, frugality; and for folly, wisdom. Significantly what he promises them if they follow his advice is not really so much materialistic gain but true *liberty*, which is the opposite of taxation. His speech is no less about freedom than Daniel Webster's dedicatory address. "When you run in Debt," he warns, "*you give to another, Power over your Liberty.*" Poverty is enslaving, and it "deprives a Man of all Spirit and Virtue." When you buy on credit, you put yourself under a kind of "Tyranny." Toward the end of his remarks, he cries out to his listeners: "Disdain the Chain, preserve your Freedom, and maintain your Independency: Be *industrious* and *free;* be *frugal* and *free.*"[48] *Wealth* thus becomes a code word for liberty and survival, *poverty* for enslavement and destruction; and the way to wealth is through self-knowledge and discipline, not through ignorance and indulgence. We must practice genuine "Circumspection," Father Abraham insists; we must "oversee our own Affairs *with our own Eyes.*"[49]

Wealth in this sense is "the Philosopher's Stone," and when you have explored your heart and disciplined your complex self so as to obtain it, "you will no longer complain of bad Times, or the Difficulty of paying Taxes."[50] "Happiness," Franklin said in a letter to Hugh Roberts in 1758, "in this life rather depends on internals than externals."[51] Though not generally acknowledged, Franklin stressed the point that externals—material riches—will not bring "wealth"; money without inner plentitude is merely a second form of poverty. Citing a French saying, he remarked in 1742: "Dog's dung and silver marks / Are all one at the day of judgment."[52] The nonmaterialistic basis of "The Way to Wealth" was perceived by a French religious society in Franklin's day. The

48. Ibid., pp. 287–88.

49. Ibid., pp. 233, 284.

50. Ibid., p. 288.

51. *Franklin Reader*, p. 780.

52. Quoted in Alfred Owen Aldridge, *Franklin and His French Contemporaries* (New York: New York University Press, 1957), p. 44.

Théophilantropes, a group of Deists, regarded "The Way to Wealth" as "a religious and moral system" and included it in a collection of writings for the contemplation of their members.[53] Franklin's insistence upon not going too far in practicing industry, frugality, and reason stems from his fundamental conviction that excesses of whatever sort are destructive. Toward the end of "The Way to Wealth," Father Abraham admonishes his audience not to forget God and their fellow men on the way to wealth. In *Poor Richard's Almanack* for 1742, Franklin expressed the essence of his theory of survival: "Excess in all other things whatever . . . is also to be avoided."[54] He is, then, very much another Plotinus Plinlimmon, one who follows the Greek way—know thyself and nothing in excess. He is an accomplished follower of the middle way, which is for him the path to survival with dignity, self-esteem, and power. Thus in describing where Franklin lives in Paris, Melville writes: "In this congenial vicinity of the Latin Quarter, and in an ancient building . . . *at a point midway* between the Palais des Beaux Arts and the College of the Sorbonne, the venerable American Envoy pitched his tent" (pp. 47–48, italics mine).

Melville's treatment of Franklin in *Israel Potter,* then, is closely akin to his characterization of Plotinus Plinlimmon. He admires both for their extraordinary knowledge and command of their inner resources and their vast superiority to the dead level of the masses. He views both as genuine survivors in a world where "9 men in 10 are suicides." On the other hand, their mode of coping with themselves and life is not his, and he senses that their self-compromising to find the middle way in all things has resulted in a loss he would not want to sustain, the loss of a certain wildness that he treasures as the Azzageddi spirit of creative fire. Plinlimmon writes nothing, and Franklin is no poet (nor could he ever be). Melville would have agreed with William Carlos Williams that Franklin paid a high price for his greatness: "the shutting

---

53. Aldridge, p. 52. "Poor Richard," points out Bell, "ceaselessly condemned greed, avarice, mere money-getting. 'The excellence of hogs is fatness, of men virtue' " (*Complete Almanacks,* 1:xvi).

54. *Franklin Reader,* p. 540.

out of the wild spirit of the American continent."[55] Franklin, writes Melville, was a "Jack of all trades, master of each and mastered by none" (p. 48). His diversity prevented excessive involvement in any one area; it warded off the passion and wildness that might have broken down his system for survival.

Though Benjamin Franklin's way to wealth was not Herman Melville's, they journeyed toward similar destinations. Israel Potter moves toward quite another. Had he been a different sort of man, he might have profited greatly from his exposure to the elderly Franklin and his philosophy of wealth. But here as elsewhere he sees only the surface and understands little of what lurks under it. What he himself is remains for him the greatest mystery of all. Franklin seeks to guide him to self-understanding and survival; he would be Abraham (his pseudonym in "The Way to Wealth") to Israel. When he shows his young guest to his room, he gives him two works to read. "But you must not be idle," he tells Israel. "Here is Poor Richard's Almanac, which in view of our late conversation, I commend to your earnest perusal. And here, too, is a Guide to Paris, an English one, which you can read. Study it well" (p. 45). The two writings form a contrasting rather than a complementing pair. Franklin furnishes Israel with them as if to say, "Here is the way to the inner world; here is the way to the outer world. Note the profound difference and choose accordingly." Israel reads first in the guidebook, and the possibilities for self-indulgence in Paris are presented with such attractiveness that "reading about the fine things in Paris" makes him extremely restless to leave Dr. Franklin behind and enjoy the world he sees depicted in the book. Then he picks up Franklin's own "little pamphlet," which fascinates him as Plinlimmon's pamphlet does Pierre. "But here's 'Poor Richard,'" he says. "I am a poor fellow myself; so let's see what comfort he has for a comrade" (p. 53). Franklin's formula for escaping the bondage of poverty remains inscrutable for Israel, who exclaims, "Oh confound all this wisdom! It's a sort of insulting to talk wisdom to a man like me" (p. 54). He marks the saying "God helps them that help

55. Quoted in Michael Kammen, *A Season of Youth: The American Revolution and the Historical Imagination* (New York: Alfred A. Knopf, 1978), p. 228.

themselves," but he never understands what it means. He has only a single momentary glimmer into the symbolic meanings and differences inherent in the two pieces of writing: "So here is the 'Way to Wealth,' and here is the 'Guide to Paris.' Wonder now whether Paris lies on the Way to Wealth? if so, I am on the road. More likely though, it's a parting-of-the-ways" (p. 54). He suspects that Dr. Franklin had a reason for putting "these two books" in his hands, but he is never to profit, never to undergo any self-revelation, from understanding what that reason is. He leaves "The Way to Wealth" open at "God helps them that help themselves," having been impressed with the advice, but he walks away from it without heeding. In doing so, he is duplicating the action of the multitude in Franklin's pamphlet. "Thus the old Gentleman ended his Harangue," writes Poor Richard. "The People heard it, and approved the Doctrine and immediately practised the contrary, just as if it had been a common Sermon; for the Vendue opened, and they began to buy extravagantly, notwithstanding all his Cautions, and their own Fear of Taxes."[56]

What the doubloon is to *Moby-Dick,* "The Way to Wealth"—and more particularly its most famous maxim, "God helps them that help themselves"—is to *Israel Potter.* For Benjamin Franklin, the saying expresses his conviction that the way to fulfillment is through self-knowledge—one finds God from the inside, not from the outside. To Israel Potter, Poor Richard's memorable thought underscores a truth that but adds to his frustration, for he believes that his destiny is determined by external happenings. How, then, he asks, can he help himself when he appears always to be a pawn of fate? He feels that physical freedom is the absolute prerequisite to happiness, certainly not an extreme or unusual view but one that nevertheless misses the point that Melville makes over and over in his writings, namely that we largely form our own destinies. The third major character of the novel, John Paul Jones, considers the maxim an expression of his own most fundamental philosophy. When he reads it for the first time in Israel Potter's room, he exclaims: "'God helps them that help themselves.' That's a clincher. That's been my experience. But I

56. "The Way to Wealth," p. 288.

never saw it in words before" (p. 61). So taken is he with "The Way to Wealth" that he tells Israel: "I must get me a copy of this, and wear it around my neck for a charm" (p. 61). Later, when Jones is awarded command of the larger ship he has been agitating for, Israel points out to him that the ship's name—*Duras*— sounds like "durance vile," a term used for imprisonment. Jones cannot tolerate the idea of commanding a ship that carries such a suggestion, for liberty is his highest ideal. "Paul Jones," he boasts to Israel when Dr. Franklin introduces them, "never was captured" (p. 58). Therefore, he and Israel decide to change the name of the *Duras* to the *Bon Homme Richard*, "in honor of the saying," Jones exclaims, "that 'God helps them that help themselves,' as Poor Richard says" (p. 115). It is general knowledge that the *Richard* was actually named for Benjamin Franklin, and Melville found the fact stated in his two principal sources for the particular sections of the novel involving Jones (which constitutes, incidentally, nearly a third of *Israel Potter*): Cooper's *History of the Navy of the United States of America* and Sands's *Life and Correspondence of John Paul Jones*. Melville, however, made a significant alteration. Cooper says merely that the name of the *Duras* was "changed to that of the Bon Homme Richard, in compliment to Dr. Franklin,"[57] but the *Life and Correspondence* states: "This ship was given to Captain Jones; and at his request called *Le Bon Homme Richard*, in compliment to a saying of Poor Richard; 'If you would have your business done, come yourself; if not, send.'"[58] Melville made the change in maxims because he wished to place Franklin's other one, which deals with the necessity of knowing oneself and of realizing the true nature of destiny, at the center of the novel.

By doing so, he created a poignant irony. Seeking to avoid "durance vile," Israel and his captain change a name but not themselves. They who cherish the liberty that Franklin espouses cannot obtain it because they do not truly understand its nature.

57. James Fenimore Cooper, *History of the Navy of the United States of America*, vol. 1 (Philadelphia: Lea and Blanchard, 1840), p. 154.

58. *Life and Correspondence of John Paul Jones, Including His Narrative of the Campaign of the Liman* (New York: Chandler, 1830), p. 149.

Jones, unlike Israel, is not disgusted with Poor Richard's "wisdom" as pointing up how much he is controlled by others and by outward circumstances; but neither does he grasp the true import of Franklin's philosophy. He cannot because he does not understand his own divided personality. Like Ahab, he is characterized as a man driven by two overpowering and conflicting sets of motivations, a complex and titanic figure doomed to destruction because he does not know and therefore cannot adequately control himself.[59] The nature of these conflicting sides is suggested in the motto he so cherishes, "God helps them that help themselves." The two aspects of his being agree that Poor Richard's saying is an affirmation of the truth, but they are attracted to the maxim for opposing reasons. One side focuses upon "God helps," and backs Jones up in his conviction that he is aligned with the angels in his fight for liberty; he is God's instrument and avenger. "I will rain down on wicked England," he prophesies to Franklin, "like fire on Sodom" (p. 56). This is the unselfish, idealistic, and crusading John Paul Jones, the man who refuses to be bound by the jingoistic allegiance to a single nation, even his homeland. "I would teach the British," he boasts to Franklin, "that Paul Jones, though born in Britain, is no subject to the British King, but *an untrammelled citizen and sailor of the universe*" (p. 56, italics mine). The real Jones said much the same thing, though it was not to Franklin but to the countess of Selkirk in his noble letter to her and though it was to America rather than to Britain that he disclaimed any narrow allegiance: "Though I have drawn my sword in the present generous struggle for the rights of men, yet I am not in arms as an American. . . . I profess myself a citizen of the world, totally unfettered by the little, mean dis-

59. Richard Chase comments that "Jones is, in Melville's final estimation, more an Ahab than a Bulkington" and embodies "Melville's deepest fear about the American character: that it would turn out to be inorganic, unstable, possessed by an enormous impatience which would lead it to plunge violently into undertakings for which it was unprepared." *Herman Melville: A Critical Study* (New York: Macmillan, 1949), p. 182. Robert Zaller, in "Melville and the Myth of Revolution," *Studies in Romanticism* 15 (1976), points out that "Paul is a kind of Ahab, with George III as his white whale" (p. 610).

tinction of climate or of country, which diminish the benevolence of the heart and set bounds to philanthropy."[60]

He plays a double role, however, though he does not realize it. His other side centers its attention on the second half of Poor Richard's maxim, which seems to command, "help thyself." This is the side that makes him cry out, "Why was I not born a Czar!" (p. 57). If as an idealistic campaigner for liberty he desires, on the one hand, to punish Great Britain for the wrongs it has inflicted on America, a weaker and younger nation, he aches, on the other hand, to avenge the wounds that Britain inflicted on him personally. "Bad stories" circulate about him in Whitehaven, lies of how he "flogged a sailor, one Mungo Maxwell, to death." Though he was acquitted, his reputation there was ruined. "But let 'em slander," he sneers. "I will give the slanderers matter for curses. When last I left Whitehaven, I swore never again to set foot on her pier, except, like Caesar, at Sandwich, as a foreign invader. Spring under me, good ship; on you I bound to my vengeance!" (p. 91). Thus he is Ahab on a minor scale, a split being who seeks revenge not for himself but because of high principles but who is concurrently motivated, and just as strongly, by an insatiable desire to strike back at those who have insulted him and degraded him personally. Because he is moved by unselfish sentiments, love of liberty and justice and abhorrence of tyranny and wrong, he throws his lot with America, wishing for no material gain whatsoever.[61] Because he is moved by selfish egotism of extreme magnitude, he will brook nothing over him, no principle or country or force whatsoever. He tells Franklin that he wants no orders but "a separate, supreme command." He will have "no leader and no counsellor but himself" (p. 57). It is this aspect of his character that produces his puzzling behavior when he sails near the steep, thousand-foot-high Crag of Ailsa. The great crag stands like a lonely giant or a profound genius, "who, even in overthrow, har-

60. *Life and Correspondence*, p. 91.
61. "Nor am I in pursuit of riches," Jones wrote to the countess of Selkirk. "My fortune is liberal enough, having no wife nor family, and having lived long enough to know that riches cannot ensure happiness." *Life and Correspondence*, p. 91.

bors none but lofty conceptions" (p. 97). Though in hot pursuit of an enemy vessel, Jones discontinues the chase when near the crag. Israel comments on his changing his mind "rather queerly about catching that craft," and assumes that Jones believed the enemy ship "was drawing us too far up into the land." What causes Jones to turn back, however, is not the other ship's maneuvers. He tells Israel that he is not fearful of the British vessel, "nor of King George"; he turned away because he had come under "the domineering shadow of the Juan Fernandez-like Crag of Ailsa": "As the Ranger shot nigher under the crag, its height and bulk dwarfed both pursuer and pursued into nut-shells." Under this shadow, causing a kind of "general eclipse," Captain Jones suddenly changes and orders his crew to give up the chase (p. 97). Pride, not fear, is his motivation. He cannot bear to feel small and insignificant.

As Melville learned more about the historical John Paul Jones from reading in the *Life and Correspondence* and other writings, he discerned that here was a man who seemed to be heroically pursuing universal human rights but who was at the same time running away from something; an outspoken and "frank" man—as he claims to be in *Israel Potter* when talking with Dr. Franklin— and yet a person who had something to hide; a "Chevalier," as he is referred to in the *Life and Correspondence,* and yet a man capable of murderous violence once his quick temper was aroused. About three years after the Mungo Maxwell episode, when Jones was in command of a ship named the *Betsy,* then harbored at Tobago in the West Indies, he killed a man who attacked him aboard ship. He left the island in 1773, probably intending then to return later in order to stand trial. Instead, he went to America and lived in relative secrecy, having changed his name from John Paul to Paul Jones, *Jones* being a common name that allowed him a great degree of anonymity. Later he reassumed his old first name but kept his new (and false) surname. He was a brilliant warrior, and young America needed such men too badly to worry about what appeared to be shady pasts. Consequently, he was given an unfettered command and "left alone," as Benjamin Franklin in his wisdom recognized that he should be; and he became a national hero. But the depth, complexity, and contradictions in his character did not escape Melville, who was never one to accept recorded history on its face value.[62]

Melville was concerned to depict the real John Paul Jones as he saw him, not the one of patriotic legend, a man with a kind of double division—split internally between two competing factions and that internal chaos in turn overlaid with an external facade of high civilization, gentility, and control. Suggestions of this second form of division pervade Melville's characterization of him. He is a person of "poignant feelings, buried under an air of care-free self-command" (p. 91). When Israel first sees him, he is "elegantly and somewhat extravagantly dressed . . . with a superinduced touch of the Parisian *salon*" (p. 56). The next morning, after speaking with Franklin, "he left the place with a light and dandified air, switching his gold-headed cane, and throwing a passing arm around all the pretty chambermaids he encountered" (p. 63). He sports ruffles and lace, carries a "small, richly jewelled lady's watch" (p. 59), and wears several "Parisian rings" (p. 63). If he can be rakishly civilized with the chambermaids, he can be gallantly civilized with Lady Selkirk toward whom he conducts himself with gentility and for whom he goes to considerable expense to set right the ungentleman-like act of his officers in taking her silver as booty.

62. In fact, Melville felt that recorded history if not a lie is a distortion, a kind of corpse from which all true life and truth have escaped. Paradoxically, only through distorting the written record of history can some of the substance and vigor of the past be restored. Consequently, *Israel Potter* is a book that plays free and loose at times with sources and records so that Melville can de-mummify his materials. For example, the *Life and Correspondence* identifies the man that Paul Jones took with him to spike the cannons at Whitehaven as "Mr. Green" (p. 81). Melville gives Israel the assignment. Cooper describes a young man that had escaped from the British and joined Captain Jones to become a kind of favorite, but he is not Israel Potter but a Lieutenant Dale (*History of the Navy*, 1:157). In Cooper's description of the fight between the *Richard* and the *Serapis*, Melville read: "At length one man, in particular, became so hardy as to take his post on the extreme end of the yard, whence, provided with a bucket filled with combustibles, and a match, he dropped the grenades with so much precision that one passed through the main-hatchway. . . . The effect of this explosion was awful" (1:168). Israel becomes this brave sailor as Melville again takes liberty with official history.

Peeping through his dandified air of civilized control, however, is what Melville refers to frequently as the "savage." He has a "savage" eye, the look of "a disinherited Indian Chief" (coincidentally, the ship that he desires to command is called the *Indian*), and he sits in his chair like an "Iroquois" (p. 56). At one point in his first conversation with Israel, he looks like "a parading Sioux demanding homage to his gew-gaws" (p. 58). That night in Israel's room he appears "wrapped in Indian meditations," and as he passes a mirror, he rolls up his sleeve and exposes for his own admiration an arm covered with tattoos: "It was a sort of tattooing such as is seen only on thorough-bred savages—deep blue, elaborate, labyrinthine, cabalistic" (p. 62). In other places, Melville associates Jones with Fejees (p. 90), cannibals (p. 91), and a "prowling *brave*" (p. 95).

In great and deep men, contrary emotions and thoughts are not uncommon, and it is not necessarily fatal to possess two distinctly different clusters of motivations for our actions and philosophies for our reasoning. Indeed, Melville himself was such a divided man, as we have seen. To survive, however, such a person must become intimate with the selves within the self, must see lucidly and realistically what is there and accept these quarreling children of the self with love and wise understanding. Only after this close familiarity can control of some sort be applied so that the frequent fights will not tear down the house. First, then, comes self-knowledge, then control. Plinlimmon and Benjamin Franklin have both become intimate with themselves, and they have both worked out a method of control, the system of bringing extremes of self into a compromising middle way, the Greek Golden Mean—"nothing in excess." Melville's way was to oscillate from one aspect of his being over to the other and back, in that way retaining all the qualities of both emotional states but not allowing either to dominate or exist undetected in a state of war with the other. In John Paul Jones, Melville depicts a character, like Ahab and Pierre, who is incapable of exerting either method of control because of self-ignorance; consequently, he is doomed to self-destruction—one of those nine men in ten, as Franklin put it, who are in a sense "suicides." The point in associating him frequently with savages is to emphasize the fact that

below an exterior of civilization is an uncivilized domain, uncivilized, that is, because it is savage, not under human control.
It is this connotation of *savage* that Melville seems to have uppermost in mind in the strange scene where Jones views his tattoos in
the mirror and in those other places where he is associated with
Fejees or Indians.

Because he is himself uncontrolled, he proves to be a poor
controller of others. Like Ahab, he can be magnetic, however,
and attract other men who might be subject to his spell, as is
Israel. He so appeals to Israel that the youth for a time forgets all
about his zeal to return to America and is happy to follow his
captain anywhere and to carry out any orders he may give. The
savage element in Jones—the inner selves not under control—is
dangerous to others, like a fire burning out of control that catches
up other buildings as it spreads or like a carrier of a disease who
brings his contagion to others. He does not lead; he infects.
Jones's savage voice puts Israel up to the terrible killings aboard
the English vessel. Israel explains this to one of Jones's officers,
who replies, "Captain Paul is the devil for putting men up to be
tigers" (p. 89). Furthermore, Israel is not able to profit from his
exposure to Jones as Ishmael gains from his experience with
Ahab. He does not learn the way to wealth from Franklin, and he
cannot learn it from Jones; he remains "poor Israel." After Jones
conquers the *Drake,* he receives great fame, "especially at the
court of France, whose king sent Paul a sword and a medal. But
poor Israel, who also had conquered a craft, and all unaided too—
what had he?" (p. 113). Even with his new position as quarter-
master, with close "official contiguity to Paul" (p. 94), and
aboard a greater ship (the *Bon Homme Richard*), he is still "poor
Israel" (p. 115). The influence of Jones in his life is "like a crimson thread" that simply "flits and re-flits" through an "otherwise
blue-jean career" (p. 131). The image is one of the most suggestive in the book, for red is the color associated with blood,
rebellion, savagery, and fire. Jones proves to be an ineffectual military organizer and administrator because his inner world has become crimson. He operates best alone, without orders. His subor-
dinates in the expedition that sails from Groix prove to be
insubordinate; he cannot hold them together or make them into

an effective fighting unit. The insubordination within his fleet is but a metaphor for the insubordination within his tumultuous being.

Two other metaphorical patterns point up with artistic deftness and subtlety—qualities that are seldom associated with this remarkable book, though they should be—the nature of John Paul Jones's inner world: the chase and fire. Even before Israel sees Jones, he senses that the man who is about to enter Dr. Franklin's room is involved in a chase, in this instance a flirtatious one, for he is pursuing the chambermaid (p. 55). Whether chasing romantically or warringly, he is constantly trying to overtake something. His adventures involve many chases—after the revenue cutter on which Israel has been forced to serve (p. 87), after the revenue wherry that sails close to the Crag of Ailsa (pp. 96–97), after the letter-of-Marque on which Israel by accident becomes a crew member, and so on. Such activity suggests one in control, one who is free or, as Jones himself likes to put it, "unfettered." Yet, he does not understand nor enjoy true liberty, for frequently he is, like Ahab, himself chased, "repeatedly," in fact (p. 113). While he is pursuing the enemy without, the enemy within seeks to overtake him. "Jones beware of Jones," he could say if he but had the insight.

Similarly, while he is associated frequently with fire and is characterized as a kind of human flamethrower, he is also, metaphorically, being burned. He had, Israel notices in their first meeting, the look of "an unflickering torch" (p. 56), but at the same time, he has been burned by the sun, his "tawny cheek" speaking "of the tropic" (p. 56). When Dr. Franklin suggests that he act as a decoy so that French ships can capture British vessels, Jones hisses his displeasure "in a fiery rage," and Israel sits "rapt at the volcanic spirit" (p. 57). He is not capable of giving fire, however, without being himself consumed by it. He is "flaming with wild enterprises" during the night that he walks the floor in Israel's room. Once in bed, Israel feels "an uneasy misgiving sensation, as if he had retired, not only without covering up the fire, but leaving it fiercely burning with spitting faggots of hemlock" (p. 62). Melville's interest in the John Paul Jones of history was doubtlessly intensified by the degree to which the great warrior was himself burned in his efforts to spread conflagration among the enemy. Whitehaven is an excellent example. Jones took the bold step of sailing into this British port with the intention of firing the shipping there and leaving the town itself in flames. The editor of the *Life and Correspondence of John Paul Jones* states that "it was one of the most impudent attacks since the times of the sea-kings."[63] Though the bold move succeeded in showing Britain its vulnerability, it did not wreak the havoc Jones desired, for he could not produce a widespread fire. In Melville's treatment of the episode, fire is the central metaphor: the lamps that the American force brings go out, and the men forget to bring along matches. Jones commands Israel to produce fire, and he does—by lighting his pipe from the hearth of one of the citizens. They are able to set ablaze a single ship and to cause considerable confusion, but the reputation Jones leaves behind is merely that of an "incendiary," a label he finds degrading.

If the fire—what there is of it—is in a sense self-generated, since the source of it is a hot coal from a Whitehaven home, the spreader of the blaze is in a symbolic way burning himself. At least, that is what the irate British press accused him of doing. How could any decent and civilized man, they asked, attack his own people, those whom he knew intimately in his youth? How could he try to burn the very place from which he first sailed as a boy? With disgust, they accused him of treachery against that which had nurtured him. Even in America, many felt that there was something unnatural about Jones's desire to burn Whitehaven. The stigma remained, and when the *Life and Correspondence* was published in 1830, the compiler felt obliged to come to Jones's defense for his actions at Whitehaven: "The sentimental disgust of those who censured him for availing himself of that very knowledge [his "thorough acquaintance with the localities"], and of 'stiffling his early associations,' is natural enough. But war is not waged upon sentimental principles. . . . He conquered the repugnance he might have felt at making a hostile entry among the scenes of his infancy."[64] With its suggestion of self-warring, this

63. *Life and Correspondence*, p. 88.
64. Ibid.

incident presented itself to Melville as one that manifested in concentrated form Jones's internal situation.

Whitehaven is merely a prelude, however, to the event that most dramatically projects Jones's inner conflict and his course toward self-destruction. From Melville's handling of the famous battle between the *Bon Homme Richard* and the British frigate *Serapis,* it is clear that he perceived it in terms of a blind and wasteful combat between kindred forces. He explains at the beginning of his account of the engagement that he sees in it "something singularly indicatory" because "it may involve at once a type, a parallel, and a prophecy" (p. 120). Overtly he is comparing Jones to America and this particular battle to the Revolutionary War for the purpose of prophesying concerning his country's future: it may not be very bright if we engage too much in this sort of conflict, which is really a kind of "Civil War," as Cooper referred to it in the book Melville seems to have used as his main source of information on the engagement.[65] In such a civil strife, no one stands to win. It would be tragic, he implies, if America turned out to be "civilized in externals but a savage" internally, in other words, "the Paul Jones of nations" (p. 120). If such proved to be the case, we could expect the same destiny for the country as for the man—heroism, "boundless ambition," obstinacy, self-ignorance, internal chaos, and, finally, destruction from the inside. On a less obvious level, the battle between the *Richard* and the *Serapis* is "indicatory" because Melville makes it a parabolic revelation of Jones's private war.

That psychological strife within an individual person is Melville's fundamental subject is partly evinced by his repeated emphasis upon the physical interconnectedness of the two ships as they fight. "Never was there a fight so snarled," he writes. There was a "bewildering entertanglement of all the yards and anchors of the two ships, which confounded them for the time in one chaos of devastation" (p. 120).[66] Not like an ordinary battle between two forces unrelated to each other, "it seemed more an

65. *History of the Navy,* 1:138.
66. Cooper describes how the two ships became interlocked, but he does not emphasize this aspect of the engagement to the extent Melville does (1:166–67).

intestine feud than a fight between strangers. Or, rather, it was as if the Siamese Twins, *oblivious of their fraternal bond,* should rage in unnatural fight" (p. 125, italics mine). The Siamese twins are the two sides of Jones's being engaged in "unnatural fight." In another place, Melville says that the "belligerents" seem more like copartners in a kind of "joint-stock combustion-company" than like "an English ship, and an American ship." It is not a happy endeavor, however, for the copartners are "divided, even in participation" (p. 126). Trope is piled on trope, but they are all closely related to the notion of a deadly feud between kindred factions that need to exist in harmony with each other lest the individual mind, a business enterprise, or a country collapse through internal strife. As he recounts the mutually destructive encounter, Melville suggests that the combatants are of a single blood, in this metaphor, Italians (the Guelphs and the Ghibelines); that they have been occupying a house with a common wall between them (a "party wall"); that openings have been cut in this wall; and that the neighbors, now aware of each others' natures and finding themselves at odds, are in open battle.[67] In such a fight, "neither party could be victor. Mutual obliteration from the face of the waters seemed the only natural sequel to hostilities like these" (p. 129).

Among other things, then, Melville's account of the terrible combat between the *Bon Homme Richard* and the *Serapis* is another of his psychological parables showing the "mutual obliteration" that results from "hostilities like these," man against himself in blind rage. Smoke is the principle metaphor for this state of self-blindness. The fires that burn within Jones warm a few (such as Israel) and for a time draw them toward him, but they destructively flame out toward others and consume. Ultimately they consume him, yet he is unaware that they are so close to home because of the smoke they produce. Significantly, Jones abhors smoke and wishes to find a way to avoid it, not recognizing its

67. The Guelphs and the Ghibelines were two factions in Medieval Italy. The Ghibelines were aristocrats and as a political party supported the authority of the German emperors. The Guelphs made up a party that was papal and popular in its leanings and opposed the German emperors.

true source. Dr. Franklin tells him: "To have less smoke in time of battle, especially on the lower decks, you proposed a new sort of hatchway. But that won't do" (p. 59). Franklin, the sage of self-knowledge, knows how to prevent smoke from rendering one sightless and bewildered, but Jones's attempts to avoid it are futile because smoke represents his permanently clouded psychological state. Consequently, Melville emphasizes the cloud of smoke that engulfs the "Siamese Twins" as they destroy each other. To know what is happening in Jones's deepest internal being, "to get some idea of the events enacting in that cloud, it will be necessary to enter it; to go and possess it, as a ghost may rush into a body" (p. 124). That cloud of smoke, "incessantly torn in shreds of lightning, then fusing together again, once more to be rent," is the lurid and turbulent atmosphere of John Paul Jones's psyche, and enter it Melville did.

In view of his characterization of John Paul Jones, Melville must have found his most famous words, "I have not yet begun to fight," charged with irony. Not only was he in the service of America for ambivalent reasons—one admirable, unselfish, and idealistic but the other egotistical and vengeful in a personal sense—but while carrying on an outer war with an enemy that probably should not have been one, he failed to recognize that he was psychologically fighting himself. His defiant and memorable words, then, which Melville quotes in *Israel Potter* (p. 128), signify nobility, courage, and victory only on the surface. His continuing self-war led to more personal chaos. After the Revolutionary War, he seemed more desperate than ever to chase some elusive image of liberty at the expense of a clear sense of who he was. Insubordination and frustration continued to be mixed with his accomplishments as he served as rear admiral in the Russian navy, fighting against the Turks, and then as an American representative in Paris, where he died shortly after reaching his forty-fifth birthday.[68] His difficulty in establishing his own personal

68. William Carlos Williams, who shared Melville's view of history and who was fascinated with several of the same characters that caught Melville's imagination, commented that Jones had "to leave the American navy, we feel, to go to Russia, for release." *In the American Grain* (New York: New Directions, 1956), p. 155.

identity seems curiously reflected in the fact that he lay in an anonymous grave in Paris for a hundred years. Closing his account of the engagement between the *Richard* and the *Serapis,* Melville asks a fundamental question: "In view of this battle one may well ask—What separates the enlightened man from the savage?" (p. 130). The answer, of course, is clear self-appraisal and effective control over psychological disparates. John Paul Jones remains a savage, flying "hither and thither like a meteoric corposant-ball" and "blacked and burned" through self-conflict, revealing as his "Parisian coat, with its gold-laced sleeve" is laid aside, the unmistakable tattoos of the untamed savage (p. 126). But Melville asks one other question: "Is civilization a thing distinct, or is it an advanced stage of barbarism?" (p. 130). Civilization as we know it is not made up of enlightened people as it should be, but is, indeed, merely an advanced stage of barbarism because of men who, like Jones, appear to be civilized but do not understand the forces that sway them and therefore cannot, as barbarians cannot, control them.

Jones's foil in *Israel Potter* is Ethan Allen. Melville found no mention of Colonel Allen, leader of the Green Mountain Boys and hero of Fort Ticonderoga fame, in Trumbull's account of Potter's life, but he could not resist the temptation to imagine that Israel saw the extraordinary Vermont giant while the two were in England, one as an escaped prisoner, the other as a manacled exhibit to the British people. From his reading of *A Narrative of Col. Ethan Allen's Captivity* (1779), Melville received not only all the information he needed for his treatment of Allen's imprisonment in Pendinnis Castle but also an impression of the man's deep character, which he delineates in a brief but highly significant episode near the end of *Israel Potter.* Probably what fascinated him about Allen was the way his savagery differed from that of John Paul Jones. Jones is a man who often appears highly civilized but who is internally not under control. Allen, on the other hand, seems wild, even bestial at times, but in reality he is always in command of himself. No other episode in his life reveals this fact more clearly than his British captivity. He treats his guards "with barbaric scorn." He "taunted them, with cramped gestures of his manacled hands" (p. 143). From outside the walls of Pendinnis

Castle, Israel is startled at Allen's violent ragings "as of the roar of some tormented lion" (p. 143). On the grass of the castle green, he looks "like some baited bull in the ring"; all around him the sod is "trampled, and gored up" (p. 144). Not only his manner but also his dress convey the impression that he is an untamed savage, for he is "outlandishly arrayed in the sorry remains of a half-Indian, half-Canadian sort of a dress, consisting of a fawn-skin jacket—the fur outside and hanging in ragged tufts—a half-rotten, bark-like belt of wampum; aged breeches of sagathy . . . old moccasins riddled with holes" and a faded cap (p. 144). With a matted beard, "his whole marred aspect was that of some wild beast" (p. 144).

Melville knew from his reading of Allen's *Narrative* that this bestial-like violent behavior was turned on and off at will.[69] Allen in captivity evinced strongly the characteristics of a survivor. In several places, he indicates in various ways that his "design was not to die" but to retain his control over himself, to manipulate his captors, and to survive.[70] When he was prisoner on board a Gaspee schooner, he was, he explains, "obliged to throw out plenty of extravagant language, *which answered certain purposes, at that time*" (italics mine).[71] At one point, he confesses that as a result of his behavior, "the enemy gave out that I was crazy . . . but my vitals held sound, nor was I delirious any more than I had been from youth up; but my extreme circumstances, at certain times, rendered it politic to act in some measure the madman."[72] *Politic,* he certainly was, for he had his mind made up to survive this ordeal. When the British brought him back to America and allowed him to associate with other prisoners, a young soldier came to him and bade him farewell because he expected

69. Alfred Kazin perceives correctly that Allen "is *willfully* mad" (p. 10, italics mine).

70. *Narrative of Col. Ethan Allen's Captivity,* 4th ed. (Burlington: Chauncey Goodrich, 1846), p. 30. His motive, he says a little later, is his "preservation" (p. 39). Again, "Consequently the reader will readily conceive I was anxious about my preservation," and so "I had recourse to strategem" (p. 42). He speaks of "pretended resentment" (p. 44) as having "a more probable tendency to my preservation than concession and timidity" (p. 45).

71. Ibid., p. 33.

72. Ibid., p. 77.

soon to die. He had been commanded by the British to enlist in their armed service, but he told Allen that he had rather die first (he was of the patriotic ilk of Israel Potter). Allen took him aside and gave him a survivor's advice: enlist by all means, as a "duty to himself," and then deceive the British all he could.[73]

Melville picked up on Allen's own explanation of his wild behavior and echoed it in *Israel Potter*. When he compares Allen to David just come from the "outlawed Cave of Adullam" (p. 144), he is referring to 1 Samuel 21 and 22: "And he changed his behavior before them, and feigned himself mad in their hands, and scrabbled on the doors of the gate, and let his spittle fall down upon his beard." By seeming mad, David escaped to the cave of Adullam. Melville concludes that there were two reasons "for the Titanic Vermonter's singular demeanor abroad" (p. 149). The first is that Allen did have a wild, powerful, rebellious, and prideful side to his nature. His violent defiance of his British captors, therefore, was partly the result of his real resentment at the cruel treatment he was receiving. He was genuinely irate. But as his own *Narrative* makes clear, his anger was also a tool that he used on some occasions but not on others. It was genuine, but he could and did turn it on or off. By letting his wild side loose, he knew that he could "better sustain himself against bullying turnkeys than by submissive quietude" (p. 150). "When among wild beasts," Allen knew that he must "be a wild beast" (p. 150). With startling suddenness, however, he could control his defiant self and allow a milder disposition to emerge, as he does when he turns from a heated verbal attack on General Howe delivered to a "wasp-waisted officer," who is "blown backwards as from before the sudden burst head of a steam-boiler" (p. 144), to a much calmer conversation with a minister, who is so moved at having "his religious courtesy appealed to" that he orders a servant to bring Colonel Allen a bowl of punch (p. 145). To the young woman who visits him, he "talks like a beau in a parlor," and she desires to have a lock of his hair. He is courtly and chivalrous, encouraging her to take the lock and calming her fears. Mixed with his hair is straw from the place he has been kept. "But the wearer is no man-of-straw, lady," he assures her (p. 146). His

---

73. Ibid., p. 82.

conduct again procures for him certain advantages, for this time, "a worthy, judicious gentleman," noting Allen's "knightly" behavior, "suggested a bottle of good wine every day, and clean linen once a week. And these, the gentle Englishwoman . . . did indeed actually send to Ethan Allen, so long as he tarried a captive in her land" (p. 146). The most pronounced aspect of Allen's character as Melville delineates it is this shifting back and forth at will from wildness, anger, and defiance to conviviality, good spirits, and calm sophistication.

Since he is described as performing "a mocking bow" to the kind minister who orders punch for him, and since he admits that he has "dabbled in your theologies" when "not better employed braiding" his beard (p. 145), then Melville must have known something of his notoriety as a religious thinker. "In my younger days," he tells a curious visitor, "I studied divinity, but at present I am a conjuror by profession" (p. 146). Whether Melville read Allen's *Reason, the Only Oracle of Man* (1784) or not, he was certainly aware of its existence and of its author's religious bent. In the preface to that book, Allen boldly states: "I am no Christian."[74] He was a sneering Deist, a believer in God but a mocker of Christianity as it was practiced in the churches. His biographer has called his *Oracles* "the first major work published in the Western Hemisphere" to deliver "well-aimed and telling blows at Christian orthodoxy."[75] Consequently, one encounters in history two Ethan Allens, the American patriot who took Ticonderoga and defied the British while he was their prisoner, and the iconoclast who defied the Christian world with his loud and aggressive Deism. Timothy Dwight, representing American Christian orthodoxy, painted a portrait of Allen that does not even resemble the one that hangs in the gallery of patriotism. To the Reverend Mr. Dwight, Allen was "licentious in his disposition. . . . In his conversation he was voluble, blunt, coarse and profane. . . . He early obtruded himself upon the public as an opposer and ridiculer of Christianity, and gloried in the character of an infidel."[76] Dwight found the *Oracles,* which he designated "the first

---

74. *Reason, the Only Oracle of Man; or, A Compendious System of Natural Religion* (Boston: J. P. Mendum, 1854), p. ii.

75. Charles A. Jellison, *Ethan Allen: Frontier Rebel* (Syracuse: Syracuse University Press, 1969), p. 311.

formal publication in the United States openly directed against the Christian religion," to be "brutal nonsense."[77] If Melville used the third edition of the *Narrative* (1838), he read in the "Advertisement" a defense of Allen against Dwight's charges. At any rate, he clearly knew that Allen was not an orthodox Christian, yet he has him say several times in *Israel Potter* that he is. Allen calls himself "a true gentleman and Christian" (p. 143), a "meek-hearted Christian" (p. 145), and a "Christian gentleman" (p. 145). "You Turks," he cries at the British, "never saw a Christian before" (p. 144). It is important to understand here that in his acting, Allen is not simply a liar. The contexts for his claims make it clear that he is using the term *Christian* metaphorically to suggest not a specific theological position but a high degree of culture and civilization, which he wishes to claim for himself. Though he may seem untamed and savage, he is saying that he is not. The term *Deist* simply would not convey his meaning in this regard. But his claim also is carefully calculated, as are other aspects of his behavior, to assure his survival, for he knows that his captors will be shamed by his contention that he is a true Christian and that they are Turks.

Allen is thus no mere player of parts. He is a consummate actor who calls upon a true aspect of himself when he performs. When he needs to be irate, he does not feign anger but unleashes what is already within him; when the occasion demands skill in physical combat, he does not fake it but becomes a dexterous fighter; when he should be bold but chivalrous, he is truly as knightly as a Bayard. Melville says that he did not play the part of but *was* actually a "curious combination of a Hercules, a Joe Miller, a Bayard, and a Tom Hyer" (p. 149). The combination is "curious," indeed, for two of these names are practically household words— Hercules and Bayard—while the other two references are to obscure figures. Melville chose Joe Miller (1684–1738) to suggest not only Allen's acting ability—Miller was a popular London actor—but also his talent for wit and humor, his deep sense of

76. Timothy Dwight, *Travels in New England and New York*, ed. Barbara Miller Solomon (Cambridge: Harvard University Press, 1969), 2:283.

77. Ibid.

farce, for the man he compares him with was "a natural spirited comedian," of "convivial disposition," a man widely known as "The Factitious Gentleman."[78] Tom Hyer (1819–64) is now forgotten except in sporting circles. To Melville, who read about Hyer's pugilistic deeds in the New York papers, the great boxer was a figure not only of indomitable courage but also of wiry craftiness and physical skill. He was the first white boxing champion of America, a title he gained when he defeated Yankee Sullivan in 1848, a brutal bout that "aroused great interest both in this country and abroad."[79] Allen does not merely resemble these various figures; he has their power and talent within him that he can unleash and then leash as he wills. He is, therefore, one of the forerunners in Melville's fiction of the Confidence Man.

Israel Potter, Benjamin Franklin, John Paul Jones, and Ethan Allen are connected by a single ideal that motivates all of them— the principle of liberty. In the opening words of his *Narrative,* Allen reflects this concern: "Ever since I arrived at the state of manhood, and acquainted myself with the general history of mankind, I have felt a sincere passion for liberty."[80] In *Israel Potter,* Melville has him say, "I love freedom of all things" (p. 146). He understands, however, that liberty results primarily from understanding of self, from tapping the power that is there, and from keeping firm control over it so that one does not give over his identity to any one of the elements within that are always ready to take command. He never loses his identity, never becomes a "man-of-straw" or any other kind but what he has been. Toward the end of his *Narrative,* he speaks of his last days with the British when they began to treat him civilly: "I was admitted to eat and drink with the general and several other of the British field officers, and treated for two days in a polite manner. As I was drinking wine with them one evening, I made an observation on my transition from the provost criminals to the company of gentlemen, adding that I was the same man still."[81] Though he did

78. "Joseph Miller" in *Dictionary of National Biography.*

79. Alexander Johnston, *Ten—and Out!: The Complete Story of the Prize Ring in America,* 3d ed. (New York: Ives Washburn, 1947), p. 28.

80. *Narrative,* p. 11.

81. Ibid., p. 118.

not devote much of his novel to this man who "overshadowed" others "as St. Paul's dome its inferior steeples" (p. 142), Melville nevertheless thought of him as one of those extraordinary figures whom he calls in *The Confidence-Man* "original" characters.

Israel's exposure to Benjamin Franklin, John Paul Jones, and Ethan Allen does not alter his limited understanding of the nature of true liberty. He feels imprisoned when Franklin tries to teach him the way to wealth, and he fails to see that the ostensibly free Jones is a prisoner of himself while the manacled Allen is freer than those who taunt him. Melville deviates from Trumbull and devotes nearly all of his novel to Israel's pre-London years because he wants to detail the numerous opportunities his young hero had to see the light before he was engulfed in the eternal fog of the big city, opportunities for self-revelation not only from being thrown with men who could and should be, in a way, his teachers, but also from being placed into situations that ought to force him into deep inner exploration. Time and again Melville departs from his source and invents such episodes in order to show Israel repeatedly failing the test of self-knowledge and, consequently, moving toward that terrible state of death-in-life that results from a lack of personal identity. Israel's imprisonment in the secret chamber of Squire Woodcock's house is a good example. The small cell where the Squire hides Israel was once part of a "religious retreat belonging to the Templars" (p. 70). Those members of the order who did not understand the real meaning of freedom and who sought greater liberty by breaking restraints, who in other words were "convicted of contumacy," were confined in this space, about the size of a coffin in those days. A small hole served for ventilation and a means for getting food in. It opened in on the chapel so that the errant Templar could "overhear the religious services at the altar," explore his own nature, and change his thinking (p. 71). A burial rite accompanied this entombment, and when the penitent emerged weakened in body almost to the point of actual death but renewed and strengthened in spirit, the event was celebrated as a kind of resurrection. Israel knows of this ancient use of his cell, but he makes no connection between those once placed there and himself. Three days in the tomb brings him no real resurrection.[82] He emerges not with a greater understanding of himself but with another false identity, that of the squire. When he is first placed in the cell, he tells Squire Woodcock that he wishes a mirror. Furnished with one, he gazes at himself but fails to see deeply. "What a pity I didn't think to ask for razors and soap. . . . How it would pass the time here. Had I a comb now and a razor, I might shave and curl my hair, and keep making a continual toilet" (p. 69). His escape from the hidden chamber is not cause for celebration, though in concluding the chapter Melville writes ironically that Israel pushed the door open and "stood at liberty" (p. 72).

While he remains in the secret room, Israel articulates to himself the paradox of liberty without realizing the import of his thoughts. "Poverty and liberty, or plenty and a prison, seem to be the two horns of the constant dilemma of my life, thought he. Let's look at the prisoner" (p. 69). But he regards only his outside as he peers at his unshaven face in the mirror. He does not re-evaluate his concept of freedom. What he should see is that the kind of liberty he has been seeking, shallow and brief, leads but to a form of poverty and destruction while "plenty" or plentitude, that state of feeling full or complete that results from a strong sense of identity, is always accompanied by discipline, restrictions, denials—"prison." It is one of the oldest and truest of paradoxes given new and subtle form in this strange and greatly underrated brief novel.[83]

---

82. Edgar A. Dryden suggests that the numerous biblical analogues in the novel reveal "the absence of meaning in Israel's life of wandering." *Melville's Thematics of Form: The Great Art of Telling the Truth* (Baltimore: Johns Hopkins University Press, 1968), p. 145.

83. Percy H. Boynton, in *More Contemporary Americans* (Chicago: University of Chicago Press, 1927), called *Israel Potter* "a perfunctory piece of work not as interesting as the book it was based on" (p. 45). John Freeman found Melville attacking and sneering at his own "natural exuberance" and writing in such a way as "to restrict himself to the dry husks of language, putting an unnatural constraint upon his genius." *Herman Melville* (New York: Macmillan, 1926), pp. 137–38. In his *Herman Melville* (New York: William Sloane, 1950), Newton Arvin impatiently concluded: "Naturally the product is not a narrative with any profound unity or serious inner coherence of its own" (p. 245). More recent

Instead of seeking his own identity and receiving plentitude, Israel, in his frantic desire for external freedom, goes from one disguise to another and ends up without substance. Melville's frequent references to Israel's change in clothing projects this theme.[84] He leaves Woodcock's house dressed as the squire and is taken for a ghost, which in effect he is. Then he exchanges this disguise for that of a scarecrow, a man of straw, which also in a sense he is. At this point he is in stark contrast to Ethan Allen, who claims to the young woman with justification that he "is no man-of-straw" (p. 146). In someone else's clothes, Israel feels "comparatively safe in disguise" (p. 20), more comfortable than when in his own garb not only because he is averting detection by others but also because he is such a stranger to himself. Avoidance of self-confrontation leads either to inner war (as with Ahab, Pierre, and John Paul Jones) or to such a silencing of the inner voices that one becomes a shell, a hollow man. That Israel has reached this terrible state is suggested in "The Shuttle" chapter, where he mistakenly jumps aboard a British ship and tries to disguise himself as an English sailor. He goes from the main-topmen above to the waisters below, trying to find a place, but he has no identity. Finally, the officer of the deck asks the questions that by implication characterize Israel Potter as Melville conceived him. " 'Who the deuce *are* you?' at last said the officer of the deck, in added bewilderment. 'Where did you come from? What's your business? Where are you stationed? What's your name? Who are you, any way? How did you get here? and where are you going?' " (p. 137). After commenting that "he don't seem to belong anywhere," the master-at-arms leads him away with "Come along, then, my ghost" (p. 139).[85] When Melville

critics tend to evaluate *Israel Potter* higher, though some continue to feel that it is inferior fiction. Edwin Fussell refers to it as Melville's "last potboiler." *Frontier: American Literature and the American West* (Princeton: Princeton University Press, 1965), p. 294.

84. For a discussion of Israel's frequent change of clothes, see Alexander Keyssar, *Melville's Israel Potter: Reflections on the American Dream* (Cambridge: Harvard University Press, 1969).

85. See John Seelye's treatment of Israel's lack of identity as revealed in "The Shuttle" chapter. *Melville: The Ironic Diagram* (Evanston: Northwestern University Press, 1970), pp. 113–15.

claimed in his dedicatory preface that the *Life and Remarkable Adventures of Israel R. Potter* was "now out of print," he was referring not only to Trumbull's book (which was not so rare as he pretended)[86] but also to the book's hero, a man "himself out of being" (p. 169), a ghost.

Whereas many of the principal characters in Melville's fiction perceive their experience as epiphanic, Israel appears deadened to any universal implications in the events of his life. By the time he finally reaches London, he has had experiences that would have convinced Ahab or Pierre that man is an alien amid hostile forces, that he is born into a world created by an inferior and unseeing God, and that the proper course for him is to denounce both nature and the Creator and to glory in his own innate superiority as a creature untouchable by the material filth that surrounds him. To some, a night like the one Israel spent trying desperately to find a place among the crew members of a British ship would have pointed up that society remains indifferent, uncaring, and foreign to the special souls cast among them. Israel realizes that to those on the ship he has "an alien sort of general look" (p. 136), but he is incapable of raising the kinds of questions that lead some of Melville's characters to a Gnostic way of thinking. At times, Melville practically rubs his nose in the strong scent of Gnosticism in order to show that he lacks the qualities of other characters who smell the odor and madly rush off in pursuit. To do so, of course, would be to move toward destruction, but Israel's failure to assume Gnostic attitudes is not, as it was with Ishmael and Melville himself, the result of his having been tempted by and his having consciously rejected them. He is simply insensitive to the call.

But he is exposed to one, or at least he is placed in a situation so highly charged with suggestiveness that it might lead deeper and more imaginative characters to believe that they had glimpsed a fundamental truth about man's terrible entrapment in universal nature. Israel, however, simply remains consistently deadened to

86. An editor of *Putnam's*, in fact, claimed that he had a copy before him as he composed his "Editorial Notes" (issue for May 1855). He implies that Melville felt free to depart from his source because he thought it was so rare that no one could check up on him!

any such philosophical or theological connections. The brickyard outside London where he labors for thirteen weeks is described from a Gnostic orientation, projecting the enslavement of mankind in the machine of inexorable natural laws, the most obvious of which is the process of human reproduction. Brick-making is actually man-making, and it is depicted with such Gnostic disgust as to render the subject repulsive.[87] The "mill" consists of a "hopper, emptying into a barrel-shaped receptacle." A "muddy mixture" is introduced into the hopper "by spavined-looking" men and ground up "till it slowly squashed out at the bottom" as a "doughy compound, all ready for the moulds" (pp. 154–55). Once in the moulds, the clay that is the basic substance of average man is then exposed to the fire that is life, some burned beyond recognition by it, others made just right to fit the needs of the world, and still others too remote from the blaze and thus of less use to society. About the same time that Melville created this metaphor, embodying the Gnostic's abhorrence of natural processes, he invented an even more elaborate trope to suggest the same idea in the second part of a bipartite story. The paper mill in "The Tartarus of Maids" is situated in a hopper-shaped setting, desolate and forbidding. The "great machine" is described in terms that suggest conception, gestation, and childbirth. But the machine here, as in *Israel Potter,* is more than the womb. It is universal nature, and the two striking passages in these works develop from a Gnostic perspective the plight of ordinary mankind caught in its steady, grinding, relentless process. The narrator of "The Tartarus of Maids" receives this revelation with such force that he nearly faints, and he feels that he must not tarry lest his epiphany convert him to Gnostic thinking. Israel, however, is not so threatened. He feels like a slave, not of universal nature but merely the British people; he feels degraded but instead of discovering his gold in the mud, he concludes: "What signifies who we be? . . . Who ain't a nobody?" (p. 157).

His response to a sense of enslavement and poverty, therefore,

87. Melville writes that "each man" is a "brick." "Brick is no bad name for any son of Adam. . . . What is a mortal but a few luckless shovelfuls of clay, moulded in a mould, laid out on a sheet to dry, and ere long quickened into his queer caprices by the sun?" (p. 156).

is drastically different from that of characters like the narrator of "Cock-A-Doodle-Doo!" and Merrymusk, who feel victimized on a cosmic level and who hear the call of a supernatural cock conveying *gnosis* or knowledge of their true worth and of the proper way for them to conduct themselves in a world that strives to debase and control them. Poverty makes them feel spiritually rich and thus sets them apart from others; it causes Israel to conclude that as a "nobody" he is like everyone else. They cannot survive mentally and physically because their Gnostic-like attitudes encourage self-blindness and inner warring; Israel does live a long life, but it is an existence devoid of that power and plentitude that accompany genuine inner probing and hard-won self-knowledge and self-love.

Whereas the title of Trumbull's book emphasizes vitality and experience (*Life and Remarkable Adventures of Israel R. Potter*), Melville's title—*Israel Potter: His Fifty Years of Exile*—suggests a long separation from home. In the literal sense, his exile is from America, but more important, "home" is Israel's inner world represented by the Berkshire Mountains in chapter 1. In "The Shuttle" chapter, where Israel is clearly seen as a man who lacks identity, he feels a "wide gulf between him and home" (p. 132). There is no life worth living apart from that home. Its opposite is London, where Israel makes his way in an attempt to find the false liberty of anonymity, the illusion of freedom and security that comes from loss of identity. Chapter 1, "The Birthplace of Israel," and chapter 24, "In the City of Dis," make for a startling contrast when juxtaposed; one depicts life, the other psychic death. Israel does not have to die in order to die. His funeral takes place on a Blue Monday in November, Guy Fawkes' Day, the procession crossing London Bridge into "Erebus," where one can see coalscows looking like "awaiting hearses," where everything is foggy and black, and where the flagging on streets resembles "tombstones minus the consecration of moss" (p. 159). This is "Dis," the city of the dead, "Phlegethon" (p. 159). Israel makes his way hither with others who are nameless, without substance: "On they passed; two-and-two, along the packed footpaths of the bridge; long-drawn, methodic, as funerals. . . . One after the other, they drifted by, uninvoked ghosts in Hades" (p. 160).

Melville saw no need to detail, as Trumbull did, Israel's long stay in London any more than there would be a need to describe forty-five years in a grave.[88] London, adversity, and the sea "slay, and secrete their victims" (p. 160). Israel emerges from London as he had done from his premature burial in the "black bowels" of an old British hulk, "sunk low in the sunless sea" (p. 15), in his lonely room in Paris, and in the secret chamber in Squire Woodcock's house, but without receiving new life.[89] Before his literal death, he is like the half-cord of hemlock that he encounters upon his return to America: "It preserved the exact look, each irregularly defined line, of what it had originally been," but it was "abandoned to oblivious decay" and now represented "a long life still rotting in early mishap" (p. 168).[90] So by the time Israel was allowed to leave London, it was too late for him to find "home." He dies a man without identity, unrecognized by his country as he was aboard the British ship when he sought a place among its crew. The Bunker Hill Monument, which should commemorate his love of country, becomes a giant tombstone to suggest the fate of one who practiced patriotism rather than self-exploration. He should have listened to Ben Franklin: "Bravery in a poor cause, is the height of simplicity, my friend" (p. 43). At the height of his bravery (and "simplicity"), he unfurls an American flag aboard the *Ranger,* and he is enveloped in its "red ribbons and spangles, like upspringing tongues, and sparkles of flame," but it is actually only a "glorified shroud" for him (p. 112).

Israel Potter reveals a Melville deeply concerned about both his country and himself. In the novel he depicts the four spirits of America. Benjamin Franklin embodies its great variety of pursuits and its adeptness at all of them, but he is no poet (p. 48). Melville worries that "America is, or may yet be, the Paul Jones

88. "Just one 'significance' is left him," comments Charles Feidelson, Jr., and that is "the evaporation of significance." *Symbolism and American Literature* (Chicago: University of Chicago Press, 1953), p. 183.

89. For a discussion of the confinement motif in *Israel Potter,* see John T. Frederick, "Symbol and Theme in Melville's *Israel Potter," Modern Fiction Studies* 8 (1962): 265–75.

90. Israel, who in a sense rots internally like the half-cord of hemlock, is thus set in contrast to John Paul Jones, who rapidly burns up internally like a fire "with spitting faggots of hemlock" (p. 62).

of nations," that is, "civilized in externals but a savage at heart" (p. 120). After all, France had seemed the most cultured and disciplined of countries but proved that it was untamed right below the surface. The French Revolution "levelled the exquisite refinement of Paris with the blood-thirsty ferocity of Borneo" (p. 63). When *Israel Potter* was published, America was sounding the trumpet of liberty, just as it had done before the Revolutionary War. As a house obviously divided against itself, it was about to go the way of a person torn by inner forces not controlled or even understood. In the Western spirit, as manifested in Ethan Allen, Melville saw some hope. Retaining a certain wildness but keeping it within bounds and exercising alternately more gentle and civilized qualities, Allen represents what should be "the true American" spirit (p. 149). But Melville's frustration with his homeland is evident from his use of Israel himself as the character who most consistently stands for America. The parallel begins early in the novel as Melville writes of Israel trying to throw off the yoke of a "king," his father, just as America is about to do. Israel's Independence Day, when he rebelled against the tyranny of his parents and left home, is in July just as is America's. Nations as well as people sometimes do not understand themselves. Melville views America's history as similar to the life of Israel Potter, who fights and suffers to be free from external restraints, not realizing that, paradoxically, this fierce insistence upon physical freedom is taking him further and further away from indispensable self-knowledge. On a superficial level, *Israel Potter* was intended to appeal to Americans. The appearance of its first installment in *Putnam's* coincided with the celebration of national independence in July, and it carried the subtitle (changed when published as a book) of "A Fourth of July Story." It *seemed* to glorify the unsung ordinary American as *Moby-Dick seemed* to glorify the lowly whaleman. In both instances, the deeper intention is elsewhere. If Melville wanted Israel to be America personified, it was not so much to elevate his protagonist to heroic proportions or to proclaim with patriotic fervor his country's fundamental superiority but to offer a subdued and camouflaged warning. *Israel Potter,* then, is conservative and traditional in its observation that one form of liberty is precious and essential for survival of the whole self of a person or a nation and that another form, deceptively attractive but elusive, often brings on destruction, but the novel is subversive in its implied charge that America with its preoccupation with freedom, freedom, freedom, has chosen to pursue exclusively the wrong kind of liberty, the form that leads to poverty of spirit.

But *Israel Potter* is mostly a warning to Melville himself about the horror of premature death. The cross of scars that marks Israel's body, scars from wounds received first at Bunker Hill and then in the fight with the *Serapis,* suggests that he is a kind of Christ figure, a sacrificial victim. Melville identified with Israel because he, too, felt victimized, unrecognized, and misunderstood; but his sympathy and understanding did not lead him to make a great man of Potter. Indeed, Israel is not only America's sacrificial lamb; he is Melville's as well. If America used Israel to help save itself, Melville sacrifices him—through character delineation—so that his own horror of self-ignorance can be expressed and eased.

The Five Virtues
of the Confidence Man

Chapter 9

A few years before Melville began writing *The Confidence-Man: His Masquerade,* an item appeared in the New York *Journal* under the headline "Curious Fraud: Personating the Author of 'White-Jacket.'" The article recounts the story of a man traveling in the South and claiming to be Melville: "It appears that some individual ambitious of notoriety has become enamoured of the good name and reputation of our townsman, Herman Melville . . . and has been so far successful in his attempts to pass himself off for that gentleman, in remote parts of Georgia and North Carolina, that persons near the scene of his exploits have been induced to correspond with the Messrs. Harper, of this city, Mr. Melville's publisher, for the purpose of getting reliable information on the subject of this stranger's claims to the authorship of Mr. Melville's books."[1] One of the disguises of this confidence man pretending to be Herman Melville was that of a deaf mute. In the spring of 1850, he entered the home of a merchant in

1. Jay Leyda, *The Melville Log: A Documentary Life of Herman Melville, 1819–1891* (New York: Harcourt, Brace, 1951), 1:377–78.

North Carolina who had two deaf and dumb sons and effectively convinced the good man that he was actually the well-known New York author and that he was himself a deaf mute. Sarah Ann Tillinghast, daughter of the gullible merchant, wrote a letter to her brother expressing her suspicions about the stranger: "There is a man in town that is deaf an dumb, or pretends to be he says he is the Author of Typhee and Omoo his name is Mr *Herman Melville* he was here last night and staid all night, Pa is delighted with him. I think *'that'* he is an imposter, he says that every place he visits the people think he is an imposter, but such people ought to be treated with *pity* if not *contempt*." She goes on to relate some of his claims about his abilities, his background, and his friendship with influential people, all of which she finds suspect.[2]

Since inquiries were made to the Harpers and since the exploits of this confidence man with literary interests reached the New York papers, Melville almost certainly knew that someone using his name was abroad in the land. Such a situation would frighten many people and infuriate others, but it was the kind of event that would stimulate Melville's imagination. Here was a shrewd operator proclaiming pity for those who did not trust him. To a mind sensitive to the prevalence of farce in the affairs of life, this imposter would prove interesting indeed.[3] After the initial shock, amazement, and amusement upon hearing that there was a second Herman Melville traveling through the South seeking acceptance from all those whom he encountered, Melville would have pondered much on the metaphorical potentiality of the situation and then allowed it to grow and develop gradually in the

2. This letter and another one relating to the imposter that called himself Herman Melville are in the William Norwood Tillinghast Papers in the Duke University Library. See Paschal Reeves, "The 'Deaf Mute' Confidence Man: Melville's Imposter in Action," *Modern Language Notes* 75 (1960): 18–20.

3. The appearance of an imposter upon the scene probably affected Melville even more deeply because he was having a difficult time anyway proving to some that his name really was Herman Melville. A British reviewer commented that it was obviously too distinguished a name for an American. In the same article in a New York newspaper that announced the presence of an imposter, the reporter affirmed that Melville did not write under a pseudonym.

rich soil of his creativity. It bloomed and became manifest in his final full-length novel, which was completed in 1856 and published the following year.[4]

The Confidence-Man is precisely the sort of book that would have developed from such a seed, as if Melville had heard of the imposter using his name and then started to wonder what it would be like if he really were a confidence man of a certain unusual order traveling through the land probing and affecting others through his conversation. Upon occasion he could indeed be a brilliant conversationalist, as Maunsell B. Field discovered during the summer of 1855 when he and the artist Felix O. C. Darley visited with Melville and Oliver Wendell Holmes in Pittsfield: "Soon there arose a discussion between Holmes and Melville, which was conducted with the most amazing skill and brilliancy on both sides. It lasted for hours, and Darley and I had nothing to do but listen. I never chanced to hear better talking in my life."[5] Others marveled at the same ability. Evert Duyckinck described in his diary for October 9, 1856, an evening spent in conversation with Melville and a few others: "Good talk—Herman warming like an old sailor over the supper."[6] A few days earlier Melville and Duyckinck (just the two of them) had passed an evening in such stimulating conversation that Duyckinck

4. The "deaf-mute" imposter was probably not Melville's only source for the confidence man, however. Johannes Dietrich Bergmann points out that in 1849 the New York papers carried wide coverage of the career of a petty thief named William Thompson who asked his victims to have confidence in him. "The Original Confidence Man," *American Quarterly* 21 (1969): 560–77. See also Michael S. Reynolds, "The Prototype for Melville's Confidence-Man," *PMLA* 86 (1971): 1009–13, which identifies the same source. Jane Donahue Eberwein links the confidence man with Joel Barlow's portrayal of the Incan hero Manco Capac: "Barlow told how Capac and his sister imposed on their subjects' superstition to guide them toward civilization." "Joel Barlow and *The Confidence-Man*," *American Transcendental Quarterly* 24, supplement (1974): 28–29. P. T. Barnum claimed in 1850 that he had discovered a Negro that used a weed to transform black people into whites. William M. Ramsey feels that this well-publicized hoax may have been a source for Black Guinea, who is changed into the man with the weed. "Melville's and Barnum's Man with a Weed," *American Literature* 51 (1979): 101–4.

5. Leyda, *Melville Log*, 2:506.

6. Ibid., 2:524.

called it "a good stirring evening—ploughing deep and bringing to the surface some rich fruits of thought and experience."[7] The entry in his diary goes on to mention some of the diverse topics on which Melville spoke so interestingly and impressively. Speaking, in fact, was soon to become Melville's chosen source of livelihood, for after he returned from his journey abroad upon completing *The Confidence-Man,* he took up lecturing (only to find that he was less effective at it than at engaging in give-and-take conversation).

Much of the difficulty that readers experience with *The Confidence-Man*—especially in regard to the identity and motivations of the protagonist—stems from the fact that the book is in essence a fantasy, a waking dream of the sort highly imaginative people sometimes have when they begin to wonder what they might do if they could become invisible or if they could fly. Melville is fantasizing about himself in the role of an extraordinary man in complete control of himself and thus in command of great insight and power. Numerous references to dreams, masquerades, and role playing enhance the impression that the book is an extended and detailed authorial reverie.[8]

It is not, however, a bitter reverie though critics have frequently called it Melville's bleakest work. Newton Arvin found it "completely nihilistic, morally and metaphysically."[9] To Richard Chase, it was "a disillusioned and savage book,"[10] and Ronald

7. Ibid., 2:523.

8. Walter Dubler discusses the novel's similarity to a play in "Theme and Structure in Melville's *The Confidence-Man" American Literature* 33 (1961): 307–19. Joel Porte argues that the work is a "romance" in which "our author will reappear in his own fantasy as a gaudy reincarnation of Satan." *The Romance in America: Studies in Cooper, Poe, Hawthorne, Melville, and James* (Middletown, Conn.: Wesleyan University Press, 1969), pp. 159–60. Warner Berthoff complains that unlike a good novel, this work is "tiring to get through," but he concludes that while "it is not finally a good *novel . . .* it is an altogether extraordinary exercise of creative imagination, and an absorbing book." *The Example of Melville* (Princeton: Princeton University Press, 1962), p. 60. A. R. Humphreys shrewdly comments that "the total effect is less of gloom than of a shifting satiric fantasy of which the keynote is entertainment." *Melville* (Edinburgh: Oliver and Boyd, 1962), p. 110.

9. Newton Arvin, *Herman Melville* (New York: Sloane, 1950), p. 251.

10. Richard Chase, *Herman Melville: A Critical Study* (New York: Macmillan, 1949), p. 205.

Mason discovered in it a "bitter theme."[11] *"The Confidence Man,"* William Ellery Sedgwick argued, "is what Prospero called Caliban, a 'thing of darkness.' " He found "savage indignation" there and "spiritual anguish at the book's core."[12] F. O. Matthiessen felt that when Melville composed *The Confidence-Man,* he was in "a mood of Timonism."[13] Joyce Sparer Adler agrees that it was written in a "bitter state of mind,"[14] as does Richard Boyd Hauck[15] and Joel Porte.[16] "This is a despairing book, a bitter book," says Daniel G. Hoffman.[17] According to Paul Brodtkorb, Jr., the work "must be read as an expression of its author's despair,"[18] and Alan Lebowitz thinks it a novel written by a "tired author," a "grim book and a tedious one."[19]

Among the loud roar of voices proclaiming that *The Confidence-Man* is a despairing work composed in a mood of severe depression, only a few scattered disclaimers are heard, but they should be listened to attentively, for though Melville produced a dreamlike work, it is no nightmare.[20] To be sure, Melville did undergo

11. Ronald Mason, *The Spirit Above the Dust: A Study of Herman Melville* (London: John Lehmann, 1951), p. 202.

12. William Ellery Sedgwick, *Herman Melville: The Tragedy of Mind* (Cambridge: Harvard University Press, 1944), pp. 187, 189.

13. F. O. Matthiessen, *American Renaissance: Art and Expression in the Age of Emerson and Whitman* (New York: Oxford University Press, 1941), p. 411.

14. Joyce Sparer Adler, *War in Melville's Imagination* (New York: New York University Press, 1981), p. 111.

15. "He was not well; his vision was deteriorating. He was bitterly disappointed by the critics' reception of *Pierre* and the indifference of his readership at large." Richard Boyd Hauck, "Nine Good Jokes: The Redemptive Humor of the Confidence-Man and *The Confidence-Man,*" in *Ruined Eden of the Present, Hawthorne, Melville, and Poe: Critical Essays in Honor of Darrel Abel,* ed. G. R. Thompson and Virgil L. Lokke (West Lafayette: Purdue University Press, 1981), p. 254.

16. "It is a complex exercise in self-satire such as only the bitterest, most disappointed and most brilliant romancer could ever have conceived" (Porte, p. 160).

17. Daniel G. Hoffman, *Form and Fable in American Fiction* (New York: Oxford University Press, 1961), p. 281.

18. Paul Brodtkorb, Jr., *"The Confidence-Man*: The Con-Man as Hero," *Studies in the Novel* 1 (1969): 430.

19. Alan Lebowitz, *Progress into Silence: A Study of Melville's Heroes* (Bloomington: Indiana University Press, 1970), pp. 187, 188.

20. Merlin Bowen, for example, suggests that Melville reveals no mental

a crisis of despair during which he was lonely, disappointed, depressed, and physically exhausted, a time when he felt himself in danger of withdrawing from the world around him into his own shell. The question is whether he wrote *The Confidence-Man* during this crisis and thus whether it embodies the terrible pessimism that must have gripped him.

Exactly when this mental and physical crisis of the 1850s began and when, precisely, it ended is difficult to determine. We know from Elizabeth Melville's notes about her husband that he suffered "his first attack" of severe back trouble in February 1855 after he had completed *Israel Potter*.[21] That June, Elizabeth recorded that he had such pain from sciatica that Dr. Oliver Wendell Holmes was called in to examine him. Over a year later, on September 1, 1856, Lemuel Shaw (Melville's father-in-law) wrote to his son, Samuel: "I suppose you have been informed by some of the family how very ill Herman has been." He describes the problem as "severe nervous affections" and tells of Melville's plan to go abroad.[22] It seems likely, however, that by the time Judge Shaw had written this letter indicating that Herman "has been" ill (rather than "*is* ill"), Melville had pretty much worked his way through his physical and mental trial. As early as September 14, 1855, a writer for the *Berkshire County Eagle* (probably J. E. A. Smith) described a kind of masquerade picnic in Pittsfield and commented that Melville was there and that he was "just recovering from a severe illness."[23] It was an occasion that Melville "apparently greatly" enjoyed, indicated the reporter. The gala could well have been another suggestive incident that provided a basic idea for *The Confidence-Man,* where the narrator comments that "life is a pic-nic *en costume;* one must take a part, assume a char-

---

blocks or confusion in the style, where such problems often manifest themselves as aberrations in syntax and loose verbosity. Melville's style in *The Confidence-Man* is "poised, precise, and at all times under easy control. Here, at least, there is no hint of confusion: this is the voice of a man who knows perfectly well what he is about." "Tactics of Indirection in Melville's *The Confidence-Man,*" *Studies in the Novel* 1 (1969):401.

21. Jay Leyda, *Melville Log,* 2:498.

22. Ibid., 2:521.

23. Ibid., 2:507.

acter, stand ready in a sensible way to play the fool" (p. 133).[24]
Another indication that Melville was a good deal improved in
mind and body by the time that he was fully engaged in writing
The Confidence-Man[25] is that during that period he seemed to be
ebullient and sociable in the conversation recorded by Maunsell
B. Field mentioned above.

In addition, he appeared to be looking *back* upon a period of
enervation and "severe nervous affections" with the perspective
that comes with time when he wrote "The Piazza," the last of his
short stories and the introductory work for his book *The Piazza
Tales*. Merton Sealts points out that "The Piazza" was composed in
January or February 1856.[26] By that time Melville could discern
clearly what had happened to him, and he could record how he had
regained his equilibrium, for this is one of his most intimately
personal stories, an account of a multidimensional crisis in his life.

24. *The Confidence-Man: His Masquerade,* ed. Harrison Hayford et al. (Evanston and Chicago: Northwestern University Press and the Newberry Library, 1984). All page references to *The Confidence-Man* are to this edition.

25. In *Herman Melville: A Biography* (Berkeley and Los Angeles: University of California Press, 1951), Leon Howard suggests that the Pittsfield fancy masquerade picnic gave Melville his initial idea for *The Confidence-Man* and argues, therefore, that the novel was started in the fall of 1855. Elizabeth S. Foster, on the other hand, feels that writing began in the summer of 1855. Introduction, *The Confidence-Man: His Masquerade* (New York: Hendricks House, 1954), p. xxiii. Merton M. Sealts, Jr., states that Melville "had apparently begun" *The Confidence-Man* during the summer of 1855. "The Chronology of Melville's Short Fiction, 1853–1856," in *Pursuing Melville, 1940–1980* (Madison: University of Wisconsin Press, 1982), p. 231. This essay was originally published in the *Harvard Library Bulletin* 28 (1980): 391–403. Alma A. MacDougall has succeeded in determining the date of a previously undated letter from George William Curtis to Joshua A. Dix (the publisher of *Putnam's*) as June 29, 1855. This is the letter in which Curtis advises Dix: "I should decline any novel from Melville that is not extremely good." MacDougall argues that this comment refers to a proposal Melville had made to Dix about a new novel, which was, she argues, *The Confidence-Man*. However, she concedes that there is no absolute proof when the novel was actually begun and that Curtis's statement could refer to "an idea for a work Melville never developed, or, like the 'Agatha' story, never published." "The Chronology of *The Confidence-Man* and 'Benito Cereno': Redating Two 1855 Curtis and Melville Letters," *Melville Society Extracts,* no. 53 (1983):3–6.

26. Sealts, p. 231.

The narrator has been weary, suffering from an unhealthy state of mind. Though he attempts first to find relief in the wrong places, he ends by undergoing, in a sense, a rebirth, gaining a renewed sense of the value of retaining his identity without losing touch with the actual world around him. Though Melville mentioned to Hawthorne during the first leg of his journey abroad in the fall of 1856 that he had just about reconciled himself to annihilation, he did not act as if he had and his old friend recognized that fact. It is probable, therefore, that his decision to take a trip abroad was not so much a desperate act to recover mental health as it was the act of a man who had already largely recovered and was anxious to re-establish contact with the world, a sign of health achieved or on the way rather than of health despondently sought.

At any rate, *The Confidence-Man,* completed before Melville sailed on October 11, 1856, for Liverpool, is not the bitter book so many critics assume that it is, though, to be sure, it crackles often with social satire and with aspersions on human nature. It is highly unusual among Melville's works, however, because it reverses the usual order of appearance and reality. Most of Melville's works of fiction seem on the surface brighter than they are; *The Confidence-Man* appears to be darker than it really is. In it, the sun is hidden but it is there nevertheless. That sun at the center is the theme of self-knowledge stressing that power and insight can come from understanding and mastering the self. The book reverberates with allusions to this basic idea from the moment when Black Guinea says that several men on board the steamer *Fidèle* know him well. He is actually referring to other manifestations of himself, and his hidden point is that in whatever outward form he is observed, and there are eight of them in all as most critics of the book now agree,[27] he is intimately acquainted with himself: "God bress 'em; yes, and what knows me as well as dis poor old darkie knows hisself, God bress him! Oh, find 'em, find 'em" (p. 13).[28] A few pages later, as the man with the weed, John Ring-

27. They are the deaf-mute, Black Guinea, John Ringman, the man in a gray coat collecting for the Seminole Widows and Orphans Fund, the man in a tasseled traveling-cap who is president and transfer-agent of the Black Rapids Coal Company, the herb doctor, the Philosophical Intelligence Office representative, and Frank Goodman the Cosmopolitan.

28. The idea to have the confidence man appear as a black man may have

man, the confidence man approaches Henry Roberts, a merchant, on the suggestive note of knowing oneself. He asks the merchant to determine who he is. Irritated, Roberts replies: "I hope I know myself." But John Ringman senses that he does not: "And yet self-knowledge is thought by some not so easy. Who knows, my dear sir, but for a time you may have taken yourself for somebody else?" (p. 20). That he is right is evident shortly thereafter when the merchant makes a statement that surprises even himself. He departs, "mortified at having been tempted by his own honest goodness, accidentally stimulated into making mad disclosures—to himself as to another—of the queer, unaccountable caprices of his natural heart" (p. 68).

In encounter after encounter, the confidence man uncovers this common denominator of character in those with whom he converses—they are strangers to themselves. As the man in a tasseled traveling-cap (the president and transfer-agent of the Black Rapids Coal Company), he tries to sell an arrogant young collegian on the idea of investing in "New Jerusalem," a metaphor for the inner kingdom. He assures the sophomore, who is foolishly proud that, as he puts it, "no appearances can deceive me," that New Jerusalem is *bona fide.* "All terra firma," he exclaims, but he realizes that the collegian does not "seem to care about investing" in that which is truly substantial and real but only in that which is of the outside world (p. 50). In debating with the man wearing a brass plate (of the Philosophical Intelligence Office), Pitch, a Missouri bachelor, shows himself to be like "a thunder-cloud with the inkept unrest of unacknowledged conviction" (p. 123). He is a man who believes that he knows himself but truly does not. The philosopher Mark Winsome claims that he receives self-knowledge through a disciple, Egbert, but the idea is tenuous. "Indeed, it is by you," he says to Egbert, "that I myself best understand myself" (pp. 197–98). In probably what was meant to be a sardonic or even an off-color comment, an unseen speaker, annoyed with Frank Goodman and an old man as they converse about the Apocrypha, shouts, "If you want to know what widsom is, go find it under your blankets" (p.

come to Melville as a result of his interest in the word *Masquerade,* which many etymologists believe derives from *mascarar,* to black the face (*OED*).

243). He has spoken far better perhaps than he realizes, for this is the central message of Melville's later novels.

It is not a new theme, then, that constitutes the heart of *The Confidence-Man*. Melville had realized how important it was to try to fathom his inner world, to discover what was going on there and to control it, but he also found that his search for self-understanding did not keep him invulnerable to doubts, depression, and physical suffering. He had become aware that power and perception derive from self-knowledge, but he also knew that he had not yet reached that stage of mastery whereby he could transcend frailties of mind and body. He was especially sensitive to this fact during and immediately after the crisis that occurred, as I have suggested, before he wrote *The Confidence-Man*. Whereas he had manifested in Ahab, Pierre, and Israel Potter the destructiveness of self-blindness, he fantasized in *The Confidence-Man* about an extraordinary figure who has obtained the extent of self-knowledge and control that he wishes he had. This character is the confidence man himself, who is not Satan, nor Christ, nor a trickster God, nor Vishnu, nor some mythic folk figure,[29] but Mel-

---

29. Critics who interpret the confidence man as Satan include the following: Elizabeth S. Foster, p. xxi; Edward H. Rosenberry, *Melville and the Comic Spirit* (Cambridge: Harvard University Press, 1955), p. 153; Thomas L. McHaney, "The *Confidence-Man* and Satan's Disguises in *Paradise Lost*," *Nineteenth-Century Fiction* 30 (1975): 200; James E. Miller, Jr., "*The Confidence-Man:* His Guises," *PMLA* 74 (1959): 111; Hershel Parker, "The Metaphysics of Indian-hating," *Nineteenth-Century Fiction* 18 (1963): 172; Joel Porte, p. 156; Charles Feidelson, Jr., *Symbolism and American Literature* (Chicago: University of Chicago Press, 1953), p. 210; Daniel G. Hoffman, p. 293; Susan Kuhlmann, *Knave, Fool, and Genius: The Confidence Man as He Appears in Nineteenth-Century American Fiction* (Chapel Hill: University of North Carolina Press, 1973), p. 122; John W. Schroeder, "Sources and Symbols for Melville's *Confidence-Man*," *PMLA* 66 (1951): 370. Paul McCarthy sees the confidence man as the Devil, but argues convincingly that many of those with whom he comes in contact are better and more noble than most critics have recognized. "Affirmative Elements in *The Confidence Man*," *American Transcendental Quarterly*, no. 7 (1970): 56–61. Richard Boyd Hauck feels that the confidence man is not actually Satan but the Devil's advocate (pp. 255–56). John Bernstein avoids the pitfall of oversimplification about the confidence man with his shrewd observation that "there is no one-to-one relationship between the Confidence Man and either Christ or Satan" but that he "contains elements of both." *Pacifism and Rebellion in the Writings of Herman Melville* (The Hague: Mouton, 1964), p. 156. According to Lawrance Thompson, the confidence man is

ville's rendition of not only how a man with the highest possible degree of self-understanding might actually be but also how he would appear to be to the world at large. He would be a demigod but appear to be something entirely different.

To say that *The Confidence-Man* is a kind of fantasy is not to suggest that it is flighty or loosely controlled fancy though much is unsaid or hidden. It is, in truth, a book of theories about what would be possible under certain conditions. In unfolding the nature and activities of his protagonist, Melville had nothing to go on but theories. He had never seen or known anyone like the confidence man; nor is this extraordinary figure, strictly speaking, based on Melville's own character. That is, he is not Melville

---

God's "Agent," but God has "malicious purposes." *Melville's Quarrel with God* (Princeton: Princeton University Press, 1952), p. 305. Edgar A. Dryden finds the confidence man to be "a satanic harlequin with a Christian message." *Melville's Thematics of Form: The Great Art of Telling the Truth* (Baltimore: Johns Hopkins University Press, 1968), p. 167. Helen P. Trimpi agrees that the confidence man is a harlequin figure, but she sees him operating not for evil but for the purpose of satire in the conventions of commedia dell'arte and pantomime. "Harlequin-Confidence-Man: The Satirical Tradition of Commedia Dell'Arte and Pantomime in Melville's *The Confidence-Man*," *Texas Studies in Literature and Language* 16 (1974): 147–93. Among those who interpret the confidence man as God or Christ are Merlin Bowen, pp. 401–42; and Carolyn Lucy Karcher, *Shadow over the Promised Land: Slavery, Race, and Violence in Melville's America* (Baton Rouge: Louisiana State University Press, 1980), pp. 186–257. R. W. B. Lewis sees the confidence man as a kind of Hermes, "the Muse responsible for inspiring the rhetoric of salesmanship." *Trials of the Word* (New Haven: Yale University Press, 1965), p. 69. William Bysshe Stein also links the confidence man with Hermes or Mercury, "who superintends the ludicrous plot of existence, but with a touch of merciful grace." "Melville's *The Confidence-Man*: Quicksands of the Word," *American Transcendental Quarterly* 24 (1974): 50. Warwick Wadlington considers the confidence man a Trickster god: "The trickster tricks because everything . . . is immaterial to him." *The Confidence Game in American Literature* (Princeton: Princeton University Press, 1975), p. 159. In *The Wake of the Gods: Melville's Mythology* (Stanford: Stanford University Press, 1963), H. Bruce Franklin makes an elaborate case for the various forms of the confidence man as avatars of Vishnu in Hindu mythology. Richard Chase argues that the confidence man is a "composite figure" embodying "the Westerner," Brother Jonathan, Uncle Sam, and others (p. 186). See Mary K. Madison's summary of the various positions critics have taken in regard to the identity of the confidence man: "Hypothetical Friends: The Critics and the Confidence Man," *Melville Society Extracts*, no. 46 (1981): 10–14.

as he is but Melville as he conceives that he could be if he could master the art of self-development. The confidence-man represents the end-product of that art. Therefore, concepts about the self in its relationship with the outer world constitute the basic material of the book. Melville formulates and illustrates through the confidence man in his various forms and as he interacts with society five theories, all of which deal with the central theme of self-knowledge.

 1. The more one understands and is in control of oneself the more likely is it that he will be an "original" person, original being used in the sense of primary, not copied or derivative or dependent but "proceeding immediately from its source, or having its source in itself." (*OED*)

 2. The more one understands and is in control of oneself, the more likely is it that he will exercise a sense of charity or philanthropy toward the world and the more highly will be developed his sense of humor toward it.

 3. The more one understands and is in control of oneself (and is confident in that self-knowledge), the less likely is it that he will be debased or victimized.

 4. The more one understands and is in control of oneself, the more likely is it that he will be honest, for every act of dishonesty is an act of self-ignorance or a loss of self-control or both.

 5. The more one understands and is in control of oneself, the more likely is it that he will be consistent and the less likely that he will be truly understood by others although they will often think—erroneously—that they do understand him.

The five great virtues stemming from knowledge and mastery of a deep and complex inner self are thus originality, charity (or philanthropy), confidence, honesty, and consistency. These fundamental concepts occupy the foreground of *The Confidence-Man*.

Originality, Melville insists, is not what it is ordinarily perceived to be. The point of chapter 44, Melville's famous discussion of the rarity of original characters in literature, is that there is a vast discrepancy between the world's opinion of what constitutes originality and what truly does. "Quite an Original" is a phrase loosely used by the uninitiated and the "untraveled" in the inner realms of self to apply to anyone who appears different from the common run. "The man who has made the grand tour," however (and Melville here refers to inner travel, voyaging into self), realizes that "odd characters" in life or literature are seldom original ones. They are merely "novel, or singular, or striking, or captivating, or all four at once" (p. 238). They derive much of what goes into their makeup from the outside, whereas truly original beings manifest outwardly what comes from inside them. If "there is discernible something prevailingly local, or of the age" about a person or a fictional character, he cannot be original in the sense Melville means because he takes in light from his environment rather than radiating it upon his surroundings from inside: "The character sheds not its characteristic on its surroundings, whereas, the original character, essentially such, is like a revolving Drummond light, raying away from itself all round it" (p. 239).

Though Melville's ostensible purpose in chapter 44 is to refute that Frank Goodman, the Cosmopolitan, is what the barber's friends call him, "quite an original," in reality he confirms that he is.[30] Melville wishes "to show, if possible, the impropriety of the phrase, *Quite an Original,* as applied by the barber's friends" (p. 239). That is, he wants to make the point that the barber's friends would not recognize an original being if they saw one. The phrase is inappropriate in their mouths because they do not grasp what it means. Thus they give the right designation to the confidence man for the wrong reasons, understanding neither the concept of originality as it applies to character nor the Cosmopolitan himself. They have no inkling that "original" is synonymous with "first cause." To be original, one must have uncovered the core of extraordinary psychic energy and insight, recognized it for what it is—a power akin to God—and allowed it, rather than any other influence, to operate. Rarely does such a development

30. In *Melville's Confidence Man: From Knave to Knight* (Columbia: University of Missouri Press, 1982), Tom Quirk argues that in the first half of the novel, Melville based the confidence man on the petty criminal William Thompson, whose exploits Melville probably read about in New York papers and elsewhere, but switched his concept in the last half of the book and in the Cosmopolitan "sought to create a truly original character" (p. 15).

take place, however. When those who understand what they are seeing witness originality, it is like watching the divine creation of form and beauty from chaos: "In certain minds, there follows upon the adequate conception of such a character, an effect, in its way, akin to that which in Genesis attends upon the beginnings of things" (p. 239). Melville's frequent intuition that somewhere hidden within him was a God-like being formed the basis for his conception of originality as a superhuman quality which he associates with the Creation and with divine light.

Besides directing his attention in chapter 44 to the erroneous assumption on the part of the world that originality is mere oddity or eccentricity and to a true definition of the concept, Melville also discusses the condition under which an author can create an original character. He must above all understand what originality is and where it comes from even though he himself has not developed to that extent: "To produce such characters, an author, beside other things, must have seen much, and seen through much" (p. 239), and, of course, he must have the good fortune that always is an ingredient in successful artistic creativity. The representation of originality in character does not derive from the writer's imagination. That is, an original character cannot be made up but must be born from the seed that already exists within the author. If that seed is not there, the novelist stands no chance of being the creator of such a rare and memorable character. "It cannot be born in the author's imagination," for "all life is from the egg" (p. 239).

Each of the five distinct attributes of self-knowledge and self-mastery carries with it certain rewards of magnitude affording those few who have reached this rare stage of development enormous advantages over the mass of humanity. With originality go a high degree of independence and superhuman powers. Perhaps the most obvious aspect of the confidence man in his several roles is the easy freedom that he enjoys, not encumbered either by heavy biases or heavy luggage on his journey through life. Not desperate like Ahab to be totally free of all restraints, he appears to have gained a measure of independence that the blinded and rebellious captain cannot obtain. He comes and goes in the world, selecting his own roles and moving at his own pace. His unusual freedom is evident whenever he is juxtaposed to characters who are in some way enslaved, as almost all are. The one-legged man who accuses Black Guinea of dishonesty is enslaved by his cynicism, the collegian by his juvenile arrogance and greed, the miser by his avarice, the sick man by his disease of body (and perhaps of mind), the Missouri bachelor by his disillusionment, Thomas Fry by the legal system that crippled him and then by his bitterness, China Aster by debt and depression, and so forth throughout the book. Most of them permit their enslavement because of self-ignorance. The confidence man escapes it through self-awareness.

The extraordinary power exercised by the confidence man is largely responsible for his being misinterpreted as Satan, Christ, or other supernatural figures. In whatever form he appears, he is in charge even when he appears to others as deferential, naive, or weak. Only he really seems to know what is happening. He takes command of conversations and directs them while seeming to be led. If the characters whom he encounters realized that he is one person playing eight different roles and if they could see him performing in all of these parts, they would be so frightened by his total command of the situation that they would desert the *Fidèle* before it made its first stop. His practice of preparing for a new role (as he does when as Black Guinea he mentions in a list most of the disguises he will take on as the day passes) is not merely to have others believe that he is what he seems nor simply to acquire needed information for his next contact (as he appears to be doing when Black Guinea uses his leather stump to cover and thus secrete the country merchant's calling card). In such acts he is exhibiting the same kind of complete control over events that the skillful novelist exercises when he creates foreshadowing. The confidence man deliberately and repeatedly indulges in foreshadowing and in harking back or echoing. The effect is that of interconnectedness within seeming randomness, purpose within haphazardness. Black Guinea's "geniality" foreshadows that of the Cosmopolitan. John Ringman is in "need," as Frank Goodman claims to Charlie Noble that he is. The man in a gray coat collecting for the Seminoles is a philanthropist, as is the Cosmopolitan. The agent of the Black Rapids Coal Company wears, as does the Cosmopolitan, a strange hat and invites a dried-up man he speaks with to drink wine and tell stories—acts Frank Goodman later indulges in. The man in gray also foreshadows the Cosmopolitan's going into the men's quarters and finding an old man when in chapter 15 he enters the emigrant's quarters and discovers an aging miser. The herb doctor speaks of doing good to the world (p. 94), and so does the Cosmopolitan. In conversation with "a prim-looking stranger," who is outraged that Thomas Fry pretends to be a disabled veteran of the Mexican War, the herb doctor makes a comment which later becomes the theme of a story he narrates in the role of the Cosmopolitan. He explains that Fry does not tell others of his real woes because such troubles would repel, not attract (p. 97). This is exactly the reasoning behind Charlemont's refusal to let his friends know of his severe financial difficulties. When the herb doctor states that the Black Rapids Coal Company agent had turned an investment for him into gold eagles (ten-dollar gold coins), he foreshadows the Cosmopolitan's possession of gold eagles (which he places around Charlie Noble). The confidence man looks backward as well as forward, however, and ties his words already spoken to those he is speaking, these echoes acting as reminders that he is consistently and firmly in control. The herb doctor links himself with one of his previous roles when he tells Fry that he "prescribed" for Black Guinea and that he anticipates that the cripple will be "able to walk almost as well as myself" (p. 99), which of course is true since they are one and the same person. The herb doctor's words in chapter 19 to the prim-looking man echo precisely those that the deaf-mute writes on his slate in chapter 1: "Charity never faileth" (pp. 97, 5).

In the first four of the eight roles he plays, the confidence man makes his plea to humanity in the name of charity, the second virtue of self-awareness. The deaf-mute holds up to a suspicious public the words of Saint Paul on charity. Black Guinea plays "this game of charity," trying in a different way from the deaf-mute to get his fellows to taste the flavor of benevolence by throwing him coins. When distrust develops among contributors, a Methodist minister speaks out for putting "as charitable a construction as one can upon the poor fellow" (p. 13). In response, a bitter one-legged man argues heatedly that charity has no place among men. After Black Guinea disappears, John Ringman approaches a country merchant and asks for charity to aid him in his plight. With chapter 6 comes the man in gray, asking charity for the Seminole Widow and Orphan Asylum, but several "passengers prove deaf to the call of charity" (p. 28). Ironically, they are deaf whereas the deaf-mute can, in this sense, hear. The man in gray is successful, however, with others, including a clergyman; a gentleman with gold sleeve-buttons, to whom the collection agent describes his philanthropic scheme for a world charity; and "a charitable lady," who donates twenty dollars to the Seminole fund. In his last four roles, the confidence man makes his theme that of sound and rewarding investment. The representative of the Black Rapids Coal Company sells stock for greater wealth; the herb doctor sells investment in better health; the man from the Philosophical Intelligence Office asks his clients to invest in boys; and the Cosmopolitan argues repeatedly and lengthily for investing in humanity in order to escape the blight of cynicism and bitterness. In effect, however, what the Cosmopolitan is espousing is the same as that of the confidence man in his first manifestation, the deaf-mute, for charity and philanthropy are essentially the same virtue.

The degree to which the confidence man is successful in getting people to be charitable or to "invest" (in the larger and more humane sense) is secondary to Melville's wider purpose, which is to delineate the true nature of this virtue of charity-philanthropy as opposed to how the world often conceives of it and to link it with the development, understanding, and control of one's psychic forces. The mature, examined, and disciplined mind inevitably develops a benevolent stance toward humanity and poignantly intuits the necessity of such an attitude, but because that mind is so greatly superior to those of ordinary humanity, patience and kindness would be impossible without the quality that accompanies charity, namely a "saving" sense of humor. Humor, therefore, is an essential ingredient in *The Confidence-Man,* revealing the way in which the extraordinary man of self-knowledge deals with and retains his necessary connection with the world around him.

Melville obviously relies heavily upon Saint Paul's concept of charity, especially in chapter 1 when the deaf-mute writes five statements on his slate from 1 Corinthians 13: "Charity thinketh no evil," "Charity suffereth long, and is kind," "Charity endureth all things," "Charity believeth all things," and "Charity never faileth" (pp. 4–5). What is less obvious is Melville's use of another verse in that same chapter of 1 Corinthians: "When I was a child, I spake as a child, I understood as a child, I thought as a child: but when I became a man, I put away childish things." Paul is clearly linking the feeling and practice of charity to spiritual maturity and by implication charging those who lack true benevolence and long-suffering patience with being childish. Melville picked up on this association of charity with maturity and conveyed it in a scene charged with some of the most effective irony in the book. The deaf-mute is described as a child and treated as one by those aboard the *Fidèle* when in actuality he is a mature man of self-knowledge who has put away childish things, and they are mental and spiritual toddlers in the guise of adults. The deaf-mute's "cheek was fair, his chin downy, his hair flaxen," like that of an infant. He stands near a placard "offering a reward for the capture of . . . an original genius" (p. 3), but it is he who is the original genius, even if he appears to be a babe. Toward the end of the book, Melville remarks that "the sense of originality exists at its highest in an infant" (p. 238). As such, the man in cream colors appears to be cut off, for one cannot communicate with him in the ordinary ways. He seems to have been recently born, to have come from a far place. And like a child in his innocence and helplessness, he is now and then jostled aside or impatiently abused by the adults around him. Yet their "buffets" are all "unresented" as he offers a lesson in charity and then, again like a small child or infant, goes off to sleep without caring much where. Resembling a toddler, he is constantly in the way, and two porters with a trunk almost run over him, but he accepts it all with "lamb-like" forbearance. Though considered a "simpleton," he is the opposite.

The reason that charity grows out of self-knowledge is not merely that the great and ordered mind senses its superiority to society in general and thus is moved to a feeling of pity but more fundamentally that such a highly developed and self-aware mind realizes that it has to exist among the ordinary and will become unstable without some connection with the world of common people. Therefore, an original person cannot long remain so in aloof isolation. One comes to value company, even though not of the highest order, as necessary for self-understanding. This is what the Cosmopolitan means when he tells Charlie Noble that there is "a kind of man who, while convinced that on this continent most wines are shams, yet still drinks away at them; accounting wine so fine a thing, that even the sham article is better than none at all" (p. 162). He then compares the inferior wine with inferior company and draws a parallel between the drinker and a "good-natured" person who "might still familiarly associate with men, though, at the same time, he believed the greater part of men false-hearted—accounting society so sweet a thing that even the spurious sort was better than none at all" (p. 162).

But this is not to say that the confidence man loves each person he encounters. To feel a sense of charity toward humanity and to value the company sometimes even of false-hearted people is not to cherish or even to like every individual. With few exceptions, however, the confidence man remains tolerant and friendly, perhaps even benevolent, toward those he meets. He can do so because they are as children to him. He sees what they are up to, what they want, and he plays with them, not as the Devil toys with the damned but as a good-natured mature adult talks with a child and, without letting the child know it, amuses himself by manipulating the immature (and often selfish) mind. Throughout, the confidence man is in this way amusing himself, but in a good-natured, not satanic, vein. When John Ringman tells the merchant, Henry Roberts, that he has "a hundred times" laughed over something that passed between them, he may be indulging in the kind of storytelling that adults frequently practice with children, but he nevertheless reveals that indispensable quality that is the companion of charity, a highly developed and mature sense of humor as opposed to that pseudohumor characteristic of the immature or sick mind.

In fact, the confidence man is repeatedly contrasted with those who appear to have little sense of humor or a warped or childish one. The country merchant, for example, sees none of the humor in John Ringman's assertion that Roberts must have suffered an "unfortunate brain fever" since he has no recollection of their prior meeting. Similarly, the collegian, who takes himself so seriously that he is something of a comic figure anyway, suffers surprise and embarrassment when John Ringman tries with exaggerated heat and amusing mock concern to get him to give up reading Tacitus. A sense of humor would certainly have spared him such discomfort. Occasionally the characters who encounter the confidence man are heard to laugh, but more often than not, it is laughter without joy or good humor. The one-legged man's "ha, ha, ha!" is described as "A sort of laugh more like a groan than a laugh; and yet, somehow, it seemed intended for a laugh" (p. 29). Similarly, a shaggy giant, an "invalid Titan in homespun" (p. 85), meets the herb doctor's amusing greeting with a smile, but one that is "hypochondriacally scornful" (p. 86). Thomas Fry's laughter is "strangely startling" with something of the wild hyena in it (p. 95). Charlie Noble's laughter is cruelly directed toward "a pale pauper-boy on the deck below, whose pitiableness was touched, as it were, with ludicrousness by a pair of monstrous boots, apparently some mason's discarded ones, cracked with drouth, half eaten by lime, and curled up about the toe like a bassoon" (p. 163). Laughter is thus not always indicative of the kind of mind and heart which the confidence man possesses. "It is said," he comments to Charlie Noble, "that a man may smile, and smile, and smile, and be a villain; but it is not said that a man may laugh, and laugh, and laugh, and be one" (p. 163). Yet he knows that this is true, and he is referring to Charlie, whom he recognizes for what he is, a petty and pitiable sharper without a true sense of humor, which is a reward and byproduct of the virtue of charity.

The Cosmopolitan clearly links charity and humor when he says that "humor has something, there is no telling what, of beneficence in it, it is such a catholicon and charm . . . and in its way it undeniably does . . . a deal of familiar good in the world" (p. 163). Not only do those who lack charity also lack a sense of humor but they also seem to possess "a disrelish," a "hatred" for those who do enjoy healthy laughter. The Cosmopolitan gives the example of Phalaris, "the capricious tyrant of Sicily," who had one of his subjects beheaded for laughing. Charlie Noble reveals his lack of charity by exclaiming, "Funny Phalaris!" to which the Cosmopolitan, in one of his deeply felt statements, replies, "Cruel Phalaris!" (p. 164). "According to my principle," the Cosmopolitan later explains, "humor is in general to be held a saving quality" (p. 172). Its absence marks at one extreme the simpleton and at the other Timon, the lost man-hater. To lack it, and its parent, beneficence, as the confidence man tells the collegian, is "the sign of a hardening heart and a softening brain" (pp. 50–51). Melville goes to surprising lengths to emphasize that genuine love of laughter and profundity are not alien characteristics but wedded traits of the extraordinary man of self-understanding. The anecdote that Melville relates in chapter 13 about "a grave American savan" mistaking the great Sir Humphrey Davy for a mere "jackanapes" because of his lightheartedness underscores the point that there is no discrepancy between the man who indulges in what may pass as "jaunty levity" and the person who is "capable of philosophic and humanitarian discourse—no mere casual sentence or two as heretofore at times, but solidly sustained throughout an almost entire sitting" (p. 64). Otherwise learned and intelligent, Mark Winsome lacks a well-developed sense of humor and is consequently a foil to the much superior Cosmopolitan. Winsome is a "stranger," who is "constitutionally obtuse" to the confidence man's "drollery" (p. 196). William Cream, the barber, proves likewise.

In one of his three chapters that deal with the writing of fiction, Melville pauses and, taking the position of his readers who may complain about the unreality of the confidence man, asks: "Who did ever dress or act like your cosmopolitan?" (p. 182). His answer is "harlequin," who "can never appear in a coat too particolored, or cut capers too fantastic" (p. 183). The suggestion that the Cosmopolitan is similar to the harlequin figure in Italian commedia dell'arte is highly revealing.[31] The confidence man and the characters in commedia dell'arte travel widely, rely heavily on masks and improvisation, and value laughter as mankind's

31. See Trimpi, "Harlequin-Confidence-Man."

unique gift and tool. Yet, harlequin, a principal figure in commedia dell'arte, is sometimes victimized (especially in matters of
the heart) whereas the confidence man is not vulnerable. As a
devotee of roles and laughter, a philanthropist in the guise of a
fool, he more closely resembles one of Melville's most cherished
authors, Rabelais, a profound man who believed "that true
wisdom often disguises itself as foolishness."[32] Colin Wilson has
remarked that the sixteenth century was so dominated by men of
action that the true thinker, the prober, "had to don the disguise
of the charlatan to make his mark."[33] Rabelais, he points out,
was "more or less at home in it."[34] Melville marked in his Bible a
passage in 1 Corinthians that bears on the relationship between
wisdom (self-knowledge especially) and "foolishness": "Let no
man deceive himself. If any man among you seemeth to be wise
in this world, let him become a fool, that he may be wise"
(3:18).[35] Melville's admiration for Rabelais is well documented,
but critics of *The Confidence-Man* have, as far as I can determine,
overlooked the strong possibility that Rabelais is one of the
sources for the central figure, especially in the role of the Cosmopolitan.[36] A widely circulated story about Rabelais concerns his
donning of a ridiculous costume in order to be seen and heard. An
article in the *American Whig Review* (May 1850), an essay Melville
almost certainly read since it compares *Mardi* with the work of
Rabelais, describes this incident: "He dressed himself in a cos-

32. Florence M. Weinberg, *The Wine and the Will: Rabelais's Bacchic Christianity* (Detroit: Wayne State University Press, 1972), p. 149.

33. Colin Wilson, *The Occult: A History* (New York: Random House, 1971),
p. 243.

34. Ibid.

35. The New English Bible translates the passage: "Make no mistake about
this: if there is anyone among you who fancies himself wise—wise, I mean, by the
standards of this passing age—he must become a fool to gain true wisdom. For the
wisdom of this world is folly in God's sight." The New American Bible offers the
following translation: "Let no one delude himself. If any of you thinks he is wise in
a worldly way, he had better become a fool. In that way he will really be wise, for
the wisdom of this world is absurdity with God."

36. I am not suggesting here that Rabelais is the sole figure on which Melville
modeled the Cosmopolitan. Indeed, in the next chapter I offer an additional
model.

tume calculated to attract attention, a long green gown, an Armenian bonnet, oriental breeches."[37] Melville has the Cosmopolitan dressed in different attire but equally garish and strange: "a vesture barred with various hues, that of cochineal predominating, in style participating of a Highland plaid, Emir's robe, and French blouse" with a "flowered regatta-shirt," large trousers of white duck, "maroon-colored slippers, and a jaunty smoking-cap of regal purple" (p. 131). So jovial was Rabelais in disposition and yet so deep was his learning that some of his fellow friars, according to the nineteenth-century translators and editors of his work, believed him to be "a conjuror."[38]

The Cosmopolitan's connection with Rabelais is suggested when the Missouri bachelor calls Goodman's theories about life part of "Rabelais's pro-wine Koran" (p. 135). The Cosmopolitan, like Rabelais, seems to have "a disposition ungovernably bacchanalian" (p. 162), and both hold to humor as man's saving quality. For both, wine is deeply symbolic. In Rabelais's writings, the "boozers" are "those who truly seek."[39] And wine represents the marrow of truth; those who tipple are led "to discover the hidden divinity within."[40] The confidence man drinks heartily but he never becomes drunk in a physical sense. His great praise of wine drinking is in actuality commendation of truth seeking. An understanding of Rabelais's wine symbolism leads to important revelations about Melville's use of wine in *The Confidence-Man*. For both, imbibing is the metaphor for discovering the hidden sun.

Melville also seems to have picked up on another of Rabelais's unusual symbols for the seeker, the dog. In his prologue to *Gargantua*, Rabelais asks his readers: "Did you ever see a dog with a marrow-bone in his mouth? . . . If you have seen him, you might have remarked with what devotion and circumspectness he wards and watcheth it: with what care he keeps it: how fervently he holds it: how prudently he gobbets it: with what

---

37. Eugene Lies, "An Essay on the Life and Writings of Francois Rabelais, the Good Curate of Mendon," *American Whig Review*, n.s., 5 (1850): 489.

38. *The Works of Francis Rabelais*, trans. Sir Thomas Urquhart and Motteux, vol. 1 (London: H. G. Bohn, 1854), p. 2.

39. Weinberg, p. 28.

40. Ibid., p. 44.

affection he breaks it: and with what diligence he sucks it."[41] The marrow for Rabelais is truth, and he urges his readers to imitate the dog and seek the essence. Melville repeatedly associates the confidence man in his several roles with dogs. Black Guinea is compared to a Newfoundland dog, and he speaks of himself as "der dog widout massa" (p. 10). Since he "seemed a dog, so now, in a merry way, like a dog he began to be treated" (p. 11). The Black Rapids Coal Company representative comes into the ship's cabin gleefully, as if to say, "What dear, happy dogs are we all!" (p. 53), and later he refers to himself in another role (John Ringman) as a "lucky dog" (p. 67). He takes the part of a dog again as the PIO man, whom the Missouri bachelor calls to "as if to his pointer" (p. 114). Saint Augustine, says the PIO man, was for a time "a very sad dog" (p. 125), and the Cosmopolitan tells the barber that "to tell a dog," probably meaning himself, "that you have no confidence in him" is a "matter for affront to the dog" (p. 226).

A great deal of the confidence man's talk appears conceived in mischievousness: he is saying something or implying something that the person he is speaking with cannot perceive. Frequently he seems to emote and to appear dead serious when one senses that under the cover of gravity is a strong current of lightheartedness. Such was the technique Melville so admired in Rabelais. In fact, Eugene Lies, in the article about Rabelais that compares Melville with him, defines the humor of which Rabelais is "the prince" as "a veil of mock gravity cast over pleasantry to make her more attractive."[42] The confidence man resembles Rabelais not only in his philosophy and use of humor, his symbolic concepts of the drinker, wine, and the dog, but also in his underlying serious and philanthropical intention, for he follows Rabelais in being keenly and often painfully aware of the sham, selfishness, and ridiculousness of humankind, which he is committed to reveal, but at the same time concerned enough never to separate himself from that world he often scorns. Indeed, he is a kind of castigating well-wisher to it. Eugene Lies's article in the *American Whig*

41. Rabelais, 1:95–96.
42. Lies, p. 487.

Review is largely a defense of Rabelais along these lines. As a doctor, Rabelais made his patients laugh because he wanted to cure them. Humor is the "catholicon," as the confidence man puts it, for the human race. Lies depicts him as a rambler who "passed several years in travelling from place to place, without any other aim or object than to enjoy life or to investigate some curious subject."[43] But, Lies insists, there was always a strong moral basis for his actions, and he resents the tendency to declare Rabelais's writings immoral. Once you understand this, "his apparent licentiousness no longer scares your propriety, and you surrender up your judgment to him, feeling like a child in the hands of an intellectual giant, or like a candidate for initiation at the mysteries of Eleusis, following your guide through passages and labyrinths of dismal obscurity, yet never doubting that you will soon emerge into the broad light of Heaven."[44] If Melville did indeed read these words, he would have agreed, as he would have with Coleridge's assessment (included in the English translation of Rabelais's works): "I could write a treatise in praise of the moral elevation of Rabelais' work, which would make the church stare, and the conventicle groan, and yet would be truth, and nothing but the truth."[45] Eugene Lies argues that Rabelais pursued his "disinterested activity" to such lengths "that entitle him to be considered a benefactor of humanity."[46] For the confidence man, as for Rabelais, laughter was both the instrument and the reward of charity-philanthropy.

But charity begins at home. It grows outward from genuine compassion for oneself; it is impossible without self-love, not egotism or Narcissism, but that which Melville calls in his poem "Shelley's Vision" "self-reverence":

> Wandering late by morning seas
> When my heart with pain was low—
> Hate the censor pelted me—
> Deject I saw my shadow go.

43. Ibid., p. 492.
44. Ibid., p. 496.
45. Rabelais, 1:23.
46. Lies, p. 491.

In elf-caprice of bitter tone
I too would pelt the pelted one:
At my shadow I cast a stone.

When lo, upon that sun-lit ground
I saw the quivering phantom take
The likeness of St. Stephen crowned.
Then did self-reverence awake.[47]

William H. Shurr points out that "though the vision is attributed to Shelley, nothing similar can be found in his writings. One realizes again that this poem projects a thin disguise for Melville's own emotions."[48]

Just as the philanthropist is first a lover of self in the best and most positive sense of the term, so is the confidence man (that is, the *man of confidence*) infinitely self-confident. Confidence in self derives from the knowledge of what one truly is and a consistent refusal to fool oneself even though fooling others sometimes proves necessary. The third virtue that Melville explores, therefore, is closely akin to charity. Comments about confidence occur so frequently in the book and are so lightly made that Melville seems almost determined to trivialize a deeply felt conviction. The man of confidence asks the shallow collegian: "Could you now, my dear young sir, under such circumstances, by way of experiment, simply have confidence in *me?*" (p. 27). The question appears playful or insincere; it is generally considered an attempt to set the young man up so that he can be relieved of some of his money. It goes far beyond that, however. The confidence man asks this same question with slight variations several times. In doing so, his motive appears to be twofold, to manifest and, in his own particular and peculiar way, to serve.

He wishes in a sense to show off, to place himself in stark contrast to people around him by manifesting the ultimate degree of confidence, a mental attitude that is more powerful and far-reaching than ordinary humankind realizes. As with originality

47. First published in *Timoleon* (1891).
48. William H. Shurr, *The Mystery of Iniquity: Melville as Poet, 1857–1891* (Lexington: University Press of Kentucky, 1972), p. 163.

and charity, Melville is bent upon showing that the world has only a superficial sense of what it is to have confidence. In the man of confidence it takes the form of "assurance, boldness, fearlessness, arising from reliance (on oneself . . .)," as the *OED* defines it in one of its many meanings. When John Truman, the man with the traveling cap, asks the country merchant if the unfortunate John Ringman desponded or had confidence, he is clearly speaking of self-confidence. The herb doctor later understates the degree of his "assurance, boldness, and fearlessness" when he says that he is a person "with some little modest confidence in himself" (p. 107). As one of the five virtues derived from self-understanding, confidence provides a priceless reward to one who truly possesses it—immunity from excessive fear and insecurity, those destructive emotions that plague ordinary mankind.

The confidence man rests easy in his knowledge that because he knows and controls the forces within himself, he will be able to know and thus keep ahead of other people. He who has developed beyond the stage of being a victim of himself—Pierre is such a victim—will no longer be victimized by the world. There is never the slightest possibility that the Cosmopolitan is going to become another one of Charlie Noble's dupes. Though Charlie plies the Cosmopolitan with wine and exercises all the guile of which he is capable, he proves to be comically ineffectual in his attempts to fool his superior companion, who appears always two steps ahead of him. In each encounter, the confidence man enjoys an extraordinary advantage because he understands the mind with which he is dealing. He immediately perceives the country merchant's lack of self-knowledge and his resultant insecurity. He sees clearly into the old miser, who lives in panic. "But confidence," John Truman says to him, "I fear that, even had you the precious cash, you would not have the more precious confidence I speak of" (p. 75). He means the fearlessness and security that he himself enjoys, the sense of self-possession. The Cosmopolitan states that to him "no man is a stranger" (p. 132), by which he means that he has confidence that he will be able to unveil and to see into the people around him. Such fascination and intense feeling of self-esteem derive from the exercise of this rare talent that the man of confidence cannot resist playing his game of confidence wherever he goes. The most poignant contrast between a true man of confidence and a man who lacks it comes in the final chapter where the Cosmopolitan converses with an old man in the gentlemen's cabin. The aged man has seen much of life but lives in fear of the unknown. Since he does not know himself, he cannot receive the rewards of confidence in its deepest sense. The copy of the Bible he reads represents the man himself. The man of confidence speaks of him as well as of the book when he says: "Look at this volume; on the outside, battered as any old valise in the baggage-room; and inside, white and virgin as the hearts of lilies in bud" (p. 249). The old man has never read the book of self. Consequently, the sense of security that he purports to receive from his religion is as thin as the pages of the largely unread Bible, as inadequate as the stool—life preserver that he takes to bed with him, a comic and pathetic substitute for the security and fearlessness that come from confidence. The flimsiness of his religious faith and its failure to take the place of self-knowledge in furnishing immunity to victimization are suggested in the episode where he readily buys all the security devices offered by a strange juvenile peddler, who is far more likely meant for a Satanic figure than is the confidence man. The old man is given a useless "Counterfeit Detector"; the man of confidence has an effective and infallible one—built in, as it were.

The first of the confidence man's motives, then, is simply to manifest, to show off, the powerful effects of *self*-confidence. His second motivation is more philanthropic in nature, for he attempts to do something, as he puts it, to *alleviate*. Here the word *confidence* has another meaning and refers to trust in others. He possesses both kinds. He has supreme confidence in self, and he has that unshakable security that comes from confidence in others, that is, confidence that he *understands* others. From self-knowledge comes knowledge of others. Recognizing that the ordinary man will not adequately probe the recesses of his inner being and struggle long and hard to identify, analyze, and control the complex forces there, the confidence man seeks to do what he can to help him cure the two diseases of self-ignorance before they become incurable, those two most destructive of all human emotions—fear and anger. If he cannot give those he encounters the deeper confidence, he may be able to cultivate in some a healing trust, groundless though it may often seem, that will alleviate the dread sicknesses of anxiety and cynicism.

Thus the man of confidence seeks to be a healer, not just in the role of the herb doctor but in all the parts he plays, and those he meets are nearly all described in terms of poor health or disease, persons in need of a physician. Early in the novel a drover who is amused by Black Guinea is described as "purple-faced" with a "large purple hand" (p. 10), and the one-legged man is introduced as "a limping, gimlet-eyed, sour-faced person" (p. 12). As the man in gray collecting charity, the confidence man fails with two people in chapter 6, both of whom seem to have health problems: a gentleman with a "ruby-colored" face and a "bulky" old man (p. 28). He fails to reach somewhat later a "little dried-up man" (p. 53).[49] The miser, consumed with fear of losing his money, appears to be in terrible health as does the sick man of chapter 16 who has sought cures in numerous places. Thomas Fry has suffered grave illness in prison and has become a cripple. Whereas the Cosmopolitan is described in terms of health, his "boon companion," Charlie Noble, has "something the reverse of fine in the skin" and a "bilious" countenance (p. 139). There seems to be a correlation between the readiness and degree of trust in these characters and their health. Those who are lost in anger or cynicism are the least healthy. The herb doctor recognizes that the giant invalid who comes on board in chapter 17 has "pain, strong pain, somewhere" (p. 87), and he connects this physical pain with "cases of mental suffering" (p. 88). The Titan's bitterness has gone too far, however, for any alleviation. He is, as the confidence man accurately states, "lost to humanity!" (p. 88). The Cosmopolitan angers the Missouri bachelor when he comments that a person who bitterly separates himself from mankind is like a rooster "that has the pip" (p. 135). The same point is made in the Cosmopolitan's story of the old woman of Goshen who takes on a cynical outlook and concurrently becomes physically ill. Her

49. Playing the part of physician, the president and transfer-agent of the Black Rapids Coal Company encourages the dried-up man to greater geniality and adds: "Hope you will do well, *as the doctors say*" (p. 53, italics mine).

recovery is brought about because of a renewed intoxication with life. Again in this episode, the confidence man links bitterness with sickness. "Disease," he says, springs from "a certain lowness, if not sourness, of spirits" (p. 133). "A sick philosopher," says the herb doctor, "is incurable" because "he has no confidence" (p. 80). In one place, the Methodist minister unquestionably speaks for Melville when he warns against destructive cynicism. He says that he has seen in madhouses "the cynic, in the moody madness muttering in the corner; for years a barren fixture there; head lopped over, gnawing his own lip, vulture of himself" (p. 16).

When he is not seeking to ward off or cure the diseases of anxiety and cynicism, the man of confidence is attempting to bring his hidden sun to bear upon coldness, which is along with sickness the most frequent problem of those he meets. The man with the gold sleeve buttons, for example, is quite healthy, and he takes every precaution to stay that way. He touches nothing: "like the Hebrew governor," he knows "how to keep his hands clean" (p. 36). Though his habits and dress ostensibly reflect cleanliness, they more directly suggest coldness. The whiteness of his glove and skin and "the inner-side of his coat-skirts" is that of snow. He listens attentively to the man in gray who speaks of philanthropy, and he gives his money willingly, but it is clear that no sun can thaw the ice that has capsulated him and permanently separated him from others. Goneril, John Ringman's supposed wife, is similarly rosy in complexion with a cold nature. Her eyes some described as "cold as a cuttle-fish's," and "like an icicle-dagger, Goneril at once stabbed and froze" (p. 61). Her strange habit of touching young men derives from her instinctive desire for a moment of warmth. In whatever role he plays, the confidence man's heated conversation and activity contrast with the chill of certain other characters. Completely to reject the world, he tells the Missouri bachelor, is "cold" and "loveless" (p. 136). Even the enthusiastic Charlie Noble is associated with "gamblers and all sorts of subtle tricksters sticking to cold water, the better to keep a cool head for business" (p. 164). Melville's masterpiece of coldness, however, is Mark Winsome. Like the man in gold sleeve buttons (who has a "winsome aspect") and

Goneril, Mark Winsome is healthy in appearance but cold of eye and emotion, another of the confidence man's failures because the sun cannot reach him any more than medicine can help the lame Titan of an earlier episode. He sits with the Cosmopolitan, "coldly radiant as a prism" and refusing wine for ice water, "its very coldness, as with some is the case, proving not entirely uncongenial" (p. 194). His iciness sends away a poet-beggar trying to sell his poem.

These two imagistic clusters involving disease and coldness serve to differentiate the two categories of people in *The Confidence-Man* who have not developed the virtue of confidence. Some of them will not trust others because of emotional reasons. They have been abused in some way by society or cheated. They have been hurt and victimized, and that suffering has left within them a dark suspicion that colors their vision; or they may be so obsessed with obtaining more money or so consumed with the fear of losing what they have that they passionately distrust all others until they can see a use for them. These generally are the characters who do not appear physically healthy, disease connoting emotional distrust or even cynicism. The other group seems not to have gone through the same kind of experiences that taught them the hard way not to trust other people. They appear to have escaped the emotional ravages that have left many in the other group bitter. Yet because of intellectual reasons, they are unwilling to reach out to the world. They are the characters described in images of coldness. One segment lacks confidence because of the heart, the other because of the head.

Those whom the confidence man cannot move are not depicted as profounder or smarter or even more wisely shrewd but as sicker or colder than those who succumb to his appeal. Those who successfully resist him, therefore, are the lost, not the saved. Among the several articles and news items in 1849 that commented on the escapades of the swindler who approached others in New York and asked for confidence was an especially enlightening commentary published first in the *Merchant's Ledger* and reprinted in Evert and George Duyckinck's *Literary World,* which Melville at this period read regularly. The author takes a point of view with which Melville was obviously sympathetic: "The man who is *always* on his guard, *always* proof against appeal, who cannot be beguiled into the weakness of pity by *any* story—is far gone, in our opinion, toward being himself a hardened villain. He may steer clear of petty larceny and open swindling—but mark that man well in his intercourse with his fellows—they have no confidence in him, as he has none in them. He lives coldly among his people—he walks an iceberg in the marts of trade and social life—and when he dies, may Heaven have that confidence in him which he had not in his fellow mortals."[50] Melville's concurrence with this position is suggested by an annotation that he made in his copy of Crabb Robinson's *Diary.* Robinson mentions that William Blake told him "that careless people are better than those who, etc., etc." Melville wrote as a conclusion to the unfinished sentence: "are coldly, selfishly, and malignantly prudent—which is a truism to the wise."[51]

Even if one assumes more than there is actual proof for in the novel, namely that the confidence man is not what he claims and is taking something from others to use himself, still there is no question but what those who donate or invest are better off than those who refuse. The act of donating or investing is a kind of signal that they have not lost their compassion or hope or trust in something. Melville probably realized that his man of confidence would be seen as a confidence man (in the sense of a malignant swindler) because he knew that most people cannot conceive of a man whose motivation would be high enough and pure enough actually to take something from his fellow beings to help them rather than to cheat and diminish them. Nevertheless, that is indeed the situation in the book. It may be likened to that of a certain kind of priest whose actions toward his parishioners bespeak selfishness and contempt but whose explanation is that whatever he does is best for them in the long run. For example, he might enjoy a long, leisurely, and sumptuous meal complete with fine wine and cigars while some of his parishioners, heavily

---

50. Quoted in Paul Smith, "*The Confidence-Man* and the Literary World of New York," *Nineteenth-Century Fiction* 16 (1962): 334.

51. Quoted in William Braswell, *Melville's Religious Thought: An Essay in Interpretation* (Durham: Duke University Press, 1943), pp. 116–17.

laden with guilt and anxious to confess their sins, are kept waiting much longer than necessary. If asked why he allowed them to wait so long, he might explain that it was good for their souls to do so. The point is that most humane and perceptive people would not believe him. They would conclude that the priest is squandering the time of his poor parishioners and their money for his own pleasure and comfort while pretending to do good, and to be sure, in most instances such an assumption would prove accurate. All outward signs cause one to suspect that this priest is a fraud who is not really interested in the welfare of his people though his method does, indeed, appear to work—the waiting has a salutary effect on the sinners. What most of those who understandably criticize this priest fail to realize is that once in a while there may come along a person who knows the mind and heart of others well enough and whose aims are noble enough to do actually what the priest in our example does and for the reasons he gives. He would have to be an extraordinary man, unshakable in his confidence in himself as well as in his ability to see into and move others. He could count on being almost universally misunderstood, as is Melville's man of confidence.

Inevitably such a person is considered dishonest though in reality honesty of a high order is one of his cardinal virtues. The illusion of dishonesty creates a heavy atmosphere that surrounds him, a haze through which one has to penetrate to perceive the truth. The illusion has been taken for the truth in *The Confidence-Man* principally because Melville's definition of honesty has a different emphasis from that of the world at large. Like the other four concepts—originality, charity, confidence, and consistency—honesty is not quite what it is generally perceived to be, for its highest form is not openness and straight-dealings with others but with oneself. With his extraordinary degree of self-understanding and control, the confidence man is above all else honest with himself, never self-deluding. That he creates the illusion of dishonesty is an indication that deception and dishonesty are not always synonymous. Others are deceived as to his nature and intent, and he knows this, but he realizes the impossibility of anyone's perceiving him truly who is not equal to him in the mastery of inner forces.

One insistent theme in *The Confidence-Man* is the futility of honest dealings with others when self-honesty is not practiced. The trait most stressed in the characterization of China Aster, for example, is his honesty. His father was known as Old Honesty, and he inherited a reputation for the same quality. Orchis admonishes him: "don't be so honest" (p. 209), and declares that his "honesty is a bore" (p. 210). When he begins to sink into debt, his honesty induces a money lender to make him a loan. At one point, the narrator of China Aster's story implies that had the poor candlemaker not been so honest, he would never have carried himself and his family to financial ruin (pp. 214–15). The analysis is faulty, however. China Aster needed not less honesty but a different and deeper form of it, namely fidelity to self. But since that is impossible without intimate understanding of what comprises the self, China Aster was doomed. No amount of honest dealings with others can take the place of genuine trueness to oneself. The confidence man rejects Egbert's "moral of the story," namely "the folly, on both sides, of a friend's helping a friend" (p. 221) for two reasons. First, that is not the true lesson of the story, which actually teaches that honesty without self-knowledge is futile. Secondly, the confidence man realizes that the philosophy of Mark Winsome and Egbert leads to "ice of the heart" (p. 223).

If one, like China Aster, can be honest with others without exercising self-knowledge, it does not follow that one who is dishonest with others can also be a deep understander of self, for Melville holds that the two are incompatible and contradictory. Charlie Noble, for example, practices but a shallow shrewdness; he does not and probably cannot probe the recesses of his own being to discover what is there to harness and to use. Self-ignorance lies at the heart of his dishonesty, and misanthropy is, as Frank Goodman puts it, a coordinate with "infidelity" (p. 157).

Knowledge and control of self, then, lead to the most fundamental kind of honesty, and that virtue in turn makes one a truth-teller, though the method is often one of indirection. His hearers may not perceive the truth of what he is saying, but the confidence man tells the truth. His method closely resembles that which Melville employed on many occasions in *Moby-Dick*. What was only one of a number of modes in the earlier novel, however, has become dominant in *The Confidence-Man:* one line of argument calculated to communicate on three levels of perception. In chapter 82 of *Moby-Dick,* for example, Melville proclaims "The Honor and Glory of Whaling" in terms that create three different strata of response. On one level, he appears actually to be praising the ancient vocation of whaling. When examined carefully, however, his praise seems mock heroic, and thus the praise turns to condemnation. Still further probing, however, reveals that the first impression is correct; he is, indeed, glorifying whaling, not the literal kind but deep diving. Everything that Ishmael says of whalers and whaling in this chapter is therefore true from his point of view if his definition of whaling is understood.

The confidence man speaks consistently in exactly this way. Much of what he says can be interpreted on three levels: as honest, as dishonest, and, again, as honest. He is widely misunderstood as Satan or some other evil figure because the third and final level of his language—the one which reveals his true stance—is simply not discerned. He says, for example, that he does not accept the moral Egbert draws from the China Aster story. That could be because he is all-trusting and resents any aspersion at all on human nature. But the general context of his remark—he has just tried to borrow money himself—suggests that he is being devious for selfish and dishonest reasons. Time after time in the book, a character will accept his reasoning or his claims on face value because he has appealed or argued persuasively. But each time this happens, the other person appears as a dupe, a victim, because something about the confidence man's actions and words creates a suspicion that things are not as they seem. Consequently, critics most frequently see him as a dishonest manipulator. No one in the novel is able to rise above the second level of perception. Some see him as honest, or take a chance that he is, but they do not even remotely understand the nature of his honesty. Others think him dishonest and pride themselves on their insight, but they are even more misled than the others. Recognition that the confidence man is actually practicing the fine art of telling the truth is the most astounding discovery that a reader can make about the book. And the irony of ironies is that he is the only character in the novel who is *not* in some degree a confidence man in the sense of a fraud or cheater because all but he—the man of confidence—practice varying degrees of self-deception.

The fifth virtue deriving from self-knowledge is consistency, a subject that shares the foreground of *The Confidence-Man* with originality, charity, confidence, and honesty. Melville devotes an entire chapter to its consideration. Chapter 14 explores and explodes the idea that ordinary people are (or can be) consistent. In a moment of deep discontent, the merchant Henry Roberts seems to violate his chief personality traits of optimism and confidence. Melville feels it necessary to explain why he allowed an obvious inconsistency in characterization to stand. Mr. Roberts "may be thought inconsistent, and even so he is" (p. 69). To portray a man like the merchant as consistent would be contradictory to life, for "in real life, a consistent character is a *rara avis*" (p. 69). Therefore, "that fiction, where every character can, by reason of its consistency, be comprehended at a glance, either exhibits but sections of character, making them appear for wholes, or else is very untrue to reality; while, on the other hand, that author who draws a character . . . much at variance with itself . . . may yet, in so doing, be not false but faithful to facts" (pp. 69–70). Now, to be sure, not all writers depict their characters as inconsistent because they understand human nature. Some authors are mere bunglers; so it calls "for no small sagacity in a reader unerringly to discriminate in a novel between the inconsistencies of conception and those of life" (p. 70).

Though this chapter may appear to address itself largely to the inscrutability of human nature, Melville's point is rather that it is better to consider ordinary people "past finding out" than to think of them as consistent. Yet an extraordinary person—like the confidence man—sees even beyond the inscrutability and understands others in all their inconsistencies. Such insight and perception, however, is reserved for those few who first understand themselves. Melville establishes, then, a hierarchy of perception regarding human nature, each representing a higher degree of wisdom. Ordinary people, who are themselves unknowingly inconsistent, demand that novelists create what is in effect an illusion of consistency with regard to their characters, and when writers first project inconsistency only to untangle it all in the end, they have the admiration of the reading public. With biting irony, Melville says that they throw open the complications of humankind "to the understanding even of school misses" (p. 70). Nevertheless, all those novelists who seek to portray "human nature on fixed principles," that is, with an underlying consistency, violate truth, and "the studious youth" who relies on such fiction to teach him the ways of humankind will find himself lost when dealing with actual people. A higher level of perception sees through the illusion of consistency and pronounces all beings unfathomable. These wiser and deeper souls claim that human nature is too variable to be charted, and they look with disdain upon those who think they have mathematically determined "the longitude" of the human heart. Rejecting consistency as illusory, they posit as the nature of man an inconsistency that cannot be understood. On the other hand, the special few who perceive at a level even higher than this also recognize consistency in human nature as an illusion, but they disagree that the inconsistency cannot be deciphered.[52] To such a profound seer, the "streets" of an ordinary mind "may be very crooked," but in following them, "he does not hopelessly lose his way" (p. 71).

If Melville forcefully rejects in chapter 14 the popular theory that people are basically consistent if we but could understand them, elsewhere he refutes the somewhat more sophisticated position that inconsistency is somehow a higher expression of intelligence than is consistency. This second theory he attacks mainly in his treatment of Mark Winsome and Egbert. Both are advocates of the proposition that other persons are unknowable because of their inconsistencies, and both justify their own inconsistencies of thought by holding consistency in contempt. When Frank Goodman asks Winsome to give his opinion of Charlie Noble, the ice-water philosopher answers: "What are you? What am I? Nobody knows who anybody is. The data which life furnishes, towards forming a true estimate of any being, are as insuf-

52. Paul Brodtkorb, Jr., correctly perceives Melville's view that "the essence of human nature is probably inconsistency" (p. 426), but he confuses, as do most readers, inconsistency with inscrutability and does not allow for the higher understanding of others that the confidence man possesses.

ficient to that end as in geometry one side given would be to determine the triangle" (p. 193). Though Winsome's insight here exceeds that of the oversimplifiers who see or think they see fundamental consistency in human nature, and though his words even appear to reflect an idea that Melville may have found congenial, the flaw in his argument is laid bare by the fact that the confidence man *does know him,* does see him for what he truly is. Frank Goodman understands him and points out to him his inconsistency in first trying to label Charlie Noble and then in saying that he is unknowable, but Winsome replies: "I seldom care to be consistent" (p. 193). What he reveals is that he *cannot* be consistent because he lacks the depth of self-knowledge that it requires. His disdain for consistency is thus, as the confidence man recognizes, a rationalization that he passes down to his disciple. Egbert echoes Winsome's message of man's inconsistency when he argues that a friend who makes a loan today may turn into an enemy tomorrow. He tells Frank Goodman that the difference between one man and another "is not so great as the difference between what the same man be to-day and what he may be in days to come" (p. 222), and he attributes much of this inscrutable unpredictability to "some chance tip of Fate's elbow in throwing her dice" (p. 222). Frank objects that such a position goes against what Egbert earlier said about the possibility of man having "a will, a way, a thought, and a heart of his own," and he complains that Egbert indulges in "an inconsistency." Egbert's Winsome-like reply is merely, "Inconsistency? Bah!" (p. 222). Melville's objection to Winsome and Egbert is not only that they espouse a coldhearted and hackneyed philosophy hypocritically held up in the guise of nobility and originality but also that as perceptive as they are in seeing inconsistency as the lot of common humanity, they fail to value true consistency for the supreme virtue that it is. They deny its existence—even in the extraordinary person—and they arrogantly proclaim that they would not want to be consistent even if they could.

Melville's probings into the nature of consistency and inconsistency in humankind collectively constitute a theory that consistency is impossible without self-knowledge and without the presence of those virtues that result from self-knowledge. For example, persons who may appear self-confident but who are highly distrustful and insecure in their intercourse with others because of their suspicions—such persons are actually "inconsistent," which is to say that their apparent self-confidence is an illusion and that they do not actually enjoy that virtue in the true sense because it cannot coexist with suspicious tentativeness in estimating and dealing with other people. Similarly, Melville finds it a given that self-love in the highest and best sense cannot coexist with misanthropy, nor self-fidelity with dishonesty in conduct. *Inconsistency* then, is another word for contradiction.

The confidence man's reaction to the story of Colonel John Moredock, the Indian hater, is calculated to reveal that certain things claimed for Moredock in Judge Hall's account (as related by Charlie Noble) could not possibly be: they are self-contradictory.[53] Only a superficial understanding of Moredock could lead to the conclusion that he was both a man of love and a man of hate. The world observes such a person and thinks that it sees there strange and inexplicable combinations. Although the confidence man seems to be speaking from a position of naive idealism

53. Melville's rendition of Judge Hall's description of John Moredock has created as much disagreement among critics as any other aspect of *The Confidence-Man*. John W. Schroeder argues that the Indian hater is a noble figure, "the world's only remedy against the confidence-man," whom Schroeder considers the Devil (p. 379). On the other hand, Roy Harvey Pearce submits that "there is nothing but distortion in the Indian-hater's vision of spiritual reality" and points out Melville's humane stance toward Indians in his review of Parkman's *The Oregon Trail*. "Melville's Indian-Hater: A Note on a Meaning of *The Confidence-Man*," *PMLA* 67 (1952): 942–48. William Ellery Sedgwick feels that Moredock is a character with whom Melville deeply sympathized (p. 193). Hershel Parker, however, sees this section of the novel as "a tragic study of the impracticability of Christianity, and, more obviously, a satiric allegory in which the Indians are Devils and the Indian-haters are dedicated Christians, and in which the satiric target is the nominal practice of Christianity" (p. 166). Generally, critics fail to take into account the confidence man's reaction to the story of Moredock. In that reaction, I believe, is the best hint with regard to Melville's own attitude and intentions. Because Hall has depicted a person who could never exist, William M. Ramsey perhaps comes closer to the truth than most commentators when he writes that the section on the diluted Indian hater "is a sham or mock fiction in which *authentic* Indians and Indian-hating do not even appear" (p. 226, italics mine). "The Moot Points of Melville's Indian-Hating," *American Literature* 52 (1980): 224–35.

when he disputes the reality of a Moredock as Charlie delineates him, he is actually developing Melville's theory that the true virtues deriving from self-knowledge are never accompanied by contradictory traits. Either the virtue was not really there to begin with (though it seemed to be), or the traits that appear contradictory to it are not so in actuality. The story of Colonel Moredock says Frank Goodman, "strikes me with even more incredulity than wonder. To me some parts don't hang together. If the man of hate, how could John Moredock be also the man of love? Either his lone campaigns are fabulous as Hercules'; or else, those being true, what was thrown in about his geniality is but garnish" (pp. 156–57). He seriously questions whether "ever there was such a man as Moredock," such a man, that is, as he has been conceived by the ordinary world. He is saying that Judge Hall's depiction is in error insofar as it attributes to Moredock a genuinely loving heart, a philanthropic attitude toward society, an honest nature, and a high degree of self-knowledge which made him realize that he could not be true to himself and accept the governorship of Illinois. He perhaps possessed these qualities to a degree. He exemplified them as the world understands them. But Melville's point is that it would be *impossible*—not merely inconsistent—for a person to have attained the self-knowledge of the confidence man and to have been blessed with the resultant virtues of originality, charity, confidence, honesty, and consistency and then to pursue a course of partial misanthropy that takes command over the mind at times and completely controls it. "Colonel Moredock, as you and the judge have painted him," Frank tells Charlie, is not believable because too much of a positive nature has been claimed for him.

The confidence man makes the same point to the Missouri bachelor and to the barber William Cream. To the bachelor's claim that he has respect (or love) for himself but none for mankind, the confidence man replies: "Now don't you see, my dear fellow, in what inconsistencies one involves himself by affecting disesteem for men" while claiming self-esteem (p. 135). The two, he insists, simply cannot coexist in the same mind. Similarly, he tries to get the barber to see that his sign, "No Trust," is inconsistent with his claim that he trusts himself to know others,

a knowledge he is confident in because of long experience in dealing with the public. Self-trust and insecurity in dealing with the
world are impossible coordinates; the barber, then, does not actually possess the virtue of self-trust or he would not post the sign
of "No Trust" in others.

The by-product of true consistency, which only the confidence
man possesses, is, ironically, an impenetrable surface. Though
the people with whom he converses frequently consider him
transparent, they are entirely blind to his nature. He understands
them, but they are incapable of understanding him. His disguises
are really metaphors for the surface of the consistent man, a surface that is always deceptive to those ordinary human beings who
view it. Melville conceived the idea of a man appearing in several
different guises not because he wanted to create a skillful swindler
but because he wished to emphasize the fact that the consistent
man is always in disguise to the world. Frank Goodman tells the
Missouri bachelor that to him "no man is a stranger" (p. 132),
but because he is original, charitable, confident, honest, and consistent, he must remain a stranger to all those around him.

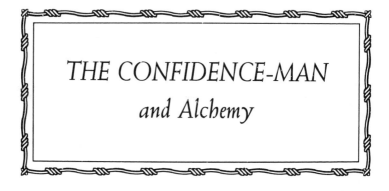

THE CONFIDENCE-MAN
and Alchemy

Anyone who knew, as Melville certainly did, the fundamental tenets of Gnosticism would also be aware of the rudiments of alchemy, for the two systems of belief had a great deal in common up to a certain point. They clothed their doctrines in mystery and secrecy. They used many of the same basic symbols, such as the sun, gold, the uroborus, and so forth. Both posited the discovery of self as the basis for spiritual fulfillment. That is, they directed the seeker to go contemplatively within himself rather than outside to some external pseudotranscendental experience, for they considered the core of self to be the true source of light since it was conceived to be a piece of God. Both held that there was deliverance and power to be derived from that discovery. But whereas Gnosticism viewed man as alone in an alien nature, encouraged separation from the world, and ultimately stimulated bitterness toward society, alchemy required its followers to accept nature as an ally and to carry on one's progress toward truth and fulfillment within the realm of nature in order to understand it as a step toward understanding oneself. Furthermore, it taught a benevolent attitude not only toward those who possessed the secrets of its art but also toward those who were skeptical of its validity. One who, like Melville, dallied with the principles of Gnosticism, felt a strong personal affinity for its world view, but who on the other hand sensed its dangerous tendency to provoke a hostility that isolates and an arrogance that unbalances, might well have cast a longing eye on the attractive and profound alternative of alchemy. Indeed, there is some evidence that Melville did so, for he indicates his familiarity with alchemy by referring to one of its most prominent figures, Paracelsus, in *Moby-Dick* and in other places by alluding to such offshoots of alchemy as Rosicrucianism. And, as I shall argue below, he may have had a definite adept in mind when he created the confidence man. But even though he possibly did not actually realize that the protagonist of his fantasy about self-mastery (and, consequently, mastery of the world) is so like an adept that he could have come from the pages of hermetical history, the confidence man nevertheless manifests the qualities of that type to such an extent that an exploration of alchemical beliefs furnishes a new way of understanding this seemingly enigmatical character.

Melville read in Goethe's autobiography of that writer's youthful enthusiasm for alchemy and of his actually setting up a laboratory to pursue the art of transmutation of base metals into gold, for the true seeker an outward manifestation of the change taking place within the aspiring adept. There is no reason to believe that Melville went that far or that he was at all concerned with the metalurgical side of alchemy, though intelligent and prominent men besides Goethe (such as Newton) unashamedly had been. In addition, he would have been less interested in alchemy as a program for his future development than as a set of beliefs that paralleled his own thinking in many ways. Alchemy was not, in other words, the cause for these beliefs in Melville but an expression, an echo, of them. He had access to a good deal of information on alchemy, as he did on the subject of Gnosticism, through his copy of Chambers's *Cyclopaedia,* most of which is given without any attempt to discredit or disparage the ancient pursuit. The reference work contains numerous entries related to the general area of thought, including articles on "Adepts," "Alchymy," "Chymistry," "Elixir," "Hermetic or Hermetical Art," "Philosopher's

Stone," "Tincture," and "Transmutation." A fairly long discussion on "Rosycrucians" stresses the hermetical basis of their thinking. From Chambers, Melville could have received many of the fundamentals of alchemy together with the names of some of its most famous practitioners. In analyzing the treatment of alchemy in the *Cyclopaedia,* Philip Shorr points out that the extent and the point of view of the coverage suggest the respect Chambers had for this esoteric art:

> Alchemy is considered the "sublime part of the art of chymistry," or a higher and more refined kind of chemistry employed in the "more mysterious researches of the art." The four elements as taught by Aristotle are accepted. . . . In the article on water as one of these elements, Chambers relies on the authority of Basil Valentine, Paracelsus, Van Helmont, Sendivogius and others who maintained the principle that water is elemental matter. . . . The article on alchemy retains all the medieval science connected with it, without any change. The great objectives of alchemy are enumerated without a shadow of scepticism. These are (1) the turning of baser metals into gold, to be effected by the philosopher's stone; (2) the finding of the elixir or universal medicine; (3) the discovery of the *alkahest* or universal solvent; (4) and the search for a universal ferment which when applied to any seed will increase its fecundity. That the subject still absorbed the interest of a good many readers of a cyclopedic work is evident from the large amount of space Chambers devotes to alchemy. He is very careful in his historical account of the subject. Then he has comparatively long accounts on the *alkahest* and philosopher's stone. All in all we cannot say that very much scepticism is betrayed in the treatment of alchemy and related topics. [1]

Chambers's entry on water, as Shorr points out, owes much to the "authority of Basil Valentine, Paracelsus, Van Helmont, Sendivogius" and other alchemical adepts. Whenever Chambers feels called upon to list the most prominent alchemists, as he does in this entry and the one on adepts, he includes the last of those

1. Philip Shorr, *Science and Superstition in the Eighteenth Century: A Study of the Treatment of Science in Two Encyclopedias of 1725–1750* (New York: Columbia University Press, 1932), pp. 20–22.

names given above, Sendivogius (he spells it "Centiviglio"), the reputed author of the famous *New Chemical Light,* which was chosen for inclusion in perhaps the best known of all collections of alchemical texts, *The Hermetic Museum* (first published at Frankfurt in 1678).[2] It is not surprising that Chambers recognizes Michael Sendivogius as one of the giants of alchemy, for a legend of great richness had grown up around his name by the time the *Cyclopaedia* was composed. "The folklore of alchemy," comments one historian of hermeticism, "is not without its apostolic heroes who wander about the world preaching its truths and using the methods of direct evidence to convert the skeptics and cynics."[3] The example used of such an apostolic hero is the man who until the beginning of the present century was known as Michael Sendivogius. He was widely called, however, the "Cosmopolite."[4] In "the annals of alchemy his name is The Cosmopolite, because of his extensive travels and international activities on behalf of alchemy."[5] History of course abounds with instances of greedy deceivers (like Edward Kelly, 1555–97, for example) who passed themselves off as adepts but who were mere "charcoal burners" or "puffers," as they were often called. The Cosmopolite stands in stark contrast to these materialistic confidence men, for he commanded the respect of great men of his time and appeared more like an itinerate missionary with extraordinary powers than an avaricious fraud. Wolfgang Dienheim, a respected professor at Fribourg and one-time hater of alchemists, recorded his experiences with the Cosmopolite at Bale, and ended by calling him "this saint, this demi-god."[6] While on a boat, Dienheim had

2. For a modern edition, see Arthur Edward Waite's English version (1893) in two volumes (New York: Samuel Weiser, 1973).

3. Mark Graubard, *Astrology and Alchemy: Two Fossil Sciences* (New York: Philosophical Library, 1953), p. 306.

4. The Cosmopolite is now thought to have been Alexander Seton, a seventeenth-century Scot who was a noble adept and genuinely skilled in the alchemical arts. Michael Sendivogius was a Pole who became a follower of Seton and used the name of Cosmopolite when the former died. Whenever authors of past centuries refer to the travels of the Cosmopolite or to the theories and accomplishments of Sendivogius, they probably have Seton in mind.

5. Graubard, p. 306.

6. Quoted in Jacques Sadoul, *Alchemists and Gold,* trans. Olga Sieveking

laughed at the premises and claims of alchemy. The Cosmopolite heard him out patiently and later "by a philosophical demonstration" convinced him of his error. The Cosmopolite's goal, he explained, was to persuade the "adversaries of alchemy" to "dismiss their *distrust* of the Art" (italics mine).[7] In 1742, the Abbé Lenglet du Fresnoy portrayed the Cosmopolite as an unselfish and untiring man of mystery who conceived his mission to travel through the world obliterating distrust wherever he encountered it and creating confidence in the art he had mastered. "We know nothing of his early life," writes Lenglet du Fresnoy, "and his story begins with the seventeenth century. He appears before us a fully adept alchemist and, as we shall see, a Past Master in his Art, by whatever means he may have come by his knowledge. A quality for which he particularly deserves admiration is his disinterestedness. In every place to which the need he felt to make Hermetic propaganda took him, he justified his mission by successes that might in all conscience be regarded as miraculous." All his efforts were directed toward sceptics so that he might "dispel their doubts." Lenglet du Fresnoy then places the Cosmopolite in the context of other serious seventeenth-century adepts: "This indeed is characteristic of most of the Adepts of the time. It appeared to them that alchemy had been evolved, not to pander to men's baser instincts but to be the glory of men of learning and high ideals. They went from place to place, preaching their Science as though it were a religion—that is, never neglecting anything that would demonstrate its truth, though never profaning its mysteries. In a word, it was a sort of apostolic mission carried out by Adepts during a century that bred critics and rationalists—a mission that was always difficult, often dangerous."[8]

(New York: Putnam's, 1972), p. 122. Sadoul devotes an entire chapter to the Cosmopolite.

7. Quoted in Sadoul, p. 121.

8. Quoted in Sadoul, p. 120. Sadoul comments on the distinctive quality of seventeenth-century alchemy. "It is, indeed, shown in a completely different light from that of earlier centuries. In this period, Adepts such as the Cosmopolite, Philalethes or Lascaris are no longer found as isolated Seekers, concerned to carry out the Great Work alone; they are transformed, as it were, into

The missions of the Cosmopolite and those extraordinary few like him were difficult because adepts met distrust everywhere. The theme underlying all that they did and said was that the better side of the human heart can be brought out just as base metals can be transmuted into gold. Their main object, that is, was to open the eyes of humanity, to show what freedom and power are possible to one who understands and relies upon his own originality. Their journeys could be dangerous because of the greed of influential people who sometimes held them captive seeking to have them reveal the secret of transmutation. The Cosmopolite himself was the victim of such a person, Christian II, the Elector of Saxony, who had him imprisoned and tortured but never learned how to create the philosopher's stone. Because of the widespread distrust of one who called himself an adept and because of the greed among the rich, the Cosmopolite and other adepts frequently hid their identity. Traveling widely in Germany, the Cosmopolite "was careful to preserve his anonymity by using a variety of aliases."[9]

Though in many ways similar to other seventeenth-century alchemists, the Cosmopolite also stood out distinctively. Colin Wilson has called his career among alchemists "perhaps the most startling of all."[10] That Chambers mentions him (or, rather, the man who at that time was thought to have been the Cosmopolite) in company with the premier alchemists guarantees that Melville had opportunity to know of him. That he did so is suggested by the fact that he calls Frank Goodman, who dominates the latter half of *The Confidence-Man,* the "Cosmopolitan" and endows him and the other manifestations of the confidence man with attributes highly suggestive of those possessed by an adept.

The supreme goal of alchemy was the philosopher's stone, sometimes called, as Chambers explained in various entries in the

---

emissaries of the Hermetic Art for the benefit of their fellow-scientists. It is impossible to say why Adepts of the seventeenth and early eighteenth centuries acted in this way. The fact remains that they devoted themselves to proselytising" (pp. 120–21).

9. Ibid., p. 124.

10. Colin Wilson, *The Occult: A History* (New York: Random House, 1971), p. 246.

Cyclopaedia, the "Aqua Vitae," the "Grand Elixir," the "Powder of Projection," the "Universal Medicine," the "Vegetable Seed of Nature," or the "Way of Excellence."[11] It was the culmination of the "Great Work," the nature of which has been widely misunderstood, for the route to the philosopher's stone was clearly internal. Alchemy was fundamentally the science of self-knowledge. All that went on in the retorts, crucibles, and ovens was merely the "projection" of what was being accomplished within the aspiring adept. Whereas some who pursued the secret of the stone worked diligently with metals and chemical substances, other serious alchemists "never went near a workshop and concentrated entirely on spiritual progress."[12] Rudolf Bernoulli points out that "There are then two kinds of alchemy: the one strives to know the cosmos as a whole and to recreate it; it is in a sense the precursor of modern natural science. It aspires to create gold as the supreme perfection in every sphere, the *summum bonum.*" He considers the other alchemy an even higher form of endeavor. "It strives for the great wonder, the wonder of all wonders, the magic crystal, the philosophers' stone," which is neither a chemical that can be scientifically analyzed nor some simplistic psychological trick: "It is something more than perfection, something through which perfection can be achieved. It is the universal instrument of magic. By it we can obtain to the ultimate. By it we can completely possess the world." It marks the stage of self-development in which one soars above the ordinary world. This is the form of alchemy, Bernoulli adds, that was practiced by those like "the Rosicrucians of the seventeenth century, but also (if we read the sources correctly, between the lines as it were)" by many alchemists "in the Byzantine and Arabic period."[13]

11. E. Chambers, *Cyclopaedia; or, An Universal Dictionary of Arts and Sciences,* 2 vols. (London: James and John Knapton et al., 1728).

12. Richard Cavendish, *A History of Magic* (New York: Taplinger, 1977), p. 63. Titus Burckhardt comments that "spiritual alchemy was not necessarily involved in outward metallurgical operations, even if it made use of them as similes" (p. 92). *Alchemy: Science of the Cosmos, Science of the Soul,* trans. William Stoddart (Baltimore: Penguin, 1971).

13. Rudolf Bernoulli, "Spiritual Development as Reflected in Alchemy and Related Disciplines," in *Spiritual Disciplines: Papers from the Eranos Yearbooks,* ed. Joseph Campbell, Bollingen Series 30 (New York: Pantheon, 1960), p. 318.

Other historians and philosophers have denied that there was such a clear split among genuine hermeticists, but none disputes the fact that *all* true alchemists realized that the quintessence of their art was self-examination and mastery of one's own inner world.[14] Stanislas Klossowski de Rola has commented that "the Great Work is, above all things, the creation of man by himself, that is to say, the full and entire conquest of his faculties and his future. . . . He who would find the answer, not only intellectually but as a way of Life—indeed as a way *to* Life—must begin by taking a long, hard, unblinking look at himself. He will, if he is honest, see that the root cause of all his troubles lies in his almost total ignorance of that which matters most: his true self."[15] This is the theme of alchemy and the theme of Melville's later novels. C. J. Jung complained in one of his volumes on alchemy that in the modern world, "no one has time for self-knowledge or believes that it could serve any sensible purpose. Also, one knows in advance that it is not worth the trouble to know oneself, for any fool can know what he is." Consequently, "Western man confronts himself as a stranger" and "self-knowledge is one of the most difficult and exacting of the arts."[16] Melville was not, strictly speaking, an alchemist, but he was a fellow pilgrim on their journey, deeply involved as they were in what Jung has called "the wearisome process of self-knowledge."[17]

14. Burckhardt concedes that "one can observe two currents in alchemy," the one "predominately artisanal in nature," where the symbolism of an "inward work" is not stressed, and the other mystical, where references to "metallurgical processes" serve as "analogies," but he argues that these are two aspects of the same tradition, two different manifestations of the same idea (pp. 17–18).

15. Stanislas Klossowski de Rola, *Alchemy: The Secret Art* (London: Thames and Hudson, 1973), pp. 8, 14.

16. C. G. Jung, *Mysterium Coniunctionis: An Inquiry into the Separation and Synthesis of Psychic Opposites in Alchemy*, trans. R. F. C. Hull, Bollingen Series 20 (New York: Pantheon, 1963), p. 498.

17. Ibid., p. 499. Jung explains that the aim of alchemy was "knowledge of oneself. In contradistinction to the modern prejudice that self-knowledge is nothing but a knowledge of the ego, the alchemist regarded the self as a substance incommensurable with the ego, hidden in the body, and identical with the image of God" (*Mysterium*, p. 499). For Jung, the alchemist was a prime example of the person who sets out "consciously and intentionally" to seek "wholeness or completeness" and to understand clearly what is happening to him so that he will not suffer the fate of the unknowing. The alchemist de-

He was seeking, with them, "the guide and leader within him," as Bernoulli puts it. "Down through the centuries this transmutation, this metamorphosis of the imperfect into the perfect and perhaps even the supraperfect, has been the task and goal of mystical alchemy. But much as we read about it, however much we seek to apprehend its essence, it will always remain a mystery."[18] That is, its essence cannot be adequately communicated from one person to another.

From the acquisition of the philosopher's stone, then, comes power and grave responsibility. The power consists of those attributes exhibited by Melville's confidence man, the first of which is the ability to break the bonds that enslave most of the human race, to exercise a measure of control over the world rather than allowing it to be in command. This is what Bernoulli means when he says that through the philosopher's stone, one can "possess the world" and in large measure "make ourselves free from the world."[19] If Melville's confidence man often appears to be a manipulator, it is because he is in the world but not of it; he is aware of all the attitudes and emotions that ensnare ordinary beings but he is caught by none of them. The second power has made adepts both attractive and awesome through the centuries—the ability to perform extraordinary, indeed magic, acts. "The image of the Stone," writes Mircea Eliade, "integrated all the magical beliefs. The man who carried the Stone was deemed to be invulnerable," and through its agency, one could change himself or even become invisible.[20] It was "the universal instrument of magic."[21]

The confidence man has this magical ability to change himself from one form of human being to another, from a white man to a

---

scended into the "deep pit" of self "with all the necessary precautions"; he did not, like others, "risk falling into the hole backwards." "When an inner situation is not made conscious," Jung adds, "it happens outside, as fate." *Aion: Researches into the Phenomenology of the Self*, trans. R. F. C. Hull, 2d ed., Bollingen Series 20 (Princeton: Princeton University Press, 1959), pp. 70, 71.

18. Bernoulli, p. 319.

19. Ibid., p. 318.

20. Mircea Eliade, *The Forge and the Crucible,* trans. Stephen Corrin (New York: Harper, 1962), p. 168.

21. Bernoulli, p. 318.

black man and then back again. His changes are not merely disguises with different clothes and new makeup but something akin to transmutations, for he completely molds himself to each new part. In addition, he appears to have the power to read others' minds. "I know just what is in your mind," he says to the speechless collegian, and doubtlessly he does (p. 26). As the Cosmopolitan, he anticipates Mark Winsome's words before they are spoken: "As reading his argument in his eye, the cosmopolitan, without waiting for it to be put into words, at once spoke to it" (p. 191). Later, he is able to discern what the barber is thinking: "What was passing in his mind seemed divined by the other" (p. 226). Though he pretends to be completely taken by surprise when Charlie Noble's "eulogy of the press" turns out to be a lighthearted tribute to wine, he is not at all fooled. His preliminary comments, spoken before Charlie gives his panegyric, are supposedly directed in praise of newspapers, but given the confidence man's high opinion of wine as metaphor for inspiration, each statement could apply equally well to the wine press as to the printing press. He anticipates Charlie's joke, speaks approvingly but in cloaked terms of wine, and then acts surprised. Not the least of his power is the ability to remain sober even though he drinks a great deal more port wine than Charlie, who is trying to get him intoxicated. That he does not change under the influence of alcohol is evidence of his complete self-mastery.

In what Melville refers to as the confidence man's "manner" is a magical power capable of fascinating others, swaying them, frightening them, or simply transfixing them. John Ringman casts a "spell" of fascination over the collegian. "Noting something in his manner," a prim-looking man changes his mind after the herb doctor forbids him from exposing the crippled Thomas Fry. When the Cosmopolitan fails in his arguments to convince the barber to trust humanity, he resorts to his mesmeric "manner": "Hard to say exactly what the manner was, any more than to hint it was a sort of magical; in a benign way, not wholly unlike the manner, fabled or otherwise, of certain creatures in nature, which have the power of persuasive fascination—the power of holding another creature by the button of the eye, as it were, despite the serious disinclination, and, indeed, earnest protest, of the victim. With this manner the conclusion of the matter was not out of keeping; for, in the end, all argument and expostulation proved vain, the barber being irresistibly persuaded to agree to try, for the remainder of the present trip, the experiment of trusting men, as both phrased it" (p. 234).

That the confidence man possesses powers that can only be called "magical" is evident in several places.[22] The barber refers to him as "the man-charmer—as certain East Indians are called snake-charmers" (p. 237). The title of chapter 32 is "Showing That the Age of Magic and Magicians Is Not Yet Over." The magician referred to is the Cosmopolitan who calms the irate Charlie Noble by showing him a great deal of money. Though largely humorous in intent, this brief episode nevertheless gives a glimpse of the confidence man as practitioner of the alchemical art. With "the air of a necromancer, an air heightened by his costume," he places ten gold pieces in a circle around Charlie, waves his hand, and murmurs "cabalistical words" (p. 180). Since Charlie is a riverboat sharper out for quick gain, he is naturally impressed by this show of gold, but beyond this Melville hints that the Cosmopolitan has actually cast a momentary magical spell over him: "Meantime, he within the magic-ring stood suddenly rapt, exhibiting every symptom of a successful charm—a turned cheek, a fixed attitude, a frozen eye; spellbound, not more by the waving wand than by the ten invincible talismans on the floor" (p. 180). A bit later, the Cosmopolitan is called a "necromancer" (p. 181).

The confidence man's possession of the philosopher's stone, then, gives him such magic power that he is unquestionably more than merely an ordinary man. In a moment of unusual revelation he reacts to the barber's calling him "only a man": "But don't be too sure what I am. You call me *man,* just as the townsfolk called the angels who, in man's form, came to Lot's house; just as the Jew rustics called the devils who, in man's form, haunted the

22. Edwin M. Eigner is one of a very few critics who have noticed that "Melville's Cosmopolitan in *The Confidence-Man* is both a mesmerist and a magician." *The Metaphysical Novel in England and America: Dickens, Bulwer, Melville, Hawthorne* (Berkeley and Los Angeles: University of California Press, 1978), p. 185.

tombs. You can conclude nothing absolute from the human form, barber" (pp. 225–26). He is neither divinity nor devil, however, but one who, having taken the grand tour of self and mastered the conflicting forces there, can now be termed a true adept.

By arriving at that stage which is often metaphorically represented by the stone or the powder of projection, the adept gains a third power, that of the intellect. The great alchemical adepts were not merely tricksters but were frequently considered among the wisest men of their age. They were masters of many fields including chemistry, medicine, philosophy, theology, astronomy, law, and numerous others. They often wrote prolifically and talked with such proficiency on so many subjects that they astounded their listeners. They were, in other words, men "of vast learning," who were "philosophers and theologians preoccupied with debates and conversations," as Melville's confidence man certainly is.[23] His is clearly "a superior mind," as Melville states (p. 170), one that encounters little real competition from those around him; his is a "mature" mind consorting with "immature" ones (p. 171).

The best-known power of the adept was his ability through the philosopher's stone to transmute, and this miraculous capacity included not only the ability to perfect metals—to change lead or copper or zinc into gold or silver—but perhaps more important, the talent to change both the body and mind of human beings to bring the physical and mental conditions into healthier states. Nearly all noted alchemists were sought-after physicians, and the philosopher's stone was also known as the universal medicine. It took the form of both powder (powder of projection) and liquid (elixir or Aqua Vitae). As Chambers explained, "These two Things, most Alchymists take to coincide; so that what will make Gold, will cure all Diseases."[24] Melville's herb doctor is his adept in the role of healer. In other roles he is also a transmutor, sometimes of money into more gold (though we do not see this process) but more often of unhealthy suspicions and other negative mental states into a more positive frame of mind. In his

23. Graubard, p. 287.
24. Chambers, 1:293.

conversation with a sick man, the herb doctor outlines his philosophy of transmutation. Medicines, he explains, do not work directly upon the body but must be changed in order to produce health. He mocks "an eminent physiologist in Louisville" who instructed the sick man to take iron: "For what? To restore your lost energy. And how? Why, in healthy subjects iron is naturally found in the blood, and iron in the bar is strong; ergo, iron is the source of animal invigoration. But you being deficient in vigor, it follows that the cause is deficiency of iron. Iron, then, must be put into you" (p. 78). The theory behind such practice the herb doctor questions. His art is that of the alchemist, based on the idea that "conversion of one thing to a different thing" must take place (p. 78); materials must be transmuted, and the physician must know what to prescribe to affect that change.

Melville realized that most readers would perceive the herb doctor as a charlatan just as the Cosmopolite and his fellow adepts were met with charges of quackery and fraud wherever they went. They had to prove themselves repeatedly, and this job was made more difficult by the fact that there were so many actual quacks claiming the same cures but unable to perform them. The charcoal burners abounded. The herb doctor is alluding to them when he speaks of those whose "motives come from the purse" (p. 83) and of "these chemical practitioners with their tinctures, and fumes, and braziers, and occult incantations" (p. 79). He, on the other hand, practices "the genuine medicine" (p. 83) and is "not unfamiliar with essences" (p. 79). He refers to a "powder" (perhaps the Powder of Projection) given to a patient. His repeated references to his "art," his insistence upon the role of nature in bodily healing, his theory that "from evil comes good" (another way of describing transmutation), his conviction that distrust is the enemy of health, his refusal to take the credit for cures ("done by power divine"), and his determination not to reveal the ingredients of his Omni-Balsamic Reinvigorator—all are distinctive marks of the alchemist. The herb doctor exhibits the same attitudes when he offers another form of his philosopher's stone, the Samaritan Pain Dissuader, which is "pure vegetable extract" (p. 84) and suggestive of the alchemist's vegetable seed of nature. He meets with doubts and hostility even when he argues that his medicine does not cover up but actually transmutes: it does not merely bring on insensibility as a painkiller but changes the pain into health. If one will not allow the alchemist to demonstrate the power of what he has discovered, that person, like the giant who strikes the herb doctor, is "lost to humanity" (p. 88). He has better luck with Thomas Fry, who finally agrees to try his medicine. Though most readers and critics of *The Confidence-Man* apparently assume that the herb doctor is an archdeceiver who practices his deviousness either for materialistic or malicious reasons, there is just as much evidence that he possesses genuine powers and wishes to help those he encounters who are unhealthy in both mind and body. What has been missed in interpretations of his role in the novel is that he espouses many of the essential ideas of alchemy, and though he is often perceived as the equivalent of a "puffer," he may well be an adept.

If the philosopher's stone was thought to bestow upon the adept deliverance, magical abilities, intellectual depth, and the secrets of healing (as well as of other forms of transmutation), it also deepened the alchemist's sense of responsibility. His first obligation was to don a cloak of secrecy, to speak and write indirectly about the method whereby he developed the philosopher's stone. He was anxious to demonstrate the power of the stone but elusive and, in a sense, deceptive when it came to explaining the sources of the stone. Klossowski de Rola points out that alchemical writings are "full of promises" about directing the reader to the philosopher's stone, but "these texts invariably contain elaborate devices to deter the unworthy. They are couched in a language often so obscure and so impenetrable that their study requires years and years of devoted attention, of reading and rereading, before their exegesis may even be attempted. For secrecy is inextricably woven into the fabric of alchemy."[25] It was not uncommon for an adept to be imprisoned and questioned under physical pain, as was the Cosmopolite, in an effort to get him to reveal his secrets. They were surprisingly tenacious in their determination to protect the mystery. This sense of responsibility derived from their awareness of at least three facts. First, the al-

25. Klossowski de Rola, p. 9.

chemists realized that if they attempted to speak directly and clearly, "they would, throughout history, have been persecuted for their unconventional ideas and beliefs" in the same way that the confidence man would have been attacked immediately had he revealed just how different his thinking really is from those around him.[26] Secondly, they knew that it was not possible to describe precisely and to communicate fully a person's internal experiences as he undergoes the process of self-examination and self-mastery; consequently, methods of symbolism and indirection became the necessary vehicles for expression. Thirdly, the alchemists developed a profound respect for mystery, a conviction that faith brought one closer to truth than fact. Melville's confidence man remains steadfast in his allegiance to the code of elusiveness. The herb doctor tells a sick patient who asks him for the makeup of his medicine: "It cannot be made known" (p. 80), and when an old miser asks him how, exactly, Mr. Truman, who has taken some of his money, will turn it into a greater amount, the herb doctor answers that it is "a secret, a mystery" (p. 103).

Of the several analyses offered by critics of the confidence man's motivation, including the frequently stated theory that he is the Devil out to win souls to Hell and mock Christianity, it seems to me that none elucidates his behavior and describes his underlying reason for being on the *Fidèle* as well as the perception of him as an adept carrying out his deeply felt sense of responsibility to the world though he is far superior to it.[27] He has appeared suddenly upon the scene, as adepts frequently did, having "come from a

26. Ibid.

27. Philip Drew's perceptive article, "Appearance and Reality in Melville's *The Confidence-Man*," *ELH* 31 (1964), convincingly shows "how even the most dubious of the Confidence-man's transactions are susceptible of an innocent explanation," which requires "those who affirm his diabolic nature to produce unequivocal evidences," and points "to a number of incidents, some major, some minor, where it seems clear not only that the Confidence-man's conduct is technically irreproachable but that his actions and sentiments carry the weight of Melville's sympathy" (p. 424). Tom Quirk states that the Cosmopolitan "often serves as a spokesman for Melville's own deeply held convictions and at times represents the author's feelings toward his own situation." *Melville's Confidence Man: From Knave to Knight* (Columbia: University of Missouri Press, 1982), pp. 16–17.

very long distance" (p. 6), in order to carry out his mission, which is to transmute the minds of those who will allow adequate demonstration from the negativism of "No Trust" to a belief in the alchemy of life. "To my fellow-creatures," he confesses to an insensitive collegian, "I owe alleviations" (p. 26). Such a motivation seems either false or unfathomable to many readers, who assume that he must be maliciously lying or so mysterious that nothing can be known about him.[28] Yet, to anyone familiar with the history of alchemy, the confidence man's mission, which he states repeatedly, is neither evil nor puzzling, for it parallels closely the activity of an adept like the Cosmopolite, who felt keenly the two-pronged responsibility to be secretive and allusive on the one hand but enlightening on the other as he traveled on his mission as "honest envoy," an "ambassador" of light (p. 138).[29]

The confidence man is also suggestive of an adept because Melville associates him with three of the basic symbols of alchemy: the seed, the sun, and gold, all representative of the godlike core of being. Though he intends an unfavorable connotation, the Missouri bachelor refers to the confidence man as "that seedy Rosicrucian" (p. 130). More frequently, however, the confidence man is linked with gold and the sun. "That there is an inward gold, or rather, that gold has an inward as well as an outward reality," writes Titus Burckhardt, "was only logical for the contemplative way of looking at things, which spontaneously

28. See, for example Edgar A. Dryden, who argues that the confidence man "may have no real or enduring self at all but may be merely a set of changing profiles." *Melville's Thematics of Form: The Great Art of Telling the Truth* (Baltimore: Johns Hopkins University Press, 1968), p. 183. Similarly, Michael Paul Rogin concludes that "There is no self under the confidence man's disguises." *Subversive Genealogy: The Politics and Art of Herman Melville* (New York: Knopf, 1983), p. 224.

29. See Graubard's discussion of various traveling adepts. Alfarabi, for example, a tenth-century adept, "was reputed to have been the wisest man of his age and to have travelled extensively. . . . He proved himself the possessor of vast knowledge of alchemy, astrology, theology, and philosophy, and outwitted all who dared debate with him" (pp. 280–81). Rhasis, "a celebrated physician and chemist," also "journeyed in many lands" not only acquiring new information but also "surpassing all practitioners of his time in knowledge and skill" and exhibiting generosity, nobility, and kindness to the poor (p. 281).

recognized the same 'essence' in both gold and the sun. It is here, and nowhere else, that the root of alchemy lies."[30] As the man in cream colors, the confidence man is associated with the sun on the first page of the novel, where he appears "suddenly as Manco Capac at the lake Titicaca" (p. 3). Manco Capac was supposedly a child of the sun, a god who founded the Inca civilization in Peru, but he was also widely perceived not as an actual god but as a powerful man, who identified himself with the sun and taught reverence for it and who benignly led his subjects to a higher form of life.[31] As an ambassador of light, Manco Capac's mission was thus parallel to both that of adepts and the confidence man. The same "essence," the inner self, is represented by both the sun and by gold. The confidence man in another role, as the Cosmopolitan, refers to himself as one of the "golden boys" (p. 175). In fact, these two images, the sun and gold, lend distinctive qualities to the two halves of the book and function structurally as well as thematically. The image of the sun provides a suggestive backdrop for the action of part one (that is, up until dusk, when the Cosmopolitan appears on the scene). The novel opens at sunrise, when the man in cream-colors arrives on the *Fidèle*, and throughout this section, Melville makes us aware of the sun's presence. Black Guinea uses the alchemical symbol of the oven and refers to the sun as the "good baker" (p. 11). How a character perceives the sun is a measure of his self-understanding. To the adept, the sun is a projection of the light within, and he tries to get others to see it the same way. But most do not. A sick man that the herb doctor approaches sits in the sun, which is "a golden huzzar, from his tent, flashing his helm on the world" (p. 77). The setting is one of warmth and promise, but the sick man is "not warmed, by

---

30. Burckhardt, p. 15.

31. Jane Donahue Eberwein shows in "Joel Barlow and *The Confidence-Man*," *American Transcendental Quarterly* 24 (Supplement 1974), that Melville's conception of Manco Capac may have been derived from Joel Barlow's *The Vision of Columbus* and *The Columbiad*, where that Peruvian hero is depicted as a "pious fraud" with "mystic charm" (p. 28) who did much for a superstitious people. The impact of her argument is lessened, however, because she does not see that the confidence man is on a similar mission. His, she believes, is an entirely different purpose.

the sun," which is to say that he does not partake of the health of self-knowledge, does not experience the vitalizing power of self-mastery. The sun is not helping him just as the miser's gold is not making that character happy because neither reads the image as a projection of what truly could be obtained, the Great Work. Still, the herb doctor persists in his efforts to make others see, and he points out to the crippled Thomas Fry that he can reap the benefits of a "gracious sun" (p. 99).

Darkness characterizes the setting of the second half of the novel, but the idea of gold is now in the foreground as the sun was earlier. Just as Melville shows the two ways of regarding the sun, so he indicates the difference between the healthy and the unhealthy perception of gold. This distinction, in fact, is set up even before the sun disappears. In two episodes in part one, we see how the confidence man thinks of gold metaphorically and in opposition to how others perceive it. The officer of the Black Rapids Coal Company takes gold from an old miser, who calls it "My gold, my gold!" (p. 76). It is not *real* gold, however, because the miser sees it materialistically and literally. He views gold as the sick man sees the sun. The "transfer-agent" (another name for an adept) would like to transmute the miser's gold into the real thing, would like, that is, to change the miser's perception so that he views gold as does a true alchemist. Inadvertently, the Missouri bachelor later suggests what gold truly stands for to an adept like the confidence man—knowledge or more precisely self-knowledge. "I am of opinion," he says to the "philosopher with the brassplate," "you should be served like a Jew in the middle ages with his gold; this knowledge of yours . . . should be taken from you" (p. 125). Knowledge and gold have entirely different meanings to the bachelor and to the "philosopher," who wears an insignia made of an alloy of base metals as a reminder of the process of transmutation: the change that occurs in boys as they mature is nothing but a manifestation of the miracle that is the basis of alchemy. The terms associated with the confidence man in his several forms, the name he is called, the descriptions of his activities, aims, and occupations—all are strikingly suggestive of alchemy.

Throughout the centuries, the true adept has been among the

most widely misunderstood of all great figures. Since he sought pure gold, many of those who heard of him believed that he sought wealth. The situation of the adept in his environment is duplicated in *The Confidence-Man.* Many readers and critics assume that because he seeks and acquires gold, he is in pursuit of riches. It appears axiomatic that anyone who devotes his efforts successfully to the acquisition of gold must be materialistic and cunning. If he carries out his search well enough, he must also be evil. The further removed we become from the tradition of alchemy, the more difficult it becomes to see the confidence man as anything other than a sharper or a devil. "I will take what you give me," the alchemist said to the unbelievers, "and I will turn it into gold for you." But the act of transmutation was for him a projection of inner possibilities. The base metal was not real gold; what came from it was real gold but *only as long as it was viewed symbolically.* The moment that pure gold ceased to be seen as manifestation and was perceived simply as precious metal, it became fool's gold. Consequently, material wealth was never the motivation of a genuine adept, nor is it for the confidence man. Though gold in the materialistic sense may try its "blandishments on me," he says, he will not be moved by it (p. 159). He spends a good deal of time trying to explain to Charlie Noble that mankind is desperately in need of correct perception about gold. They need to find the pure gold, but, even more critically, they need to recognize it for what it is, not the means of worldly wealth but the outward sign of inward richness. He metaphorically depicts the situation by recalling that Pizarro and his men found a great quantity of "precious gold in old Peru" (p. 175), so much of it, in fact, that they could not believe it real: "You remember that when the Spaniard first entered Atahalpa's treasure-chamber, and saw such profusion of plate stacked up, right and left, with the wantonness of old barrels in a brewer's yard, the needy fellow felt a twinge of misgiving . . . as to the genuineness" (p. 177). He satisfied himself that all was pure gold, but the fundamental point, one that Charlie is entirely incapable of grasping, is that this "pure gold, good gold, sterling gold" was then perceived by the raiders only as loot and thus lost its true preciousness. Therefore, all those of humankind who find solid gold, think it false, then realize that it is gold after all are actually right the first time unless they have adequately mastered themselves to view it other than materialistically. And this, precisely, is the reason that it is more difficult for a rich man to enter the kingdom of heaven than for a camel to go through the eye of a needle. What the "small Pizarros," the "needy minds" need in order to transmute them is a circle of gold around them, as the Cosmopolitan places about the irate and disappointed Charlie Noble, and then the degree of self-understanding and command of inner forces that will enable them to associate that circular image of "divine inertness" outside with the sun hidden inside.

The story of China Aster is actually a parable on this subject though Mark Winesome's disciple, Egbert, narrates it with the stated purpose of showing the evils of lending and borrowing money. With pervasive allusions to the alchemical symbols of gold and light, it tells the story of one who futilely engages in the production of a pure substance for materialistic gain, never understanding himself nor the world. China Aster is a candlemaker, "one whose trade would seem a kind of subordinate branch of that parent craft and mystery of the hosts of heaven, to be the means, effectively or otherwise, of shedding some light through the darkness of a planet benighted" (p. 208). His name is that of a common flower, but it also suggests ironically "astra" or "astrum," which means *star* and could refer to a key concept in alchemy—the light that is in nature. He fails both in giving and receiving light, however. His friend Orchis, who has lately won a large amount of money in a lottery and who now sports a gold-headed cane, resembles numerous rich men in the annals of alchemy who often forced their money upon anyone they believed would be able to transmute base metals into gold. They furnished the person they hoped would increase their fortune with all the materials to produce pure gold, appearing not to be anxious to profit themselves but in truth desperately greedy to add to their wealth. More often than not, they ended up with nothing, for the person they invested in proved to be a mere charcoal burner rather than a true adept. "You must drop this vile tallow," Orchis tells China Aster, "and hold up pure spermaceti to the world" (p. 209). Spermaceti candles are more costly but bring greater profits. In other words, spermaceti will become the magic means for changing the thousand dollars Orchis forces upon China Aster into ten thousand. It will be the philosopher's stone. The would-be alchemist thus obtains "a good lot of spermaceti," through whose "operation he counted upon turning a better penny than he ever had before in his life" (p. 212).

Gold as wealth rather than as a sign of spiritual development is therefore the end China Aster seeks, an aim that illustrates his lack of self-perception. Light and gold are combined in a dream that he has twice, but they merely alert him to his materialistic desires. He dreams of a "smiling angel" with a "cornucopia in her hand . . . pouring down showers of small gold dollars, thick as kernels of corn." She tells him that she is "Bright Future" and urges him to go ahead with the plan to make money. He seems to wade about in the shower of gold "like a maltster in malt" (p. 212). After he tries the new venture and fails, he is about ready to listen to his friends Old Plain Talk, Old Prudence, and Old Honesty and turn away, but he dreams of "his bright friend, the angel, in another dream." She showers the gold upon him again from her cornucopia, and again he is deceived by his own dream of wealth. When he finally gives up his attempt to produce gold, it is too late, for his sense of misdirection and failure destroy him. A lesson in the necessity of self-knowledge, the story is told in the words of its "original" narrator (p. 207), words that Egbert merely repeats. Consequently, the Cosmopolitan picks up on the key symbols and alchemical suggestions in the language and reads the parable aright, whereas Egbert perceives its message as a warning against trusting and helping others. That moral, exclaims the Cosmopolitan, is unacceptable. He means not only that the principle appears to him wrong but also that Egbert, who has the common ailment of misperception, has deduced the wrong moral from the words of the original narrator.

References to primary alchemical symbols abound in this story-within-the-story. In fact, they constitute its imagistic framework. The seed and the flower, frequently encountered in alchemical texts, are suggested by the names of the chief characters. *Orchis* designates both a flower (as does *China Aster*) and the male producers of seed, the testes. In addition, seeds are referred to in

China Aster's dream, where coins like kernels of corn pour down upon him. Gold images recur throughout the story in the form of Orchis's thrice-mentioned cane and the contents of the angel's cornucopia. Light is an important motif as well, for China Aster is a candlemaker and attempts to create a fortune by producing purer and more precious light through spermaceti candles. This alchemical imagistic network serves to contrast the characters to real adepts and thus to throw into perspective the reasons for the pathetic failure of China Aster and his shallow sponsor. They never truly manifested bloom from the inner seed, never discovered that core of being that could have grown outward into a life of profound beauty. They sought gold as wealth, not as the manifestation and fulfillment of the Great Work taking place within. They could no more "make" this gold than could the charcoal burners who pursued their aim for the wrong reason. The light they sought was a mere flicker compared with the drummond light of the self or the hidden sun.

The theme and symbols of the China Aster section are strikingly parallel to those of "The Happy Failure," a story Melville composed in 1853 and published the following year in *Harper's*. So similar is his use of a framework of alchemy in these two pieces that one wonders if he did not write the China Aster story earlier than the rest of *The Confidence-Man* as a companion piece of "The Happy Failure" (which "The Fiddler" turned out to be) or even with the purpose of combining the two works into one as a bipartite story such as "The Two Temples." Both are stories of failure, the one hero made happy by it, the other destroyed because of it. Both heroes attempt more than they are capable of, these attempts garbed in the imagery of alchemy. The old man of "The Happy Failure" labors on a mechanism contained in a box that is "hermetically sealed." Mystery and secrecy surround his "experiments." He wants no one to know the secret of how he arrived at his marvelous accomplishment. All in all, it is highly suggestive of the alchemist at work producing the philosopher's stone. But the point in this story, as it is of the China Aster section, is that the hero is not a true adept but a mere bungler. Melville read with great interest his friend Hawthorne's tale of an alchemist, "The Birthmark," and he marked passages that fascinated him. In

"The Happy Failure" and the China Aster story, he created a backdrop of alchemy but made the actors far cries from Hawthorne's Aylmer, who fails but who is tragic, not comic or pathetic, in doing so. The old experimenter in "The Happy Failure" seeks to develop a converter, a transmutor in a sense, for it is supposed to convert worthless swampland into fertile fields by draining them. Suggestions of the philosopher's stone emerge when the old man's nephew accuses him of having "stones" in the hermetically sealed box. References to alchemy in both "The Happy Failure" and the China Aster story serve as a means of indirect contrast, the experimenter in the first work with the great figures of hermetic history and the candlemaker in the second with the powerful adept who listens to the tale.

The man Aster is a foil to Astral Man, a term in alchemy for the hidden essence of being, divine in origin and nature and symbolized by the seed, gold, and the sun. It is that pure and powerful core which the Cabala refers to as Adam Kadmon or Original Man.[32] It is *homo maximus,* the discovery of which is the real goal of all serious alchemists. Now the confidence man in his several roles constantly praises "man" and strongly objects to disparaging remarks about man. He tells of his love for him and his confidence in him. So effusive is his glorification of "man" that readers frequently assume that he is insincere since one would have to be naive to the point of instability or retardation to live in the world and really believe that mankind with its myriad and multifold sins and weaknesses deserves such faith, such admiration. The confidence man is not maliciously lying nor is he a fool; he is simply using the abstraction "man" in a special sense. His praise is not directed toward outer man but inner man. Whenever he expresses his love for and confidence in "man," he speaks as an adept and uses the term as alchemists frequently did to mean Original Man, the hidden sun, that which a person might be capable of discovering if he were wise enough, persistent enough, and humble enough.

32. See Jung's discussion of this concept in *Alchemical Studies,* trans. R. F. C. Hull, Bollingen Series 20 (Princeton: Princeton University Press, 1967), pp. 165–67.

That is what Melville perceived in Shakespeare, what made the great bard, as the confidence man says, "a kind of deity" (p. 172). In a conversation with Charlie Noble, the Cosmopolitan confesses that he does not always understand Shakespeare because in him is something "at once enlightening and mystifying." It "appears to be a certain—what shall I call it?—hidden sun" (pp. 171–72). Though he claims that he does not wish to say what "that hidden sun might be," he actually does so when Charlie asks him whether he believes it to be "the true light," and the Cosmopolitan answers that he thinks of Shakespeare as "a kind of deity." Shakespeare, in other words, had reached that stage in self-knowledge where he could tap the divine energy within him, and it was awesome to witness the results. The intensity of divine light, believed the alchemist, was indescribable; he found that illumination and energy within himself and saw it projected in the sun of nature. Melville's splendid short poem "In the Desert," which was included in *Timolean* (1891), creates the effect that the desert sun has upon a mind given to alchemical perception. Melville first suggests the irresistible power of the sun and then connects it to the awesome, unspeakable energy of God:

> Never Pharoah's Night,
> Whereof the Hebrew wizards croon,
> Did so the Theban flamens try
> As me this veritable Noon.
>
> Like blank ocean in blue calm
> Undulates the ethereal frame;
> In one flowing oriflamme
> God flings his fiery standard out.
>
> Battling with the Emirs fierce
> Napoleon a great victory won,
> Through and through his sword did pierce;
> But, bayonetted by this sun
> His gunners drop beneath the gun.
>
> Holy, holy, holy Light!
> Immaterial incandescence,

Of God the effluence of the essence,
Shekinah intolerably bright!

No adept could express more beautifully and more compactly the function of the sun in alchemy than Melville has done in the final stanza of this poem. The concept of "Immaterial incandescence" as the light of God and the idea of the sun as "Shekinah"— presence of the divine as manifested in nature—both lie at the heart of alchemy, which taught as one of its fundamentals that the sun was an emanation "of the essence." And the sun that radiates on the barrenness of the earthly desert also is what beams forth as a powerful drummond light in those who through the long and often painful process of understanding and controlling their inner world develop the attributes of "a kind of deity."

In contrast to this hidden sun is the temporary light produced by China Aster's candles and the various lamps that dimly illuminate the external world of the *Fidèle* after dusk. Melville sets up a notable opposition between the hidden sun he speaks of in chapter 30 and the solar lamp that he describes in the final episode of the book: "In the middle of the gentlemen's cabin burned a solar lamp, swung from the ceiling, and whose shade of ground glass was all round fancifully variegated, in transparency, with the image of a horned altar, from which flames rose, alternate with the figure of a robed man, his head encircled by a halo" (p. 240). As Elizabeth Foster and others have pointed out, the lamp suggests the horned altar of Exodus, which Moses had constructed, and the figure of Jesus.[33] Since this lamp does not illumine a very big area ("the rays died dimly away") and since it goes out at the end of the book, it has appeared to many readers to be Melville's metaphor for the ineffectualness and the artificiality of the Christian message. Such an idea appears supported by other comments that Melville makes about it. For example, it is set among "other lamps, barren planets, which had either gone out from exhaustion, or been extinguished" (p. 240). In other words, it is among other forms of religious enlightenment, none of which proved

33. Elizabeth S. Foster, ed., *The Confidence-Man: His Masquerade* (New York: Hendricks House, 1954), p. 363.

true or lasting. This is merely the "last survivor of many" religions that now "burned on" but to inevitable extinction itself. In the end, it begins to produce an unpleasant odor, dims, and finally expires. Then the confidence man and the comely old man he has been conversing with leave the cabin and stroll forth in the darkness.

Melville did not, however, create the solar lamp as part of some quarrel with God, for it has nothing to do with that "immaterial incandescence" of the divine. It does not represent God or the profound teachings of Christ but that which the ordinary world settles for when it could have the real thing. It is what the mass of mankind uses for its light instead of the hidden sun. It, like the other lamps, is used by men who "want to sleep, not see" (p. 240). As the superficial and artificial aspects of organized religion with its mere trappings of holy symbols, the solar lamp "burned on, inwardly blessed by those in some berths, and inwardly execrated by those in others," but doomed to extinction because it is not the real light. Men receive its pale illumination outwardly, but the search for light begins within the self. In the midst of this setting is the representative figure of the "clean, comely, old man," who, like most people, is untraveled in the inner realm of gold and light. Melville compares him to a man from the country who puts up at a London inn "and never stirring out of it as a sight-seer, will leave London at last without once being lost in its fog, or soiled by its mud" (p. 241). He reads the Bible but by the light of a religion he has brought himself to rather than by that of one which has come to him—through the inside. He is one of the loneliest and most pathetic figures in the book, professing belief in the light but lost in darkness and torn by doubts and insecurity. The only hope for someone like him is that in his darkness will appear a man of light, who perhaps can impart some of it to him. In fact, the Cosmopolitan is described as just such a person when Melville writes that the confidence man seemed "to dispense a sort of morning through the night" (p. 241). Therefore, the final words of the book that describe the Cosmopolitan leading the unseeing, unenlightened figure of human typicality through darkness, his shallow concept of divinity having failed him, do not mark Melville's nadir of bitterness as is often supposed. Instead, they suggest both the problem with ordinary humanity and something of a solution for those who will accept a guide when he appears.

Melville's mood when he composed *The Confidence-Man* must have been parallel to that reflected in poems of his later years like "Gold in the Mountain" and "Disinterment of the Hermes," where he metaphorically projects through the discovery of Praxiteles' famous sculpture the possibility of man's finding within himself "demigod and god" if he will give up searching for the wrong kind of gold and "dig for these" within the self. There he will excavate not the "barren" but the true gold.

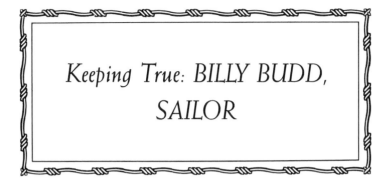

Chapter 11

A curious but little-noticed fact from Melville's last years furnishes a valuable clue to the theme of *Billy Budd, Sailor.* His
granddaughter Eleanor remembered that he composed his final
work on "an inclined plane that for lack of more accurate designation one must call 'desk'; for though it had a pebbled green-paper
surface, it had no cavity for inkwell, no groove for pen and pencil,
no drawer for papers, like the little portable desks that were cherished as heirlooms in the late nineteenth century." It was "open
underneath" and rested upon a "paper-piled table" in Melville's
room at Twenty-Sixth Street in New York. On one of the inside
walls of the inclined plane, he pasted a maxim: "Keep true to the
dreams of thy youth."[1] Most biographers and critics overlook or
ignore this detail probably because of its seeming triviality. But
Melville was not the kind of person given to pasting wise sayings
about his house; so the discovery of this piece of paper attached to
his writing desk should have stimulated far more discussion than

---

1. Eleanor Melville Metcalf, *Herman Melville: Cycle and Epicycle* (Cambridge:
Harvard University Press, 1953), pp. 283, 284.

it has. [2] The maxim—placed for his eyes only—suggests that this was a subject much on his mind during the last years of his life. *Billy Budd* is his final portrayal of a man who failed to know and to be true to himself.

That man is Captain the Honorable Edward Fairfax Vere, a person of pronounced intelligence, unusual depth of feeling, splendid education, impeccable credentials as a naval officer, and unswerving commitment to principles. The context for his life as Melville delineates it is mutiny, a constantly recurring subject in the novel. [3] Melville set the story in a time when bloody revolutions had shaken the world outside England; when England itself was engaged in a war; when within the British navy the shadow of mutiny loomed threateningly; when on an individual ship, the *Bellipotent,* mutiny was in the air; and, finally, when the captain of this ship was concerned that a mutiny of sorts may be imminent within his own thinking. Mutiny thus is a stone dropped into a calm pool, causing a series of concentric disturbances. The

2. Eleanor Metcalf believes that the "dreams" were "religious in nature" (p. 284). Charles J. Haberstroh, Jr., disagrees and posits the theory that Melville had in mind memories of his lost father. *Melville and Male Identity* (Rutherford, N.J.: Fairleigh Dickinson University Press, 1980), p. 133. Closest to my own interpretation is Martin Leonard Pops, who argues that Melville was expressing again, as he did to Hawthorne, his preference for the "heart" over the "head." *The Melville Archetype* (Kent: Kent State University Press, 1970), p. 255.

3. A group of critics, of which Lawrance Thompson has been the most vehement, takes the position that the narrator of *Billy Budd* is a fictional character separate and distinct from Herman Melville. Thompson is somewhat unusual, however, in his insistence that not only is there a "difference between the narrator's overt meaning and Melville's covert meaning," but also that "Melville takes bitter pleasure in permitting his stupid narrator to continue . . . to praise and defend Captain Vere, even while Vere is making an ass of himself." *Melville's Quarrel with God* (Princeton: Princeton University Press, 1952), pp. 382, 390. Though he does not exhibit Thompson's extreme distaste for the narrator, a recent commentator, James Duban, makes a similar point, namely that the narrator is not Melville but a character, "conservative" in nature, who sides with Vere. *Melville's Major Fiction: Politics, Theology, and Imagination* (DeKalb: Northern Illinois University Press, 1983), pp. 221–48. See also Robert Merrill, "The Narrative Voice in *Billy Budd,*" *Modern Language Quarterly* 34 (1973): 283–91. My position in this chapter is that the narrator is for all practical purposes Herman Melville, or, at least, a character that expresses so closely Melville's views that a distinction would not be productive.

largest circle is the outside world, the smallest, the inner world of Captain Vere. [4]

Mutiny, in fact, was in Melville's thoughts from the work's very inception, from the time when he began the original ballad and the accompanying prose headnotes that would evolve over the next few years into the novel that he left in manuscript at his death. [5] Through the various stages of composition, new materials were added and the emphasis shifted from Billy to Captain Vere, but the idea of mutiny remained a constant, the work's central concept from first to last. The editors of the scholarly Chicago edition of the novel explain that in the earliest stage "the focal character was Billy (Billy Budd in the prose headnote), a sailor on the eve of his execution. . . . This Billy was an older man, condemned for fomenting mutiny and apparently guilty as charged." [6]

Melville's concern with mutiny, insurrection, and revolution is evident on nearly every page of the final version of *Billy Budd*. He could not have chosen a year for the happening in his story when there was a greater anxiety in England over the prospect of disruption than 1797, which has come to be known as the year of "The Great Mutiny" (p. 54). [7] Partly because of the French Revolution a few years before, England was at war with France. It was involved in "those wars which like a flight of harpies rose shrieking from the din and dust of the fallen Bastille" (p. 66). To add to the urgency and disorder of the times, sailors in the British navy mutinied at Spithead in April, and in the following month, a "yet more serious outbreak in the fleet at the Nore" shook the country: "To the British Empire the Nore Mutiny was what a

---

4. Kingsley Widmer points out that though Melville apparently had "no sense of revolution," he did possess a lifelong interest in mutiny and once did "engage in mutinous behavior" himself. Furthermore, when such rebellion "appears in his fictions," it is presented as "positive." *The Ways of Nihilism* (Los Angeles: California State Colleges Publication, 1970), p. 52.

5. For an excellent summary treatment of the background of *Billy Budd*, see Merton M. Sealts, Jr., *Innocence and Infamy: Resources for Discussing Herman Melville's Billy Budd, Sailor* (Madison: Wisconsin Humanities Committee, 1983).

6. *Billy Budd, Sailor (An Inside Narrative)*, ed. Harrison Hayford and Merton M. Sealts, Jr. (Chicago: University of Chicago Press, 1962), p. 2.

7. Page references to *Billy Budd* are to the Hayford-Sealts edition.

strike in the fire brigade would be to London threatened by general arson" (p. 54). The idea of change, of reform, was in the air as perhaps at no previous time in history. "Reasonable discontent growing out of practical grievances in the fleet had been ignited into irrational combustion as by live cinders blown across the Channel from France in flames" (p. 54). The atmosphere was such that even servile sailors began to question the treatment they received and the ultimate wisdom of those in authority over them. They sought drastic changes.

But the Great Mutiny came to naught. Most of the military service remained loyal, and "final suppression . . . there was" (p. 55). The mutineers wanted reform, but the "authorities" considered their demands "not only inadmissible but aggressively insolent" (p. 55). Those who had mutinied resumed their servile obedience. Indeed, many of them were ordered into battle under Nelson and won for him "the naval crown of crowns . . . at Trafalgar" (p. 56). So the Great Mutiny amounted to no more than a challenge. Melville compares it to a temporary illness in a human being: "To some extent the Nore Mutiny may be regarded as analogous to the distempering irruption of contagious fever in a frame constitutionally sound, and which anon throws it off" (p. 55).

This context of mutiny in *Billy Budd* serves as an analogue to a like challenge within the heart and mind of Captain Vere that comes only a month or two after the rebellion at the Nore. This interval—from May 1797 to the following summer, when the action of the novel takes place—was marked by a sense of unusual alertness among officers of the fleet to the least sign of unrest among the men: "So it was that for a time, on more than one quarter-deck, anxiety did exist. At sea, precautionary vigilance was strained against relapse. At short notice an engagement might come on. When it did, the lieutenants assigned to batteries felt it incumbent on them, in some instances, to stand with drawn swords behind the men working the guns" (p. 59). Captain Vere is thus highly sensitive to the threat of mutiny because of the world situation and, more particularly, the outbreaks at Spithead and the Nore: "For it was close on the heel of the suppressed insurrections, an aftertime very critical to naval authority, demanding from every English sea commander two qualities not readily interfusable—*prudence and rigor*" (pp. 102–3, italics mine). In one sense, Vere's haste in calling a drumhead court to try Billy, instead of waiting until the ship rejoined the squadron and referring the case to the admiral, is understandable. The times are right for rebellion: "Feeling that unless quick action was taken on it, the deed of the foretopman, so soon as it should be known on the gun decks, would tend to awaken any slumbering embers of the Nore among the crew, a sense of the urgency of the case overruled in Captain Vere every other consideration" (p. 104).

Still, Vere's decision appears to his officers as an overreaction, and indeed it is, one brought on not only by his awareness of the general climate of insurrection but also by the long-standing prospect of mutiny *within his own mind*. Through "prudence and rigor," that is to say, rationalization and discipline, he maintains his steady allegiance to king and country. His prudence and rigor—those nemeses of mutiny—are manifested especially in his glorification of what he calls "forms." He is fond of saying: "With mankind . . . forms, measured forms, are everything; and that is the import couched in the story of Orpheus with his lyre spellbinding the wild denizens of the wood" (p. 128). Vere himself has been spellbound by an Orpheus of sorts, and he will not allow anything to break the spell: he is committed to this music wherever it takes him and no matter what it demands of him.[8] It is represented by the martial tunes played immediately after Billy's execution, tones "subserving the discipline and purposes of war" (p. 128). It comes, however, from an Orpheus inimical to his deepest nature and puts him under a spell that he maintains to his death, a spell that makes him into something that by instincts he is not.

Vere's name suggests the two broad areas in which the spell

8. Edgar A. Dryden, *Melville's Thematics of Form: The Great Art of Telling the Truth* (Baltimore: Johns Hopkins University Press, 1968), sees Orpheus as a negative figure, "a kind of confidence man" (p. 211). John Seelye points out that the music that Vere follows is not like that in the myth of Orpheus but "harsh, discordant, 'unnatural'—like the system it enforces." *Melville: The Ironic Diagram* (Evanston: Northwestern University Press, 1970), p. 170.

operates, *veritas* and *vir*.[9] He is committed to what, in his enchanted condition, he believes to be truth, to things as they actually are—*veritas*. Even his preference in books illustrates this
fidelity to reality: "His bias was toward those books . . . treating
of actual men and events no matter of what era—history, biography, and unconventional writers like Montaigne, who, free from
cant and convention, honestly and in the spirit of common sense
philosophize upon realities" (p. 62). Under the heading of *veritas*,
he has filed away in his intellect certain convictions that act as
blinders to keep him on the path that his spell leads him and as
filters to keep out any music but that of his false Orpheus. He had
"established in him some positive convictions which he forefelt
would abide in him essentially unmodified so long as his intelligent part remained unimpaired" (p. 62). By "his intelligent
part," Melville means his "prudence," or his ability intellectually
to rationalize his actions to match his convictions and thus to
achieve thereby a sense of self-justification.[10] Consequently, when
stirrings within him threaten mutinously to break the spell and
to reform his inner world, his intellect—enchanted as it is—
strongly meets the challenge of the insurrection and triumphs
like a strong human body over a temporary fever. Just as England
meets the mutineers at the Nore head-on and represses them, so
does Vere always manage to meet any threat of drastic changes
within his own inner realm: "His settled convictions were as a
dike against those invading waters of novel opinion social, political, and otherwise, which carried away as in a torrent no few
minds in those days, minds by nature not inferior to his own" (p.
62). Melville makes it clear, however, that Vere does not take this
position merely because he is a member of the aristocracy. Many
of those who, like him, are highborn resisted changes and were
"incensed at the innovators mainly because their theories were

9. Norman Holmes Pearson suggests that Vere is "*vir* . . . as well as *veritas*."
"Billy Budd: 'The King's Yarn,' " *American Quarterly* 3 (1951): 112.

10. For a more positive interpretation of *prudence* as Melville uses it in connection with Vere, see Marjorie Dew, "The Prudent Captain Vere," *Studies in the
Minor and Later Works of Melville,* ed. Raymona E. Hull (Hartford: Transcendental Books, 1970), pp. 81–85. Dew argues that in *Billy Budd, prudence* "is no
longer the pejorative term it has always been in Melville" (p. 81).

inimical to the privileged classes" (p. 62). But Vere's commitment is not to material wealth or to maintaining an aristocratic class structure; he is following what he has determined to be the truth, and the reforms espoused by contemporary voices represent to him mutinous threats to "the peace of the world and the true welfare of mankind" (p. 63). He is entirely sincere and high-principled—all the more tragic that he exists under a kind of spell, that what he believes to be strains of noble music issuing from his heart come from another source and are in disharmony with his true inner self.

Vere is also spellbound in his firm commitment to those things represented by *vir*, which connotes in Latin a man of character and courage. In Latin writings the word is frequently used to designate a military man. Whenever his allegiance to all those areas of thought and conduct suggested by *vir* comes in conflict with some deep impulse within his being, he prevents mutiny through the exercise of "rigor." He tells the officers who try Billy: "Our vowed responsibility is in this: That however pitilessly that law may operate in any instances, we nevertheless adhere to it and administer it" so that "private conscience should not yield to that imperial one formulated in the code under which alone we officially proceed" (p. 111). His Orpheus, he is saying, is the "imperial conscience," not his "private conscience." Through rigor he succeeds in stifling the latter in order to preserve his fidelity to "the code," but in doing so he blocks self-understanding and acts contrary to his true self.[11]

Indeed, if he followed his "private conscience," which, Melville implies, should be in control but is not, he would not even be a military officer. Only by violating his essential nature can he remain faithful to the "imperial conscience." By becoming a practitioner of war he has abnegated his real self, and that is the underlying meaning of Melville's comment about a military officer's similarity to a monk: "But a true military officer is in one

---

11. According to James Duban, "the stance that the narrator imposes upon Vere . . . is almost identical to conservative Whig arguments offered in defense of Judge Lemuel Shaw, Melville's father-in-law, for subordinating private conscience to constitutional mandate in the surrender of fugitive slaves to their owners" (p. 246).

particular like a true monk. Not with more of *self-abnegation* will the latter keep his vows of monastic obedience than the former his vows of allegiance to martial duty" (p. 104, italics mine).

The further apart the imperial and the personal consciences, the more is "rigor" required to prevent inner mutiny. Some naval officers do not need to stress severe military discipline to ward off insurrection, either within their actual command or within themselves. There may be so little tension between their imperial and personal consciences that mutiny is not a threat. Melville gives Admiral Nelson as an example of this type and recounts an incident to reveal that he did not need to practice a high degree of rigor: "In the same year with this story, Nelson, then Rear Admiral Sir Horatio, being with the fleet off the Spanish coast, was directed by the admiral in command to shift his pennant from the *Captain* to the *Theseus;* and for this reason: that the latter ship having newly arrived on the station from home, where it had taken part in the Great Mutiny, danger was apprehended from the temper of the men; and it was thought that an officer like Nelson was the one, not indeed to terrorize the crew into base subjection, but to win them, by force of his mere presence and heroic personality, back to an allegiance if not as enthusiastic as his own yet as true" (p. 59). That Nelson does not need to exert severe discipline to keep his men obedient signifies that he does not need to keep constant watch over himself lest he neglect his martial vows. Throughout *Billy Budd,* what happens on the outside is a reflection of what occurs on the inside, and it is in this sense that Melville gave his novel the subtitle *An Inside Narrative.* [12]

12. William Braswell sees Vere, Billy Budd, and Claggart as aspects of Melville: "as Billy symbolizes the heart, so Claggart roughly symbolizes 'the head' " and Vere, "the later Melville." "Melville's *Billy Budd* as 'An Inside Narrative,' " *American Literature* 29 (1957): 135, 144. Similarly, Milton R. Stern sees the conflict between Billy and Claggart as "the internal war between heart and mind which constantly tears Vere apart." *The Fine Hammered Steel of Herman Melville* (Urbana: University of Illinois Press, 1957), p. 233. On the other hand, the novel's subtitle, according to Joyce Sparer Adler, "refers to what is occurring inside the heart of man in the critical modern era, continuing into Melville's day, which *Billy Budd* exemplifies." *War in Melville's Imagination* (New York: New York University Press, 1981), p. 177.

The portrait of Admiral Nelson in *Billy Budd* is somewhat deceptive, for it is not nearly so flattering as it first appears. Though Melville seems to be defending him against the charges of the "Benthamites of war," he depicts the Admiral as a man who has raised the "excessive love of glory" almost to the height of a personal religious conviction. Indeed, words with religious connotations mark his characterization. Nelson had "a sort of priestly motive" and "adorned himself for the altar and the sacrifice" (p. 58). That Melville does not place a high premium on such love of glory is indicated in his comments on Nelson in *White-Jacket:*

> Thinking of all the cruel carnal glory wrought out by naval heroes . . . I asked myself whether, indeed, that was a glorious coffin in which Lord Nelson was entombed—a coffin presented to him, during life, by Captain Hallowell; it had been dug out of the mainmast of the French line-of-battle ship *L'Orient,* which, burning up with British fire, destroyed hundreds of Frenchmen at the battle of the Nile. Peace to Lord Nelson where he sleeps in his moldering mast! but rather would I be urned in the trunk of some green tree, and even in death have the vital sap circulating round me, giving of my dead body to the living foliage that shaded my peaceful tomb. [13]

Furthermore, he says, "the whole matter of war is a thing that smites common sense and Christianity in the face; so every thing connected with it is utterly foolish, unchristian, barbarous, brutal, and savoring of the Feejee Islands, cannibalism, saltpetre, and the devil." [14] His opinion of the "he-man" aspect of a military hero, that which is suggested by the word *vir,* is that it exists in an officer only after loftier traits have been chased away: "Courage is the most common and vulgar of the virtues; the only one shared with us by the beasts of the field; the one most apt, by excess, to run into viciousness. And since Nature generally takes away with one hand to counterbalance her gifts with the other, excessive animal courage, in many cases, only finds room in a character vacated of loftier things. But in a naval officer, animal courage is

13. *White-Jacket,* ed. Harrison Hayford et al. (Evanston and Chicago: Northwestern University Press and the Newberry Library, 1970), p. 316.

14. Ibid., p. 315.

exalted to the loftiest merit, and often procures him a distinguished command."[15]

To his credit, Vere has to struggle with himself constantly to remain a good military officer whereas Admiral Nelson, to his discredit, appears to have no such problem.[16] The discipline that

15. Ibid., p. 314. Melville continues in this passage: "Hence, if some brainless bravo be Captain of a frigate in action, he may fight her against invincible odds, and seek to crown himself with the glory of the shambles, by permitting his hopeless crew to be butchered before his eyes, while at the same time that crew must consent to be slaughtered by the foe, under penalty of being murdered by the law. Look at the engagement between the American frigate *Essex* with the two English cruisers, the *Phoebe* and *Cherub*, off the Bay of Valparaiso, during the late war. It is admitted on all hands that the American Captain continued to fight his crippled ship against a greatly superior force; and when, at last, it became physically impossible that he could ever be otherwise than vanquished in the end; and when, from peculiarly unfortunate circumstances, his men merely stood up to their nearly useless batteries to be dismembered and blown to pieces by the incessant fire of the enemy's long guns. Nor, by thus continuing to fight, did this American frigate, one iota, promote the true interests of her country. I seek not to underrate any reputation which the American Captain may have gained by this battle. He was a brave man; *that* no sailor will deny. But the whole world is made up of brave men. Yet I would not be at all understood as impugning his special good name. Nevertheless, it is not to be doubted, that if there were any common-sense sailors at the guns of the *Essex*, however valiant they may have been, those common-sense sailors must have greatly preferred to strike their flag, when they saw the day was fairly lost, than postpone that inevitable act till there were few American arms left to assist in hauling it down. Yet had these men, under these circumstances, 'pusillanimously cried for quarter,' by the IV. Article of War they might have been legally hung" (pp. 314–15).

16. Critics have generally found Melville's treatment of Admiral Nelson to be favorable, however. Wendell Glick, for example, sees Nelson as the best possible representation of "social expediency," which Melville is espousing in *Billy Budd*. "Expediency and Absolute Morality in *Billy Budd*," *PMLA* 68 (1953): 109. For John B. Noone, Jr., Nelson is the "ideal synthesis of instinct and reason." "*Billy Budd*: Two Concepts of Nature," *American Literature* 29 (1957): 261. Milton R. Stern states that in Nelson, Melville depicts the "kind of heroism that . . . may lead to salvation" (p. 208). For the view that Nelson serves as a contrast to Vere, whom Melville portrays unfavorably, see Phil Withim, "*Billy Budd*: Testament of Resistance," *Modern Language Quarterly* 20 (1959): 117, and Merlin Bowen, *The Long Encounter: Self and Experience in the Writings of Herman Melville* (Chicago: University of Chicago Press, 1960), pp. 216–33. On the issue of Nelson's exposing himself in battle, Warner Berthoff writes: "Nelson's conduct was, Melville insisted . . . altogether natural and fitting,

Vere demands of others suggests the severe rigor that he applies to himself. He never tolerates "an infraction of discipline." He is "resolute" (p. 60). He feels that Billy must be condemned to die or else the crew of the *Bellipotent* would think its captain soft, and that in turn would be "deadly to discipline." He is, in brief, "a martinet as some deemed him" (p. 128). His unusual action in calling a drumhead court, therefore, results from his sensing that a revolution may be imminent within his own being; his true self is stirring and threatening to take over. He thus meets his own personal Great Mutiny and crushes it before reform can take place. It is not a victory to be celebrated.

The surgeon's suspicion that Captain Vere may be "affected in his mind" is well grounded (p. 101).[17] His actions suggest that he may indeed be "unhinged," and Melville hints that a careful reading of the novel will reveal the nature and source of his form of madness: "Whether Captain Vere, as the surgeon professionally and privately surmised, was really the sudden victim of any degree of aberration, every one must determine for himself by such light as this narrative may afford" (p. 102). The light that the narrative affords shows that the "mental disturbance" (p. 108) which Vere's officers note in him is an intensification of the spell that he has been under all along. Vere has not been Vere. His is "a mind resolute to surmount difficulties even if against primitive instincts strong as the wind and the sea" (p. 109), and that resolution to ward off the challenge of his most basic intuitive urges (his "primitive" self) shows the power of the spell that has him. His spellbound condition is suggested in another way in Melville's

---

coming from that 'exaltation of sentiment' which is the mark of the truly heroic action." "'Certain Phenomenal Men': The Example of *Billy Budd*," *ELH* 27 (1960): 345. In Nelson, Ralph W. Willett argues, Melville chose "to create a perfect hero." "Nelson and Vere: Hero and Victim in *Billy Budd, Sailor*," *PMLA* 82 (1967): 370. On the other hand, Ray B. Browne, *Melville's Drive to Humanism* (Lafayette, Indiana: Purdue University Studies, 1971), writes that "Melville thinks that Nelson may have been a vainglorious fool" (p. 375).

17. But see Stern, who insists that Vere is Melville's "complete man of action, mind, and heart" who "never passes from the way of understanding" (p. 225). My own interpretation of Vere is closer to those of Merlin Bowen and Joyce Sparer Adler.

description of his dying moments: he is drugged. Though he dies with Billy Budd's name on his lips, "these were not the accents of remorse" (p. 129). He is confident even as he faces death that he has remained true to the "imperial conscience." And he has; the spell retains its control over him to the end. [18]

There is something in Vere, however, that wants to break the spell of the false Orpheus, something that occasionally attempts to usurp the ruling imperial conscience and take its place. It is the genuine Vere, the "King's yarn in a coil of navy rope" (p. 63); the "Starry" Vere. He is being himself more when he gazes out at the sea in what appears a "certain dreaminess of mood" (p. 61) than when he acts the part of a devotedly patriotic officer leading his men in combat or when he prudently philosophizes "upon realities" (p. 62). Only in rare moments does he seem to allow his instinctive being rather than his spellbound intellect to dominate. Always the music of the false Orpheus breaks in, and Vere shows "more or less irascibility" (p. 61) because he must again become something that he is not. His prudence and rigor immediately control his irascibility, which is actually the outward sign of mutinous stirrings within. [19] If Vere could have prolonged

18. The details surrounding Vere's death have stimulated a long-standing controversy. Norman Holmes Pearson's view is typical of one group of critics who read Vere's death scene as the crowning glory of his heroic life (pp. 113–14). Others have not been so charitable. Merlin Bowen, for example, sees no signs of redemption in the way Vere dies. He is "a uniformed and conscientious servant of 'Cain's city,' an overcivilized man who has stifled the sound of his own heart and learned to live by the head alone as his calling requires, who has abdicated his full humanity in the interests of a utilitarian social ethic and postponed the realization of truth and justice to some other and more convenient world" (p. 217). According to Joyce Sparer Adler, Vere's "death on the heels of his sacrifice of Billy to Mars is Melville's Judgment upon him for his denial of God" (p. 177). The fact that Vere is mortally wounded in an encounter with a ship named the *Athée* suggests to Edgar A. Dryden that Vere has been destroyed by the same "forms" he devoted his life to, *seeming* forms, that is, but in actuality formlessness and nothingness (p. 212).

19. C. B. Ives believes that Vere is irritable in these moments because he is embarrassed at being caught in a dreamy mood. See "*Billy Budd* and the Articles of War," *American Literature* 34 (1962): 38. Though her frame of reference is somewhat different from mine, Marlene Longenecker comes close to expressing my view of Vere's reveries in her cogently argued essay "Captain Vere and the

these times of introspection, that "king" within him, his real self, might have gained ascendancy, but it remains captive and buried away.

Since in the novel what happens on the outside parallels what occurs on the inside, the abrupt intrusion of Billy Budd into his captain's life suggests that what I have called the real "king" in Vere is suddenly challenging the imperial conscience, the false king. Consequently, Billy is described in royal, kingly terms. "Noble descent," writes Melville, "was as evident in him as in a blood horse" (p. 52). He has a "natural regality" (p. 43). His bearing is "suggestive of a mother eminently favored by Love and the Graces," and it hints at "a lineage in direct contradiction to his lot" as a common sailor. What Vere is fighting after he witnesses Billy's act of mutiny is the instinctive urge to let this regal young sailor go free. He thinks that he must remain resolute against "primitive instincts strong as the wind and the sea." But what Vere is fighting back—his sympathetic tendency toward Billy—is the attempt of his truest and deepest self to emerge and take control. In addition, Melville suggests that it is not only the true Vere that is being stifled but also the *best* in Vere, his "youth," a pristine force of great power. If Vere had given in to his yearning to free Billy, he would at the same time have freed himself from the spell of the false Orpheus and been able to sense the ineffable wonder and power of the hidden sun within.

Melville thus meant two things by the maxim pasted on his writing desk: "Keep true to the dreams of thy youth." First, he was reminding himself of the necessity to find out what and who you are and of acting and thinking in fidelity to that self-knowledge. Secondly, he was expressing his conviction that once that has been achieved, one is in position to probe this true self through the process of deep diving in order to discover the light and strength within, the primitive, Unfallen Man. By "youth,"

Form of Truth," *Studies in Short Fiction* 14 (1977): 337–43: "The atavistic longing represented by Vere's moody gazing at the blank sea is the 'true' content of 'uncompromised' vision. That uncompromised vision is incompatible with civilization, and as we know it results in the conflict between truth and law" (p. 342).

therefore, Melville did not mean a previous time in his life, that is, before he reached maturity.[20] He was not reminding himself to call upon his memory and reconstruct early ideals that he felt he should follow in his old age. It is not youth remembered but youth within him at the moment that he is interested in. Something alive and vigorous within him, which he calls his "youth," sends forth impulses, which he calls his "dreams," and to them he knows that he should adhere, for they are the only source of truth on which he can rely. He refers to this force within him as his youth because it, unlike his body, never ages. In a general sense, the concept is not unusual. In "Rhapsody of Life's Progress," Elizabeth Barrett Browning expressed a similar idea when she wrote: "The soul keeps its youth / But the body faints sore."[21]

So pronounced are the suggestions of the extraordinary and the phenomenal in *Billy Budd* that it takes on the essential qualities of a myth. Extraordinary people come together in a moment in time that is phenomenal because external reality both initiates and mirrors crucial internal conflicts. Billy is a phenomenon because he causes things to happen inside people who are able to recognize him for what he is. On the *Bellipotent*, only Vere and Claggart are "capable of adequately appreciating the moral phenomenon presented in Billy Budd" (p. 78). They instinctively recognize Billy as a kind of miraculous real-life version of what may be termed original human nature, pristine and unaffected by the process of "civilization." How they respond to this phenomenon is the essence of the novel.

To suggest Billy's role as the projection of man's original human nature, his unfallen nobility, Melville characterizes him with images and references that not only point up kingly qualities, as we have seen, but also his purity and spiritual appeal. So pure is his mind and his heart that he is utterly incapable

20. Indeed, he wrote Hawthorne that there was little in his early years that was memorable: "Until I was twenty-five, I had no development at all. From my twenty-fifth year I date my life." *The Letters of Herman Melville,* ed. Merrell R. Davis and William H. Gilman (New Haven: Yale University Press, 1960), p. 130.

21. *Complete Works,* ed. Charlotte Porter and Helen A. Clarke, vol. 3 (New York: Society of English and French Literature, 1900), p. 116.

of sarcasm or satire: "the will to it and the sinister dexterity were alike wanting. To deal in double meanings and insinuations of any sort was quite foreign to his nature" (p. 49). His face is "all but feminine in purity of natural complexion" (p. 50). In general, he has "an untampered-with flavor like that of berries" (p. 53). This basic and unspoiled purity makes him as appealing as if he were almost a god. Indeed, he is the center of attention wherever he goes, a "cynosure" (p. 44). The point in stressing his great beauty as a Handsome Sailor is to show his appeal. Terms like "homage" and "spontaneous tribute" create a religious aura in Melville's description of Billy and the Handsome Sailor as a type. One such sailor he compares with a "pagod," a deity (p. 43). The closest we can come to God, Melville seems again to be saying, is through the discovery of our *original* human nature. Consequently, Billy (and the sort of whom he is an example) is associated with such venerated objects as the "grand sculptured Bull" worshiped by the Assyrians (p. 44) and such gods as Apollo, as Lieutenant Ratcliffe of the *Bellipotent* calls him.

Apollo was the Greek god of music as well as of light and prophecy, and, indeed, the appeal of music is an implied metaphor for Billy's magnetism. "He could sing," Melville writes, "and like the illiterate nightingale was sometimes the composer of his own song" (p. 52). Under usual circumstances, Billy's voice is "singularly musical, as if expressive of the harmony within" (p. 53). His last words, "God bless Captain Vere," are "delivered in the clear melody of a singing bird on the point of launching from the twig" (p. 123).[22] His music stands in opposition to the martial strains to which Vere marches. Billy thus represents the true Orpheus whom the Captain should follow. In *Clarel,* Melville writes of a singing Cypriote who joins the band of travelers:

> Orpheus of heavenly seed
> Adown thrilled Hades' gorges singing,

22. The father of ironist readings of *Billy Budd,* Joseph Schiffman, finds "piercing irony" in Billy's final words, which cause the reader to "gag." "Melville's Final Stage, Irony: A Re-examination of Billy Budd Criticism," *American Literature* 22 (1950): 133.

> About him personally flinging
> The bloom transmitted from the mead.[23]

Such is Billy aboard the hellish ship of war. Orpheus-like he flings about him a bloom; in fact, his very name, Budd, suggests this function. He is a bud or a flower deriving from the "heavenly seed," a vigorous, life-giving force. Lieutenant Ratcliffe calls him "the flower of his [the King's] flock" (p. 48), and Claggart compares him with a daisy (though not intending a compliment).

The seed-flower imagery used to characterize Billy is part of an extensive system of references that reveals Melville again employing the most fundamental symbols of alchemy to suggest an alchemical-like idea: the sustaining and rejuvenating power of what he calls "the hidden sun." Billy is also associated with the jewel and with gold, two of the most common symbols in alchemy for the aims of the "inward work," the realization through self-knowledge of "an extra-ordinary spiritual state."[24] To Captain Graveling, Billy is "the jewel of 'em," the loss of which will leave his ship lusterless and quarrelsome. The Handsome Sailor of Liverpool wears "big hoops of gold" in his ears, and Billy is compared to "a goldfinch popped into a cage" when he is impressed aboard the *Bellipotent* (p. 45). He is more frequently referred to, however, in connection with light and the sun. He is tanned by the sun (p. 50), and his arm is like "lightning" (p. 47). Claggart, on the other hand, remains in "seclusion from the sunlight" (p. 64). If Billy's face was "without the intellectual look of the *pallid* Claggart's, not the less was it lit, like his, *from within,* though from a different source. The bonfire in his heart made luminous the rose-tan in his cheek" (p. 77, italics mine). He frequently produces a smile that "sunned him" (p. 87). At his death, he seems to merge back into the light that is his source: "The vapory fleece hanging low in the East was shot through with a soft glory. . . . Billy ascended; and, ascending, took the full rose of the dawn" (p. 124). He is reclaimed by that which had sent him:

23. *Clarel,* ed. Walter E. Bezanson (New York: Hendricks House, 1960), III.iv.37–40.

24. Titus Burckhardt, *Alchemy: Science of the Cosmos, Science of the Soul,* trans. William Stoddart, (Baltimore: Penguin, 1971), p. 204.

"The fleece of low-hanging vapor had vanished, licked up by the sun that late had so glorified it" (p. 128). That the sun or the light with which Billy is linked at his death is meant to have connotations of divinity is suggested by the fact that "the full rose of the dawn" into which Billy ascended at his death was at one time in the manuscript "the full shekinah of the dawn."[25] Melville had used the term *shekinah* before in his poem "In the Desert" to stand for the "fiery standard" of God, and in *Clarel* he employed the word to name the presence of God in nature (IV.ix.33–47).[26]

Billy Budd, then, is presented as the Man of Light, not the source of light itself but one who brings the light of nature, which is also the force that to the alchemist was hidden within the self. He is the bringer of the *lumen naturae.* As such, he should be the guide and teacher of those who recognize him for what he is. He is the manifestation of that which can lead to the source of truth, which is within. In *Mardi*, Babbalanja called this guide "the prompter": "Within our hearts is all we seek: though in that search many need a prompter."[27] What Melville refers to as "all we seek" is in the heart, at the center, where, according to the alchemist Michael Maier, one finds light and fire, the "physical counterpart" of which is gold and the sun.[28] As the bringer of light, Billy is referred to as a kind of instrument of the divine, a messenger or angel. When he strikes Claggart dead, Captain Vere

25. Hayford and Sealts, pp. 191–92.

26. See, however, Harry Modean Campbell, "The Hanging Scene in Melville's *Billy Budd, Foretopman*," *Modern Language Notes* 66 (1951): 378–81, who argues that Melville changed "shekinah" to "rose" because he wished to tone down "the religious symbolism" so that he would "have just enough to point up the irony" in a bitter, pessimistic novel. See the response of G. Giovannini, "The Hanging Scene in Melville's *Billy Budd*," *Modern Language Notes* 70 (1955): 491–97, and Campbell's reply, "The Hanging Scene in Melville's *Billy Budd:* A Reply to Mr. Giovannini," *Modern Language Notes* 70 (1955): 497–500.

27. *Mardi*, ed. Harrison Hayford et al. (Evanston and Chicago: Northwestern University Press and the Newberry Library, 1970), p. 637. For an entirely different (and negative) view of Billy's function, see Rollo May, who argues that no form of spirituality is represented in him but that his is a "Pseudoinnocence." *Power and Innocence* (New York: Norton, 1972), pp. 49–50.

28. See C. G. Jung's discussion in *Alchemical Studies,* trans. R. F. C. Hull (Princeton: Princeton University Press, 1967), pp. 148–52.

exclaims that "it is the divine judgment on Ananias" (p. 100). Claggart, says Vere, has been "struck dead by an angel of God!" (p. 101). Billy even seems to be speaking for God when he tells his captain, "God will bless you for that, your honor!" (p. 106). In another place Billy is compared to those "British captives" whom the Romans called angels (p. 120).

Such allusions to Billy as a messenger or angel, however, do not lead to the implication that Melville is taking a Christian position in the novel, for the focus of his attention is not upon God, the external Creator, but upon the hidden sun, a mighty and creative power akin to God within the human heart. Melville has decided that one can never know God, the mystery of all mysteries, but he can attempt to probe to the center of his own being and discover there what was once the original potency and nobility of man's nature. It is this attitude that makes him more in tune with the philosophical alchemists seeking self-knowledge and understanding than with more traditional forms of Christianity of his time. The aim of the alchemist was to discover within himself original man, that is to say, Adam before the Fall. As Titus Burckhardt points out, "Spiritually understood, the transmutation of lead into gold is nothing other than the regaining of the original nobility of human nature."[29] Though Billy in some ways suggests Christ, Melville is far more insistent in his linking him with prelapsarian Adam.[30] He has "virtues pristine and unadulterate," which are not "to be derived from custom or convention" but are "out of keeping with these, as if indeed exceptionally transmitted from a period prior to Cain's city and

29. Burckhardt, p. 26.

30. Newton Arvin remarks that Melville creates "variations" on the story of Adam in Genesis, for "There is no Eve in this Eden." *Herman Melville* (New York: William Sloane, 1950), p. 296. The variation that Arvin notices derives from Melville's following the alchemical myth of prefallen Adam rather than the biblical account. Milton Stern sees Billy as prelapsarian Adam but finds such a figure unappealing: "Melville repeatedly suggests that innocence, in the need for a knowledge of the history of the only world there is, is not a saving virtue, but a fatal flaw" (p. 215). Thomas J. Scorza argues that Billy is not like Adam, either "old or new," but an example of Rousseau's "noble savage." *In the Time Before Steamships: Billy Budd, the Limits of Politics, and Modernity* (DeKalb: Northern Illinois University Press, 1979), pp. 28, 34.

citified man" (p. 53). When Melville writes that Billy "is not presented as a conventional hero," he means that such a character is not a product of convention but pristine, *found* (Billy is a foundling) rather than being introduced into the world in the ordinary way. Several times Melville links him with "young Adam before the Fall" (p. 94). When terms like "primitive" or "primeval" are used to apply to Billy or to the instinct in Vere that the young sailor arouses, or when he is referred to as a "barbarian," Melville's meaning can best be understood by recognizing the similarity of Billy's role to that in alchemy of the prefallen Adam.[31]

Seeing Billy in this sense accounts for one of the most puzzling details about him in the novel—the presence in his highly masculine nature of distinct feminine qualities. Lieutenant Ratcliffe refers to him as "my beauty" (p. 48), and Melville says that "Billy Budd's position aboard the seventy-four was something analogous to that of a rustic beauty transplanted from the provinces and brought into competition with the highborn dames of the court" (pp. 50–51). Typically, a detail stressing his masculinity will be followed by one suggesting femininity. For example, his face is like that of "Hercules," but "this again was subtly modified by another and pervasive quality," such as his ear, "small and shapely, the arch of the foot, the curve in mouth" (p. 51). He has "as much of masculine beauty as one can expect anywhere to see," but Melville compares him to the delicate Georgiana in Hawthorne's story "The Birthmark" (p. 53). He is called "heroic" in form (p. 77) on the one hand, and "sweet" (p. 73) on the other. He exercises "manly forwardness" (p. 89), but has an expression like a "vestal priestess" (p. 99). He is capable of striking a man dead with the force of "a discharged cannon" (p. 99), but he has the "faint rosebud complexion of the more beautiful English girls" (p. 121). If Billy is to be the messenger, the "angel," an objectification of the hidden sun and, consequently, to reflect the nobility,

31. Vere, writes Melville, is not prepared (or "authorized") to view Billy and his conduct on a "primitive basis" (p. 103). In a moment when he puts aside his "imperial conscience," Vere feels the pristine appeal of Billy: "The austere devotee of military duty, letting himself melt back into what remains primeval in our formalized humanity, may in end have caught Billy to his heart" (p. 115).

purity, and appeal of original human nature, of a prelapsarian Adam figure, he must, in effect, be androgynous. Such was Adam always presented in the writings and symbolic drawings of the alchemists.[32]

Billy's extraordinary strength and physical quickness, which sometimes lead to acts of violence, do not reveal flaws in his makeup but project the superhuman power of the force he represents, a force capable of dealing summarily with evil but incapable of being "the prompter" unless it is recognized for what it is, accepted, and followed. It is not evil that keeps it from being the prompter it could be but blindness. Billy's stutter has been called the mark of a "noncommunicating mindlessness" that Melville found to be a sin.[33] Another critic writes: "Surely Billy's stutter, then, symbolizes stupidity and ineffectiveness as well as Edenic imperfection."[34] Such readings fail to go beyond the literal level of the novel by regarding the stutter as a fundamental quality in Billy whereas in a deeper and more important sense it represents not what he is but the faltering of his function in the world. And that faltering is brought about not because of his character but because of the world's failure to regard him for what he is. Of course, Melville himself is responsible for confusing scores of readers and critics because he plainly attributes Billy's "organic hesitancy" to "just one thing amiss in him" and goes on to make the point that because of our nature all human beings are flawed in some way (p. 53). A bit of double-dealing is going on here, for

32. "Alchemy . . . is based on the view that man, as a result of the loss of his original 'Adamic' state, is divided within himself. He regains his integral nature only when the two powers, whose discord has rendered him impotent, are again reconciled with one another. This inward, and now 'congenital,' duality in human nature is moreover a consequence of its fall from God. . . . The regaining of the integral nature of man . . . alchemy expresses by the symbol of the masculine-feminine androgyne" (Burckhardt, p. 149). Others have noted the suggestions of Billy's androgynous qualities. See, for example, Richard Chase, who sees Billy as "the innocent hermaphrodite Christ." "Dissent on Billy Budd," *Partisan Review* 15 (1948): 1217. B. L. Reid comments that Billy is "not effeminate so much as androgynous or angelic." "Old Melville's Fable," *Massachusetts Review* 9 (1968): 538.

33. Stern, p. 215.
34. Widmer, p. 26.

a flawed and very "human" Billy, such as Melville appears to want to make him in this particular passage, does not correspond to the pure Billy we see elsewhere. Melville was torn between his desire to present Billy as a character in a kind of extended parable or myth—where symbolism rather than reality would be all that counted—and his wish to keep the novel grounded in the familiar and the real. He consequently tries to have it both ways. He creates Billy as the messenger of the hidden sun on the parabolic and profounder level, but he knows that he must not make him perfect on the literal level because Billy would then not be believable as one of the participants in a drama of real life. Thus he *implies* that Billy's stutter is the responsibility of a world that rejects him, but he *says* that it is the mark of Billy's own imperfection.

Melville's most fundamental reason for having Billy stutter is closely akin to Hawthorne's purpose in having his spiritualized butterfly falter in "The Artist of the Beautiful." When the butterfly comes in contact with old Peter Hovenden, the representative of all those forces alien to and contemptuous of what the butterfly stands for, it "drooped its wings, and seemed on the point of falling to the floor." Even its "bright spots of gold . . . grew dim."[35] The artist Owen Warland, who has come to see that the butterfly is a projection of something within him, explains that "in an atmosphere of doubt and mockery, its exquisite susceptibility suffers torture," not because of any flaw within it but because of the detrimental effect of an unaccepting world. When it comes near the grandson of old Peter, the butterfly exhibits "a wavering movement" and "struggled, as it were."[36] And it is the hand of this child, suggesting the alien world, that destroys it. Billy stutters for the same reason that the golden butterfly struggles and wavers. The butterfly's glow is like Billy's musical voice. It is when the music stops that the stutter begins. It is brought on by the rejection of the world rather than by an inherent flaw in Billy himself.

35. Nathaniel Hawthorne, *Mosses from an Old Manse*, ed. William Charvat et al. (Columbus: Ohio State University Press, 1974), p. 473.

36. Ibid., pp. 473, 475.

When Billy delivers his final words, however, he does not stutter but pronounces them so melodiously that they have a "phenomenal effect" (p. 123). Just as there is no stutter when he says "God bless Captain Vere!" so is there no struggle or spasm during his hanging. This, too, is "phenomenal" (p. 125) because Billy is the manifestation of a phenomenon. What happens to him is, indeed, "euthanasia," as the ship's purser suggests: that is, "a gentle and easy death" (*OED*) if it can be called death at all.[37] The phenomenon of the hidden sun continues to exist; only a ray of it has ceased to shine here. Consequently, Billy does not confront his own demise with the same frustration that he exhibits when he encounters the concentrated poisonous atmosphere of the world. It would have been highly inappropriate if Melville had had him stutter and struggle at that point when he is simply taken back into his source, when the hidden sun, symbolized by the "shekinah," reclaims him, his having been rejected by one whom he could have rescued from a world of lies.[38]

The reason that Captain Vere rejects him is that Billy is a muti-

37. Walter Sutton argues that in using the word *euthanasia*, Melville was following Schopenhauer, who expressed affinity for Buddhism and thought of euthanasia in terms of *Nirvana*. "Melville and the Great God Budd," *Prairie Schooner* 34 (1960): 128–33. See also Duban's treatment of this idea (pp. 243–44).

38. Billy is no such potential saviour in the view of Vern Wagner, who argues that he is merely "another manifestation that nature 'paints like the harlot,'" that he represents a kind of "emptiness" that "repels" the reader. "Billy Budd as Moby Dick: An Alternate Reading," in *Studies in Honor of John Wilcox*, ed. A. Dayle Wallace and Woodburn O. Ross (Detroit: Wayne State University Press, 1958), pp. 157–74. See also Barbara Johnson, "Melville's Fist: The Execution of *Billy Budd*," *Studies in Romanticism* 18 (1979): 567–99. The position of Rowland A. Sherrill is closer to my interpretation: "a promise of redemption appears in the world of human experience but is repudiated by the regnant, martial perception of experience; but the very presence of the 'radiant visage,' having been refused, itself grows in moment and power to the extent that it casts into radical doubt the validity of the man-of-war world which spurns its promise." *The Prophetic Melville: Experience, Transcendence, and Tragedy* (Athens: University of Georgia Press, 1979), p. 221. An argument encountered with some frequency in criticism of *Billy Budd* is that Melville gave Vere no choice; therefore, the question of what he could have done or should have done is really a false issue. See, for example, Charles A. Reich, "The Tragedy of Justice in *Billy Budd*," *Yale Review* 56 (1967): 368–89, and B. L. Reid, "Old Melville's Fable."

neer. He brings peace, but before he can be a peacemaker, he must instigate change, sometimes with violence. A revolution of sorts occurs aboard the *Rights-of-Man* when Billy becomes a member of the crew. Frustrated and quarrelsome sailors undergo a metamorphosis as they allow the Handsome Sailor to, in a sense, rule their lives. What they feel for him brings out the best within them: "a virtue went out of him, sugaring the sour ones" (p. 47). His bitterest foe, the man with the fire-red whiskers, becomes his most devoted follower after Billy strikes him in a fight. Explains the captain of the *Rights-of-Man:* "They all love him. Some of 'em do his washing, darn his old trousers for him; the carpenter is at odd times making a pretty little chest of drawers for him. Anybody will do anything for Billy Budd; and it's the happy family here" (p. 47). Captain Graveling has to suppress a sob as he expresses his final complaint to Lieutenant Ratcliffe: "You are going to take away my peacemaker!" (p. 47). Billy, then, or what he stands for ("the moral phenomenon presented" in him), commands allegiance, and that in turn requires internal change, a usurpation of whatever it is that rules the mind and heart by other inner forces. In some simple minds this mutiny takes place quickly and is often essentially bloodless. The crew members of the *Rights-of-Man* do not understand Billy as a moral phenomenon nor do they anticipate and object to the change that he will effect in them. He is to them merely a refreshing daisy, and they are changed without their conscious awareness.

Captain Vere and John Claggart, however, perceive that for them Billy represents a threat to the internal hierarchy they have established. In their radically different ways, they both sense that "a mantrap may be under the ruddy-tipped daisies" (p. 94). In short, Captain Vere is afraid that if he allows him to go free after an act of mutiny, striking and killing a superior officer, Billy will take over his *ship,* not just the *Bellipotent* (where the crew might give Billy their allegiance as the sailors did aboard the *Rights-of-Man*) but also his inner command. He could himself become a subject of Billy Budd, and to do so would mean breaking the spell of his false Orpheus, changing all that he has talked himself into believing, going against his martial vows. In sum, this is the greatest threat that he has ever had to his "settled convictions";

this is the time of his personal Great Mutiny. His prudence and rigor prove to be strong enough to suppress a mutiny that would have brought him peace rather than war.

Billy Budd, then, is a psychological study of how two extraordinary men respond to a phenomenon, a flesh-and-blood version of original human nature (without the corruption of the City of Cain) who is placed suddenly in their midst.[39] He forces them both to the test: either they must align themselves with him or get rid of him. Vere loves him, but the call of his false Orpheus prevails. Claggart *could* love him but his perverted nature prevails. He cannot think or see except in terms of perversion. When Melville writes that he is an example of Plato's concept of innate depravity, he is using *depravity* in its true and original sense of the perversion of truth. Not so much a representative of fallen human nature as a Calvinist would envision it, he is rather an illustration of a phenomenon, a person with an inborn compulsion to distort the truth to himself as well as to others, but he does not understand this about himself any more than Vere understands that his "imperial conscience" is drastically violating his deepest and best instincts and making him play a false role. Claggart is thus not an "evil" person in the commonly received meaning of the term, a person who practices vice. He is even "without vices or small sins." He is not "mercenary or avaricious," not "sordid or sensual" (p. 76). He is not the kind of man who is likely to end up in prison for either major or minor crimes. He is not brutish or violent (p. 74) or given to strong drink. He flourishes in a civilized environment, which "is auspicious" to men like him. Melville uses words that describe noncivilization (*primitive, pagan, barbarian*) and the term *civilization* as metaphors for man's original state (or original human nature in the alchemical sense) as opposed to what that noble and pristine condition has become: corrupt and perverted. Claggart is a highly civilized man whereas Billy is an "upright barbarian."[40]

39. A slightly different phrasing of this issue is expressed by Christopher W. Sten: "Does the end—civilization—justify the inevitable sacrifice of the natural man?" "Vere's Use of the 'Forms': Means and Ends in *Billy Budd,*" *American Literature* 47 (1975): 38.

40. Billy "was wholly without irrational fear of it [death], a fear more preva-

Perversion is thus the essence of Claggart's character, the most fundamental of all his traits, and it is this innate tendency that causes and feeds his madness: "But the thing which in eminent instances signalizes so exceptional a nature is this: Though the man's even temper and discreet bearing would seem to intimate a mind peculiarly subject to the law of reason, not the less in heart he would seem to riot in complete exemption from that law, having apparently little to do with reason further than to employ it as an ambidexter implement for effecting the irrational. That is to say: Toward the accomplishment of an aim which in wantonness of atrocity would seem to partake of the insane, he will direct a cool judgment sagacious and sound. These men are madmen" (p. 76). Melville is concerned so frequently with madness in his characters that it seems almost to amount to a preoccupation, but it is what brings on madness that is his more essential interest—lack of self-understanding. Madness as Melville conceived it may be defined as a condition marked by the absence of self-knowledge. The greater the difference between what a person is and what he thinks he is, the higher the degree of insanity and, consequently, the more difficult to cure.

Ordinarily Claggart's mind functions without challenges to the systematic perversions it creates. But once in a while "some special object" will appear that causes an inner crisis, one that is not usually manifested in drastic external excitement but "self-contained, so that when, moreover, most active it is to the average mind not distinguishable from sanity" (p. 76). Billy Budd is this "special object." Melville explains that the reason why Claggart finds the handsome youth such a profound threat is that it is extremely difficult for him to pervert the image of Billy Budd. The master-at-arms tries first to twist Billy's image into some distorted form, to read into him something that would justify his abhorrence of him: "Probably the master-at-arms' clandestine persecution of Billy was started to try the temper of the man; but it had not developed any quality in him that enmity could make

---

lent in highly civilized communities than so-called barbarous ones which in all respects stand nearer to unadulterate Nature." Thus, "a barbarian Billy radically was" (p. 120).

official use of or even pervert into plausible self-justification" (p. 80). For this reason, Billy's accident with his soup is a welcome occurrence to Claggart, for he perverts a trifle into a momentous insult and thus gains a motive for pursuing vengeance. Animosity has now become justified "into a sort of retributive righteousness" (p. 80). He thus imagines himself entirely in the right.

In order to see how he could possibly think that, it is necessary to determine how he views himself, and to do that one has to examine him not from the outside but from the inside, using what clues Melville has offered about background and personality as guideposts. Though almost nothing definite is known about John Claggart, four characteristics are strongly suggested by his bearing, manner, and actions. First, he appears to be more intelligent and more educated than most seamen. His brow is the kind "associated with more than average intellect," and "his general aspect and manner" are "suggestive of an education and career incongruous with his naval function" (p. 64). Secondly, he unlike the typical sailor is probably a man of widely varied experiences and occupations. He did not go to sea until he reached "mature life" (p. 65). Because of a "superior capacity [that] he immediately evinced," he did not long remain at the lower grade level but rose quickly "to the position of master-at-arms" (p. 67). In addition to his intellectual superiority and his wide-ranging experience, he appears to be and to feel alienated, a foreigner wherever he goes in the world. The slight accent with which he speaks English suggests that he is a foreigner in a far more significant sense than the obvious. He appears to be out of his native element, to be, as Melville puts it, "keeping incog" (p. 64). Finally, he seems to have had his troubles with life (though only rumors are offered about their nature) and to have developed a rebellious attitude toward authority, though he keeps these emotions well hidden.

These are the basic traits—superior intellect that searches for answers ("a peculiar ferreting genius"), restless disposition that carries one over the world, a sense of victimization arising from a history of deep troubles, and a prideful, contemptuous, rebellious spirit—of a type of extraordinary person who is likely to formulate for himself a set of convictions that resembles the Gnostic heresy. Though they are vastly different, Ahab and Claggart share the four characteristics listed above, and both adopt Gnostic-like beliefs that tend to justify them in their own minds. Consequently, an examination of these beliefs as they apply to Claggart may get us further within him than critics have been able to go thus far. Indeed, Melville hints at one point that if we were familiar with theological history and beliefs, we might have a better chance to understand a man like Claggart: "If that lexicon which is based on Holy Writ were any longer popular, one might with less difficulty define and denominate certain phenomenal men" (p. 75).

Perverted from birth and preoccupied with a need to justify himself, Claggart has arrived at the basic Gnostic position that the God who created the world is unworthy of his worship. As a victim of the world's hostility, Claggart has to place the blame for what he considers the maliciousness aligned against him. The responsibility for that evil he assigns to the Creator. When Melville comments that "the Creator alone is responsible" for "the scorpion" (p. 78), in a passage that explains how Claggart's mind works, he is expressing his character's point of view. It is Claggart, not Melville, who has talked himself into believing that the Maker of the world botched the job and is thus an inferior and contemptible God. The alienation that he feels—Melville states that he has "alien eyes" (p. 98)—is typical of those with Gnostic convictions. Gilles Quispel comments that "this is the fundamental experience of the Gnostic, who knows that he is an alien in this world and that the world is alien to him."[41] If there is anything more commonly stated in Gnostic writings than the feeling of the world's foreignness to one of the elect, it is the belief that the Creator—or Demiurge—is blind, arrogant, unfair, and inferior to a higher spirit.

The "phenomenal pride" (p. 76) that Melville attributes to Claggart and those like him is a further suggestion of his Gnostic-like stance. One of the single most important facts about him is that he does not consider himself evil. Melville reports that he is,

41. Gilles Quispel, "Gnostic Man: The Doctrine of Basilides," in *The Mystic Vision,* ed. Joseph Campbell (Princeton: Princeton University Press, 1968), p. 238.

but that observation must be separated from Claggart's own per-verted vision of himself as one who has seen the light—*gnosis,* as the Gnostics called it—and is consequently a very special person, one of the elect. An emerging, destructive pride, as we saw in a previous chapter, thus represents a major danger of the Gnostic way of thinking. If one is to get at Claggart it must be understood that he genuinely considers all that he does to destroy Billy Budd, all the scheming and lying, to be eminently right and entirely warranted.

He justifies his plan of persecution by his Gnostic-like view of Billy as an enemy to truth. He intuits that Billy is a kind of logos, a spirit given form; he senses that a manifestation of un-fallen human nature has confronted him. Billy's personal beauty, he knows, is the result of the spirit within. To Claggart, "the spirit lodged within Billy, and looking out from his welkin eyes as from windows, that ineffability it was which made the dimple in his dyed cheek, suppled his joints, and dancing in his yellow curls made him pre-eminently the Handsome Sailor" (p. 78). As a human being, Claggart is not immune to Billy's magnetism. As a highly intelligent and unusually sensitive man, he even realizes from where Billy's appeal comes—that it is of a spiritual nature. Consequently, with the appearance of Billy upon the *Bellipotent,* Claggart faces, as does Vere, the mental crisis of his life. It is the year of his Great Mutiny as well. If he allows himself to be drawn emotionally to Billy, he will then have to face up to what he is by nature. An acceptance of Billy would mean a rejection of himself. That is, he cannot admit Billy's goodness without at the same time being honest about his own corrupt nature, which he cannot change: "With no power to annul the elemental evil in him," since it is inborn ("though readily enough he could hide it"), "apprehending the good, but powerless to be it," he therefore must find a way once again to rely on perversion to keep him from honestly confronting himself, for to do so would unquestionably be to bring on his self-destruction. Judas Iscariot hanged himself after his treachery because Christ the Logos had made him see into his own nature. The vision was too horrible to bear.

The form of perversion that Claggart applies to Billy is essen-tially the Gnostic heresy. He cannot pervert Billy into something other than what he represents, pre-fallen Adam, but he *can* justify his feeling of Billy's being his enemy by conceiving of original human nature in Gnostic terms. That is, he cannot twist the fact of Billy's innocence, so he distorts that innocence into something pernicious. To the Gnostic, innocence was the opposite of *gnosis*. Adam was made by the Creator and placed subserviently in the Garden of Eden to obey and worship an inferior God. His ignorance of the true nature of the Demiurge was to keep him in bondage. Only after "the reactionary bite of that serpent," as Melville calls it—a bite that Billy as prelapsarian Adam has never experienced—did the first man realize the truth about the Creator and himself, namely that he had within him a spark of the higher God and should not remain in bondage to a second-rate deity and a corrupt universe with its physical laws conspiring to hold him. The serpent in the Gnostic myth consequently represents not Satan but a messenger of the higher God, the Unknown or Abyss. If Claggart had a need to pervert Innocence into something threatening and abhorrent, he could not have found a more convenient justification than the Gnostic position.[42] Seeing Billy for what he is, he must condemn that quality: "And the insight but intensified his passion, which assuming various secret forms within him, at times assumed that of cynic disdain, disdain of innocence—to be nothing more than innocent!" (p. 78).

This gnosticizing of innocence furnishes Claggart with a philosophical basis for rejecting Billy, but it does not equip him with a rationalization for persecuting him. His real reason for wanting him destroyed is that he senses Billy will force him to die in his own vomit of self-revulsion upon being forced to view what he really is, but he must pervert this reason into a more noble and acceptable motivation. He does so by imagining that innocence is not passive but active and that it has consciously insulted him. With the pride of a Gnostic who has come to consider himself a kind of god, he reacts to Billy's accidental spilling of soup across his path with the righteous anger that comes from deeply injurious insult. Now his perversion has supplied him with both the

42. When Melville writes that Claggart is "the direct reverse of a saint" (p. 74), he may be suggesting that the master-at-arms is a heretic, the opposite of one canonized by the Church.

motivation to reject Billy's appeal and to destroy him. Truth *and* Justice, as he now sees them, must be served. That Claggart's rationalization for his conspiracy to destroy Billy is, in a sense, theologically based is suggested by the fact that Melville compares him to Guy Fawkes. Claggart has a Guy Fawkes "prowling in the hid chambers underlying" his nature (p. 80). Guy Fawkes (1570–1606) joined a conspiracy to destroy the British Parliament building (while King James I and his ministers were meeting) because he convinced himself that this was retributive justice for England's victimization of his own religious sect, the Roman Catholics. Though he confessed under great torture the names of the other conspirators, he remained until his death by hanging sure in his own mind that what he attempted was right. He was a maddened Catholic striking out at what he considered pernicious Protestantism as Claggart is a maddened Gnostic striking out at Christian orthodoxy with its deceptive and enslaving principles. Both men felt themselves eminently justified and were, therefore, so much the madder.

Melville's comment that "Claggart could even have loved Billy but for fate and ban" (p. 88) has led to a fairly widespread interpretation of the master-at-arms as a homosexual.[43] There appears no valid reason to object to this view of Claggart as long as it is kept in perspective. Indeed, Melville's linking of him with Titus Oates strongly supports the theory. The reference to Oates serves foremost, however, to place Claggart in the context of infamous men who acted destructively in the name of a theological ideal. Titus Oates (1649–1705) was the English Protestant clergyman who fabricated the details of the Popish Plot in 1678 in order to stir up animosity and action against Roman Catholics. Incredibly, he charged that an insurrection was being planned whereby Charles II would be assassinated and his Roman Catholic brother James, duke of York, would become king of England, which would be turned over to the Jesuits. Afraid in the extreme of usurpation and rebellion, those from the king on down be-

---

43. F. O. Matthiessen may have been the first to discuss this possibility. See *American Renaissance: Art and Expression in the Age of Emerson and Whitman* (New York: Oxford University Press, 1941), pp. 506–7.

lieved Oates and executed a number of people charged in the supposed scheme. Not until after the death of these innocent people was Oates seen to be a liar. Claggart thus has much in common with Titus Oates beyond the broad, protuberant chin that Melville mentions (p. 64). He can, like the English clergyman, lie with amazing coolness under pressure. Oates, like Claggart, served in the British navy. Both had severe differences with the world that left them emotionally scarred and periodically cast out. Their pasts cannot stand much looking into. One of the most significant reasons for Melville's associating Claggart with this famous English villain, however, may be the fact that it was widely known that Titus Oates was a homosexual.[44] Though there may be support for the view of Claggart as a homosexual, homosexuality is not the focus of his characterization or a major theme in the novel. It is merely part of a larger, profounder issue. If Melville dropped a suggestion that Claggart is sexually perverted, it was intended to fill out the portrait of this man who is perverted in *every* way. Revealing obliquely that facet of his personality is simply a method of showing the extent to which perversion enters every aspect of John Claggart's being. Essential to an understanding of his characterization is the distinction between his and what might be termed the ordinary form of homosexuality. With the usual homosexual, a different sexual orientation is the reason for one's so-called perversion; with Claggart, it is the result.

Captain Vere has an instinctive abhorrence of Claggart. When the two meet on the quarter-deck, something in the master-at-arms "provokes a vaguely repellent distaste" in his captain (p. 91). Yet despite the obvious distance between a good man like Vere and a twisted one like Claggart, Melville goes out of his way to create an undercurrent of similarity. Vere is curiously like this man for whom he feels such repugnance. He is just slightly older ("forty or thereabouts" compared to Claggart's thirty-five). The

44. See John Kenyon, *The Popish Plot* (London: Heinemann, 1972), pp. 46–47; Douglas C. Greene, Introduction to the *Diaries of the Popish Plot* (Delmar, N.Y.: Scholars' Facsimiles and Reprints, 1977), pp. viii–ix; and John Harold Wilson, *The Ordeal of Mr. Pepys's Clerk* (Columbus: Ohio State University Press, 1972), p. 20.

two stand out on board the *Bellipotent* for their obvious superiority of intellect and education. They exhibit an unusual degree of patriotism. In fact, it is Claggart's "austere patriotism" that helps to "abruptly" advance "him to the position of master-at-arms" (p. 67). Melville typically mentions one aspect of personality in Vere, drops a hint of the same trait in Claggart, and then—sometimes directly, sometimes indirectly—comments much later on the characteristic itself. For example, after showing Vere's devotion to country and then stating that Claggart appeared patriotic, he later in the novel impugns the sincerity of the "patriotic impulse" by having it praised in a published article that is full of lies about Billy Budd. According to this falsified account, John Claggart's noble character "signally refutes, if refutation were needed, that peevish saying attributed to the late Dr. Johnson, that patriotism is the last refuge of a scoundrel" (p. 130). Since Claggart has been shown to be a scoundrel, Melville implies that Dr. Johnson's theory was probably correct.

Captain Vere is no scoundrel, but time and again Melville stresses some area of likeness with Claggart. They are both advocates of discipline, carrying out quickly orders given to them and demanding strict obedience to their own. After characterizing Vere as a "martinet," Melville presents Claggart as the man most responsible for preserving discipline among the crew, "a sort of chief of police" (p. 64). And it is obviously a job that Claggart relishes and accomplishes with a high degree of success. What, then, can be the virtue inherent in the act of discipline itself when it is apart from values that need to imbue it? Melville follows the recurrent pattern here: he shows Vere as a man believing wholeheartedly in discipline, Claggart as also a stern disciplinarian, and then drops a condemning note about this quality of mind. "True martial discipline," he says a few pages before the end, "long continued superinduces . . . a sort of impulse whose operation at the official word of command much resembles in its promptitude the effect of an instinct" (p. 127). This is to say that the true "prompter" has been usurped, that the instincts are no longer allowed to guide as they should. Thus discipline causes Vere to see to it that Billy hangs, though his instincts cry for the release of this image of unsoiled human nature.

Similarly, Melville links these two disparate characters through their attitudes toward justice and the law.[45] Legal terms abound in descriptions of Claggart and Vere. Claggart's "conscience" is "but the lawyer to his will" (p. 80). He makes "a strong case against Billy" in his mind and decides that justice demands the sailor's death. Vere exclaims that Billy "must hang" (p. 101) even before he is put on trial, revealing that he, like Claggart, has made a "prejudgment" (p. 108). It is "the law," Vere states, that he is "prompted by" (p. 113). Justice and legality are thus easily perverted and become the wrong prompters, as they have for both men, though in different ways and degrees. Both characters are also advocates of fate as the dominant force in our lives, but like patriotism, discipline, and justice, fate has been perverted and has become a scapegoat. Claggart implicates fate as the source of his victimization; it is a collective term that includes for him all the enslaving powers of a hostile universe and pernicious deity. He can blame it for all his woes and resist it. Vere can also blame it and take comfort that it, not he, was in charge of Billy's future from the time when he struck Claggart. "Fated boy," he whispered when Billy struck the master-at-arms.[46] Melville makes both characters blind to what he knew to be the essential truth about fate: "Events are all in thee begun— / By thee, through thee."[47] To a very large extent, a man is his own fate. Thus, the fact that Vere dies with no remorse, blaming Billy's death on fate, constitutes one of the most striking ironies of the novel and undercuts, as elsewhere, one of the most cherished attitudes of his principal character.

45. Melville may well have indirectly associated the respectable Vere with the persecuting figure of Claggart through his choice of the captain's two given names, Edward Fairfax. In a work by William Godwin, an author with whose writings Melville is known to have been familiar, the following information is presented: "It is a painful task to record, that Edward Fairfax, the harmonious and elegant translator of Tasso, prosecuted six of his neighbours at York assizes, in the year 1622, for witchcraft on his children." Fairfax "afterward drew up a bulky argument of and narrative in vindication of his conduct." *Lives of the Necromancers* (New York: Harper and Brothers, 1835), p. 280.

46. Joyce Sparer Adler comments that "so thoroughly has Vere been dedicated to the ritual of war that to him it seems Fate" (p. 164).

47. *Clarel*, II.xxxvi.103–4.

It does not appear greatly troublesome that Vere is, as Melville calls him early, a man of "settled convictions" until we realize that this term could apply just as well to Claggart. The petty officer is as convinced that he is right and justified as is the commander. Furthermore, Claggart uses the precise same means of arriving at that self-justification as Vere—prudence and rigor. It should be expected, therefore, that they share an abhorrence of mutiny. Vere is overtly concerned with mutiny in the British navy and with preventing it aboard the *Bellipotent,* but his great underlying anxiety is that a mutiny will occur within him and that all those things he has sworn allegiance to will be overturned. Claggart appears to be inventing a conspiracy in which Billy is the villain, but in his perverted mind, he is simply helping along in his own way the progress of justice.[48] He actually perceives Billy as a potential mutineer, a person who is capable of upsetting the order and discipline on the ship because of his ability to command adoration from the crew. But more importantly, Claggart senses, as does Vere, that Billy will force him to face himself squarely. With mutiny as with all the other areas of common interest to Vere and Claggart, Melville begins by explaining Vere's position and making it sound reasonable, then suggesting that Claggart is as much against mutiny—of sorts—as is Vere, and finally implying that because the villain's position is basically the same as that of the man of nobility, the subject should be rethought. And so it should, for Vere needs nothing so much as an inner mutiny where his imperial conscience will be overthrown by those better impulses stirred up in his contact with Billy Budd. That he will not allow such a mutiny brings him into another area of kinship with Claggart. As they share so many other things, they are both perverters and madmen.

The shock value of *Billy Budd,* arising from the recognition of all those ways in which the hero is like the villain, has been scarcely recognized in criticism of the novel, but it leads one with

48. Critics do not agree unanimously, however, that Claggart is behind the plot to make it appear that Billy is fomenting mutiny. Terrence J. Matheson argues that Claggart is himself misled by what he hears of Billy's encounter with the afterguardsman and is thus victimized. "A New Look at Melville's Claggart,"*Studies in Short Fiction* 17 (1980): 445–53.

rare force—even for a work by Melville—to the heart of the matter. How dutiful and brave one is, how conscientious and intelligent, how fair and strong, how upright and ethical—none of these things is very important without true knowledge of self and self-fidelity. Indeed, one can possess all of those qualities so admired by the civilized world and still be shockingly similar to the most depraved villain. Keeping true to the dreams of your youth—only that will decisively separate you from other men, even the most corrupt. This it was that Herman Melville reminded himself again and again. The essence of all that he had learned in a long life of probing and suffering was tersely expressed in that scrap of paper pasted on the inside of his desk. It was his struggling to follow that insight that kept him writing and kept him living.

Conclusion

Herman Melville's later novels—*Moby-Dick, Pierre, Israel Potter, The Confidence-Man,* and *Billy Budd, Sailor*—reveal a mind occupied with the idea of survival. His interest was not merely clinical or artistic but profoundly personal. In each novel, he writes indirectly about himself, identifies motivations and strong proclivities, weighs their value or danger, and frequently projects what could happen to him if certain inner forces gain sway. These works constitute a sort of experimental laboratory of the mind where hypotheses about survival and perishing are developed and tested through the facilities of a brilliant creative imagination functioning with high artistic skill.

In Ishmael, Melville created a character much like himself. He represents what Melville had learned about his own large choir of voices within him and what he must do to keep those strong singers in harmony and under the direction of the leader. Solos were permitted but not usurpation of the role of the conductor. Ishmael manages this control but not without struggles and suffering. He knows the importance of seeking truth by probing the center of self instead of futilely butting his head against the unopened door of external reality. Through Ishmael, Melville reflects his fundamental philosophy of life. He is, in a sense, a solipsist. It is necessary, however, to distinguish among three forms of solipsism, two of which Melville was strongly attracted to but resisted. Egoism as a kind of solipsism is marked by the highest degree of self-pride, selfishness, and self-serving. Melville was frequently drawn in this direction (as is Ishmael), but he warned himself through the characterizations of Ahab and Pierre that bitterness and contemptuousness are the fruits of egoism. Metaphysical solipsism denies that there is any reality outside the self. Melville was also tempted to accept this hypothesis, often suspected its truth, but he realized that it led to mental suicide and he fought its appeal. This struggle is also projected in Ishmael who sometimes envisions universal nothingness or whiteness. Epistemological solipsism does not steadfastly deny that there is reality outside the self but posits that we are incapable of knowing whether there is or not. If external reality exists, man is never able to learn its secrets. Wisdom and insight therefore derive only from hard-won self-knowledge. This is the position Ishmael accepts, and he retains his mental balance largely because through self-control he resists the first two seductive forms of solipsism for which he had definite affinities. He is thus a survivor, a man like Melville himself, who was not consumed with a desire for self-destruction but determined to get through his private hell with sanity and dignity.

If in Ishmael, Melville worked out the formula of survival for a complex mind like his own, in Ahab he imaginatively projected the opposite fate of such a mind when it lacks the essential element for survival: self-knowledge. Melville considered the Great Destroyer to be self-deceit, and this is the central feature in the characterization of Ahab, whose perception of himself, God, and the world is depicted in terms of the fundamental tenets of Gnosticism, a destructive Christian heresy, as Melville saw it, because it justified pride and alienation.

Pierre is a younger version of Ahab in a different setting, but self-deceit remains the Great Destroyer, and a Gnostic-like view dominates Pierre's mind in one of the several stages he passes through to his destruction. As still another means of suggesting Pierre's blindness to what really motivates him, Melville develops an elaborate pattern of allusions to the then popular pseudo-science of physiognomy for the purpose of showing that Pierre falls prey to the same kind of erroneous thinking wherein surfaces are believed to reveal eternal truths.

Though they lack self-understanding Ahab and Pierre each has a conviction of personal identity, wrong though it is. In the next novel, *Israel Potter,* Melville portrays a character who in his lack of self-knowledge and his poverty of soul dies internally long before his physical demise. Potter is Melville's version of the hollow man who lives physically for a long period but is a mere cipher. In this much-underrated novel, Melville makes it clear that survival is not merely a matter of existing, nor are the concepts of poverty and liberty as simple as the world thinks.

In an essay that he wrote in 1850 at the very beginning of this final phase of his career as a novelist, Melville reveals his vision of the riches resulting from self-understanding and self-command. His review of Hawthorne's *Mosses from an Old Manse* is really a sort of credo, a concise statement of what it was that occupied the center of his value system, and it foreshadows and prefigures *The Confidence-Man,* published seven years later. His attitude toward Hawthorne changed in the years following his laudatory review. His enthusiasm cooled, and he decided that Hawthorne was not, after all, what he had thought him to be—the ideal man. But he did not stop thinking about such an ideal. The mode of thinking that had created his original enthusiasm for Hawthorne became, if anything, more pervasive. The things that he *thought* he saw in Hawthorne are significant, then, because they represent Melville's ideal attributes, the fruits of self-knowledge and self-mastery.

From reading Hawthorne's fiction, Melville imagined him to be, first of all, a man of a "deep and noble nature," a person who possessed "a great, deep intellect, which drops down into the universe like a plummet."[1] Melville envisioned him not as a man who occasionally exhibited these qualities of mind and heart, but one who manifested them consistently. Therefore, Hawthorne's

---

1. "Hawthorne and His Mosses," in *The Norton Anthology of American Literature,* 2d ed., ed. Nina Baym et al., 2 vols. (New York: Norton, 1985), 1:2169, 2163. Page references to this essay are to this text, which is based on Melville's manuscript.

works are not uneven in quality but consistent because they come from a base that is deep and constant. In the final pages of his essay, Melville writes that he has gone back over the stories in *Mosses* "picking up many things here and there that had previously escaped me" (p. 2171). Even the seemingly trivial in the works of such a genius can yield with examination that which calls forth "wonder and admiration" (p. 2171).

One of life's great and curious truths is that a person with the kind of fundamental consistency Hawthorne has is likely to be vastly misunderstood by the world. He will almost inevitably be deemed much less profound than he really is. Though Hawthorne was much admired, seldom was he seen for what he was because "it is the least part of genius that attracts admiration." The world, continues Melville, regards Hawthorne as "a pleasant writer, with a pleasant style,—a sequestered, harmless man, from whom any deep and weighty thing would hardly be anticipated:—a man who means no meanings" (p. 2163). Time and again, Melville reiterates this point—that Hawthorne is taken to be pleasantly changeable and superficial whereas he is of a single mind, though profoundly complex: "Nathaniel Hawthorne is a man, as yet, almost utterly mistaken among men" (p. 2165).

Since true consistency is almost never understood as such by the ordinary world, it requires charity in a man like Hawthorne not to become disgusted and contemptuous. Speaking of "The Old Apple Dealer," Melville writes: "Such touches as are in this piece can not proceed from any common heart. They argue such a depth of tenderness, such a boundless sympathy with all forms of being, such an omnipresent love, that we must needs say, that this Hawthorne is here almost alone in his generation" (p. 2163). Though misunderstood, Hawthorne still exhibits love, sympathy, and generosity toward society. A kind of by-product of that genuine philanthropic spirit is a sense of humor in describing others and dealing with them. Therefore, Melville finds that the two characteristics are intertwined: "But there is no man, in whom humor and love, like mountain peaks, soar to such a rapt height, as to receive the irradiations of the upper skies;—there is no man in whom humor and love are developed in that high form called genius" (p. 2163). Consistency thus produces misunderstanding in the commonality; but love and sympathy produce a sense of humor that prevents alienation.

Hawthorne's third major characteristic, as Melville then analyzed him, was basic honesty. Hawthorne was speaking of himself, Melville claims, when in "The Intelligence Office" he describes a character as possessing "stern sincerity" (p. 2170). Melville could not have bestowed higher praise than to claim for Hawthorne an "honest heart" (p. 2166). Yet coexisting with this quality is another trait, again in a way a complement characteristic, that may give the impression of a deceiver rather than a person of fundamental honesty. Hawthorne, states Melville, has powers to bewitch, to charm. He seems almost a magician or a "wizard" (pp. 2162, 2163). Furthermore, he appears to enjoy his little game of deception. He "takes great delight in hoodwinking the world,—at least, with respect to himself" (p. 2171). An example of this "hoodwinking" is his choice of titles for his stories: "but with whatever motive, playful or profound, Nathaniel Hawthorne has chosen to entitle his pieces in the manner he has, it is certain that some of them are directly calculated to deceive— egregiously deceive the superficial skimmer of pages" (p. 2171). Melville sees Hawthorne as a sort of benign confidence man, consistent, charitable, and honest with himself and with others where it most counts but given to a mischievous deceptiveness that traps the unwary and the unworthy and hypnotizes many others. Confidence is indeed one of his chief attributes as Melville judged him, confidence in himself and in his ability to read others. It does not bother him, Melville writes, that he is "esteemed but a so-so sort of author" because he is "willing to reserve the thorough and acute appreciation of what he is, to that party most qualified to judge—that is, to himself" (p. 2171). His insight into the workings of the ordinary mind leads him to believe that if he were more highly praised by society, he would lose part of his self-confidence: "At the bottom of their natures, men like Hawthorne, in many things, deem the plaudits of the public such strong presumptive evidence of mediocrity in the object of them, that it would in some degree render them doubtful of their own powers, did they hear much and vociferous braying concerning them in the public pastures" (p. 2171). Hawthorne views mankind benevolently, but he has no illusions about average people. He has an uncanny ability to measure and see into them.

Finally, this ideal man is in the truest sense of the word original, though in this he is also greatly misunderstood. "For, mark it well, imitation is often the first charge brought against real originality" (p. 2167). Melville waxes eloquent as he exalts this trait: "Let us boldly contemn all imitation, though it comes to us graceful and fragrant as the morning; and foster all originality, though, at first, it be crabbed and ugly as our own pine knots. . . . As an excellent author, of your own flesh and blood,—an unimitating, and, perhaps, in his way, an inimitable man—whom better can I commend to you, in the first place, than Nathaniel Hawthorne" (p. 2169).

In his review of *Mosses,* Melville was not analyzing a person that he had closely observed over a long period of time. He was describing what he considered the ideal man. He had already established his criteria, and when he read Hawthorne, he believed that he had discovered someone who illustrated them. If Hawthorne later disappointed him, that did not invalidate the formula. He was actually more interested in the attributes that he discussed in his essay than in Hawthorne, for they were the characteristics of a seeker into self who had explored that vast and beautiful terrain and unleashed some of the resources to be found there. It is important to realize that Melville had formulated his idea of what constitutes the ideal man—consistency, love, honesty, confidence, and originality—as early as the essay on Hawthorne because these are precisely the qualities that he discusses extensively in *The Confidence-Man* and builds into the central character, a hoodwinker of the world. The confidence man of that novel is not some satanic swindler but a fuller and deeper version of what Melville had once imagined Hawthorne to be. The novel is thus not an expression of a black and bitter mood experienced by the author when he composed it, as many critics suppose. It germinated not from hopelessness and despair but from speculation about human possibilities that Melville had been preoccupied with at least as far back as 1850, when he wrote his review on Hawthorne. Near the end of the essay, he expressed an idea that reverberates through his final five novels: "I somehow cling to the strange fancy, that, in all men, hiddenly reside certain wondrous, occult properties—as in some plants and minerals—which by some happy but very rare accident (as bronze was discovered by the melting of the iron and brass in the burning of Corinth) may chance to be called forth here on earth; not entirely waiting for their better discovery in the more congenial, blessed atmosphere of heaven" (p. 2174).

The discovery of these "wondrous, occult properties" is a happy "accident" in the same sense as is finding buried treasure, even though one is consciously searching for it and knows something of its general location. Consciously search and dig one must, and if successful, he discovers the gold within. If this process appears to resemble that of philosophical alchemy, it is because Melville's way of thinking was perhaps more in tune with that of the true and sincere alchemists (as opposed to the notorious charlatans) than with any other single system of thought. He had no laboratory to work in; he did not attempt to transform base metal into gold. But he shared the fundamental beliefs of the alchemists that "wondrous, occult properties" were within and that one could discover them by following the long and painful and laborious process of understanding and mastering oneself. Melville's kinship with the alchemists is, I believe, an area that has not previously been explored. Yet an understanding of the alchemical vision leads to insights into Melville's thinking that might otherwise be all but inaccessible. The confidence man, who is puzzling to nearly all readers and unfathomable to many, comes into focus when seen in the light of Melville's interest in those powers that were acquired by the genuine alchemist, an adept. Alchemy, as well as the Gnostic heresy, is also important for an understanding of *Billy Budd, Sailor,* for Melville's treatment of Billy is influenced by the alchemists' conception of original human nature. Claggart, on the other hand, attempts to find self-justification through a Gnostic-like perception of himself, the world, and the Creator.

With Melville's final novel, he came full circle, for the voice that narrates *Billy Budd* could well be that of Ishmael—still surviving, still recognizing the need to look inward, still realizing the absolute necessity for knowing who you are and for keeping true to that identity, and still probing and analyzing those who to their destruction fail to do so. At one point this narrator, indistinguishable in outlook from Melville himself, says: "Long ago an honest scholar, my senior, said to me in reference to one who like himself is now no more . . . 'Yes, X—— is a nut not to be cracked by the tap of a lady's fan. You are aware that I am the adherent of no organized religion, much less of any philosophy built into a system. Well, for all that, I think that to try and get into X——, enter his labyrinth and get out again, without a clue derived from some source other than what is known as "knowledge of the world"—that were hardly possible, at least for me.' "[2] What this "source" is, Melville does not say, but from the context of his later novels it is clear that he is speaking of self-knowledge. That must come before anything else. Knowledge of the world can give only superficial insights into the nature of man. To understand another heart, one must first understand his own. Melville knew that he must understand himself to survive and also to write, and he knew that he must write to understand himself and survive.

2. *Billy Budd, Sailor (An Inside Narrative)*, ed. Harrison Hayford and Merton M. Sealts, Jr. (Chicago: University of Chicago Press, 1962), p. 74.

Index

Characters from Melville's later novels are listed separately with the works in which they appear identified in parentheses and in the following abbreviated form: BB for *Billy Budd, Sailor*; CM for *The Confidence-Man: His Masquerade*; IP for *Israel Potter: His Fifty Years of Exile*; MD for *Moby-Dick*; and P for *Pierre; or, The Ambiguities*.

409

Index

415

Index

Index

Mark Twain, 30

Marovitz, Sanford E., 2*n*, 71*n*, 140*n*

Mason, Ronald, 300–301

Matheson, Terrence J., 398

Mathews, J. Chesley, 210*n*

Matter: view of, in Gnosticism, 108, 115*n*, 119, 120

Matthiessen, F. O., 148*n*, 301, 394*n*

May, Rollo, 381*n*

Melville, Elizabeth Shaw, 302

Melville, Herman: admiration for Rabelais, 318; admiration for Shakespeare, 361; aesthetic theory, 34–35; and Agatha Hatch Robertson, 129, 130–33; and alchemy, 339, 345–46, 382, 406; attitude toward Israel Potter, 296; attitude toward whaling industry, 40–57; avoidance of anger and bitterness, 133, 238–39; avoidance of isolation, 115–16, 124; awareness of power of self, 377–78; and book of Isaiah, 106–7; on books, 235; characters as sides of himself, 170–71; compared with Rabelais, 320–21; composition of *Billy Budd, Sailor*, 367; composition of *Moby-Dick*, 60–62; composition of *Pierre*, 187–88; and concept of confidence, 327–28; his concept of the "prompter," 381; concept of self-love, 321–22, 335; concept of "youth," 377–78; concern with America's future, 294–95; contrasted with Pierre, 164–65, 167; correspondence with Hawthorne, 130–33, 378*n*; credo of, 402–6; crisis of despair, 301–4, 306; and Daniel Webster, 255–56; dedication in *Israel Potter*, 253–54; and deep diving, 7, 10*n*, 36–37; and democracy, 54–57; as "digger," 11*n*; earliest ideas about Billy Budd, 367; early plans to write about Israel Potter, 245;

estimate of Benjamin Franklin, 260–68; and Ethan Allen, 285; as fantasizer, 300, 307–8; feelings of victimization, 133; fundamental philosophy, 400–401; and Gnosticism, 93–97, 111, 112–13, 122, 124, 195–96, 291, 401; and human nature, 112; ideal man to, 402–6; impersonator of, 297–99; interest in "The Birthmark," 359–60; interest in mutiny, 366–67; interest in physiognomy, 150, 152, 154–56, 162, 186; knowledge of alchemy, 338–39; knowledge of Gnosticism, 338–39; last years of, 365–66; maxim pasted in his writing desk, 365–66, 377–78, 399; and metaphysical speculation, 23, 58, 60; on methods of writing, 208; mode of survival, 236–39, 243, 267–68; motives for going abroad, 304; motives for writing, 144, 149, 181, 238, 241–43, 248; opinion of Admiral Nelson, 373–74; opinion of civilization, 47, 49, 54, 282; opinion of Hawthorne, 402; opinion of mysticism, 13; perception of reality, 184–85; period of his short fiction, 244–45; plans for the China Aster story, 359; and Plotinus Plinlimmon, 233–37; poverty in his short fiction, 246; and the psychology of his time, 241–42; reaction to Owen Chase, 129–30, 133; and repressed sexuality, 225–27; review of Hawthorne's *Mosses*, 402–6; and Romantic poets, 192–93; as sailor, 41*n*–42*n*; as seedsman, 25; self-exploration, 13–16; self-knowledge, 166, 167, 232, 236–39, 243, 248, 275, 306, 377–78, 382, 400–407; sense of specialness, 113; sexual puns,

Index

Index

Index

Index